STILL STUCK
in TRAFFIC

JAMES A. JOHNSON METRO SERIES

The Center on Urban and Metropolitan Policy at the Brookings Institution is integrating research and practical experience into a policy agenda for cities and metropolitan areas. By bringing fresh analyses and policy ideas to the public debate, the center hopes to inform key decisionmakers and civic leaders in ways that will spur meaningful change in our nation's communities.

As part of this effort, the Center on Urban and Metropolitan Policy has established the James A. Johnson Metro Series to introduce new perspectives and policy thinking on current issues and attempt to lay the foundation for longer-term policy reforms. The series examines traditional urban issues, such as neighborhood assets and central city competitiveness, as well as larger metropolitan concerns, such as regional growth, development, and employment patterns. The James A. Johnson Metro Series consists of concise studies and collections of essays designed to appeal to a broad audience. While these studies are formally reviewed, some are not verified like other research publications. As with all publications, the judgments, conclusions, and recommendations presented in the studies are solely those of the authors and should not be attributed to the trustees, officers, or other staff members of the Institution.

Also available in this series:

Edgeless Cities: Exploring the Elusive Metropolis
Robert E. Lang

Evaluating Gun Policy: Effects on Crime and Violence
Jens Ludwig and Philip J. Cook, editors

Growth and Convergence in Metropolitan America
Janet Rothenberg Pack

Growth Management and Affordable Housing: Do They Conflict?
Anthony Downs, editor

Laws of the Landscape: How Policies Shape Cities in Europe and America
Pietro S. Nivola

Low-Income Homeownership: Examining the Unexamined Goal
Nicolas P. Retsinas and Eric S. Belsky, editors

Redefining Urban and Suburban America: Evidence from Census 2000
Bruce Katz and Robert E. Lang, editors

Reflections on Regionalism
Bruce J. Katz, editor

Savings for the Poor: The Hidden Benefits of Electronic Banking
Michael A. Stegman

STILL STUCK in TRAFFIC

COPING WITH PEAK-HOUR TRAFFIC CONGESTION

ANTHONY DOWNS

BROOKINGS INSTITUTION PRESS
Washington, D.C.

Library of Congress Cataloging-in-Publication data
Downs, Anthony.
  Still stuck in traffic: coping with peak-hour traffic congestion / Anthony Downs
    p.   cm.
  Rev. ed. of Stuck in traffic. 1992.
  Includes bibliographical references and index.
  ISBN 0-8157-1929-9 (pbk. : alk. paper)
  1. Traffic congestion—United States. 2. Traffic flow—United States. 3. Land use,
Urban—United States. I. Downs, Anthony. Stuck in traffic. II. Title.
  HE355.3.C64D69   2004
  388.4'13142'0973—dc22   2004004190

Digital printing

Typeset in Sabon

Composition by Betsy Kulamer
Washington, D.C.

Contents

Foreword

Traffic congestion has almost surpassed bad weather as a malady that is universally discussed but rarely improved through public policies. Congestion now slows down virtually every U.S. metropolitan area. It also lasts longer and affects more of the transportation network than ever before. This constantly intensifying nature of congestion is extremely frustrating to the millions of citizens who daily endure it. They keep asking, "Why doesn't somebody do something about this misery?"

The bad news for disgruntled commuters, families, and businesses is that traffic congestion is a problem that requires extremely complex and iterative solutions. Many of the nation's frequent calls for more money and increased investment in transportation focus directly on the congestion crisis with "solutions" that rely on expanding capacity by building more and bigger roads, typically on the suburban and exurban fringe. Such proposals fail to recognize what is responsible for these problems in the first place.

Traffic congestion results from many factors and varies greatly from place to place. In densely settled cities like New York and San Francisco, traffic congestion exists because there are many vehicles moving about in a generally confined area. In other metropolitan areas—and particularly in the suburbs—congestion results from low-density settlement patterns, employment decentralization, shifting consumption patterns, and market restructuring. In rural areas, seasonal tourist traffic on once-bucolic country roads may generate congestion.

But more generally, worsening traffic congestion stems from the way modern metropolitan economies and societies are organized. Americans generate congestion because they place the pursuit of other goals above minimizing the time they spend moving around on the ground. Those other goals include having most people work during the same hours each day so they can efficiently interact with one another, giving people many choices of where to live and work, having most students attend classes during the same hours to optimize the use of teachers' services, and enabling some people to choose whether they travel by car, bus, or train—although, in reality, very few really possess options other than the car.

The upshot is inescapable: pursuing all those goals simultaneously requires a large segment of the nation's population to try to travel during the same few hours each day—the "peak" or "rush" hours. This overloads much of the nation's transportation network during this time, forcing people to wait in line for their turn to reach their destinations. However, as this book proves, we cannot avoid such delays by building enough roads or rails to handle all those movers at the same time, or by setting up electronic connections for telecommuting, or even by installing tolls on all main roads during peak hours. As a result, we allocate auto transportation on a first-come, first-served basis. People have to wait in line, which is essentially what congestion is.

Although governments may never be able to eliminate road congestion, there are several ways cities, states, and metropolitan areas can move to curb its increase. Such approaches include operational improvements such as clearing accidents faster, land use improvements such as permitting appropriately sited high-density development, and market mechanisms like the pricing experiment currently under way in London's central business district.

In this book, Anthony Downs reveals the fundamental nature of peak-hour metropolitan traffic congestion and analyzes its causes—not only in America but in urban areas all over the world. He collects all of the policies that have been proposed to remedy this mobility problem and then analyzes how each might at least help slow down the rate at which congestion will get worse.

This volume is a greatly expanded and updated revision of his earlier analysis, *Stuck in Traffic,* published in 1992. Downs has deepened his earlier theoretical analysis of traffic congestion, added chapters on the role of accidents and incidents in generating congestion, examined congestion around the world as well as in America, and analyzed new tactics proposed to reduce it. Among other things, this book clearly illustrates why this nation has to get beyond the transportation-only solutions of the past fifty years in order to deal with congestion. As Downs clearly illustrates, there are no quick fixes.

Perhaps Yogi Berra said it best: "If you keep doing what you always did, you'll always get what you always got." In this book Anthony Downs shows us how a new, pragmatic, and realistic set of improvements can help address the apparent hopelessness of one of this nation's most daunting metropolitan challenges.

BRUCE KATZ
Vice President and Senior Fellow, Brookings Institution
Director, Center on Urban and Metropolitan Policy

To my wife

DARIAN DOWNS

my wonderful partner in life

Acknowledgments

Several colleagues read earlier drafts of this volume and made excellent comments of immense assistance to me. The insights of Martin Wachs were fundamental in reshaping several chapters. Genevieve Giuliano and Robert Puentes were extremely helpful. Tim Lomax and the Texas Transportation Institute generously allowed me to use many results of their outstanding studies. Kara Kockelman reviewed my analysis of the dynamics of congestion. Theresa Walker edited the manuscript, and Eric Haven, Emilia Richichi, and Catherine Theohary painstakingly verified its thousands of numbers and references.

Bruce Katz and Amy Liu of the Brookings Center on Urban and Metropolitan Policy suggested revising the earlier volume and provided financial support. I am also grateful to the following funders for their financial support: the Fannie Mae Foundation for their founding support of the Center, and the Ford Foundation, George Gund Foundation, the Joyce Foundation, the MacArthur Foundation, the McKnight Foundation, and the Mott Foundation for their continued support and advice on our work on transportation and metropolitan growth issues.

STILL STUCK
in TRAFFIC

CHAPTER 1

Introduction

In recent years, millions of U.S. metropolitan area residents have come to regard traffic congestion as their most serious local and even regional problem—with good reason. From 1982 to 1999, the average percentage of daily traffic subject to congestion in seventy-five metropolitan areas nearly doubled, rising from 17 percent in 1982 to 33 percent in 1999. The Texas Transportation Institute's annual analysis of traffic congestion in 1999 concluded, "The average length of congested periods increased from about 2 to 3 hours in 1982 to 5 to 6 hours by 1999."[1]

Unlike many basically more important American social problems—poverty, hunger, low-quality education, homelessness, and drug addiction—traffic congestion is directly experienced every day by millions of American commuters of all income levels. They have become outraged over the waste of their precious time and money caused by repeated traffic delays. Their anger has been a powerful force leading many local government officials to adopt policies to manage suburban growth. However, myriad factors affect traffic flows, so the extent and intensity of congestion are still difficult to measure and track reliably. Therefore, it is hard to determine scientifically just how well existing anticongestion policies are working.

Yet most metropolitan-area residents believe traffic congestion is worse than it was five or ten years ago.[2] The statistics suggest that congestion is rising primarily in metropolitan areas that are either very large—containing more than 2 million residents—or experiencing absolutely large growth. In 2000 the Texas Transportation Institute measured congestion by the ratio of the average time required to make a trip in rush hours versus making the same trip in uncongested periods. The ten U.S. metropolitan areas with the greatest congestion, in order of severity, were Los Angeles (with a ratio of 1.82 to 1), San Francisco, Chicago, Washington, Seattle, Boston, Miami, San Jose, Denver, and New York-Northern New Jersey (with a ratio of 1.41 to 1).[3] The average annual hours of delay in travel per peak-hour traveler caused by congestion in seventy-five metropolitan regions increased from 16 hours in 1982 to 62 hours in 2000—almost quadrupling.[4]

Why Reducing Traffic Congestion—Or Slowing Its Increase—Is Important

To people who experience it, traffic congestion is exasperating because of the time they lose sitting in traffic jams and the frustration of crawling along instead of moving at "normal" driving speeds. To society as a whole, traffic congestion is undesirable because it misallocates scarce resources and causes economic inefficiency and psychological stress. The Texas Transportation Institute estimated that congestion "wasted" $67.5 billion dollars in seventy-five metropolitan areas during 2000 because of extra time lost and fuel consumed, or $505 per person, compared with what would have happened without congestion.[5] Time lost in delays (at $12.85 an hour) accounted for about 68.5 percent of that estimated total cost; the rest was fuel costs.

In reality, these social cost estimates are based on a false premise: that peak-hour travel in these regions could have been accomplished without any congestion if only society had better policies. As explained in chapter 2, modern societies are organized in such a way that so many people need to travel during peak hours, morning and evening, that no feasible arrangements or policies could accommodate them all without significant delays. In short, a major amount of daily peak-hour traffic congestion is inescapable in every large metropolitan area in the world. Therefore, it is unrealistic to conclude that all the "excess travel time" experienced during peak hours versus nonpeak times when no congestion exists could ever be eliminated—and is all therefore "wasted" because of ineffective policies. The hypothetical alternative of "congestion-free" travel during peak hours is an unattainable myth. So comparing that illusory alternative with what happens and declaring the time difference "wasted" is a misleading exercise.

Furthermore, although the Texas Transportation Institute's estimates of congestion costs appear almost staggering when aggregated over an entire year, they seem much smaller when they are viewed on a daily basis. If there are 240 working days in a year, and each worker makes two commuting trips per day, and all congestion costs computed by the Texas Transportation Institute are allocated to the resulting 480 trips, then the estimated cost of congestion per person is $1.05 per trip, of which $0.72 is in time and $0.34 is in cash. An annual average loss of thirty-six hours in delay over the same 480 trips is only 4.5 extra minutes per commuting trip each day. These costs seem much more bearable than the aggregated figures that are usually quoted in analyses of traffic congestion.

However, traffic congestion causes two other important social costs. It adds expense to countless businesses by delaying millions of goods shipments, thereby reducing the nation's productive efficiency. And the unpredictability of daily delays forces many travelers to add more-than-the-average delay to their normal trip planning in case they encounter really horrendous congestion. This causes further total losses of time.

Moreover, congestion generates other significant costs besides losses of time and fuel and delays in shipping. Government authorities tend to respond to public demands to "do something" about congestion by devoting more resources than may be socially optimal to building roads and subsidizing public transportation. Congestion also causes urban development to spread out more than it otherwise would because many firms and workers try to reduce travel time by decentralizing jobs and housing. The total costs of these distortions cannot be even roughly estimated, but they are surely large.

Such distortions arise partly because individual drivers and businesses do not have to face the true social costs of their private decisions about where and when to travel or how to influence the travel of others. Consequently, the associated market price signals do not trigger socially efficient outcomes. For example, individual commuters do not have to pay the costs of the added congestion they impose on others when they drive onto a crowded expressway during peak hours. The commuter frustration that builds up in traffic undoubtedly also helps increase interpersonal conflicts at work and at home.

The Focus of This Book

The 1992 version of this book—*Stuck in Traffic*—assessed the public policies then available for attacking this problem.[6] It provided an overview of research on the subject by transportation experts and land-use planners and examined the advantages and disadvantages of the principal strategies being proposed to reduce traffic congestion. However, many new ideas have been advanced since then, based on more recent research and experience. Therefore, the time seems ripe to take advantage of this new knowledge and visit the subject again.

This discussion focuses on five questions: how does peak-hour traffic congestion arise? Why has it become worse? What tactics might reduce it—or at least slow down its intensification? Which tactics would be the most effective? To what extent would the most effective tactics require regionwide planning and policies, rather than purely local ones? To answer these questions, one must look at the effects of congestion on the allocation of scarce resources, the relationship between land use and traffic flows in rapidly growing areas, and the benefits of regional solutions over purely local ones.

This book contains new chapters not present in the original edition on some fundamental benefits of traffic congestion, how bad U.S. congestion has become, accidents and other incidents as causes of congestion, coping with congestion by expanding public transit, and levels of congestion in other parts of the world. It also contains a new appendix on the dynamics of congestion. And I have extensively revised and updated the original chapters retained here.

CHAPTER 2

The Benefits of Peak-Hour Traffic Congestion

Almost nobody believes there is anything good about traffic congestion. This antipathy occurs mainly because people "stuck in traffic" feel frustrated when they are crawling along "going nowhere" while driving a machine capable of moving more than 100 miles per hour. Furthermore, travel delays caused by congestion worsen air pollution, raise national fuel consumption, and add heavy costs to goods delivery. Hostility toward congestion is also partly rooted in the frequent media publication of various estimates of how much congestion costs the nation as a whole and each driver in particular.

The Real Problem: "Excess Demand" for Roadways during Peak Hours

Nevertheless, peak-hour traffic congestion plays an essential and positive role in the transportation life of the nation. Congestion—which basically consists of waiting in line—is the nation's principal means of allocating scarce road space among competing users during periods when too many people want to use that limited space at the same time. That "excess demand" for roadways during peak hours is the real problem, to which congestion is the most feasible solution. The problem of excess demand arises because American society—like almost all modern societies—is organized in such a way as to generate the need for far more people to travel during certain limited times of the day than any feasible road system can handle then at maximum flow speeds. Society cannot eliminate the resulting "excess demand" for travel during these peak hours without radically reorganizing the entire economy and all our schools in ways that are totally unacceptable to most people.

To put it another way, congestion is the balancing mechanism that allows Americans to pursue certain goals they strongly desire—goals other than rapid movement during peak hours. Those goals include having a wide choice of places to work and live, working during similar hours so they can efficiently interact, living in low-density settlements, living in neighborhoods spatially separate from where other households with much lower incomes live, carrying out several errands on individual trips, and using private vehicles for movement because such vehicles seem superior to public transit under many conditions.

Many people pursuing these goals want to travel during the same hours, especially the morning and evening rush hours. A central reason is that most organizations want their staffs to be at work each day during the same hours as people in other organizations so they can all interact efficiently. Similarly, students must attend classes during about the same hours as others in their schools so those institutions can educate many people simultaneously with staffs that are relatively small compared with the number of people taught. Furthermore, many people going to or from work or school find it efficient to do other errands on the same trips.

All these factors cause a huge number of people to want to travel during the same few hours each morning and evening. Moreover, in the United States, most of these travelers want to move alone in separate, privately owned vehicles. As a result, especially in large metropolitan areas, existing roads do not have nearly enough capacity to simultaneously accommodate all the people who want to use them during such "peak periods." This is true throughout the rest of the world too. The resulting disparity between the high demand for traveling during these periods and the limited supply of roads available is the fundamental problem. Thus congestion itself is not really the problem—in fact, congestion is the only feasible *solution* to this more basic problem.

Four Conceivable Ways to Cope with Excess Demand for Roads in Peak Hours

In theory, there are four possible ways to cope with the daily peak-hour disparity between the total demand for travel and limited road space. One is to ration our limited road space by charging drivers a user fee on those roads during periods when the demand exceeds the supply. Our free enterprise society rations many other scarce goods by pricing them in markets—why not do the same with peak-hour road space? Many economists have long recommended such "road pricing" as an efficient method of allocating road space consistent with the general market orientation of the American economy.[1] It could be carried out by charging variable tolls on all the lanes of all major expressways and other commuting roads during peak hours. Those tolls could be raised high enough to restrict the number of vehicles entering each road during peak hours so that traffic on it would flow at high speed. This would end peak-hour congestion on those roads using such tolls, though not on all other roads and streets. And more vehicles could complete their commuting journeys during peak hours if those on the roads could all drive 60 miles per hour, rather than creeping along as many do now.

There are three reasons why America has not adopted this strategy. Even if variable tolls were established on nearly all major commuting roads, permitting high-speed movement there during peak hours, that might not accommodate all the commuters who wanted to travel then. Moreover, no road pricing system could charge variable tolls on every major and minor city street. Yet such streets would be burdened with travelers not able or willing to pay the tolls on expressways, or moving to and from those expressways, or simply commuting only on those streets. So peak-hour congestion might get worse on local streets while it eases on tolled expressways.

Furthermore, Americans have decisively rejected the road-pricing strategy for two political reasons. Such a toll system would benefit higher-income households while imposing a hardship on lower-income households. The former could afford to pay the tolls and thereby would enjoy rapid movement on the most direct roads during the most convenient hours of the day. But many of the latter would be forced off such roads during those periods.[2] This outcome is regarded as grossly unfair by the vast majority of American drivers. In fact, most believe they would be in the group frequently forced off the best roads during peak hours. Since more than 90 percent of all American households own cars, they form a potent electoral force. Through 2002, elected officials were unwilling to experiment with such road pricing arrangements, although the federal government has proposed funding such experiments. All state and local public officials apparently regarded even a modest experiment in all-lane road pricing as too likely to arouse the wrath of a majority of their constituents to be worth the risk.

True, interest in such experiments increased after London started using a limited road pricing scheme in its central area in 2003. Moreover, new high-tech vehicle tracking using global positioning system (GPS) satellites, combined with in-vehicle computers, may eventually permit charging every vehicle a different toll for every different road on which it travels and mailing the owner a monthly bill. Some prototypes of this system are already in use for trucks in Europe. However, it would take many years to put such a system in operation at any large scale. Consequently, as of mid-2003, no region in the United States—or anywhere else in the world—had installed areawide road pricing as a means of coping with peak-hour congestion.[3]

Americans also dislike peak-hour road pricing because its tolls seem to be added taxes on a privilege that drivers believe they have already paid for through gasoline taxes. That privilege is the ability to drive onto any road at any time, or at least to try doing so. Citizens who are skeptical of government's motives suspect that the funds collected through peak-hour tolls might be used for purposes unrelated to improving the roads involved or even to reducing congestion—as often occurs in Europe. They see such tolls as "just another tax" in an economy they feel is already burdened by too many taxes.

The second major approach would be to immensely expand the total capacity of the road system. True, a basic tenet of this book is that a region cannot "build its way out of congestion" once peak-hour congestion has appeared there. Yet in theory, enough additional road space could be created so that all those who wanted to drive rapidly during peak hours could do so simultaneously. But in reality, there are too many people seeking to use the roads at the same time each day for this approach to work without enormous financial and environmental costs. Key routes would have to be widened so much that huge portions of the entire region would be turned into giant concrete slabs. This would destroy thousands of properties along present roadways, wreaking havoc with trees, open space, and many other aspects of the physical environment. It would also be enormously expensive. In fact, no society could afford the costs involved. And after all that road space was built, much of it would stand empty most of the time when far smaller percentages of drivers wanted to move. This approach is equivalent to building a big enough parking lot in a shopping center to hold the cars of all the consumers who want to shop during Christmas week and then watching that lot stand empty most of the year. Thus expanding road capacity enough so that peak-hour rationing of road space is not necessary is totally impractical.

Another difficulty is that greater capacity might encourage many people who have currently chosen not to travel on roads during peak hours to start doing so. In the long run, it might also encourage more urban development in the region as developers take advantage of the greater mobility provided by larger roads. These forms of "induced demand" would offset much of the hoped-for gain in capacity from building more roads.

Some people believe another alternative to rationing road space that becomes overcrowded during peak hours is providing enough public transit capacity to handle much of the total peak-hour traffic flow. In theory, that could greatly diminish the number of private vehicles trying to move on the roads at the same time, thereby reducing peak-hour congestion. But in the United States, the share of all peak-hour trips made on transit is tiny compared with the share made by privately owned vehicles (POVs) on roads (figure 2-1).

Somewhat over one-third of all 1995 weekday trips were POV trips made during peak hours, whereas about 1.5 percent of all daily trips were transit trips made during peak hours.[4] Thus, during peak hours, POV trips composed about 96 percent of POV and transit trips combined (which totaled 38.5 percent of all trips). This means twenty-five times as many peak-hour trips are made in POVs as on transit. Hence, even if expanded transit capacity succeeded in tripling the number of trips made on transit during peak hours in 1995, and thereby replaced a similar number of POV trips, that would have reduced all peak-hour POV trips by only 8.0 percent (1.48 times two as a percentage of 37.1). That would not eliminate peak-hour traffic congestion on most major roadways involved, especially because many of the road users shifting to transit would be replaced by others converging onto those roadways from other times and other routes.

The main reason so few peak-hour commuters use public transit is that large parts of the nation have little or no transit service. The forms

FIGURE 2-1. Peak-Hour Trips on Public Transit and Private Vehicles

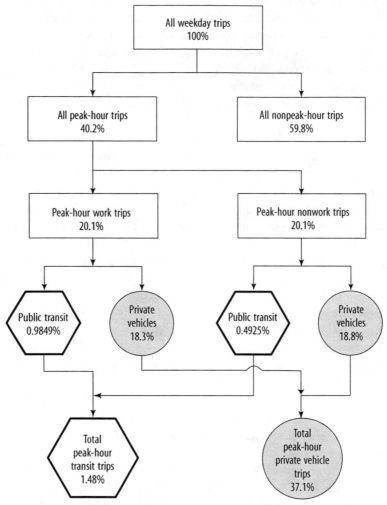

Source: Author's calculations based on Federal Highway Administration, *Our Nation's Travel: 1995 Nationwide Personal Transportation Survey, Early Results Report* (Department of Transportation, September 1977), pp. 21, 17. See note 4 in the text.

of public transit dominant in the United States cannot efficiently serve low-density settlements; yet most Americans live in such settlements. Consequently, the nation's transit services are concentrated in a few regions that contain relatively high-density settlements. In 2000, seven metropolitan regions contained 55.7 percent of all public transit commuters but only 12.5 percent of the nation's total population. Those regions were New York, Chicago, Washington, Boston, Philadelphia, Nassau-Suffolk, and San Francisco.

There is only one other feasible way of rationing road space during periods of peak demand: letting people wait in line until enough others have moved off the road so that space becomes available. That waiting constitutes traffic congestion. Thus traffic congestion is an essential ingredient in making effective use of the nation's road systems during peak travel hours. In effect, congestion is not the problem; rather, it is the solution to the real problem, which is, how can we ration our limited road space during peak hours when far more people want to travel on that space than it can handle simultaneously? Congestion may seem to be—and is—undesirable when compared with the mythical alternative of delay-free, high-speed movement at all times. But that alternative cannot possibly be achieved in most large metropolitan regions of the world.

If most Americans clearly understood the alternatives, they would undoubtedly regard congestion as much better than rationing space during peak hours by using tolls on all major roadway lanes, or building vastly more road space to avoid such rationing altogether, or trying to expand public transit systems enough to absorb all those "excess drivers" seeking to use the roads in private vehicles during peak hours.

Unfortunately, few Americans recognize that peak-hour congestion produces large benefits for society, even for those people caught in rush-hour traffic jams. Nor would such recognition make many feel much better about being stuck in traffic for long periods. Nevertheless, clearly understanding this situation is necessary to understanding why traffic congestion has arisen in our society, why it is getting worse, and why it neither can nor should be eliminated entirely.

Congestion Is Not All Bad

Traffic congestion can be viewed as a sign of prosperity and economic success, rather than as a wholly negative phenomenon.[5] Traffic becomes heaviest in economic booms, and notably declines in recessions, as dramatically demonstrated in the San Francisco Bay region during the late 1990s and early 2000s. In fact, the quickest way for a region to reduce intensive congestion is to encounter a serious recession—hardly a remedy anyone desires.[6]

Moreover, the locations and activities that society values most highly are often extremely crowded: World Series baseball games, the New

York theater district, college football games, Times Square at midnight on New Year's Eve, the most popular nightclubs and restaurants, and major shopping centers the week before Christmas. The paradox of the most popular places being plagued by congestion was summed up by Yogi Berra, who is reputed to have said: "No one goes there anymore because it's so crowded!"

Martin Wachs has pointed out that traffic congestion has a long history, dating back to ancient Rome and earlier.[7] One Roman emperor was so unhappy about commercial carts clogging Rome's streets every day that he decreed those vehicles could enter at night only. But the clatter of horses' hooves on the cobblestones, and the whinnying of countless animals, kept so many people awake that he quickly rescinded the decree. Early in the twentieth century in American cities, trolley cars jammed downtown streets. Social planners replaced trolleys with buses, which were deemed more flexible since they were not tied to fixed tracks. But buses soon caused traffic jams of their own. Eventually cars became so widespread that they were the main cause of congestion on city streets. Hence traffic engineers invented freeways to bypass those streets. Now freeways have become the locales of the worst congestion, so urban planners are proposing new "cures." These include high-occupancy vehicle (HOV) lanes, high-occupancy toll (HOT) lanes that permit single-occupant vehicles to enter during peak hours for a fee, grid street patterns to open up easier flows, light rail systems almost replicating former trolley lines, and more bike lanes and sidewalks. Thus the struggle against whatever forms of congestion are currently dominant constantly causes innovations that lead to new forms. Yet peak-hour congestion in one form or another remains an almost constant factor in civilized urban life all over the world.

Various interest groups in society even use widespread public antipathy toward traffic congestion to promote their policy agendas. Concrete and automobile manufacturers propose building more roads; transit vehicle manufacturers and transit unions propose expanding transit; and environmentalists propose requiring high-density settlements to help reduce the adverse effects of congestion.

But in reality, peak-hour traffic congestion of at least some type has become an integral part of normal life in almost all large and growing metropolitan areas in the world. So those areas are not going to get rid of congestion in the foreseeable future.

Can Nothing Be Done?

That peak-hour traffic congestion is almost inevitable in large metropolitan areas does not mean nothing can be done to reduce the costs it imposes on society. Peak-hour congestion cannot be eliminated. But its intensity can be reduced—or at least the rate at which it is intensifying can be slowed—by means of many different tactics that are analyzed in this book.

Just how bad does congestion have to become before a region should start employing such tactics? Because conditions differ greatly among regions, there is no one universal answer. Moreover, congestion in each region changes gradually over time with the growth of the region's population, citizens' incomes, investments in transportation improvements, and general prosperity. So there is no "crisis point" at which peak-hour congestion suddenly becomes so intense everyone recognizes that drastic action to reduce it must be undertaken. Rather, congestion creates a "creeping crisis" that gets worse for specific individuals and neighborhoods at different speeds.

Today in most very large American metropolitan areas, peak-hour congestion has become serious enough to motivate elected officials and other civic leaders to attack it with many policy tools. How well those tools are likely to work is the subject of this book. But all those citizens concerned with coping with congestion—including the everyday drivers "stuck in traffic"—should remember three basic facts. First, congestion performs a vital and necessary positive function in modern society. Second, congestion is not going to go away altogether, no matter what tactics are employed against it. (In fact, congestion is very likely to get worse in the future.) Third, in the long run, the most effective response is adaptation by individuals and firms through adjusting their behavior. That means changing travel times and routes, changing home or job locations, changing travel modes, even changing regions—or just getting used to it. The remaining chapters in this book should help them choose which adjustments to make and what anticongestion tactics will be most effective in at least slowing down the rate at which congestion gets worse in their region.

CHAPTER 3

How Bad Is Traffic Congestion?

Traffic congestion is extremely difficult to measure accurately because it is so variable across space and time. The degree of congestion varies widely among different metropolitan regions across the United States, among specific locations in any one region, at different times of the week at each location, and at each time of the day in each place in response to unpredictable local circumstances. These include variations in weather, accidents, other incidents, and road construction. Consequently, congestion occurring in a single metropolitan area at any given moment varies enormously across different locations. There is no simple way to aggregate these variations into a single measure of the "average degree of congestion" in the entire region for a given hour, day, week, month, or year.

Moreover, there is no one universally accepted definition of what constitutes "congested" traffic. In commonsense terms, the traffic on any given artery can be considered con-

Many of the data in this chapter have been taken from David Schrank and Tim Lomax, *The 2002 Urban Mobility Report* (College Station, Tex.: Texas Transportation Institute, June 2002). I am grateful to Schrank, Lomax, and the Texas Transportation Institute (TTI) for permitting the extensive use of their data in this analysis.

gested when it is moving at speeds below the artery's designed capacity because drivers are unable to go faster. Thus an interstate highway designed to accommodate an unimpeded flow of vehicles at 60 miles per hour is congested if most vehicles on it are, on the average, moving at any lower speed. The degree of congestion depends on how slowly the traffic is flowing compared with the road's designed capacity speed.

These basic concepts have been used by the Texas Transportation Institute (TTI) and the Federal Highway Administration to develop several measures of congestion, as shown in box 3-1. Recent changes in the degree of congestion indicated by several of these measures have been calculated by the TTI for U.S. metropolitan areas of various sizes for certain years in the period 1982 to 2000.[1] In its 2002 report, TTI analyzed seventy-five metropolitan regions from 1982 to 2000. Changes in congestion measures are shown in box 3-1 along with the definitions of those measures.

TTI's most important measure of congestion is the *travel time index*. It is the ratio of the total time required to drive a certain route during peak periods divided by the time it takes to drive the same route during uncongested periods. Thus if it takes 24 minutes to drive to work during normal peak periods, but only 20 minutes when there is no congestion, the travel time index has a value of 24 divided by 20, or 1.20. In 2000, travel time indexes varied from a low of 1.04 in the Corpus Christi, Texas, and Anchorage, Alaska, regions to a high of 1.90 in the Los Angeles region. The average travel time index for all seventy-five regions in 2000 was 1.225. This means it takes 22.5 percent longer to drive during peak periods than in uncongested periods, on the average.

The Texas Transportation Institute's whole approach to measuring traffic congestion has been criticized by the Surface Transportation Policy Project and the Washington State Department of Transportation. Both claim that TTI does not directly measure congestion empirically in each region but instead relies heavily on computerized models to estimate congestion levels. The Washington State Department of Transportation (WSDOT) has stated that TTI's data on the Seattle area do not accurately take into account the effects on peak-hour traffic speeds of several innovations implemented by WSDOT. These include extensive ramp metering and systems for signaling motorists about conditions on the roads ahead. As a result, WSDOT withdrew from the coalition of state departments of transportation that have been supporting TTI's *Urban Mobility Reports*.

Box 3-1. Measures of Traffic Congestion

The *travel time index* is the amount of additional time in minutes needed to make a trip during peak travel periods rather than other times of the day (when traffic is flowing freely at the designed speed capacity of the road). This measure is affected by both heavy flows of traffic in peak hours and incidents or accidents that disrupt traffic. The higher the travel time index, the greater the congestion it indicates. In the seventy-five metropolitan areas studied by the Texas Transportation Institute in the 2002 study, the average travel time index changed from 1.07 in 1982 to 1.24 in 2000. That means a trip that would take 20.0 minutes without undue traffic or incidents would have taken 21.4 minutes in peak hours during 1982 and 24.8 minutes in such hours during 2000, or 3.4 minutes more, a gain of 15.9 percent.

The *percentage of daily travel occurring during those hours when major roadways typically experience congestion.* In the seventy-five metropolitan areas analyzed in the 2002 study, this statistic averaged 26.3 percent in 1982 and 40.2 percent in 2000, an increase of 53 percent in eighteen years.

The *percentage of all daily travel occurring under actually congested conditions.* In the seventy-five metropolitan areas, this percentage rose from 10.5 percent in 1982 to 25.5 percent in 2000, an increase of 142.9 percent.

The *number of hours of delay per peak-hour road traveler* is the average number of hours actually traveled each year by individual drivers and passengers during peak periods, minus the number of hours it would have taken them to drive the same distance if traffic were flowing freely at each road's designed speed capacity as indicated by the posted speed limit. In seventy-five metropolitan areas studied, the average annual hours of delay per peak-hour road traveler rose from 8.7 in 1982 to 39.2 in 2000. That is an increase of 30.5 hours, or 350.5 percent.

The *roadway congestion index* is based on the ratio of the percentage of *additional vehicle miles* traveled throughout a region in any given period (say, from 1992 to 2000) to the percentage of *additional lane miles* constructed throughout the region's road system during the same period. If vehicle travel is rising at a rate faster than road construction, the roadway congestion index rises. Then peak-hour traffic congestion as measured by the *travel time index* should go up. But if road construction outpaces increases in travel, the roadway construction index declines. Then the *travel time index* should go down. Thus this index is calibrated on the overall highway *system* in a region. But it does not take into account many factors that influence congestion, such as metering entry onto expressways and faster removal of accidents from impeded lanes.

Source: David Schrank and Tim Lomax, *The 2002 Urban Mobility Report* (College Station, Tex.: Texas Transportation Institute, June 2002).

TABLE 3-1. Characteristics of Metropolitan Areas in Congestion Analysis

Size group (millions)	Number of regions	Percent of total population	Total population, 2001	Average density, 2001[a]	Average population, 2002
Very large (3.00 and over)	10	48.3	64,265,000	3,229	6,427,000
Large (1.00 to 2.99)	29	36.8	48,890,000	2,455	1,686,000
Medium (0.50 to 0.99)	22	12.0	15,930,000	2,047	724,000
Small (under 0.50)	14	2.9	3,835,000	2,013	274,000
All groups	75	100.0	132,920,000	2,356	1,772,000

Source: Data from David Schrank and Tim Lomax, *The 2002 Urban Mobility Report* (College Station, Tex.: Texas Transportation Institute, June 2002).
a. Population per square mile.

Nevertheless, this chapter relies heavily on TTI's *Urban Mobility Reports* because they are the only measures available that cover many different regions over long periods using the same basic methods in each region. Hence TTI's measures are the best available means of comparing congestion levels in different regions and tracking changes in regional congestion levels over time.

Regional Population and Congestion: Bigger Is Badder

In any given year, all measures of congestion were much higher, on the average, for metropolitan areas with large populations than for those with small populations. TTI divided the metropolitan areas it analyzed in its 2001 and 2002 studies into four population size groups: very large, large, medium, and small. The 2001 populations of each size group in the 2002 study, the number of regions in each group, the average 2001 population of the regions in each group, and the average urbanized area population density of the regions in each group in 2001 are shown in table 3-1.[2]

All the indicators of congestion measured in TTI's 2002 study (and in its earlier studies) indicate that the intensity of traffic congestion is greatest in very large regions and declines among these groups as their population sizes decrease. This is shown in table 3-2, containing 2000 averages for key congestion-measuring variables by size group.

The Surface Transportation Policy Project (STPP) has argued that the above measures do not take into account that many persons using public transportation during peak hours are not affected by traffic congestion on roads. Therefore, it developed an adjusted measure it called the

TABLE 3-2. Key Variables for Measuring Congestion Averages, by Size Group

Variable	Very large	Large	Medium	Small	All groups
Travel time index	1.46	1.28	1.18	1.10	1.24
Roadway congestion index	1.27	1.12	0.99	0.82	1.05
Annual hours of delay per person	32.90	20.83	13.90	6.29	17.79
Annual hours of delay per peak-hour road traveler	76.50	44.90	30.43	13.14	39.13
Percent peak-hour travel congested	47.40	43.40	39.14	30.07	40.17
Percent all travel congested	36.30	29.53	22.57	13.36	25.51

Source: Schrank and Lomax, *The 2001 Urban Mobility Report.*

congestion burden index, which multiplies the TTI travel rate index by the percentage of commuters who drive to work. This procedure has the effect of reducing the TTI travel rate index to a greater degree, the higher the percentage of regional commuters who use transit. Since the largest American cities have the highest percentages of commuters using transit, this adjustment might partly offset the conclusion just stated that intensity of congestion varies directly with the population of a metropolitan region.[3]

However, arranging the STPP's congestion burden index scores by the four urban area size groups used by TTI shows that the average score remains highest for very large areas, next highest for large areas, third highest for medium-sized areas, and lowest for small areas. And the STPP's calculations do not take into account that in 2002, 59.7 percent of all transit commuters rode buses, which are directly affected by roadway congestion. Hence STPP's calculations overestimate the beneficial impact of transit commuting on congestion experiences in large metropolitan areas. Correcting this error does not alter the conclusion that intensity of congestion on the average varies directly with metropolitan area population.

Further Analysis

To check the validity of the preceding conclusion on the impact of metropolitan area population on congestion, a multiple regression analysis was conducted using the 2000 travel time index of each of the seventy-five metropolitan areas used by TTI as the dependent variable and the following independent variables:
    —Metropolitan area population in 2000 and 1990;

—Absolute change in metropolitan area population from 1990 to 2000;

—Percentage change in metropolitan area population from 1990 to 2000;

—Square miles in the urbanized area in 2000;

—Total regional road system vehicle miles traveled in 2000;

—Total lane miles of freeways and principal arterials in 2000; and

—Urbanized area density in 2000 in population per square mile.

Several other variables developed by TTI were so highly correlated with the travel time index that they were not used. The statistically most significant independent variables, which yielded an adjusted r-squared of 0.6806, were total lane miles of freeways and principal arterials (positive), the absolute change in metropolitan area population from 1990 to 2000 (positive), urbanized area density in 2000 in persons per square mile (positive impact), and the number of square miles in the urbanized area in 2000 (negative impact).[4] The percentage change in area population from 1990 to 2000 was statistically significant if used instead of the absolute change, but quite insignificant when both were used simultaneously—which shows it has less influence than the absolute change. Urbanized areas with larger territory apparently spread traffic out and thus reduce congestion, although urbanized territory is highly correlated with 1990 population. However, more lane miles apparently cause people to drive more, thereby increasing congestion. Higher density apparently generates more intense congestion.

These regressions suggest that the absolute size of a region's population in 1990 or 2000 and the region's absolute growth from 1990 to 2000 had much greater positive impacts on its congestion intensity than the percentage rate at which the area's population grew or most other relevant variables. Thus congestion is likely to be the most serious in all very large metropolitan areas, since they are likely to produce absolutely large amounts of growth even if they have low percentage rates of growth, and large areas experiencing growth rapid enough to generate absolutely large gains. In contrast, small and medium metropolitan areas are likely to have less intensive traffic congestion even if they are growing at rapid percentage rates, since that will not usually produce absolutely large gains from their small initial bases.

An important implication is that intensive traffic congestion is not really a truly nationwide problem, though it is likely to be present in regions that contain a significant fraction of the nation's total popula-

FIGURE 3-1. Congestion Likelihood, by Metro Area Population Size Group

Percent of total U.S. population

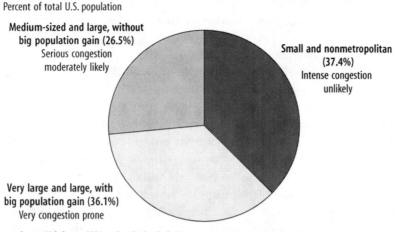

Medium-sized and large, without
big population gain (26.5%)
Serious congestion
moderately likely

Small and nonmetropolitan
(37.4%)
Intense congestion
unlikely

Very large and large, with
big population gain (36.1%)
Very congestion prone

Source: U.S. Census 2000; and author's calculations.

tion. If the 2000 populations of all very large metropolitan areas and all large metropolitan areas that had sizable absolute population gains from 1990 to 2000 (more than 250,000 added residents) are added together, this congestion-prone group contained 101.6 million residents, or 36.1 percent of the nation in 2000. At the other extreme are all small metropolitan areas and all nonmetropolitan areas combined, which in 2000 contained 105.3 million residents, or 37.4 percent of the nation. These areas are least likely to suffer from intensive traffic congestion. In between these extremes are the 74.5 million residents of *medium-sized* metropolitan areas and *large* metropolitan areas that did not have big absolute gains in population from 1990 to 2000. This 26.5 percent of the nation's total population may or may not suffer from intensive congestion, depending on specific regional conditions. The relative sizes of these three groups as of the 2000 Census are shown in figure 3-1.

Changes in Intensity over Time

Most Americans believe that traffic congestion has become worse over time, and substantial evidence supports that view. The average time Americans spent commuting each day has risen from 18.2 minutes in 1983 to 22.4 minutes in 1990, 20.7 minutes in 1995, and 25.5 minutes in 2000.[5] That is an increase in average commuting time per trip of 40.1 percent in eighteen years. But the average distance traveled in commuting rose from 8.5 miles in 1983 to 10.6 miles in 1990 and 11.6 miles in 1995 (data for 2000 were not available when this was written). Thus the average speed of movement during commuting trips increased from 28.0 miles per hour in 1983 to 33.6 miles per hour in 1995. These data do not prove that congestion has gotten worse. Rather, they may show that people take longer commuting time because they are enjoying a wider variety of choices of where to live and where to work

Another possibly relevant aspect of commuting is the percentage of all commuters who must travel very long times each day, say, more than forty-five minutes each way. A steady rise in that percentage over time might indicate greater traffic congestion—though it could have other causes, such as higher percentages of workers living in far-out locations. Forty-five minutes per one-way trip is about double the overall average commuting times that prevailed in 1990, 1995, and 2000. In 1990, 12.5 percent of all U.S. commuters commuted forty-five minutes or more each way; while 5.9 percent traveled 60 minutes or more. In 2000, these figures had risen to 14.6 percent and 7.3 percent respectively. This suggests, but does not prove conclusively, that congestion worsened in the 1990s.[6]

The Federal Highway Administration has measured the average number of vehicles per lane on interstate and other major expressways each year from 1993 through 2001.[7] These data show a steady increase in traffic flows per day (not confined to peak hours). During this nine-year period, average daily vehicle counts rose 32.1 percent on rural interstate highways and 22.9 percent on urban interstates. The percentage increases during peak hours were probably even greater.

Other measures show persuasively that congestion has increased in metropolitan areas in all four size groups defined by TTI. The percentage of all daily travel occurring under congested conditions has been estimated by TTI from 1982 through 2000 for seventy-five metropolitan areas classified into the four population size groups defined earlier. These percentages are shown for the four years 1982, 1987, 1992, and 2000 in figure 3-2.[8] This measure of congestion has soared in all four groups over this eighteen-year period. However, because congested periods were initially such a small fraction of the total among small areas, even a 174.9 percent increase from 1982 to 2000 produced congestion for only 13.4 percent of daily travel in 2000. In contrast, in very large areas, that percentage was 36.5 percent.

Similarly, TTI estimated the annual hours of delay owing to congestion per person for each of the four metropolitan area size groups for

FIGURE 3-2. Percent of Daily Travel in Congestion, by Regional Size Group[a]

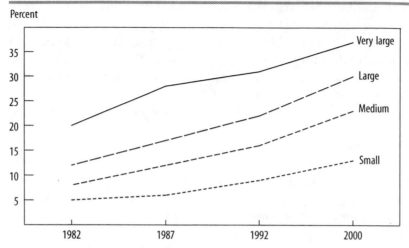

Source: Based on data from David Schrank and Tim Lomax, *The 2001 Urban Mobility Report* (College Station, Tex.: Texas Transportation Institute, 2001).

a. Sample includes seventy-five areas. Figures are averages for each group.

the years 1982 through 2000. The results are shown in figure 3-3. Absolute increases in hours of delay from 1982 to 2000 averaged 53 hours per year per peak-hour road traveler for very large areas, 36 for large areas, 26 for medium areas, only 10 for small areas, and 45 for all areas combined. That estimated national average increase was a 275 percent rise in eighteen years.[9]

It is easy to see why so many people think congestion has gotten much worse, even if they live in small-sized metropolitan areas where absolute congestion delays were still minor in 2000. Percentage increases in delay have been great in all four size groups, very large, large, medium, and small, even in just the most recent period.[10]

From 1992 to 2000, congestion delays per peak-hour road traveler rose eighteen hours, or 41.2 percent, in all four size groups combined (based on dividing the total annual delay in all seventy-five areas by the total number of peak-hour road travelers). People experiencing such relatively large increases in delays in just eight years are likely to conclude that congestion has become "bad" or "very bad" in their areas, even if it has not reached absolutely high levels—as in most small areas.

The view that congestion is becoming nearly intolerable—even in small areas—has been encouraged by TTI's practice of aggregating congestion delays and costs into annual totals that seem staggeringly large.

FIGURE 3-3. Annual Hours of Congestion Delay per Peak-Hour Traveler, by Regional Size Group[a]

Hours

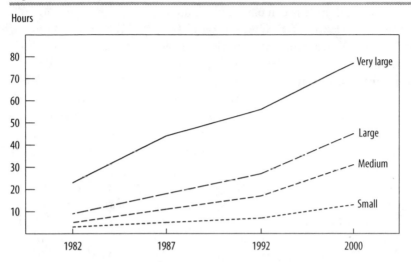

Source: Based on data from Schrank and Lomax, *The 2001 Urban Mobility Report.*
a. Sample includes seventy-five areas. Figures are averages for each group.

The media like to broadcast such fearful totals as part of their general bias to make facts seem as shocking as possible in order to attract attention. For example, TTI's *2002 Urban Mobility Report* states that 3.569 billion hours of peak-hour congestion delay occurred in all seventy-five of the areas studied combined in 2000.[11] That is equivalent to 148.7 million wasted days, or 21.3 million wasted weeks, or 409,615 wasted years. These sound like gigantic losses of one of life's most valuable resources: time. The institute also converts this estimate into an annual average delay per peak-hour road traveler of 61.5 hours over all four area size groups combined, or 17.8 hours per person.

A Different Perspective

However, other ways of looking at these same data lead to quite different conclusions. As noted earlier, TTI's whole analysis of the "costs" of congestion is based on the false premise that there is some alternative state of the world in which everyone who wants to travel during peak hours could do so freely without delays. As British traffic expert P. B. Goodwin pointed out, "I cannot endorse statements of the form 'congestion costs the economy 15 billion pounds per year, updated from time to time by inflation,' implying an annual dividend of 1,000 pounds waiting to be distributed to each family. This is a convenient, consensual fiction. It is calculated by comparing the time spent in traffic now, with the reduced time that would apply if the same volume of traffic was all traveling at free-flow speed, and then giving these notional time savings the same cash value that we currently apply to the odd minutes saved by transport improvements. This is a pure, internally inconsistent notion that can never exist in the real world. (If all traffic traveled at free-flow speed, we can be quite certain that there would be more of it, at least part of the time saved would be spent on further travel, and further changes would be triggered whose value is an unexplored quantity.)" [12]

Another reason such a hypothetical congestion-free peak-hour state cannot exist in the real world is that the capacity of the transport systems in many large metropolitan areas—including roads and off-road public transit facilities—is insufficient to carry without delays all the people who would like to move during those hours. And that capacity cannot be expanded enough to accommodate all of them without infeasible costs of various types.

This does not mean peak-hour congestion is costless. As Goodwin also observed, "I do not at all challenge the wide agreement that time, energy, and money spent in traffic jams is a waste, and that traffic growth's continuing current trends will have unacceptable effects on economic efficiency." [13] Even if TTI's time-delay estimates are accepted, their significance looks different when seen from a daily perspective. Take TTI's estimate that congestion wastes an average of 61.5 hours per peak-hour road traveler per year in the seventy-five metropolitan areas it studied. The typical year contains 240 working days (365 minus 104 for weekends, 10 for vacations, another 10 for holidays, and 1 for illness). If 61.5 hours is converted into minutes and then divided by 240, that means the average daily delay is 15.37 minutes. And there are two commuting trips each day, so the average 2000 delay per peak-hour road commuting trip across the nation is only 7.69 minutes. These delays do not seem to impose such a staggering cost on the average commuter or the entire nation as stating that all commuters in just seventy-five metropolitan areas lose 3.6 billion hours per year stuck in congestion.

Nevertheless, there is little doubt that congestion has steadily been getting worse in much of the nation, especially in very large and large metropolitan areas.

The Travel Time Reliability Problem

Another dimension of peak-hour road travel is the reliability or consistency of each driver's travel-time experiences. Even if the average delay per commuting trip across the United States during peak hours is just under eight minutes, on many occasions every driver runs into much longer delays. This is inescapable because traffic congestion has two basic causes: daily overloading of the roads because of recurrent excess demand during peak hours, and unpredictable incidents that block one or more lanes during those hours. These incidents include major crashes, minor "fender-benders," flat tires, motorists running out of gas, trucks overturning and spilling their cargoes all over the road, lanes blocked by repairs and construction, and hazardous weather conditions. Thousands of such incidents occur every day across the United States, but each one is unpredictable. The traffic delays because of such incidents add a random aspect to the repetitive delays because of routine overcrowding. Hence no driver can be sure that today's experience will be about average. As TTI points out, "If travelers assume each trip will take the average travel time, they will be late for half of their trips."[14] If a traveler wants to arrive at her destination punctually 90 percent of the time, she will have to add time onto what she believes is her expected average travel time to account for those unexpected delays that inevitably occur some of the time. The Texas Transportation Institute refers to this added allowance as "buffer" time. Not all commuters add large buffer allowances onto their expected average times, or else the actual average would be much higher. But commuters responding to polls do not always include "buffer time" in the estimated averages they report, unless they are specifically asked to do so.

Nevertheless, in communities where incidents are particularly frequent—which usually means very large regions—many commuters and other peak-hour travelers who must arrive punctually most of the time may have to add significant buffer allowances to what would otherwise be their average travel time. This time-consuming practice caused by the uncertainty of each person's daily travel experience is one of the most aggravating aspects of peak-hour congestion.

Estimating the Costs of Congestion to Society

In its annual reports on traffic congestion, TTI estimates the annual economic costs of congestion to American society. Its basic method is to calculate how many hours motorists in each of the regions it studies spend in traffic more than they would if there were no peak-hour congestion delays. These hourly estimates are then converted into dollars by calculating the additional fuel costs required while running vehicle engines during those hours and an estimate of the value that people stuck in traffic place on the extra time involved. In its *2002 Urban Mobility Study*, TTI estimated that congestion cost the residents of the seventy-five areas it studied about $67.5 billion, based on 3.6 billion hours of delay and 5.7 billion gallons of extra fuel consumed.[15]

However, there are several reasons to regard such cost estimates with great skepticism. As just noted, the main reason is that this analysis implies it would actually be possible for all people who want to move during peak hours to do so at free-flowing speeds without any delays. But that supposition is false. The "waste" of time and fuel generated by traffic congestion is to a great extent unavoidable; so presuming it could be eliminated is a fantasy. Using a utopian free-flowing state as a measuring rod may be useful for making comparisons of how peak-hour delays change over time. But it should not be seen as a realistic measure of costs generated by congestion that might be avoided by policy changes.

Another reason to discount these estimates is that many people do not regard the time they spend stuck in traffic as a complete waste. Recent studies show that some people have a positive desire to travel for its own sake. Moreover, many commuters see the time they spend alone in their vehicles as temporal "islands of low social pressure" compared to the hassles they experience at work and at home. They can listen to the radio, records, or tapes, or just relax, without having to respond to work colleagues or family members. A survey in 2000 of 1,900 San Francisco Bay residents by Patricia Mokhtarian and Ilan Salomon showed that, although 42 percent of the respondents disliked commuting travel, 40 percent were neutral, and 18 percent positively liked it.[16] Moreover, when asked to comment on statements about the value of their commuting time, 35 percent agreed that "I use my commute time productively," whereas 33 percent were neutral, and 32 percent disagreed. And more than 80 percent agreed that "it is nice to be able to do errands on the way to or from work." When asked whether "travel time is generally a waste of time," 47 percent disagreed, and only 30 percent agreed. When asked to compare their actual commuting time with their "ideal" commuting time, although 49 percent preferred shorter commutes, 50 percent liked about the time they were now spending, and a small percentage actually preferred longer commutes. This survey is hardly definitive, but it suggests that many Americans do not think of the time they spend commuting—or even "excess" time spent stuck in traffic—as a net loss.

A third reason to discount TTI's huge estimates of the costs of congestion is TTI's assumption that time spent stuck in traffic can be economically equated in value with time spent working. TTI used $12.85 per hour as the cost of time "wasted" in traffic congestion. In 2000, according to the Bureau of Labor Statistics, the average hourly wage was $11.48 for all goods-producing workers, and probably slightly higher for all service workers.[17] It may be an established convention among transportation economists to regard sitting in traffic for an average of eight minutes per commuting trip for a week as equivalent in economic value to working at one's job for an extra eighty minutes at one's normal wage. But if there were no congestion, converting the sixteen minutes per day saved into compensated work would hardly be feasible for most people.

Still another reason to discount these huge estimates of the congestion costs is that traffic congestion is often a sign of prosperity and economic success for an entire region, rather than an unmitigated disaster. Places from night clubs to ball games to city streets become crowded because a lot of people want to go there.[18] A contributing factor is that more people can afford to buy and use private vehicles during economic booms. Such places become uncrowded when hardly anyone wants to go there—which is usually a sign of economic decline. When the high-tech stock "bubble" burst in the Silicon Valley in 2000 and employment plunged, traffic congestion dropped markedly in much of the San Francisco Bay Area. In a sense, intensified traffic congestion is one of the prices a regional society pays for economic success.

A final aspect of estimating commuting costs is that only part of the time spent traveling to and from work occurs while the commuter is in a vehicle on major roads. Notable shares of the overall trip consist of walking to the vehicle, starting it up, moving it on local streets to major arteries, moving it off those arteries on local streets to a parking place, parking it, and walking to one's final destination. Hence even if traffic jams on major arteries could be reduced significantly, that would not necessarily reduce the overall trip length proportionately.[19]

However, TTI's estimates of congestion costs do not take into account the losses experienced by businesses because of delays in shipping goods. Some experts believe these costs constitute a serious drag on the efficiency of the entire U.S. economy.[20] Furthermore, many public officials believe congestion is a key factor influencing the ability of their regions to compete economically with other regions in the nation and around the globe. Severe traffic congestion in a region can cause firms choosing sites for production facilities to avoid locating in that region if other suitable sites are available in less congested regions. In fact, absence of intense congestion is one of the main attractions of relatively small regions to "footloose" business firms.

Thus skepticism about the magnitude of TTI's congestion cost estimates is not meant to deny that congestion is a significant economic problem in the aggregate.

Traffic Congestion and Regional Economic Competitiveness

Many business and government leaders worry about their areas becoming less economically competitive because of rising traffic congestion. Greater congestion in a region adds significantly to the costs of production there because of shipping and personal delays. That may reduce the economies of agglomeration that underlie the overall economic efficiency of any region. So regional leaders fear that rising congestion will discourage firms and households from moving in from other regions and encourage firms already located there to shift future expansions in capacity to other areas with less congestion.[21] Does the evidence support these worries?

To answer that question, one must first distinguish the competitiveness of American metropolitan areas with one another from their competitiveness with regions outside the United States. (Urban traffic congestion in most large metropolitan areas around the world is worse than that in the United States—often far worse.) This is true even though the United States has vastly more motor vehicles absolutely and per 1 million residents than any other nation. It also has vastly more roads. So rising traffic congestion is not likely to weaken the American economy's ability to compete with the economies of other nations. But intensified congestion in one American region could conceivably weaken its competitiveness with other American regions.

Analysis presented earlier shows that traffic congestion tends to vary in intensity directly with overall regional population. Thus larger regions have worse congestion, and small ones have the least congestion,

TABLE 3-3. Regional Size and Change in Population Growth, 1990–2000

Size of region	Number of regions	1990 population	2000 population	Absolute change	Percent change
Greater than 5 million	9	75,874,152	84,064,274	8,190,122	10.79
2 to 4.999 million	14	35,988,684	42,848,575	6,859,891	19.06
1 to 1.999 million	27	31,483,749	37,055,342	5,571,593	17.70
500,000 to 999,999	32	19,803,788	22,139,269	2,335,481	11.79
250,000 to 499,999	65	20,647,406	23,551,277	2,903,871	14.06
100,000 to 249,999	113	15,977,919	17,828,880	1,850,961	11.58
All regions	280	201,381,763	229,192,836	27,811,073	13.81

Source: U.S. Bureau of the Census, Census 2000 Redistricting Data (P.L. 94-171), Summary File and 1990 Census.

other things equal. If congestion intensity also directly and strongly affects economic growth, then population growth rates from 1990 to 2000 should also vary with regional size. However, this is not the case, as shown in table 3-3.

The fastest overall growth rate was among regions from 2.0 to 4.999 million, and the smallest regions had the lowest growth rate. Even the very largest regions grew almost as fast as those in several smaller categories. This is admittedly a crude measure, since many other factors besides traffic congestion affect regional population growth rates. But in the 1990s, there was no clear relationship between total regional population and population growth rates, as there was between regional population and traffic congestion.

A more sophisticated approach involves multiple regression analyses with either absolute or percentage growth in individual regions from 1990 to 2000 as the dependent variables, and several traffic-related variables and other factors as independent variables. To isolate the influence of traffic-related variables from the influence of other factors that are likely to affect regional growth, multiple regressions were first run with only standard economic factors as independent variables. These included the following:

—The population of each region in 1990 and 2000;

—Median household incomes in 1989 and 1999 and the percentage change in those incomes during the 1990s;

—Mean January temperatures;

—The gross density (persons per square mile) of the urbanized areas in each region;

—The spatial area of the major urbanized area in each region;

—Median sales prices for existing single-family homes in 2000;

—Percentage of the population 25 and over who had bachelor degrees or above; and

—Percentage of the population 25 and over who graduated from high school but went no higher in education.

The regressions using various combinations of these variables that had the best results produced adjusted r-squared values of 0.2992 when the dependent variable was the percentage gain in regional population from 1990 to 2000, and 0.6605 when the dependent variable was the absolute population gain.

Then several traffic-related variables were introduced into these regressions to see what impact they would have. These traffic-related variables were taken from TTI's *2002 Urban Mobility Report* for seventy-five metropolitan regions, based on congestion measurements from 1990 and 2000. The variables used were:

—Travel time index in 2000;

—Absolute change in the travel time index from 1990 to 2000;

—Percentage change in the travel time index from 1990 to 2000;

—Percentage of travel in congestion in 2000;

—Absolute change in the percentage of travel in congestion in 2000;

—Percentage change in the percentage of travel in congestion in 2000;

—Annual delay in hours per peak road traveler in 2000;

—Absolute change in annual delay per peak-hour road traveler from 1990 to 2000;

—Percentage change in annual delay per peak-hour road traveler from 1990 to 2000;

—Total lane miles in freeways and principal arterials in 2000; and

—Combined freeway and principal arterial lane miles per 100,000 residents in 2000.

Several of these variables were highly correlated with one another, so they could not be used simultaneously. Hence those with the best results were ultimately accepted.

Many combinations of these variables were tested with each of the two dependent variables. For both, introduction of certain traffic-oriented variables markedly increased the adjusted r-squared scores. When the percentage change in regional population from 1990 to 2000 was the dependent variable, the best regression produced an adjusted r-squared of 0.7263—more than double the earlier result. This regression contained four independent variables with t scores of 2.0 or higher. They were the percentage change from 1990 to 2000 in total daily vehicle miles traveled (positive), mean January temperature (positive), the percentage change from 1990 to 2000 in mean household incomes (positive), and number of lane miles in all major roadways per 100,000 residents (negative). The travel time index had a t score of 1.96 and a positive sign, whereas the regional population in 1990 was not statistically significant but had a negative sign. The first variable above indicates that increased driving contributes to faster population growth. The fourth variable indicates that regions with higher amounts of roadways per 100,000 residents grew more slowly than those with lower amounts. The results for the travel time index show that greater degrees of congestion are associated with faster growth. All these results imply that rising traffic congestion contributes to faster population growth.

When the absolute change in regional population from 1990 to 2000 was the dependent variable, the best regression achieved an adjusted r-squared of 0.8133 with nine independent variables with t scores above 2.0. They were the 2000 travel time index (positive), regional population in 1990 (negative), mean January temperature (positive), the percentage change from 1990 to 2000 in total daily vehicle miles traveled (positive), the total number of lane miles in 2000 in all major roadways per 100,000 residents (negative), size of the urbanized area in 2000 in square miles (positive), the percentage of residents 25 and over who graduated from high school but went no higher in education (negative), the density in persons per square mile of the whole urbanized area (positive), and the median price of single-family homes sold in 2000 (negative). The traffic-related independent variables in this regression have the same implications as they did in the one for percentage increases in population: that higher levels of congestion are associated with greater amounts of population growth.

This analysis is not wholly unambiguous, but it certainly does not show any strong linkage between greater traffic congestion and slowing population growth. If anything, greater congestion seems to contribute to faster population growth. Moreover, as shown earlier, when one analyzes the forces underlying the travel time index, rising population helps increase congestion. Hence *the rising congestion that many regional leaders fear may be a symptom of their success at stimulating growth.* Whether this success has a self-limiting aspect by creating traffic congestion that slows further growth is not yet clear. A striking example of these relationships occurred in the San Francisco Bay region during and after the dot.com boom of the late 1990s. At the peak of the boom, traffic congestion was the worst ever; two years after the bust in 2000, with unemployment and office vacancies soaring, congestion had declined perceptibly. In my view, this analysis supports the general contention that rising congestion is an inescapable accompaniment of economic and other success in growing metropolitan areas throughout the world.

This conclusion does not imply that all attempts to counteract or ameliorate rising congestion are hopeless. But these facts mean that as regions become more economically powerful and productive, they are almost sure to suffer from rising congestion. So intensifying congestion should not in itself be taken as a sign that a region is losing competitiveness. It is just as likely to be a symptom of the region's competitive success.

The Public's Perception

No matter what objective measures of congestion indicate, the American public's perception of what has been happening over time to the congestion it encounters is vitally important to public policy. Why? Because elected officials in a democracy react as much—often even more so—to public perceptions as to objective realities. There is enormous evidence that people in many parts of the nation—especially very large and large metropolitan areas—believe not only that congestion has gotten worse but that it has become a serious negative influence on their quality of life. Yet, although many Americans see traffic congestion as a serious *local or regional* problem, relatively few believe it is a major *national* issue.

This conclusion is supported by dozens of surveys of citizen views conducted across the nation by foundations, interest groups, newspapers, polling organizations, and government agencies. A recent Internet search of the linked terms "traffic congestion" and "polls" turned up more than 6,000 responses. Examination of most of those responses produced the following relevant examples.

Traffic Congestion as a National Issue

The Pew Charitable Trusts sponsored a telephone survey of 1,004 adults 18 years old and over in October 1999 conducted in the Denver, Philadelphia, San Francisco, and Tampa metropolitan areas. Respondents were asked what they believed was the most important issue *facing the whole nation* at that time. Crime and violence had the highest response (15 percent), but neither traffic congestion nor population nor urban growth received significant notice (as much as 1 percent).

In February 2001, the Gallup Poll conducted a telephone survey asking a random sample of 1,004 adult Americans to name the most important problem facing the country. This is an open-ended question with no set of answers identified in advance, though multiple answers are allowed. Gallup has been asking this question for more than sixty years. In this survey, fourteen issues or clusters of related issues received mention by at least 4 percent of respondents. Neither the environment nor traffic congestion received as much as a 4 percent mention (their percentages were not identified in this article).[22]

In May 2000, the Gallup Poll carried out a telephone survey of 1,032 randomly chosen American adults exploring their commuting behavior and their experiences with traffic congestion. About 58 percent drove to work each day, and the average time it took each way was 26.0 minutes (compared with 23.7 minutes on a similar survey in 1998). Among these 601 respondents, 19 percent thought the daily traffic they encountered was "a major inconvenience and problem," and 31 percent thought it was a "minor inconvenience and problem." But 48 percent thought it was "not a significant problem," and 2 percent had no opinion. So just half regarded congestion as "a major problem and inconvenience."

A large majority (62 percent) thought traffic had gotten worse or much worse in the past five years, and a similar majority (61 percent) thought it would get still worse in the next five years. Yet when asked how often they got stuck in traffic jams, only 11 percent said every day, 14 percent said several times a week, 22 percent said several times a month, 31 percent said a few times a year, and 20 percent said never.

Among all 1,032 respondents, 69 percent said they had not changed their lives or schedules in any way because of traffic in recent years. Among the 31 percent who did change, 36 percent left earlier, 18 percent took alternate routes, 13 percent allowed more time for travel, and 12 percent avoided driving in certain times. Another 5 percent moved, 1 percent changed jobs, 1 percent worked at home or telecommuted, and 3 percent used mass transit or carpooled.

When all respondents in this traffic-oriented survey were asked—in an open-ended question—to name what they saw as the worst problem facing their communities today, none named traffic congestion.

The Nationwide Personal Transportation Survey conducted by telephone by the Federal Highway Administration in 1995 asked people how they rated certain negative views of traffic congestion. Respondents could answer strongly agree, agree, disagree, strongly disagree, or unknown.

For all three observations, "Congestion is a major problem," "I spend too much time in my vehicle," and "Travel by vehicle is very stressful," the percentages of respondents who did not regard congestion or commuting as a problem were much larger than those who regarded it as a problem—usually by a ratio of more than two to one.[23]

The surveys clearly show that congestion is not a pressing concern among all Americans. Significant fractions of the nation's residents do not encounter heavy traffic very often or are only rarely or never delayed by it. A large majority have not altered commuting behavior because of traffic congestion. Almost none see it as a national problem comparable in importance to education, the economy, crime and violence, and drugs and alcohol.

Traffic Congestion as a Local or Regional Issue

Views on congestion as a local or regional problem are quite different from those concerning it as a national problem, as shown by the following survey results.

In January 2000, the National Association of Homebuilders reported on a telephone survey it had conducted of 500 registered voters in each of five major metropolitan areas about reactions to the pace of growth and traffic congestion. The five areas were Denver, Atlanta, San Diego, Washington, and Minneapolis-St. Paul (Twin Cities).[24] The percentages of respondents characterizing traffic congestion as a "very big problem" and "causing a negative impact on their quality of life" are shown in table 3-4.

On the most important *local* issue, the 1999 Pew Charitable Trust survey indicated that "development, sprawl, traffic and roads" was tied with "crime and violence" for the highest response (18 percent), with "economic issues and the economy" third with 13 percent. "Sprawl-related issues" were named as the most important issue by 60 percent of the Denver region residents, 47 percent of San Francisco region residents, and 33 percent of Tampa residents but only 18 percent of Philadelphia region respondents.[25]

The Bay Area Council has conducted an annual survey in the San Francisco Region in most years since 1990, asking "What do you think

TABLE 3-4. Views of Congestion in Five Metropolitan Areas
Percent

Metropolitan area	Congestion is a very big problem	Congestion has a negative impact on quality of life
Atlanta	53.5	49.9
Denver	58.6	56.8
San Diego	48.5	50.9
Twin Cities	28.7	38.3
Washington	55.5	51.2

Source: National Association of Homebuilders (www.nahb.com/news/survey.htm [December 2003]).

is the most important problem facing the Bay Area today?" Throughout the 1990s, "transportation" was most often mentioned as the "most important problem" by a wide margin except in the recession of 1992–95.[26]

In this highly congested region, people's perception of the relative importance of congestion as a problem rises sharply during periods of strong economic prosperity and declines during times of economic stress. The percentage citing "the economy" as the most important problem jumped from 4 percent in 2000 to 27 percent in 2001. Congestion rises in importance during prosperity because traffic gets worse when more people are working and economic growth is strong, and because fewer people are then worried about holding jobs and getting decent incomes.

In June 1996, the *Los Angeles Times* conducted a telephone survey of 942 adult residents of the city of Los Angeles and asked, "What's the most important problem facing your community today? Is there another problem which is almost as important?" For the city as a whole, 67 percent cited "crime" or some closely related aspect of it, making that overwhelmingly the most-cited issue, and "the economy" was second, cited by 19 percent of the respondents. Traffic congestion and inadequate public transportation combined were mentioned by only 4 percent.[27] Yet Los Angeles has consistently ranked as the region with the worst traffic congestion as measured by TTI.

Conclusions from Polling and Survey Data

I have read descriptions of dozens of other similar surveys about traffic congestion conducted all over the United States during the past decade. Most suffer from two drawbacks: they are telephone polls and therefore omit people who do not have telephones—mostly very poor households—and they are conducted with relatively small samples that result in significant probable errors. Nevertheless, examination of these polls leads to the following reasonable conclusions: most Americans do not consider traffic congestion an important national issue, such as other broad issues like education, crime, and the economy.

When asked to identify significant local or regional issues, people's responses tend to vary with the total populations of their own regions or the absolute rates at which those regions are growing. Residents of large and very large regions experiencing significant absolute population and economic growth—such as Denver, Atlanta, and San Francisco—are likely to rank traffic congestion very high among their concerns. Conversely, residents of small regions and those experiencing slow or no growth in population—such as Philadelphia and the whole state of Ohio—are much less likely to identify traffic congestion as one of their most pressing concerns.

People's perception of the relative importance of traffic congestion in their lives is greatly influenced by the economic prosperity prevailing in their regions. Even in large and very large regions, residents are much more likely to consider traffic congestion a major problem during periods of strong economic prosperity than in economic recession.

CHAPTER 4

Causes of Recent Increases in Peak-Hour Traffic Congestion

Traffic congestion is of two basic types: recurring congestion caused by high volumes of traffic trying to use limited road capacities and random congestion caused by accidents and incidents. This chapter deals with the first type, and the following chapter deals with the second.

The main causes of recurring peak-hour traffic congestion are deeply rooted in American desires and behavior patterns. Some are even built into the basic physical and social structures of U.S. metropolitan areas. Policymakers hoping to reduce recurring congestion—or at least slow its rate of growth—therefore must persuade millions of Americans to alter some of their most cherished social goals and most comfortable habits.

An Overview of the Causes

Several major causes of increases in recurring traffic congestion in America and around the world interact in myriad ways. Several very broad but simple propositions pertain to these complex interactions as follows:

—Normal human time-usage in modern societies results in the concentration of a high percentage of all the trips people want to take within a few hours of the day. They are in the morning from about 6:00 to 9:00 a.m. and in the evening from about 4:00 to 7:00 p.m.

—When overall population grows in any metropolitan area, the total amount of daily travel rises. As a result, more and more people want to make their daily trips during each of the morning and evening trip-concentration periods. From 1950 to 2000, the total population of the United States increased by more than 130 million persons (86 percent), mostly in metropolitan areas. It is currently rising more than 3 million persons per year. Hence the number of persons in each region wanting to use the roads during the same time periods keeps increasing.

—As household incomes rise in societies around the world, a higher percentage of all residents seek to use faster and more comfortable means of travel. In the United States, rising incomes during the past fifty years have been a major reason why millions more travelers use privately owned vehicles, especially because the real costs of doing so have declined.

—As incomes rise in a society, the individual citizen's desires for, and abilities to achieve, private vehicle ownership tend to rise faster than public sector abilities to create additional road and transit facilities. Consequently, growth in the capacity of roads and transit facilities tends to lag behind growth in the demands to use them. A similar divergence between private sector and public sector decisionmaking arises because individual drivers are not required to bear the full social costs of their travel decisions.

—Most American metropolitan areas consist primarily of settlements with densities too low to be effectively served by public transit. Therefore, the most efficient mode of travel for most residents there consists of privately owned vehicles with single occupants. As a result, it takes many more separate vehicles to move any given number of peak-hour travelers than would be the case if people worked and lived close enough together to make more widespread use of common vehicles possible.

As individual metropolitan areas become larger and wealthier, their economies become more complex. This complexity requires ever-greater goods shipments internally and to and from other regions and creates nodes around which traffic concentrates. These conditions generate ubiquitous heavy truck traffic and numerous traffic "bottlenecks."

TABLE 4-1. Weekday Trips

Type of trip	Percent of all trips during EACH of two major peak periods		Percent of all trips taken during the entire weekday				
	6 a.m. to 9 a.m.	4 p.m. to 7 p.m.	6 a.m. to 9 a.m.	4 p.m. to 7 p.m.	Both peak periods	All other times	Total
To and from work	45.5	49.0	7.75	11.33	19.08	26.88	45.96
To work	37.7	3.1	6.43	0.73	7.16	6.19	13.35
From work	7.8	45.9	1.32	10.60	11.92	20.69	32.61
Other business trips	3.8	1.8	0.65	0.41	1.06	2.44	3.50
All work-related trips	49.3	50.8	8.40	11.74	20.14	29.32	49.46
All non-work-related trips	50.7	49.2	8.67	11.37	20.04	30.48	50.52
All trips in this period	100.0	100.0	17.08	23.12	40.20	59.80	100.00

Source: Federal Highway Administration, *1995 NPTS Data Book,* chap. 6, "Journey to Work," table 6-17, p. 6-30.

The Concentration of Trips in Time

Certain basic human behavior patterns in modern societies cause many people to want to travel during the same limited periods each day. One is the normal tendency to sleep most of the night, which reduces the time available for travel. Another is the desire among businesses and other organizations to have all their members working during approximately the same daily hours so they can efficiently interact with one another. Similarly, schools want to have all their students in class at the same time so they can efficiently educate them with a relatively small number of teachers. These patterns cause millions of persons to want to travel during the "peak periods" of 6:00 to 9:00 a.m. in the morning and 4:00 to 7:00 p.m. in the evening. For personal efficiency, many travelers want to perform several errands on trips they must make during these peak periods. This desire adds to the length and complexity of the trips made then.

As a result, in 2000, 66.4 percent of all workers employed outside their homes left for work between 6:00 and 9:00 a.m.[1] That includes persons commuting by transit as well as by private vehicle. In 1995, 40.2 percent of all weekday trips occurred during the two peak periods: 17.1 percent in the morning and 23.1 percent in the evening (table 4-1). Thus workers traveling to and from their jobs composed 45.5 percent of all weekday peak-hour trips in the morning and 49.0 percent of all those trips in the evening. Including other business trips, work-related trips were almost exactly half of all trips in both peak-hour periods and throughout the average weekday.[2]

The net result of all this trip concentration is that more persons want to move at the same time during peak periods than can be handled without delays by the roads and transit facilities available in many metropolitan areas. So those roads and transit facilities become overloaded in relation to their designed capacity. This causes traffic on roads to slow down, and passengers on transit facilities to become densely crowded together.

Rapid Population and Job Growth

Growth in the number of households and jobs in a region inevitably increases the daily flows of traffic within it. Growth can be rapid because it is absolutely large or occurs at a high percentage rate or both. Absolutely large growth recently occurred for jobs, though not always population, in the twenty-six metropolitan areas with 2000 populations exceeding 2 million.[3] All experienced substantial absolute gains in the number and use of vehicles during the 1980s and 1990s, even if their total populations grew only slowly (two MSAs—Pittsburgh and Buffalo-Niagara—lost population from 1990 to 2000; all others gained). Absolutely large population growth, defined as a gain of 250,000 or more persons from 1990 to 2000, took place in seventeen of those large metropolitan areas and in twelve others with populations under 2 million. Rapid rates of population growth—defined as percentage gains more than double the 1990-2000 average of 13.1 percent for all U.S. metropolitan areas—happened in thirty-seven metropolitan areas with population increases of 26.2 percent or more.[4]

These two kinds of probably traffic-worsening changes occurred in sixty-three American metropolitan areas according to the Census Bureau (table 4-2).

Employment growth in the 1980s (14.4 percent) and the 1990s (13.8 percent) has perhaps had an even greater impact in causing congestion than population growth.[5] For every 1 percent increase in nationwide population during those two decades, there was a 1.49 percent increase in total jobs outside the home. This means that areas with relatively low rates of population growth nevertheless had more workers commuting daily. The Pittsburgh metropolitan area, for instance, experienced a 4.8 percent increase in employment between 1980 and 2000 despite an 8.3 percent decrease in population.[6]

Congestion is thus not growing at an alarming rate throughout the nation but primarily in areas that have very large populations or are experiencing absolutely rapid population or job growth. This conclusion is consistent with data from the Texas Transportation Institute's *2002 Urban Mobility Report*, as discussed in chapter 3.

TABLE 4-2. Growth of Congestion-Prone Metropolitan Areas, 1990–2000[a]

Metropolitan area	1990 population	2000 population	Absolute change	Percent change
1. Los Angeles–Long Beach, CA PMSA	8,863,164	9,519,338	656,174	7.4
2. New York, NY PMSA	8,546,846	9,314,235	767,389	9.0
3. Chicago, IL PMSA	7,410,858	8,272,768	861,910	11.6
4. Philadelphia, PA–NJ PMSA	4,922,175	5,100,931	178,756	3.6
5. Washington, DC–MD–VA–WV PMSA	4,223,485	4,923,153	699,668	16.6
6. Detroit, MI PMSA	4,266,654	4,441,551	174,897	4.1
7. Houston, TX PMSA	3,322,025	4,177,646	855,621	25.8
8. Atlanta, GA MSA	2,959,950	4,112,198	1,152,248	38.9
9. Dallas, TX PMSA	2,676,248	3,519,176	842,928	31.5
10. Boston, MA–NH PMSA	3,227,707	3,406,829	179,122	5.5
11. Riverside–San Bernardino, CA PMSA	2,588,793	3,254,821	666,028	25.7
12. Phoenix–Mesa, AZ MSA	2,238,480	3,251,876	1,013,396	45.3
13. Minneapolis–St. Paul, MN–WI MSA	2,538,834	2,968,806	429,972	16.9
14. Orange County, CA PMSA	2,410,556	2,846,289	435,733	18.1
15. San Diego, CA MSA	2,498,016	2,813,833	315,817	12.6
16. Nassau–Suffolk, NY PMSA	2,609,212	2,753,913	144,701	5.5
17. St. Louis, MO–IL MSA	2,492,525	2,603,607	111,082	4.5
18. Baltimore, MD PMSA	2,382,172	2,552,994	170,822	7.2
19. Seattle–Bellevue–Everett, WA PMSA	2,033,156	2,414,616	381,460	18.8
20. Tampa–St. Petersburg–Clearwater, FL MSA	2,067,959	2,395,997	328,038	15.9
21. Oakland, CA PMSA	2,082,914	2,392,557	309,643	14.9
22. Pittsburgh, PA MSA	2,394,811	2,358,695	(36,116)	−1.5
23. Miami, FL PMSA	1,937,094	2,253,362	316,268	16.3
24. Cleveland–Lorain–Elyria, OH PMSA	2,202,069	2,250,871	48,802	2.2
25. Denver, CO PMSA	1,622,980	2,109,282	486,302	30.0
26. Newark, NJ PMSA	1,915,928	2,032,989	117,061	6.1
27. Portland–Vancouver, OR–WA PMSA	1,515,452	1,918,009	402,557	26.6
28. Fort Worth–Arlington, TX PMSA	1,361,034	1,702,625	341,591	25.1
29. Orlando, FL MSA	1,224,852	1,644,561	419,709	34.3
30. Sacramento, CA PMSA	1,340,010	1,628,197	288,187	21.5
31. Fort Lauderdale, FL PMSA	1,255,488	1,623,018	367,530	29.3
32. San Antonio, TX MSA	1,324,749	1,592,383	267,634	20.2
33. Las Vegas, NV–AZ MSA	852,737	1,563,282	710,545	83.3
34. Charlotte–Gastonia–Rock Hill, NC–SC MSA	1,162,093	1,499,293	337,200	29.0
35. Salt Lake City–Ogden, UT MSA	1,072,227	1,333,914	261,687	24.4
36. Austin–San Marcos, TX MSA	846,227	1,249,763	403,536	47.7
37. Raleigh–Durham–Chapel Hill, NC MSA	855,545	1,187,941	332,396	38.9
38. West Palm Beach–Boca Raton, FL MSA	863,518	1,131,184	267,666	31.0
39. Tucson, AZ MSA	666,880	843,746	176,866	26.5
40. McAllen–Edinburg–Mission, TX MSA	383,545	569,463	185,918	48.5
41. Colorado Springs, CO MSA	397,014	516,929	119,915	30.2
42. Fort Myers–Cape Coral, FL MSA	335,113	440,888	105,775	31.6
43. Boise City, ID MSA	295,851	432,345	136,494	46.1

continued on next page

TABLE 4-2. Growth of Congestion-Prone Metropolitan Areas, 1990–2000[a]
(continued)

Metropolitan area	1990 population	2000 population	Absolute change	Percent change
44. Provo–Orem, UT MSA	263,590	368,536	104,946	39.8
45. Reno, NV MSA	254,667	339,486	84,819	33.3
46. Brownsville–Harlingen–San Benito, TX MSA	260,120	335,227	75,107	28.9
47. Fort Pierce–Port St. Lucie, FL MSA	251,071	319,426	68,355	27.2
48. Fayetteville–Springdale–Rogers, AR MSA	210,908	311,121	100,213	47.5
49. Boulder–Longmont, CO PMSA	225,339	291,288	65,949	29.3
50. Ocala, FL MSA	194,833	258,916	64,083	32.9
51. Fort Collins–Loveland, CO MSA	186,136	251,494	65,358	35.1
52. Naples, FL MSA	152,099	251,377	99,278	65.3
53. Wilmington, NC MSA	171,269	233,450	62,181	36.3
54. Olympia, WA PMSA	161,238	207,355	46,117	28.6
55. Myrtle Beach, SC MSA	144,053	196,629	52,576	36.5
56. Laredo, TX MSA	133,239	193,117	59,878	44.9
57. Richland–Kennewick–Pasco, WA MSA	150,033	191,822	41,789	27.9
58. Greeley, CO PMSA	131,821	180,936	49,115	37.3
59. Las Cruces, NM MSA	135,510	174,682	39,172	28.9
60. Bellingham, WA MSA	127,780	166,814	39,034	30.5
61. Yuma, AZ MSA	106,895	160,026	53,131	49.7
62. Punta Gorda, FL MSA	110,975	141,627	30,652	27.6
63. Auburn–Opelika, AL MSA	87,146	115,092	27,946	32.1
Total	105,645,668	123,608,295	17,962,627	17.0
Average	1,676,915	1,962,036	285,121	27.1

Source: U.S. Census Bureau website, comparisons of metropolitan areas.

a. This table breaks down CMSAs (consolidated MSAs) into their constituent MSAs and PMSAs. It includes all those metropolitan areas that (1) contained 2.0 million or more residents in 2000 or (2) had absolute growth of 250,000 or more in the 1990s, or (3) grew at least twice as fast as all U.S. metropolitan areas combined.

Some local governments experiencing worsening traffic congestion react by trying to slow their own growth. Not only is rapid growth the most visible cause of congestion, but local government officials believe—correctly—they have more control over local growth than over any other congestion cause. But the traffic flowing through most individual localities in a metropolitan area is generated by many other communities in that area too. Thus traffic congestion is essentially a regional phenomenon that cannot be effectively remedied by purely local actions.

More Intensive Use of Automotive Vehicles

Throughout the world, as people's incomes rise, many try to shift to faster, more comfortable, and more individually flexible means of transportation. In developing nations, this involves the progressive movement of individuals from walking to bicycling to public transit to motorbikes and motorcycles to private cars and light trucks. In the United States, this basic tendency has expressed itself as a strong preference among American commuters for traveling alone in privately owned vehicles and great intensification of the overall use of such vehicles over time.

Most Americans prefer traveling in private vehicles, mainly alone, in part because such travel usually provides convenience, comfort, privacy, flexibility of timing, and speed far superior to that of public transit. (An equally powerful reason concerns the dominance of low-density settlements in America.) According to the 1995 Nationwide Personal Transportation Survey, travel in privately owned vehicles (POV) accounted for 86.1 percent of all person trips and 90.8 percent of all person miles. In contrast, travel by public transit constituted only 1.8 percent of all person trips and 2.1 percent of all person miles.[7] During peak hours, the shares of both transit and private vehicles are slightly higher. Transit accounted for 5.1 percent of all workers commuting in 1995 and 4.7 percent in 2000, whereas privately owned vehicles accommodated 90.7 percent of workers commuting in 1995 and 87.9 percent in 2000, including carpools.[8] But in 2000, transit commuting trips took 45.8 minutes, on the average, while the average commuting trip in privately owned vehicles was about 23.2 minutes.[9]

This preference for private vehicles immensely increases the total number of vehicles on the roads during peak hours, compared with what would happen if public transit was more widely used. And any large increase in the fraction of commuters sharing rides in private vehicles could significantly reduce peak-hour congestion. Clearly, most Americans believe the net benefits of driving alone exceed the net benefits of public transit or ride sharing. The commuter who drives alone enjoys not only greater privacy and comfort and shorter travel times but also more convenient and flexible timing, the ability to combine several activities on a single trip, and—if parking is free—lower day-to-day cash outlays.

To persuade more commuters to shift modes without changing the locations of their homes or jobs, it would be necessary to make net benefits of solo driving less than those of travel by other modes. That would require increasing the net benefits of the other modes or decreasing those of driving alone. Unfortunately, in most regions, it is extremely difficult to increase the net benefits of using alternative modes. So the most effective course of action is likely to be decreasing the net benefits of driving alone, mainly by raising its costs. A great many of the tactics analyzed later in this book are designed to do just that.

Another cause of increased peak-hour traffic congestion during the past few decades has been much more intensive use of privately owned vehicles for all types of movement. This has greatly compounded the increase in vehicle travel resulting from population growth alone. Thus, from 1980 to 2000, the number of cars and trucks registered increased 42 percent, and the number of miles driven per vehicle increased 28 percent, whereas total population increased only 24 percent and the number of households, 33 percent. In fact, between 1980 and 2000, the U.S. vehicle population rose by 1.2 cars, trucks, or buses for every additional 1.0 woman, man, or child added to the human population. (This ratio was 1.49 to 1 in the 1980s, then declined to 1 to 1 in the 1990s.) Hence the total number of miles traveled by all motor vehicles annually soared 80 percent in these twenty years. In absolute terms, the number of cars and light trucks or sport utility vehicles available for personal driving during peak periods rose more than twice as fast as the number of households. It even rose faster than the number of licensed drivers.[10]

In most regions, this intensified use of vehicles has contributed even more than population growth to worsening traffic congestion. Consider a typical metropolitan area containing 1 million residents in 1980. Since there were 68.8 vehicles registered per 100 persons in 1980, on the average, the area would have contained 688,000 cars, trucks, and buses in that year. But the number of vehicles would have risen to 78.7 per 100 residents by 2000, or by 14.3 percent, even if there had been no population growth at all. The number of miles driven per vehicle also rose by 28.4 percent, so total miles driven would have increased 46.9 percent simply because the same number of residents as in 1980 owned more vehicles by 2000 and had changed their driving behavior. But during these same two decades, the nation's population rose by 24.2 percent. If this community had grown at that same rate, by 2000 its total population would be generating 82.4 percent more vehicle miles of driving than in 1980. That simulation corresponds very closely to the national increase in total vehicle miles traveled of 80 percent from 1980 to 2000.[11]

The widespread occurrence of this "vehicle population explosion" is shown in table 4-3. From 1980 to 2000, the absolute number of registered vehicles rose 65.6 million, or 19.6 percent more than the human population, which grew by 54.9 million. Vehicle populations increased

TABLE 4-3.   Changes in Population and Number of Vehicles, by State, 1980–2000[a]

State	Change in population, 1980–2000		Change in vehicles, 1980–2000		Ratio of change in vehicles to change in population	Vehicles per 100 residents, 1998
	Number	Percent	Number	Percent		
Alabama	557,100	14.32	1,022,149	34.79	1.83	89.05
Alaska	226,932	56.73	332,399	126.87	1.46	94.81
Arizona	2,412,632	88.76	1,877,538	97.94	0.78	73.96
Arkansas	387,400	16.95	266,193	16.91	0.69	68.83
California	10,202,648	43.11	10,824,923	64.16	1.06	81.77
Colorado	1,412,261	48.88	1,284,012	54.83	0.91	84.30
Connecticut	297,565	9.57	706,449	32.90	2.37	83.79
Delaware	188,600	31.70	233,446	58.80	1.24	80.46
District of Columbia	(65,941)	−10.34	(25,919)	−9.67	0.39	42.32
Florida	6,242,378	64.09	4,167,010	54.73	0.67	73.71
Georgia	2,722,453	49.83	3,337,006	87.40	1.23	87.40
Hawaii	246,537	25.55	167,551	29.39	0.68	60.88
Idaho	349,953	37.07	343,700	41.21	0.98	91.02
Illinois	1,001,293	8.77	1,495,584	20.00	1.49	72.25
Indiana	590,485	10.76	1,744,942	45.61	2.96	91.62
Iowa	13,324	0.46	777,223	33.37	58.33	106.15
Kansas	325,418	13.77	289,135	14.41	0.89	85.41
Kentucky	380,769	10.40	233,403	9.00	0.61	69.93
Louisiana	264,976	6.30	777,982	28.00	2.94	79.59
Maine	149,923	13.33	300,096	41.45	2.00	80.33
Maryland	1,080,486	25.63	1,044,538	37.27	0.97	72.64
Massachusetts	612,097	10.67	1,516,399	40.45	2.48	82.93
Michigan	680,444	7.35	1,947,721	30.02	2.86	84.88
Minnesota	842,479	20.66	1,538,940	49.79	1.83	94.11
Mississippi	323,658	12.84	712,411	45.18	2.20	80.48
Missouri	678,211	13.79	1,308,629	40.01	1.93	81.85
Montana	115,195	14.64	346,226	50.92	3.01	113.75
Nebraska	141,263	9.00	364,933	29.10	2.58	94.60
Nevada	1,199,257	150.09	564,725	86.22	0.47	61.04
New Hampshire	314,786	34.18	347,751	49.40	1.10	85.11
New Jersey	1,050,350	14.26	1,629,031	34.22	1.55	75.94
New Mexico	519,046	39.93	460,510	43.12	0.89	84.03
New York	1,418,457	8.08	2,232,531	27.90	1.57	53.93
North Carolina	2,175,313	37.03	1,690,503	37.30	0.78	77.30
North Dakota	(10,800)	−1.65	66,860	10.66	−6.19	108.04
Ohio	556,140	5.15	2,696,476	34.70	4.85	92.20
Oklahoma	425,654	14.07	431,491	16.71	1.01	87.36
Oregon	788,399	29.94	940,574	45.20	1.19	88.31
Pennsylvania	414,054	3.49	2,333,967	33.70	5.64	75.40
Rhode Island	101,319	10.70	136,570	21.92	1.35	72.46
South Carolina	893,012	28.63	1,098,729	55.05	1.23	77.14

continued on next page

TABLE 4-3. Changes in Population and Number of Vehicles, by State, 1980–2000[a]
(continued)

State	Change in population, 1980–2000		Change in vehicles, 1980–2000		Ratio of change in vehicles to change in population	Vehicles per 100 residents, 1998
	Number	Percent	Number	Percent		
South Dakota	64,844	9.40	191,509	31.87	2.95	104.99
Tennessee	1,098,283	23.92	1,548,799	47.35	1.41	84.72
Texas	6,623,820	46.55	3,595,096	34.32	0.54	67.48
Utah	772,169	52.85	635,606	64.07	0.82	72.88
Vermont	97,827	19.14	167,883	48.38	1.72	84.57
Virginia	1,732,515	32.41	2,420,127	66.74	1.40	85.42
Washington	1,764,121	42.71	1,890,866	58.63	1.07	86.80
West Virginia	(141,656)	−7.26	121,735	9.22	−0.86	79.73
Wisconsin	658,675	14.00	1,424,525	48.44	2.16	81.39
Wyoming	22,782	4.84	118,690	25.42	5.21	118.61
United States	54,918,906	24.25	65,679,173	42.16	1.20	78.70

Sources: Federal Highway Administration website for vehicle registration; for population data, U.S. Bureau of the Census.
a. Vehicles include cars, trucks, and buses.

more than human populations in thirty-four states and the District of Columbia.

This intensification of vehicle ownership and usage can be traced in part to the sharp increase in households having more than one person working outside the home, as more women entered the job market, especially in the 1980s. The fraction of all households owning two or more vehicles rose from 21.5 percent in 1960 to 51.5 percent in 1980 to 56.9 percent in 2000 (table 4-4).[12]

Declining Prices and Improving Quality of Private Motor Vehicles

One reason Americans have intensified their use of privately owned vehicles is that the prices of such vehicles and the costs of driving them have declined in real terms.

Transportation spending is the second largest element in total consumer spending (19.3 percent in 2001, exceeded only by 32.9 percent spent on housing). Transportation spending increased 5.0 percent from 1999 to 2001—slightly slower than overall consumer spending (6.8 percent) because of a drop in gasoline prices from 2000 to 2001.[13] Purchasing motor vehicles is the largest element in transportation spending (46.9 percent in 2001, or 9.1 percent of total consumer spending).[14]

TABLE 4-4. Vehicle Ownership per Household
Percent of households unless noted otherwise

	Vehicles per household				
Year	None	One	Two	Three or more	Total number of vehicles
1960	21.53	56.94	19.00	2.53	54,766,718
1970	17.47	47.71	29.32	5.51	79,002,052
1980	12.92	35.53	34.02	17.52	129,747,911
1990	11.53	33.74	37.35	17.33	152,380,479
2000	9.35	33.79	38.55	18.31	179,417,526

Source: U.S. Department of Energy, *Energy Data Book: Edition 22*, Chapter 11, "Household Vehicles and Characteristics," table 11.4, "Household Vehicle Ownership" (www-cta.ornl.gov/cta/data/Chapter11.html).

Therefore, what happens to the cost of buying private motor vehicles has a big influence on how much driving American households do each year. The Consumer Price Index for new cars divided by the Consumer Price Index for all items yields the relative price of new cars as compared to the general price level. Since 1980, the real price of new cars as measured by this index has steadily declined. It fell from 107.2 in 1980 to 80.7 in 2000, a drop of 24.8 percent, as shown in figure 4-1. In the same period, a similar index for used cars and trucks moved quite erratically (figure 4-1). In 2001, this index was 18.5 percent higher than in 1980 but 17.3 percent below its peak in 1984.

Improvements in the quality and durability of the private vehicles available to American consumers have also been important. The current dollar prices of new cars have risen steadily over the period from 1980 to 2001, but the Bureau of Labor Statistics (BLS) concluded that those nominal price increases have been more than offset by quality improvements. That is the main reason BLS has increased the price index for new cars less than that for all items in the past two decades.

Consumer Reports magazine has documented improvements in the quality of new cars by counting the number of "problems" per 100 new cars reported by owners in the first year after they bought a new vehicle. Among cars manufactured by American firms, this number was 104 in 1980 but declined to 36 in 1990. Among cars manufactured by Japanese firms, this number was 40 in 1980 but fell to under 20 in 1990. Similar improvements in quality occurred for used cars made by American firms. The number of "problems" encountered by buyers of five-year-old cars was 279 per 100 cars in 1980, but 191 in 1990, and less than 100 in 2000.[15] As a result of these improvements in quality, Americans

FIGURE 4-1. Motor Vehicle Prices, 1980–2001[a]

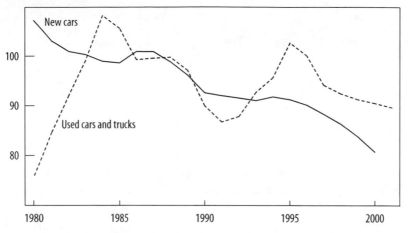

Index, 1982–84 = 100

Source: Data from Federal Highway Administration, *Our Nation's Travel: 1995 Nationwide Personal Transportation Survey Early Results* (September 1997), p. 14.
a. Index = CPI for vehicles/CPI for all items.

are retaining their vehicles longer. The average age of vehicles in use was 6.6 years in 1980 but rose to 7.8 years in 1990 and is now greater than 8.5 years.[16]

All of these developments mean it has become much easier for Americans to purchase private vehicles and to use them longer. Consequently, even relatively low-income households can afford to buy and drive a used car or light truck for commuting and other purposes, and many do so.

Declining Fuel Costs of Movement

A key reason why the amount of driving per person in the United States has risen substantially is the declining real cost of gasoline per mile of movement. This has resulted from a combination of falling real prices of gasoline and rising mileage per gallon. Gasoline prices from 1968 through 2000 are shown in figure 4-2. Gasoline prices have been relatively flat over much of this period, except for the big increases associated with the Middle Eastern oil crises of 1973 and 1979, and the ensuing inflation of the late 1970s and early 1980s. After real gasoline prices fell sharply from 1981 through 1986 because of declining crude oil prices, the retail price in constant dollars gradually declined until 1998. It then rose sharply as a result of further problems in the Middle East.

FIGURE 4-2. Retail Cost of One Gallon of Gasoline, 1968–2000

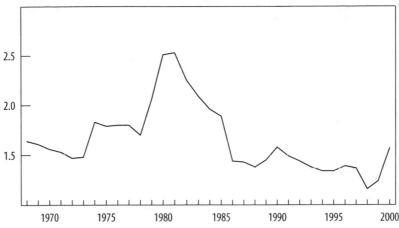

Source: U.S. Bureau of the Census, *Statistical Abstract of the United States: 2002* (2002), pp. 452–53.

However, this relative stability in gasoline prices—aside from Middle East crises—was somewhat offset by increasing mileage per gallon of the American in-use fleet of passenger cars, light trucks, vans, and sport utility vehicles. Passenger cars were getting an average of 13.4 miles per gallon in 1973 (the first year for which data are available) and 16.0 miles per gallon in 1980. But this gradually rose to 21.1 miles per gallon by 1991 and stayed at about that level until it reached 22.0 in 2000.[17] However, the overall fleet mileage per gallon was affected by the increasing share of all private vehicles consisting of sport utility vehicles and light trucks, which get fewer miles per gallon than passenger cars. The overall fleet average was 19.2 miles per gallon in 1980, rose to 22.1 miles per gallon in 1988, and slipped to 20.4 miles per gallon in 2002.[18] With gasoline about $1.40 per gallon, a change in mileage per gallon for passenger cars from 16 in 1980 to 22 in 2000 reduces the fuel cost of driving per mile (in constant 2000 dollars) from 8.75 cents to 6.3 cents, or by 28 percent. Vans, light trucks, and sport utility vehicles enjoyed a rise in mileage per gallon from 12.0 in 1979 to 17.5 in 2000—a gain of 46 percent.

When these two factors are combined, the result is a drop in the real fuel cost of driving a passenger car per mile from about 15.6 cents in 1980 to about 7.0 cents in 2000—a fall of 55 percent (about half that decline was caused by lower gasoline prices and half by greater fuel

FIGURE 4-3. Fuel Cost per Mile of Driving, 1979–2000

2000 dollars

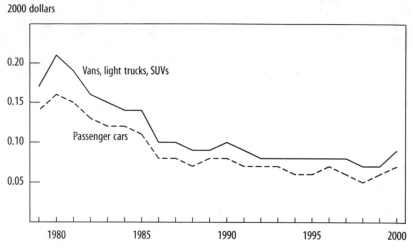

Source: Oregon Department of Transportation, "A Brief Reference on Fuel Costs and Fuel Price Elasticity," *Policy Notes*, vol. 5 (January 2001), figures A, B, C, D.

economy). In the same period, the fuel cost for vans, light trucks, and sport utility vehicles declined from 20.0 cents per mile in 1980 to 9.0 cents in 2000—also a drop of 55 percent. These changes are shown in figure 4-3. The dramatic decline in fuel costs per mile of travel caused by the above factors has certainly encouraged people to drive more miles per year than they otherwise would have.

Decisionmaking: Differences between the Private Sector and the Public Sector

A striking characteristic of transportation systems in most fast-developing nations with market-oriented economies is that private ownership of motor vehicles is increasing much faster than public construction of roads and transit facilities. The most likely reason is that private ownership of vehicles is aggressively promoted by the privately owned automotive industry to increase its profits. That industry heavily advertises vehicles and provides convenient installment financing for their purchase. Moreover, decisions about whether to own such vehicles are made by private households, based on their purchasing power and desires. Hence growth in the total number of privately owned vehicles—

and therefore in the demands for travel in them—is almost entirely dependent on private sector activities. The one exception occurs when governments deliberately impose huge taxes on such vehicles to discourage private ownership, as in Singapore.

In contrast, nearly all streets, roads, and expressways—and public transit systems—are created and operated by local, state, or national governments. Therefore, growth in such transportation facilities depends on government actions heavily influenced by political forces and encumbered by time-consuming public decisionmaking processes. This is true even where most roads are financed by gasoline taxes, and the road-building industry lobbies hard for their construction. As a result, the creation of transportation facilities tends to lag behind the creation of privately owned vehicles whose operators want to drive on those facilities.

That has also happened in the United States in the recent past. Between 1980 and 1998, total highway mileage in the United States increased by only 2.4 percent. In the same period, the number of cars, trucks, and buses registered rose by 42 percent and total vehicle miles driven rose by 80 percent. However, urban road mileage rose 36.5 percent.[19] When lane miles are measured instead of gross road length, the increase in urban mileage from 1980 to 1998 was also 36.7 percent.[20] The Texas Transportation Institute compared changes in daily vehicle miles traveled with changes in lane miles of both expressways and major arteries in seventy-five large urban areas for 1982–2000. Total vehicle miles traveled daily increased 74.5 percent, whereas total lane miles in freeways and principal arterials combined increased only 36.6 percent. Partly as a result, the percentage of daily traffic from all seventy-five areas that is congested went from 10.5 percent in 1982 to 25.5 percent in 2000.[21] From 1982 to 2000, TTI's roadway congestion index rose in all seventy-five metropolitan areas measured, by an average of 43 percent.

Another cause of traffic congestion long noted by economists but up to now ignored by government officials is that commuters are not required to pay the full marginal social costs of driving during peak periods. Every peak-hour commuter entering a congested road not only incurs the costs of her own delay but also imposes greater delay costs on all other persons using the same road at the same time. But individual commuters do not have to take that additional social cost into account in deciding whether or not to drive themselves. Unless society compels them to do so by charging a toll or parking fee for driving during the most popular periods, commuters will continue to underestimate this collective cost. They and most public officials think this way because traditionally most roads have been freely accessible to all motorists. People could certainly recognize that offering unlimited access to hearty free meals at restaurants would cause chronic overcrowding there, as happens at many shelters for the homeless. Similarly, they see that offering public housing units at below cost has generated massive waiting lists among potential occupants. But they fail to connect the congestion they abhor with free access to crowded expressways during peak hours.

Low-Density Settlements and Single-Occupancy Vehicles

One reason American peak-hour traffic congestion is intensive—and getting more so—is that in 2000, 75.7 percent of all commuters traveled singly, in privately owned vehicles, compared with 12.3 percent in car pools and 4.7 percent on public transit. As a result, far more vehicles are required to move the people who want to travel during peak hours. Why do so many people prefer driving singly to the alternatives?

A central reason is the low-density, spatially spread-out residential settlement pattern predominant in most parts of most U.S. metropolitan areas. The forms of public transit dominant in America—buses, light rail, and heavy rail—can efficiently serve only areas settled at relatively high density. Public transit needs to gather significant numbers of passengers together at its points of origin or destination or both, and that is best done when densities are high at those points. One study concluded that buses need residential densities of 4,200 persons per square mile or higher to be efficient, and fixed rail requires higher densities.[22] But most American metropolitan areas have been built with low residential and commercial densities, so they are not conveniently served by public transit. In 1995, in places with gross densities of from 1,000 to 4,000 persons per square mile, no bus service was available to 30.6 percent of households; in lower-density places, that fraction was 59 percent or higher.[23] Yet in 2000, 457 of the nation's 476 urbanized areas had average densities below 4,000 persons per square mile. Those 457 areas contained 78 percent of the total population in all 476 urbanized areas, and 54 percent of the nation's total population.[24]

To a significant degree, low-density living reflects the preferences of most American households. A goal of most American households is to own single-family detached homes with private open space next to each dwelling. In 1999, the National Association of Homebuilders asked 2,000 randomly selected households across the nation the following question:

> "You have two options: buying a $150,000 townhouse in an urban setting close to public transportation, work, and shopping or purchasing a larger, detached single-family home in an outlying suburban area with longer distances to work, public transportation, and shopping. Which option would you choose?"

Eighty-three percent of the respondents chose the larger, farther-out suburban single-family home. Similarly, significant majorities opposed building townhouses, higher-density single-family homes, or apartments in their neighborhoods.[25] The low-density pattern required to meet these preferences spreads housing over a much larger area than it would occupy in high-density settlements.

A trend contributing to lower-density settlements is that the Northeast and Midwest have long experienced major domestic out-migration of population to the West and South. One reason is warmer weather: cities in which the average daily January temperature was 50 degrees or higher gained an average of 17 percent in population from 1990 to 2000; those with average January temperatures below 30 degrees gained only 4 percent. The South and West contain more automobile-dominated metropolitan areas than the Northeast and Midwest, where most of the nation's public transit traffic is located. This move toward lower transit-oriented settlements is indicated by the fact that cities in which 65 percent or more of commuters drove to work alone in 2000 grew by an average of more than 12 percent from 1990 to 2000; cities in which 65 percent or less drove to work alone grew an average of only 1 percent. Cities in which 10 percent or more of all commuters used public transit averaged about zero growth; those in which less than 3 percent used public transit averaged 17 percent growth.[26]

In most metropolitan areas, the fastest growing suburbs are usually those at the edges of the most heavily built-up territory. These peripheral suburbs typically have residential densities much lower than communities closer in. Hence most new growth is occurring at low densities that generate more travel per resident than would higher-density settlements.

Low-density settlement is also strongly preferred for office buildings and office parks, shopping centers, industrial buildings and industrial parks, and other nonresidential structures. Many suburbs require such

FIGURE 4-4. Private Job Growth in Ninety-Two Metropolitan Areas, 1993–96, by Region[a]

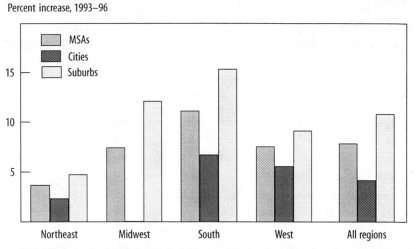

Percent increase, 1993–96

Source: "Where Are the Jobs?" Brookings Institution Center on Urban and Metropolitan Policy (November 1999), pp. 3–9.
a. Sample includes ninety-two MSAs.

facilities to be housed in low-rise structures with low ratios of floor area to ground area. Such regulations cause jobs to become widely dispersed across a metropolitan area. Since most suburbs have lower densities than their central cities, this means a higher percentage of jobs is becoming located in lower-density parts of American urban settlements. A study of employment growth in ninety-two large U.S. metropolitan areas (MSAs) during the prosperous period from 1993 to 1996 showed that in seventy-five of these regions, suburbs gained jobs at a faster rate than their central cities. Overall, suburbs had a 10.78 percent increase in jobs, while cities gained only 4.15 percent (figure 4-4). In all ninety-two MSAs combined, suburbs contained 57 percent of all private sector jobs in 1996 and captured 77 percent of total private job increases from 1993 to 1996.[27] These MSAs combined contained 50.7 percent of all U.S. civilian jobs in 1996. Clearly, jobs are spreading out across the metropolitan landscape. That undoubtedly increases commuting travel distances over what they would be if jobs were more concentrated in a few locations.

Why have jobs spread out so much in American suburbs? Both local residents and most building tenants like the adjacent free ground-level parking and attractive landscaping possible in low-density workplaces. Therefore, developers of suburban workplaces have typically found it

TABLE 4-5. Average Travel Times between Home and Workplace
Minutes

From homes located in	To central city jobs	To suburban jobs
Central city	18.8	23.0
Suburban area	16.9	19.4

Source: Alan E. Pisarski, *Commuting in America II: The Second National Report on Commuting Patterns and Trends* (Washington: Eno Transportation Foundation, 1996), p. 87.

easier to rent or sell space in these park-like settings. Exceptions are workplaces near airports, regional shopping centers, or similar amenities. Around them, developers have built clusters of high-rise office and apartment buildings in so-called edge cities like Tyson's Corner, Virginia, King of Prussia, Pennsylvania, or Irvine, California. However, a recent study by Robert Lang has shown that most suburban office space growth has occurred outside of high-density edge city clusters in scattered locations across entire suburban regions. In thirteen large metropolitan regions in 1999, 35.6 percent of all office space was scattered in the suburbs, versus 37.7 percent downtown and 19.8 percent in suburban edge cities.[28] The resulting combination of low-density residential settlements and low-density workplaces reduces the feasibility of commuting by mass transit. For the same reason, such dispersal also discourages car pools, van pools, and other ride sharing.

Some jobs have shifted to low-density workplaces because computers, fax machines, and other telecommunications devices have made it possible to separate many lower-level activities from executives without much loss of efficiency. And suburban office space generally costs less to build and to rent than downtown space. Peter Gordon and Harry Richardson contend that dispersal of suburban workplaces decreases commuting times and distances by moving jobs closer to where workers live.[29] In that case, low-density workplaces might have a beneficial effect on traffic congestion. However, Alan Pisarski concluded in his intensive study of 1990 commuting flows that flows within individual metropolitan areas had the average travel times shown in table 4-5.

These data do not appear to confirm the Gordon-Richardson hypothesis, since suburb-to-suburb trips took longer than suburb-to-city or city-to-city trips, on the average. Pisarski found the shortest average commuting time (16.5 minutes) was between homes in nonmetropolitan areas to jobs also in nonmetropolitan area.[30]

A powerful motive influencing many commuters to travel long distances or tolerate time wasted in heavy traffic is their desire to work and

FIGURE 4-5. Distribution of Commuting Times, 2000[a]

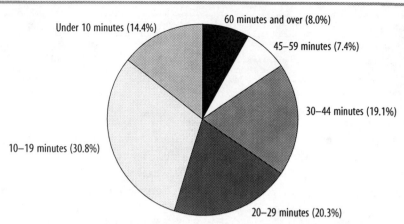

Source: Based on data from U.S. Bureau of the Census, STF (2000).
a. Overall average commute time was 25.5 minutes.

live where they choose, even if their choices do not minimize their daily travel time. In 2000, the average commuting trip took 25.5 minutes—up 5.8 minutes from 1990 and 7.3 minutes from 1983 (figure 4-5).[31] However, in 1990, 12.5 percent of all commuters traveled 45.0 minutes or more, for an average time of 58.5 minutes. By 2000, the fraction of such "long duration" commuters (excluding those who work at home) had risen to 15.4 percent, with 2.8 percent taking 90 minutes or longer. In large metropolitan areas, the average trip time is longer and the percentage of commuters traveling for long periods is higher. From 1983 to 1995, the average work trip increased from 8.5 miles to 11.6 miles (or 36.5 percent).[32] People's willingness to commute long distances has repeatedly undermined attempts to shorten commuting times by building housing near workplaces and encouraging workers to occupy that housing. Almost invariably, many local residents choose to live in distant communities, while many occupants of the adjacent housing work miles away.

The reasons for this behavior are rooted in fundamental American values. In a 1980 survey of workers commuting more than five miles to and from work daily, respondents were asked to state the most important reason they lived so far from their jobs. About 38 percent cited good schools, 24 percent said they liked their house, 17 percent said they liked their neighbors, and 10 percent said their own jobs were too far from the jobs of other family members.[33] Clearly, millions of Americans choose combinations of where to live and where to work based on goals other than minimizing their commuting times or distances.

Consequences of Complex Metropolitan Economies

As American metropolitan areas develop larger and ever-more-complex economies, technologies, political institutions, and physical structures, the resulting operational complexity has several consequences that intensify traffic congestion. One consists of increasing truck shipments of goods on highways and streets. This tendency is strengthened by economic globalization, which involves higher percentages of domestic and worldwide goods production, resulting in trading across international borders.

In 1999, total freight shipments in the United States equaled 3,715 billion ton-miles, of which 29.4 percent was supplied by trucking, 40.3 percent by railroads, 16.7 percent by oil pipelines, and the rest by water and airlines.[34] From 1990 to 1999, the amount of freight shipped by truck rose 48.8 percent—a compound annual growth rate of 4.8 percent. All other forms of freight increased at a compound annual rate of 2.2 percent in this period; hence the share of all freight done by trucking is steadily rising. So the absolute amount of freight shipments is likely to continue growing faster than the nation's gross domestic product.

Because of increased productivity in the trucking industry, the number of heavy trucks has not gone up as fast as the amount of freight they are carrying. From 1995 to 2001, the number of heavy trucks (excluding pickups, vans, sport utility vehicles, and other light trucks) rose at a compound annual rate of 2.9 percent.[35] The total number of trucks grew 27.0 percent from 1995, but most of that growth was more pickups, vans, sport utility vehicles, and other light trucks, which increased 28.05 percent. Heavy trucks grew 18.4 percent, whereas passenger cars grew only 7.2 percent.

Both the number of heavy trucks and the total miles they drove increased sharply in the 1990s compared with the 1980s. However, the proportion of all vehicles consisting of trucks did not change much over these twenty years, remaining between 3 and 4 percent. Moreover, the proportion of all vehicle miles consisting of those driven by heavy trucks has also been relatively constant: it was 7.1 percent in 1980, 6.82 percent in 1990, and 7.49 percent in 2000.[36] Although vehicle miles driven by heavy trucks rose much faster than those driven by passenger cars, that was offset by an even larger increase in vehicle miles driven by pickup trucks, sport utility vehicles, vans, and other light trucks. So the overall proportion of all vehicle movements consisting of those provided by heavy trucks has remained relatively constant.

Nevertheless, the constant absolute increase in the number of trucks on the nation's highways has undoubtedly been contributing to rising traffic congestion. Heavy trucks can be up to eighty-five feet long—four to five times the length of the average passenger car. Such vehicles take up much more space than any other type of conveyance, making it harder for other vehicles to maneuver around and past them. This is especially true of double-trailer trucks and others of extraordinary size and weight. Federal regulations limit truck weights on interstate highways to 80,000 pounds, but twenty-nine states have grandfather or other exemptions permitting greater weights, and forty-seven states permit greater weights on state roads.[37] The trucking industry plans to request an increase in this limit to 97,000 pounds in the forthcoming reauthorization of highway funding.[38] As average sizes increase, trucks take up more room on the roads. Those specific roads subject to above-average truck traffic—from 10 to 15 percent of all vehicles rather than closer to the "normal" 5 percent—pose special congestion obstacles to drivers of other vehicles. It is harder to pass several large trucks clustered close together than when they are spread out. Heavy trucks also add to congestion because they have to slow down to make wide or sharp turns, and their doing so often blocks more than one lane. True, heavy trucks actually have lower accident rates per 100 million miles driven than any other type of vehicle, as noted elsewhere in this book. This is probably because each truck is driven more miles per year, on the average, than any other type of vehicle, and they are piloted by professional drivers. Nevertheless, probable future increases in heavy truck usage on the nation's highways are likely to help intensify recurring congestion there.

A second major effect of rising complexity in metropolitan area societies is the appearance of activity nodes that attract high concentrations of vehicle traffic—thereby generating congestion.[39] These are of two types: *bottlenecks* and *strong attractions*, which may become bottlenecks. Examples of bottlenecks are parts of heavily traveled roads that are narrower than the portions on either side, such as some tunnels, and toll gates that force motorists to slow down or stop. (Toll gates are gradually being modernized by use of electronic payment cards, but many requiring vehicles to stop or at least slow down still exist.) Examples of strong attractions are airports, major seaports, events at sports stadiums, large shopping centers, outdoor concerts, and some downtown areas. All attract large concentrations of people, most arriving by automotive vehicles. The resulting concentration of traffic is endemic to such facilities and cannot be fully eliminated, though it can sometimes be offset to some degree.

Future Trends

All the factors just discussed, taken together, have generated the major recent increases in peak-hour and general traffic congestion described in chapter 3. But what will they cause in the future?

In 1990, some transportation experts predicted that congestion would not intensify as much in the 1990s as it had in the preceding two decades because some of its primary causes would abate.[40] They argued that there would not soon be another baby-boom generation coming into driving ages, the number of women obtaining driving licenses would level off in comparison with when they were first working outside their homes, and incomes would not rise as rapidly, thereby reducing consumers' ability to buy more cars. However, the third reason proved false as the U.S. economy enjoyed unprecedented prosperity in the last half of the 1990s, and the first two reasons had little noticeable impact. Hence peak-hour congestion steadily got worse in the 1990s until 2000 when the economy entered a general recession.

What will happen to recurring peak-hour congestion in the next two decades? An examination of all the above causes of recurring congestion shows that many are likely to intensify in the future, mainly because they are linked to the nation's total population. The overwhelming determinant of the future intensity of traffic congestion will be increases in the nation's population. It grew at a compound annual rate of 1.24 percent in the 1990s—compared with less than 1 percent in the preceding two decades. More than 32 million people were added to the nation from 1990 to 2000. If similar per decade population increases occur from 2000 to 2020, traffic congestion is almost certain to get worse, because the vehicle population is likely to rise commensurately, or at least significantly.

As noted earlier, from 1980 to 2000, the nation added 1.2 cars, trucks, and buses to its registered vehicle population for every 1.0 person added to its human population. Even if that ratio of vehicle addition drops to 1 to 1, as it did during the 1990s, or falls somewhat lower, millions more vehicles will appear on the nation's streets and roads during the next two decades. If the compound annual growth rate of the U.S. population falls from 1.24 percent in the 1990s to 1.0 percent in the next two decades, then the nation's total population will rise from 281.4 million in 2000 to 310.9 million by 2010 and 343.4 million by 2020. Those projections indicate decade population increases of 29.4 million and 32.4 million from 2000 to 2020. If vehicle registrations continue to rise at all close to one added vehicle for every added human being, this would put at least another 60 million cars, trucks, and buses on American roads by 2020. In 2001, there were 230.4 million vehicles registered in the United States.[41] Thus an increase of 60 million more vehicles would be a 26.0 percent gain over the 2001 total, comparable to the increase of 60 million vehicles (37.1 percent) from 1980 to 2000.

In 1997, there were 8.2 million lane miles of highway and local roads in the entire United States, of which 1.89 million were in urban areas. From 1987 to 1997, the total number of lane miles grew at an annual rate of only 0.27 percent, though urban lane miles grew at an annual rate of 1.77 percent.[42] Projecting the same rates of increase over the next twenty years indicates that total lane mileage would grow only 5.5 percent, although urban lane miles would grow 42 percent. Thus total lane mileage increases are not likely to keep up with future growth in the number of registered vehicles, but urban lane mileage might do so. Even so, that would not prevent much more intensive crowding of urban roads during peak hours, when a disproportionate share of all vehicles are trying to use the roads at the same time. Thus peak-hour traffic congestion is likely to get worse—even much worse—during the next twenty years, especially in those metropolitan areas that grow absolutely in population much faster than the national average. What, if anything, can be done to prevent or at least ameliorate this outcome is the subject of this book.

CHAPTER 5

Incidents and Accidents as Causes of Congestion

At 1:07 p.m. on a Thursday in November 1998, a depressed 32-year-old man climbed onto the railing of the Woodrow Wilson Bridge across the Potomac River south of Washington, D.C., and threatened to jump. Fearful that the man had a gun and might shoot someone, police closed the six lanes on the bridge to all traffic for five hours while they tried to talk him into surrendering. They were unable to do so. At 6:45 p.m. they shot him in the leg with a beanbag bullet, and he jumped into the river, where he was picked up by a police boat and taken to a hospital. Because this bridge is part of the Washington, D.C., beltway and normally handles close to 200,000 cars per day, its closing for more than five hours right through the evening rush hour caused one of the most massive traffic tie-ups in Washington history. Within an hour of the bridge closing, traffic on the beltway was backed up for eight miles on each side of the bridge. Police shut down many entrances to the beltway, but that simply diverted vehicles into causing gridlock on many other major roads.[1]

This event illustrates how peak-hour traffic congestion can be enormously affected by unpredictable "incidents," as well as by recurring overcrowding of the roadways. In fact, many traffic experts believe that more than half of all roadway congestion in America is caused by specific incidents rather than by sheer overloading of roads. Empirical evidence supporting that view is sparse.[2] Nevertheless, it is certain that incidents cause substantial traffic congestion every day, especially on major expressways and freeways.

What Are "Incidents"?

The *Traffic Incident Management Handbook* defines an *"incident"* as "any nonrecurring event that causes a reduction of roadway capacity or an abnormal increase in demand."[3] Examples include the following:

—Any collision or crash between two or more vehicles that blocks traffic. This is also called an *accident*, which is a subclass of the general category *incidents*.

—Any crash of one vehicle into a tree, light fixture, lane divider, or anything else that blocks traffic. This too is called an accident.

—The overturning of a truck that spills gasoline, oil, dangerous chemicals, or even live chickens or other items onto the road, thereby causing the police to close one or more lanes of traffic for safety reasons. Such overturns are also considered accidents.

—The stalling of a vehicle, a flat tire, a vehicle's running out of gas, or any other event that causes a vehicle to stop moving without actually colliding with any other object. This is called a *disablement* and is probably the most common form of incident.

—Any closure of lanes because of road construction or repairs that slows down the flow of traffic. This is also an extremely common form of incident.

—Some event on the side of the road that causes passing drivers to slow down to look more closely, thereby impeding the flow of traffic. This is often called *rubbernecking* or a *gaper's block*. It frequently occurs when a major accident has taken place and other vehicles slow down to observe it even after the vehicles and associated rescue equipment have been moved out of the road.

—Any nonrecurring special event that floods a road with extra traffic, such as a ball game, parade, or concert.

—Severe weather conditions that restrict visibility (such as fog, heavy rain, or heavy snow) or safety (such as roads made slippery by ice or rain) or road capacity (such as landslides, rock slides, or mud slides).

Though traffic accidents are a subclass of incidents, most incidents are not accidents but other events that slow traffic flows. However, since noncrash incidents slow or block traffic, they may lead to accidents involving other vehicles that run into those initially delayed by the incidents.

A Breakdown of Incidents

Different types of incidents have different effects on traffic congestion, so it would be desirable to know what fractions of all incidents are likely to be of each type. Unfortunately, there are no nationwide empirical data sets—or anything close to them—on incidents or their impacts. However, some analysts have estimated what proportion of all incidents falls into different subcategories. One such estimate is a flow chart that starts with 100 percent of all incidents and breaks them down into various categories.[4] It was developed in 1990 by Cambridge Systematics, through interviews with incident management program officials (figure 5-1). Although only 70 percent of all incidents are reported in detail, figure 5-1 extrapolates those details to the other 30 percent, which are treated as though they were the same as the ones reported in detail. All incidents are broken down into three categories: 80 percent are disablements (motorists unable to keep driving their vehicles), 10 percent are accidents, and another 10 percent are other types of incidents. Each category is subdivided into incidents that occurred on the shoulders of roads and hence did not block lanes of traffic directly, and those that occurred in traffic lanes and blocked them. The numbers next to each box in figure 5-1 show the percentages of the original 100 incidents in each of these boxes. Thus only 4 incidents out of 100 are accidents that directly block traffic lanes. All the numbers in the column of hexagons add up to the 100 total incidents broken down in the figure.

Figure 5-1 shows that 22 percent of all incidents result in direct lane blockages. True, on-the-shoulder incidents sometimes affect traffic flows by causing passing motorists to slow down to avoid the people on the shoulder or to see what is happening. So even such incidents can increase congestion to some degree. But the really big impacts of incidents on congestion usually involve serious accidents or major spills on the roadways caused by trucks turning over.

Figure 5-1 is founded on relatively old data and contains many rather arbitrary assumptions. However, based on my review of the more recent literature on the frequency of incidents, there are no incident data superior to those shown in figure 5-1. Therefore, this figure presents a reasonable approximation of the types of incidents that occur on major

FIGURE 5-1. Breakdown of Traffic Incidents and Delay Caused

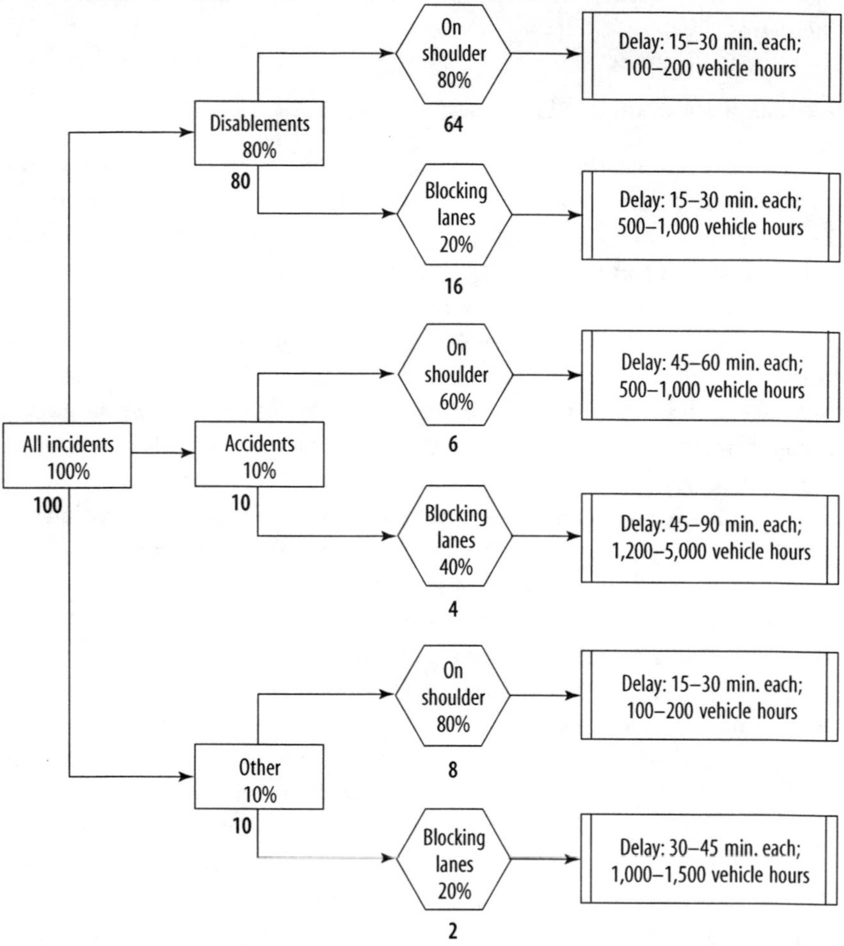

| | | Delay: 15–30 min. each; 100–200 vehicle hours |
On shoulder 80% / 64

Disablements 80% / 80

| | | Delay: 15–30 min. each; 500–1,000 vehicle hours |
Blocking lanes 20% / 16

| | | Delay: 45–60 min. each; 500–1,000 vehicle hours |
On shoulder 60% / 6

All incidents 100% / 100

Accidents 10% / 10

| | | Delay: 45–90 min. each; 1,200–5,000 vehicle hours |
Blocking lanes 40% / 4

| | | Delay: 15–30 min. each; 100–200 vehicle hours |
On shoulder 80% / 8

Other 10% / 10

| | | Delay: 30–45 min. each; 1,000–1,500 vehicle hours |
Blocking lanes 20% / 2

Source: Cambridge Systematics Inc.

roadways, and their likely impacts on congestion, and it is used as a reference in the remainder of this analysis.

Conclusions about Peak-Hour Congestion

My examination of all the evidence on the share of peak-hour congestion caused by incidents that I was able to compile leads to the following conclusions:

—The percentage of peak-hour congestion caused by incidents, including accidents, varies greatly from one region to another. In one 1984 study of thirty-seven metropolitan areas, the specific area percentages ranged from a low of 37 percent (San Diego) to a high of 100 percent (presumably because that area—Indianapolis—had no recurring congestion in 1984). The average was 60.2 percent, and the median was 57.7 percent. Thus no single quantitative estimate is likely to apply throughout the nation.[5]

—Nevertheless, incidents are responsible for a very significant share of both peak-hour and off-peak-hour congestion in all regions of the nation. Therefore, increasing the speed at which lane blockages due to incidents are removed, especially those on major freeways, can notably reduce peak-hour and overall congestion in any region.

—The majority of incidents are vehicle disablements, most of which occur on road shoulders and do not result in lane blockages.

—Roughly 10 to 15 percent of incidents involves accidents. The most serious accidents are responsible for the worst congestion arising from all types of incidents. However, some of the worst traffic-delaying accidents arise during extremely bad weather, mainly thick fog, snow, ice storms, and heavy rain.

Frequency and Nature of Traffic Accidents

Traffic accidents are surely responsible for most of the peak-hour congestion arising from incidents of all types except perhaps for road blockages because of construction or repairs. Therefore, understanding traffic accidents is crucial to coping more effectively with peak-hour congestion.

Unlike incidents in general, accidents are copiously documented by data gathered by state governments and the federal government. A whole bureau in the Federal Highway Administration, the National Highway Traffic Safety Administration (NHTSA), is devoted solely to collecting and analyzing data about traffic accidents throughout the United States and what might be done to reduce them. Nevertheless, neither this agency nor any other has expended much effort analyzing the relationship between traffic accidents and road congestion. To do that, some basic facts about the frequency and nature of traffic accidents must be noted.

According to NHTSA, in the year 2001, 6,323,000 automotive vehicle crashes were known to the police throughout the United States.[6]

FIGURE 5-2. Number of Vehicular Accidents by Damage Caused, 1988–2001

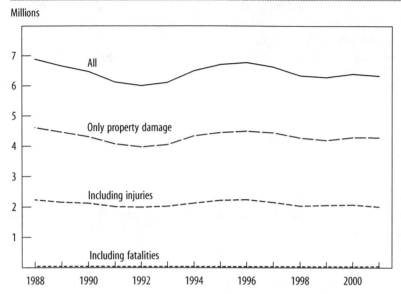

Source: National Highway Traffic Safety Administration, *Traffic Safety Facts 2000* (Washington, 2001), p. 14.

That is an average of 17,323 per day, 722 per hour, and 12.0 per minute—one every five seconds! Of these, 37,795—or 60/100ths of 1 percent—involved fatalities, killing 42,116 persons, or 115 per day.[7] The remaining 99.4 percent were nonfatal, but 31.6 percent of those resulted in injuries, while the other 67.7 percent—about 4.282 million—resulted in property damage only.

The significance of these large numbers can only be appreciated by comparing them with past numbers of accidents and the amount of driving that generated all these crashes. Figure 5-2 shows the trend in total accidents from 1988 through 2001. For crashes involving injuries and those involving only property damage, the absolute number of vehicle crashes each year has remained remarkably stable over this fourteen-year period, considering the large increases in vehicle miles driven that occurred at the same time. The number of accidents declined during the recession of the early 1990s, rose during the period of high prosperity in the mid-1990s, and then declined in the late 1990s even though strong prosperity was continuing. For both types of accidents (ones involving injuries and ones with only property damage), the absolute annual number is somewhat lower in 2001 than it was in 1988. But both numbers

TABLE 5-1. Annual Vehicle Miles Traveled, by Vehicle Type
Billions of miles per year unless otherwise indicated

| Period | All vehicles | Passenger vehicles | | | Trucks | Trucks as percent of total |
		Cars	Buses	Vans, pickups, SUVs		
1980	1,527	1,122	6.1	291	108	7.10
1981	1,555	1,144	6.2	296	109	6.99
1982	1,595	1,172	5.8	306	111	6.99
1983	1,653	1,204	5.2	328	116	7.03
1984	1,720	1,236	4.6	358	122	7.08
1985	1,775	1,256	4.5	391	124	6.96
1986	1,835	1,280	4.7	424	127	6.90
1987	1,921	1,325	5.3	457	134	6.95
1988	2,026	1,380	5.5	502	138	6.81
1989	2,096	1,412	5.7	536	143	6.81
1990	2,144	1,418	5.7	575	146	6.82
1991	2,172	1,367	5.8	649	150	6.88
1992	2,247	1,381	5.8	707	153	6.83
1993	2,296	1,385	6.1	746	160	6.96
1994	2,358	1,416	6.4	765	170	7.22
1995	2,423	1,438	6.4	790	178	7.35
1996	2,486	1,470	6.6	817	183	7.36
1997	2,562	1,503	6.8	851	191	7.47
1998	2,632	1,550	7.0	868	196	7.46
1999	2,691	1,569	7.7	901	203	7.53
2000	2,750	1,602	7.7	924	206	7.49
		Percent change				
1980–90	40.40	26.39	−5.50	97.49	34.80	−3.9
1990–2000	28.24	12.99	34.47	60.82	40.86	9.8
1980–2000	80.06	42.80	27.08	217.60	89.88	5.5

Source: U.S. Bureau of the Census, *Statistical Abstract of the United States: 2001* (2001), p. 690.

varied only in a narrow range in that period. In contrast, table 5-1 shows a steady upward trend in miles traveled. The 36 percent increase in total vehicle miles traveled (VMT) from 1988 to 2000 included an 84 percent increase by light trucks (mainly because of the increasing popularity of pickups and sport utility vehicles) and a 49 percent gain by heavy trucks, with only a 16 percent rise by passenger cars.

Figure 5-3 vividly illustrates the relative stability of the number of traffic accidents of various types, compared with the dynamic increases in people, number of vehicles, and VMT. In that decade, VMT rose by 28.6 percent, number of vehicles registered by 17.3 percent, and population by 12.8 percent.[8] These factors might have been expected to gener-

FIGURE 5-3. Changes in Key Accident Variables, 1990–2000

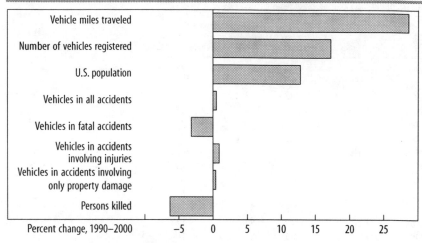

Source: National Highway Traffic Safety Administration, *Traffic Safety Facts 2000*, p. 14.

ate commensurate increases in the number of accidents, but they did not. The total number of vehicles involved in all types of accidents rose only 0.5 percent, whereas those involved in fatal accidents fell 3.2 percent. The number of persons killed by traffic accidents declined even more, by 6.3 percent. No type of accident involved even 1 percent more vehicles in 2000 than ten years earlier.

Consequently, the corresponding rates of accidents per 100 million miles traveled all declined notably in the 1990s, except for light trucks. However, large trucks had much lower accident rates in relation to their VMT, probably because they drive many more miles per year per vehicle than the other types and are driven by professional drivers. In 1990 and 2000, passenger cars had notably higher accident rates per 100 million miles of VMT than the other types of vehicles, but cars also experienced the largest percentage declines in rates during the 1990s.[9]

Why Have Accident Rates Fallen?

Why has the number of traffic accidents in the United States not risen along with total vehicle miles traveled? There is no single answer. Rather, several disparate forces have acted together to restrain the number of accidents as driving has increased.

LESS USE OF ALCOHOL BY AMERICANS GENERALLY, ESPECIALLY BY AUTOMOBILE DRIVERS. From 1980 to 1997, per capita consumption of all alcohol in the United States fell by 20 percent from 2.75 to 2.2 gallons per year.[10] Starting in the early 1980s, many states passed tougher laws imposing penalties for driving under the influence of alcohol or other substances that reduce driver capabilities. States also carried out educational and instructional campaigns publicizing those new laws.[11] Roadside surveys in 1973, 1986, and 1996 of drivers not involved in accidents show downward trends in the percentage of all age groups who had blood alcohol concentrations (BACs) of 0.10 or more, the level considered clearly unsafe for driving. True, only the under 21 age group had a statistically significant decline from 1986 to 1996, but it was a drop of 88 percent. Thanks in part to intensive media advertising campaigns against driving while intoxicated, the share of all traffic fatalities related to alcohol consumption dropped from 58 percent in 1982 to about 30 percent in 2001. About nonfatal crashes, a 2001 NHTSA report said, "The situation with respect to non-fatal crashes involving alcohol is less clear—Blood Alcohol Contents are not routinely measured in non-fatal crashes. However, data from NHTSA indicate that 9 percent of the injury crashes and 5 percent of property-damage-only crashes involved alcohol in the judgment of police officers investigating the crashes."[12]

GREATER USE OF ANTICRASH RESTRAINTS IN AUTOMOTIVE VEHICLES. Such restraints include seat belts, child and infant car seats, and air bags. In 1990, about 64 percent of car drivers in injury and damage-only crashes were using restraints. In 2000, 82 percent were using them. In fatal crashes, the usage among car drivers rose from 37.1 percent to 55.5 percent.[13] Even so, 60 percent of the passenger vehicle occupants (including nondrivers) killed in traffic crashes in 2000 were not restrained by seat belts.[14] In all ten states covered by a special NHTSA investigation of traffic safety practices that had received federal assistance, laws requiring the use of seat belts were adopted in the 1980s, and publicity programs promoting such use were also carried out. As a result, the estimated rate of use of seat belts in those states rose from 12 percent in 1980 to 65 percent in 1993.[15] Other laws requiring safety seats for children were also passed, and safety seat loaner programs were established in all ten states. The crash resistance of car designs has improved too.

True, these changes in behavior do not directly affect the total number of accidents. But they do affect the severity of damage likely to be caused by any accident. The mere buckling up with seat belts may increase drivers' awareness of safety considerations; hence more drivers may be more cautious when more of them are wearing these restraints.

INCREASES IN THE NUMBER OF LAW ENFORCEMENT PERSONNEL, INCLUDING THOSE ASSIGNED TO TRAFFIC MANAGEMENT. In 2000, both state and local police departments in the United States employed 1,019,496 full-time personnel, of whom 708,022 were sworn. That was a rise of 10.5 percent in total personnel in four years and 20.5 percent in eight years.[16] There are no reliable records about how many of these personnel were assigned to traffic policing. But it is likely that this number increased at least somewhat, since more than 98 percent of local police departments are legally responsible for traffic management in their jurisdictions.

In ten states covered by a special NHTSA investigation of traffic safety practices, the number of sworn police officers rose 19 percent from 1980 to 1993. Officers in these ten states made 33 percent more driving while intoxicated arrests and issued 14 percent more speeding citations in 1993 than in 1980. Even so, the fraction of motorists in eight of these states exceeding the 55 mile per hour speed limit then in effect rose from 44.2 percent in 1980 to 47.6 percent in 1992.[17]

IMPROVEMENTS IN ROAD DESIGN. The introduction of interstate highways after 1956 revolutionized the safety of long-distance driving in much of the nation. Many two-lane roads on which drivers passing slow vehicles risked head-on collisions with vehicles moving in the opposite direction were in effect replaced by interstate roadways with physically separated dual-or-more lanes for travel in each direction. Passing on these roadways was relatively easy and involved greatly reduced risks of head-on collisions, compared with older two-lane roads. There were no intersections at which traffic on one road crossed directly in the path of traffic on another. They were all replaced by cloverleafs or other non-confrontational interchanges. The curves on interstates were graduated enough to allow continuous high-speed movement with low risk of flying off the road at the designated speed.

These changes helped cause dramatic declines in traffic fatality rates during the period from 1956 to 1976 when interstate highways were being built across the nation. In 1966, 5.5 persons were killed for every 100 million vehicle miles of travel. By 1975, this statistic had fallen to 3.1—a drop of 43 percent. Fatality rates then leveled off for about five years until 1980, when they began falling further. From 1980 to 1992, the overall fatality rate dropped to 1.7 per 100 million miles, another decline of 45.1 percent. By 1999, it had fallen to 1.5. Thus the accident fatality rate per 100 million miles of vehicle travel fell by 72 percent from 1966 to 1999.[18] This drop was not entirely because of the building of interstates. Many other expressways and freeways were also built using the same design principles as the interstate system. And other factors like those just described were at work.

Before the advent of these modern highways, the absolute number of persons killed by traffic accidents had risen along with, but slightly slower than, vehicle miles traveled. In 1950, 34,800 people were killed at a rate of 7.6 per 100 million vehicle miles traveled. The absolute number killed rose steadily to a peak of 56,700 in 1972, though the *rate* had by then fallen to 4.5 per 100 million vehicle miles.[19] Then the absolute number killed began declining too, though it returned to more than 50,000 from 1978 through 1980. After that, the absolute number of traffic fatalities each year began a gradual decline to about 41,000 in 1998, where it has remained relatively constant since that time. Because the number of vehicle miles traveled continues to increase, this means the rate of fatalities per 100 million vehicle miles traveled is still falling.

Have improvements in road design still been improving traffic safety during the recent past? The answer is probably "yes, but more slowly than when interstates were first introduced." As newer roads are built, they embody the latest innovations in safety features, replacing older roads that were not as safe. Furthermore, as total traffic rises, higher and higher percentages of driving take place on interstates and other safely designed roads. Although interstates were originally conceived as carriers of long-distance traffic from one metropolitan area to another, they have become major local arteries carrying intrametropolitan area traffic, including millions of commuters each day. Hence the interstate system as a whole now carries more than 30 percent of all vehicle traffic in the nation.

INCREASED CONGESTION, SLOWING TRAFFIC. Increasing congestion in large metropolitan areas has two opposite impacts on the number of accidents there. On the one hand, as traffic slows down, the chances of major accidents are reduced. On the other hand, so-called secondary accidents often occur after traffic has been slowed or stopped by a "primary" accident or incident. Vehicles moving at full speed often come upon a stopped line of other vehicles unexpectedly, sometimes crashing into the latter. This is especially likely in bad weather, such as heavy fog, that obscures visibility. It seems probable that one effect of these opposite impacts is to reduce the number of fatal accidents and increase the percentage of all accidents that involve only property damage. However, there is not enough empirical information about these two impacts to determine which, if either, dominates, or by how much.

CHANGES IN THE POPULATIONS OF THE MOST ACCIDENT-PRONE AGE GROUPS. The fatality rate per 100 million vehicle miles traveled is highest among drivers over 85 (7.8), age 16 (6.7), ages 80-84 (6.0), and ages 17-18 (3.0).[20] Presumably, rates for nonfatal accidents involving injuries or only property damage are also higher for these groups. But the number of young people declined in the 1980s and much of the 1990s.[21] However, that drop was more than offset by increasing numbers of people 80 and over. Thus the total number of people in these two accident-prone groups increased from 40.0 million in 1980 to 42.3 million in 1999, a rise of 5.9 percent. Moreover, the percentage of persons in each age group with driver's licenses is notably higher among older drivers than younger ones. Hence size changes in age groups in the U.S. population cannot explain the recent decline in accident rates.[22]

Using National Statistics in Local Areas

In 2000, there were 6.394 million traffic accidents reported in the United States, and many more were unreported. This analysis assumes that unreported accidents are not serious enough to add to traffic congestion. Those 6.394 million reported accidents included 41,821 fatalities and 3.189 million injuries. In the same year, about 2.750 trillion vehicle miles were driven, according to the Federal Highway Administration. Thus there were 232.5 accidents for every 100 million vehicle miles driven, including 1.52 fatalities and 116 injuries.[23]

Since there are 365 days per year, there were 17,518 accidents per day, on the average. However, the average total accidents per weekday was higher (18,569) than the average on weekend days (15,038).

In 2000, there were 281.4 million residents of the United States. The annual accident rate per 100,000 residents was 2,272.4. That rate was remarkably constant from 1990 through 2000, varying no more than 6.7 percent from the average for that period of 2,430.1, as shown in figure 5-4. With 17,518 accidents per day in 2000, the average number per 100,000 residents per day was 6.225.

Therefore, in a metropolitan area containing 1.0 million residents, there would be an average of 62.25 accidents per day (66.00 on weekdays and 53.44 on weekend days). Analysis of the time distribution of vehicle crashes in 2000 across the twenty-four hours of each day shows that, during weekdays, about 33.6 percent of all crashes occur during

FIGURE 5-4. Crashes per 100,000 Residents, 1990–2002

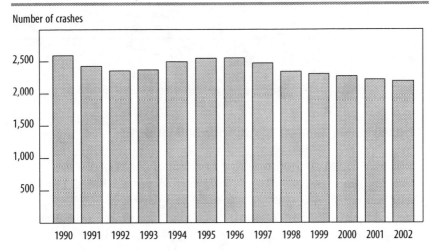

Source: National Highway Traffic Safety Administration, *Traffic Safety Facts 2002*, p. 14; and author's calculations.

the two peak travel periods of 6:00 to 9:00 a.m. and 4:00 to 7:00 p.m. combined.[24] Thus 24.2 accidents would occur each weekday during those six peak hours, or 4.0 per hour. In a metropolitan area containing 4.9 million residents, as the Washington primary metropolitan statistical area (PMSA) did in 2000, there would be about 19.6 accidents per hour during weekday peak periods, or 117.6 accidents during the six peak travel hours combined. Since this analysis is based only on accidents reported to the police, the true number might be much higher.

Earlier estimations indicated that accidents constitute about 10 percent of all the incidents that tend to disrupt the unimpeded flow of traffic, other than recurring overcrowding. So if there were 4.0 accidents per peak hour for every million residents in a metropolitan area, there would be a total of 40.0 incidents per hour—or 240 incidents in all six peak hours combined. Thus the entire Washington PMSA would typically experience about 1,176 traffic incidents (including accidents) every weekday during peak hours, or around 196 per peak hour. Assuming that 36.6 percent of all incidents occurred during peak hours, then in the course of an entire day, around 3,213 incidents of all types would take place that had the potential to disrupt traffic.[25]

These calculations show why accidents and incidents can potentially cause a great deal of traffic congestion almost every day in a large metropolitan area.

TABLE 5-2. Projected Rise in Accidents, Based on Population Growth, 2000–20

Year	Residential population	Accident rate per 100,000	Total number of accidents	Percent increase
2000	281,421,906	2,271.8	6,393,409	...
2010	310,864,864	2,300	7,149,892	11.8
2020	343,388,207	2,300	7,897,929	10.5

Source: Author's calculations.

Projected Future Numbers of Accidents and Incidents

Based on past experience, the total number of accidents in the United States will rise along with future increases in population.[26] The compound annual growth rate of the U.S. population in the 1990s was about 1.24 percent. Conservatively assuming a future compound annual population growth rate of only 1.0 percent, the residential population as of April 1 would rise from 281.4 million in 2000 to 310.8 million in 2010 and 343.4 million in 2020. If the overall accident rate remains at about 2,300 per 100,000 U.S. residents, then the number of accidents will rise as shown in table 5-2.

These projections show an expected increase in all accidents of about 11 percent per decade. But the actual accident rate per 100,000 residents has been declining slightly since 1996, at a rate of about 2.9 percent per year compounded. It is reasonable to attribute at least some of that decline to improved traffic management and accident reduction policies. If that rate of decline continues through 2010, the accident rate per 100,000 residents would drop to 1,698 in that year. Then the projected number of accidents in 2010 would be 5.810 million, rather than 7.149 million—a reduction of 1.3 million accidents per year, or 19 percent. This admittedly crude calculation provides at least an outer bound to the benefits that might be achieved by maximum use of improved traffic management policies such as those described later in this book.

These projections can also be used to estimate future changes in the likely total number of traffic incidents of all types. Assuming accidents constitute 10 percent of all incidents, there were about 64 million incidents throughout the United States in 2000. If the rates of accidents and other incidents remain the same in the future as in 2000, the number of incidents would rise to 71.5 million in 2010 and 79 million in 2020. That means there would be increases of 7.5 million incidents per decade. But if the accident rate per 100,000 residents continues to fall as just noted, the number of incidents would decline by 2010 to 58.1 million—or 13.4 million less than a continuation of the existing rate. That big a drop seems highly unlikely. But at least these calculations show there is a significant scope for decreasing current levels of incidents as related to population through improved traffic management and accident reduction methods.

CHAPTER 6

Strategies for Reducing Congestion and Four Basic Principles of Traffic

Proposed remedies for reducing traffic congestion cannot be properly evaluated without some understanding of possible strategies useful for that purpose and of four basic principles of vehicle traffic that are all too often overlooked.

Fundamental Strategies

Congestion can be tackled by supply-side or demand-side tactics. Supply-side tactics are designed to expand the means that travelers can use for commuting and other trips. An example is building more roads to increase carrying capacity. Demand-side tactics are designed to reduce the number of persons or vehicles traveling during peak periods. An example is charging high taxes on gasoline that make driving more costly. (Subsequent chapters separately analyze both types of tactics in detail.)

Another way to look at anticongestion tactics is to consider whether they are primarily *market oriented* or primarily *regulatory*. Market-oriented tactics use pricing mechanisms of some type to influence how people behave but leave choosing among the alternative courses of action up to each individual to make voluntarily. Regulatory tactics require people to behave according to certain compulsory rules that apply to everyone in the same manner.

The anticongestion tactics discussed in this book can be classified in accordance with both these schemes simultaneously, as shown in figure 6-1. The two horizontal rows divide these tactics into primarily regulatory ones or market oriented. The two vertical columns divide the same tactics into primarily supply-side or demand-side groups. Some tactics have both supply-side and demand-side elements at the same time; they are shown in boldface type. An example is making some existing expressway lanes into high-occupancy vehicle (HOV) lanes. That tactic is designed to attract more people into sharing vehicles, thereby reducing the number of vehicles traveling during peak hours. But the same tactic also alters the supply of road space available to single-occupancy vehicles.

This figure shows that most anticongestion tactics are primarily regulatory, and that there are many regulatory tactics of both supply-side and demand-side types. In contrast, fewer tactics are market oriented, and all but one of those are primarily demand side in nature. However, it is not entirely unambiguous just how every one of these tactics should be classified. The groupings shown represent my view; readers may wish to classify certain tactics differently.

The Market-Based Approach

Market-based tactics assign monetary value to different types of travel behavior and then rely on travelers to choose among them. Their goal is to achieve more efficient use of scarce resources, usually by making the prices of different travel options more nearly equal to their social costs so that marginal benefits will equal or exceed marginal costs. These tactics raise the price of the behaviors they seek to discourage in relation to the prices of those they seek to encourage.

Charging fees for using heavily congested roadways during peak hours is such a tactic. It leaves the choice of routes and travel times to individual drivers. Another example would be to have employers pay each worker a travel allowance of $75 per month but also charge $75 per month for providing each parking space formerly furnished free. Employees who wished to share rides or use public transit could profit by spending less than their travel allowances on commuting. Those who still wanted to drive alone could do so by paying the parking charge.

The underlying principle of the market-based approach is that users of specific facilities should directly pay at least some of the costs they

FIGURE 6-1. Classifying Tactics to Combat Peak-Hour Congestion[a]

	Supply side	Demand side
Primarily regulatory	Building more roads or expanding existing ones	Prohibiting certain license numbers from driving on specific days
	Building more transit facilities and increasing service and amenities in existing transit systems	Changing federal work laws that discourage people from working at home
	Improving highway maintenance	**Ramp metering on expressways**
	Adding roving response teams to remove accidents	Encouraging transportation management associations
	Traffic management centers	Encouraging more people to work at home
	ITS mechanisms for speeding traffic flows	Keeping minimum residential densities higher
	Deregulating public transit activities	Clustering high-density housing around transit stops
	Upgrading existing city streets	Limiting growth and development in local communities
	Staggering work hours for more workers	Improving the jobs/housing balance
	Developing means of transit feasible in low-density areas	**Using traffic-calming devices to slow flows**
	Building special roads for trucks only	Concentrating jobs in a few suburban clusters
		Making some lanes HOV lanes
Primarily market-oriented	Converting free HOV lanes to HOT lanes	Road pricing with tolls set to raise peak-hour flows
		Commuting allowance for employees
		Charging high taxes on gasoline
		Charging high taxes on parking during peak hours
		Eliminating tax deductibility for employers for providing free parking
		Increasing automobile license fees
		"Cashing out" free parking provided by employers

Source: Author's calculations.
a. Tactics that are to some degree both supply side and demand side in nature are shown in boldface.

impose on others when they are using those facilities. Just one additional car entering a congested highway during a peak hour can add several minutes of delay to the total travel time of each of many other commuters. By compelling drivers who choose such behavior to pay for creating that cost, market strategies discourage such behavior and collect money that can be used to compensate those on whom the cost is imposed. An example would be improving transportation facilities in the same corridor in which the money was collected. At the same time, the market-based approach permits travelers to continue socially costly behavior if they believe doing so is worth the price attached to it.

The Regulatory Approach

Regulation mandates certain behaviors or prohibits others. It does not attach varying prices to different behaviors, nor does it leave the choice up to individual travelers. Instead it prohibits or limits by government fiat the behaviors it wants to discourage and permits or requires those it wants to encourage. For example, prohibiting automobiles with license plates ending in the digit 5 from driving on Fridays, and those ending in other digits from driving on other specific days, is a regulatory tactic.

Advantages and Disadvantages of the Market-Based Approach

As an economist, I generally favor the market-based approach. Its advantages seem to far outweigh its disadvantages. Admittedly, nearly all its tactics contain some regulatory elements (for example, the choice of where and when to use road pricing is inherently a regulatory one that must by imposed by fiat). The most effective overall strategy for reducing traffic congestion should probably consist of both market-based and regulatory elements.

The principal advantage of the market-based approach is that it leaves more choice to individual travelers. Therefore it is more flexible than regulations and requires far less enforcement effort. It is also economically more efficient because it seeks to equate the marginal prices of different behaviors with their marginal social costs. Although neither approach can achieve a perfectly efficient allocation of transportation resources, the results of the market-based approach are usually closer to that ideal.

Since the tactics in this category charge for the behavior they seek to discourage, peak-hour road pricing might raise huge amounts of money that could be used to improve regional transportation facilities. Another advantage is that all drivers have the same set of choices, and groups are not treated differently, in contrast to regulations—such as the once-proposed California rule that firms with one hundred or more employees allow no more than 55 percent of their workers to commute alone in their cars. The assumption seemed to be that large firms are better able to persuade their workers to act in this manner than small firms. And it is easier for regulators to administer a rule that applies only to large firms. Tactics that treat all drivers the same way apply not just to commuters but to all vehicles traveling during peak hours. In contrast, many regulations designed to reduce congestion apply only to persons making journeys to and from work and would not deter others from traveling during the most congested period.

The market-based approach would also be easier to enforce, because it would require a smaller bureaucracy to administer, and its instruments would be more difficult to evade than most congestion-reducing regulations. It would be far easier to identify cars that fail to pay the peak-hour road price on a congested highway than to ensure that 45 percent of the workers in every large firm did not drive to work alone (as discussed in chapter 4).

The principal complaint against market-based strategies is that they put undue stress on low-income households and hence are economically regressive and inequitable. Such households are less able to pay the prices imposed than are higher-income households. Some arguments have been put forth to counter this charge, but they are not very persuasive.

One is that the many low-income workers who already commute by bus would not have to pay congestion prices but would benefit from the results. The question is, how many do use the bus? In 1995, the fraction of workers commuting by private vehicles was 84 percent among those from low-income households, versus 90 percent among those from non-low-income households. Only 5 percent of low-income commuters used public transportation, versus 2 percent of all other commuters. These outcomes were true even though the share of households with no private vehicle available was 26 percent among low-income households but only 4 percent among other households.[1] Even the suggestion that the money raised by road pricing could be used to improve transportation facilities used by low-income workers is questionable. A high percentage of all those adults who commute by public transit come from households with incomes of $20,000 or more—the figure in 1983 was 56.1 percent.[2]

Unless the funds from peak-hour tolls can be used to compensate low-income drivers directly, road pricing may have regressive effects.[3]

Advantages and Disadvantages of the Regulatory Approach

The regulatory approach to coping with traffic congestion has several advantages over the market approach. Regulations can specify exactly what type of behavior is to be encouraged or discouraged in order to reduce congestion. For example, expressway lanes can be set aside for exclusive peak-hour use by high-occupancy vehicles (HOVs), and "high occupancy" can be defined as buses or vehicles with two persons or more or three persons or more. Regulations also normally apply exactly the same way to all persons in similar circumstances, whereas the market approach usually permits similar individuals to choose among alternative courses of action. Thus a stop sign requires—at least in theory—every vehicle to stop before proceeding. Because of these two traits, regulations—when carried out as specified—create more predictable and uniform patterns of behavior than market-based approaches. And behavior patterns governed by regulations are easier to alter to fit changing circumstances. The agency issuing the regulations can modify them for a whole region simultaneously and expect fairly rapid public conformity to the changes.

But regulations also have disadvantages compared with market-based tactics. Several of these drawbacks are the obverse of regulatory advantages. Because regulations apply in exactly the same manner to all, they do not permit different individuals to choose varied actions best suited to their own preferences or immediate needs. For example, so-called high-occupancy toll (HOT) lanes are extra lanes added onto an existing expressway on which sufficiently high tolls are charged during peak hours to keep traffic volumes low enough to permit continuous high-speed movement. But the initial expressway lanes are left free from toll, so they tend to become congested during peak hours. This arrangement offers a choice to motorists between fast movement for which they must pay a significant toll or slow movement which requires no toll. Such a choice allows people in a big hurry on a particular day to move fast by paying, and those not in such a hurry to save money by moving more slowly. This permits individuals with different needs or preferences to more closely adapt their behavior to their current needs, rather than forcing all of them to do the same thing. Providing choices increases the overall welfare of all those involved.

Another drawback of the regulatory approach is that it requires stronger and costlier enforcement activities than most market-based tactics. Speed limits are a universally employed form of traffic regulation, but they are probably the most frequently violated ordinances in the nation. Getting a high percentage of drivers to conform to speed limits takes major and sustained efforts by police, courts, and administrative officials to apprehend and punish at least some of the people who do not conform. In contrast, tolls are expensive to collect but are inherently self-enforcing and also provide the revenues necessary to administer themselves.

The regulatory approach often leads to a larger bureaucracy than the market-based approach and does not automatically produce the revenues needed to support that bureaucracy, as do many market-based tactics that involve collecting fees.

Four Key Principles of Traffic Flows

A vital point to recognize in evaluating remedies to congestion—whether they follow the market-based or regulatory approaches—is that traffic flows are influenced by four principles that are usually ignored. They are the principles of triple convergence, dual swamping by growth, the imperviousness of growth to local public policies, and one hundred small cuts. Many other principles of traffic movement are also important, but they are normally taken into account by persons weighing possible congestion remedies. These four principles are discussed in detail because they have vital impacts on the potential effectiveness of specific tactics.

Triple Convergence

Most vehicle drivers search for the quickest route, one that is shorter or less encumbered by obstacles (such as traffic signals or cross streets) than most other routes. These direct routes are usually limited-access roads (freeways, expressways, or beltways) that are faster than local streets if they are not congested. Since most drivers know this, they converge on the "best" routes from many points of origin.[4]

During peak travel hours on weekdays, so many drivers converge on these best routes that they become congested, particularly in large metropolitan areas. Traffic on them eventually slows to the point where they have no advantage over the alternative routes. That is, a rough equilibrium is reached, which means that many drivers can get to their destinations just as fast on other roads. At times, the direct road may become even slower than alternative streets, and some drivers eager to save time will switch to them. Soon rough equality of travel times on both types of routes is restored at the margin. The opposite happens if travel becomes slower on alternative streets than on the expressway.

Several observations can be made about this equilibrium situation: it tends to recur, because most drivers develop habitual travel patterns; during equilibrium each limited-access road is carrying more vehicles per hour than each normal city street or arterial route because it has more lanes, more direct routing, and fewer obstacles; many drivers time their journeys to miss these periods because they do not like to waste time in heavy traffic; and at the peak of equilibrium, traffic on most expressways is crawling along at a pace far below the optimal speed for those roads.

Now suppose that the limited-access route undergoes a vast improvement—for example, its four lanes are expanded to eight. Once its carrying capacity is thus increased, the drivers using it move much faster than those using alternative routes. But this disequilibrium does not last long because word soon gets around that conditions on the expressway are superior.

In response, three types of convergence occur on the improved expressway: many drivers who formerly used alternative routes during peak hours switch to the improved expressway (spatial convergence); many drivers who formerly traveled just before or after the peak hours start traveling during those hours (time convergence); and some commuters who used to take public transportation during peak hours now switch to driving, since it has become faster (modal convergence).[5]

This triple convergence causes more and more drivers to use the improved expressway during peak hours. Therefore its traffic volumes keep rising until vehicles are once again moving at a crawl during the peak period. This outcome is almost inescapable if peak-hour traffic was already slow before the highway was improved. If traffic is going faster than a crawl on this direct route at the peak hours, its users will still get to their destinations faster than users of city streets, which are less direct and more encumbered by signals and cross streets. Total travel times on these two types of paths will only become equalized if the limited-access roads are so overloaded that vehicles on them are moving at slower speeds than those on normal streets. Triple convergence creates just such an effect during peak hours.

Even so, highway improvements that expand hourly road capacity clearly produce social benefits. The total number of vehicles moving toward their destinations during each peak hour will be greater than before. Therefore, more commuters will be able to move at their most preferred times. If there has been no growth in the total number of persons traveling each day, periods of peak traffic congestion will become shorter because the system can carry more vehicles per hour. Traffic will now move faster just before and after the peak periods. As the proportion of all commuters traveling during peak periods increases, commuter welfare will improve, because more people will be traveling during the most convenient times. And peak-hour congestion on alternative routes and on public transit will decline because more commuters have shifted to the expressway. This might even cause the public transit system to reduce the frequency of its service if its total revenues fall. Except for this possible decline in public transit service, the region's traffic situation will be better.

These effects of triple convergence are short-run impacts because they involve persons who were already traveling each day during, or shortly before or after, peak hours. But there can also be long-run impacts of increasing the capacity of a major roadway. For example, widening an expressway may encourage more intensive property development in the primary destination it serves—often a region's central business district. More commuters will arrive at that destination during each hour while encountering the same degree of traffic congestion as before. Hence the road improvement may stimulate more real estate development instead of less congestion, or some combination of reduced congestion and intensified development. This impact clearly takes a considerable time to occur.[6] Another more important long-run impact is that improving a roadway may cause more residents and businesses to locate along it in order to enjoy its upgraded access. These newcomers will then also use the expanded roadway, thereby adding to total traffic on it. This added traffic will offset some of the benefits that the original users of the road hoped to gain from expanding it in the first place. This type of long-run growth in demand caused by improving a roadway is called induced demand, since it was called forth by the roadway improvement (see chapter 8). But regardless of whether upgrading a road evokes induced demand in the long run, any upgrading is certain to evoke convergent increases in demand in the short run, as just explained. Such short-run increases in demand caused by convergence are sometimes referred to as induced traffic.

Thus, because of triple convergence, expanding a roadway's capacity does not fully eliminate peak-hour traffic congestion, or even reduce the intensity of traffic jams during the most crowded periods—although those periods will be shorter. In fact, it is almost impossible to eradicate peak-hour traffic congestion on limited-access roads once it has appeared within a nonshrinking community. In theory, such congestion could be eliminated only if the capacity of those roads were increased enough so they could carry every single commuter simultaneously at the peak minute at, say, 35 miles per hour or faster. In nearly all metropolitan areas, that is impossible. Therefore, expansions of road capacity—no matter how large, within the limits of feasibility—cannot fully eliminate periods of crawling along on expressways at frustratingly low speeds.

With one notable exception discussed later, any initial improvement in peak-hour travel conditions on high-capacity roadways will immediately elicit a triple convergence response. This is a crucial aspect of traffic flows that enormously affects how well various proposals to reduce peak-hour congestion will work in practice. Convergence will soon restore heavy congestion during peak periods, although those periods may now be shorter. Such improvements need not be made to the highway itself. For example, if a new fixed-rail public transit system is opened, it will attract some peak-hour commuters out of automobiles. That should initially reduce peak-period traffic congestion on expressways and normal streets. But as soon as drivers realize that expressways now permit faster travel, many will converge from normal streets and nonpeak periods onto those expressways during peak periods. That, in turn, will quickly overload those expressways during such periods, forcing traffic back to a crawl. Peak periods will not even be much shorter unless a new public transit system has drawn a great many commuters out of automobiles.[7] There is no evidence that new fixed-rail public transit systems in the Washington and San Francisco Bay areas have diminished peak-period congestion on any expressways there. True, those transit systems carry a lot of passengers during peak hours. By removing those people from the roads, the transit systems may have shortened the periods of greatest congestion intensity on each region's expressways. But intensely congested periods still arise daily there, and the roads are just as jammed then as they were before the transit systems were built. Other factors were also at play there, however, as I discuss later.

Similarly, if many people decide to "telecommute" by working at home one or more days a week, that would initially reduce peak-period traffic on roadways. But triple convergence would soon wipe out at least part of any resulting improvements in congestion on those roads during peak periods. All the same, many remedies to intensive traffic congestion are unquestionably worth pursuing. The point is that initial gains must not be considered permanent inroads on congestion—at least during peak periods. Furthermore, any realistic analysis of exactly what effects will emerge from proposed remedies must take the principle of triple convergence into account.

The Converse of Triple Convergence: Triple Divergence

The principle of triple convergence also operates in reverse. Any factors that increase peak-hour congestion on limited-access roads tend to cause more auto-driving commuters to shift away from those roads in peak periods to the same roads in nonpeak periods, alternative routes during peak periods, and public transit during peak periods. Such triple divergence has important policy implications.

Residents in fast-growing metropolitan areas are especially eager to limit traffic congestion because they want to prevent further expressway traffic from spilling over onto adjacent local streets. To many residents, such spillover is just as great a concern as the time lost in commuting during peak hours.[8]

It is widely assumed that high levels of peak-hour highway congestion will stimulate public transit patronage. That is why many metropolitan areas have expanded, or are considering expanding, their public transit systems to relieve highway congestion. Yet those communities that have built new public transit systems have not experienced much—if any—reduction in peak-hour automotive congestion.

Triple divergence is really an inadvertent form of demand management inherent in all intense congestion. Whenever peak-hour congestion on a roadway gets worse, the resulting decline in the desirability of using the roadway during those hours motivates some drivers to shift to other routes, other times, or other modes. This reduces the demand for that road during peak hours, thereby partially offsetting the worsened congestion until a new equilibrium is reached. Hence congestion is partially self-correcting through such triple divergence. This illustrates the basic nature of congestion as a balancing mechanism between supply and demand.

One Remedy That Avoids Triple Convergence: Road Pricing

One proposed remedy, apart from moving residences or jobs, that does not suffer from the offsetting impacts of triple convergence is road pricing. If drivers had to pay relatively high tolls for using expressways during peak periods, congestion on those roads would initially fall. Moreover, the tolls would discourage commuters now using other routes, other time periods, and other modes from converging onto those expressways during peak periods. Hence peak-hour congestion on those toll roads would remain lower, although some drivers would be diverted by triple divergence: many commuters formerly driving to work during peak hours would be induced to shift to other times, to nontolled routes, and public transit.

Dual Swamping by Growth

As already mentioned, traffic congestion is most severe in areas experiencing absolutely rapid growth in their total populations of people and vehicles in use. In fact, rapid population growth tends to offset the beneficial impacts of any particular remedies adopted to reduce traffic congestion. A remedy that successfully cuts peak-hour travel in year 1 by 5 percent will probably have no visible effects by year 3 if the number of vehicles in use is growing 2.5 percent per year. The added vehicles traveling each day will return traffic conditions to what they were before that remedy was adopted—even if the remedy is still in effect. Of course, conditions would have been worse in year 3 if the remedy had not been adopted and the growth nevertheless occurred. So that remedy would not be used entirely in vain.

Nevertheless, local residents will become increasingly frustrated if all the policies they support to reduce congestion—such as building costly new roads—fail to produce any perceptible improvements. Yet that is just what has happened in fast-growing areas such as southern California because rapid growth swamps most such remedies. In many cases, it is part of a vicious circle: authorities improve highways to fight congestion but then those improvements create incentives to increase automotive vehicle ownership and use and change the location and form of residential and nonresidential growth. Over the long run, these actions tend to intensify traffic congestion. Such increases in congestion result from induced demand caused by improving the roads. But once more population arrives, its presence may motivate authorities to build even more roads—an outcome sometimes referred to as induced growth or induced development.

For example, construction of the interstate highway system and many other expressways in U.S. metropolitan areas was a prime factor causing more citizens to buy and use automotive vehicles instead of commuting by public transit.[9] Moreover, these roadway improvements motivated many businesses to choose highly dispersed locations along expressways. As a result, such workplaces were difficult to reach by public transit and railroads. So more shippers began to use trucks and more workers began to commute in private cars. As worker ownership of cars became more widespread, housing spread further into low-density suburbs, where public transit was even less feasible to use.

Road improvements were certainly not the only causes of increased vehicle ownership and use. Massive advertising by auto manufacturers, the federal provision of mortgage insurance for single-family homes, federal tax benefits for homeownership, and rising real incomes also played major roles. Moreover, it would be inaccurate to attribute all the population and job growth along new highways to their construction. Growth in any metropolitan area is mainly the result of whatever forces are expanding employment there over the long run, not of specific new highways. The latter determine where growth will occur within the area, rather than its total amount. True, a metropolitan area well supplied with road capacity is a more attractive location for added jobs than one without such capacity. But that is only one factor governing the area's total growth. Nevertheless, past road expansions have surely contributed to the severe traffic congestion now plaguing many U.S. metropolitan areas.

Where growth is located also influences what mode of travel people use. If it is located along highways rather than in older, closer-in neighborhoods well served with public transit, it will generate more automotive traffic.

Traffic congestion resulting from rapid growth is extremely difficult to relieve if the growth has been caused by factors other than good transportation facilities. The rapid recent growth of southern California's population has resulted from such factors as good weather, proximity to Mexico and to Pacific Rim countries supplying immigrants, the presence of a large low-wage labor pool and many highly educated workers, and the huge size of the local market. The attraction of these factors remains strong even though rising congestion has made local travel increasingly frustrating and inefficient. Hence these increases in congestion have not created any self-correcting processes. They are apparently not yet bad enough to discourage further growth by other factors.

Rapid growth can also aggravate spillover effects related to traffic congestion. Since 1970, public policies have tremendously reduced the amount of air pollutants discharged into the atmosphere in the greater Los Angeles area by each automotive vehicle, factory, and other stationary source. As a result, the total air pollution there has fallen in the past three decades, despite a big increase in vehicle population.[10] But these gains could be wiped out by the massive population and vehicle increases projected to occur through 2020. Authorities dealing with air pollution there already feel they are swimming against the tide of additional growth. Peak-period traffic congestion would also be affected.

The Imperviousness of Growth to Local Policies

The preceding analysis suggests that one way to prevent the quality of life from deteriorating in a fast-growing area would be to slow its growth rate. That is the approach of "no-growth" or "antigrowth" advocates. Halting the area's growth altogether would indeed reduce some of the above problems, but such a policy would be highly impractical.

To begin with, no suburban community can hope to stop the growth of its metropolitan area as a whole if conditions favor the expansion of jobs there. A given community could ban all expansion of housing and workplaces within its boundaries, but that would not prevent nearby communities from accepting more jobs and residents. Almost every U.S. metropolitan area has at least some communities encouraging further growth. Even if none did, newcomers would continue to arrive anyway if they believed good economic opportunities were available there, as history has repeatedly proved. Such immigrants would live on the outskirts of the metropolitan area in unincorporated places with no antigrowth policies, or they would illegally double and triple up in dwelling units in communities that had formally banned further growth.

These observations indicate that regional growth is impervious to local public policy. That is to say, no one suburb can substantially affect the future growth rate of its overall metropolitan area through its own policies.[11] Therefore, attempts by any one suburb to halt growth within its own boundaries simply divert potential growth, along with its problems, to nearby communities. Even then, the problems will not be confined to the places that generate them. They will inevitably spill over into surrounding communities, as is clear from the problems associated with air pollution and vehicle traffic.

Antigrowth tactics are especially difficult to sustain because growth generates economic benefits. As incomes rise, purchasing power increases and more money is spent in local stores and businesses. With more new commercial development, local tax revenues increase and reduce the property tax burdens on existing residents. Furthermore, added jobs provide income to many existing residents. Although growth also has its drawbacks—greater traffic congestion and air pollution are but two—completely banning further growth in a community imposes sizable penalties on many of its businesses.

One Hundred Small Cuts

No one policy can fully remedy metropolitan traffic congestion. Indeed, most individual policies cannot even make a dent in such problems—especially in rapidly growing areas. That means various remedies must be combined to effect anything like a cure. Those who are striving to do so are like the woodsman who must cut down a huge tree with only one small axe. He cannot fell the tree or even make much of a cut in it with one swing of the axe. But he can eventually cut it down, with one hundred or more small cuts. A multifaceted approach offers the only hope of reducing traffic congestion significantly or at least slowing down its future growth.

However, even ten thousand small cuts will not completely eliminate peak-period congestion because of triple convergence. Hence congestion remedies should not be expected to eliminate the problem altogether. Rather, they should aim to reduce the duration of maximum congestion appreciably, reduce the average length of time required for commuting, increase the average commuting speed, increase the proportion of all commuters traveling during periods of maximum convenience, reduce the intensity of commuter frustration, and offer commuters more choices about how and when to travel to and from work.[12] Rapidly growing areas may find it impossible to achieve any of these goals. Even so, they may be better off than they were before adopting their congestion remedies.

CHAPTER 7

Reducing Incident-Caused Congestion

Incidents—including accidents—are responsible for a large share of all traffic congestion. Therefore, reducing the number of incidents and better controlling the impacts of those that occur could decrease congestion significantly.

Coping with Incident-Caused Traffic Congestion

Many strategies and tactics have been suggested for coping with incident-caused traffic congestion. Analyzing all of them in detail is not within the scope of this book. However, the most significant are listed in the following paragraphs to illustrate the variety of possible approaches.

Improving the Physical Design of Existing Roadways

This strategy includes the following tactics to reduce the probability of accidents:

—Redesigning entrance and exit ramps to reduce the severity of their curves (which often cause trucks exiting too fast to overturn);

—Building barriers separating flows of traffic moving in opposite directions adjacent to each other;

—Creating more gradual curves on existing roadways;

—Widening lanes on roadways with very narrow lanes;

—On roads containing short segments with fewer lanes than the rest of those roads, ending those bottlenecks by widening them to match the width elsewhere;

—Building more cloverleaf and other nonconfrontational interchanges at intersections of major roads;

—Replacing existing two-lane roads with four-or-more-lane roads, preferably with divided segments for traffic moving in opposite directions. The fatality rate on two-lane roads is more than double that on four-lane roads, according to the National Highway Traffic Safety Administration (NHTSA).[1]

—Providing ample shoulders—preferably paved—along all feasible portions of major roadways so that vehicles becoming disabled can be quickly removed from traffic lanes.

Coordinating Traffic Flows Better

The following tactics, by controlling signal systems on ramps, arterials, or streets, can better coordinate traffic flows:

—Instituting ramp metering on major expressways during peak hours;

—Installing systems for coordinating traffic lights along arterial streets to expedite smoother traffic flows. For example, in the Dallas area, six local governments were operating 224 uncoordinated traffic signals along a single transportation corridor. After major negotiations, they agreed to treat the whole corridor as a unified system and operate all the signals under one control plan. The results were described by one evaluator as follows:

> Travel time in the corridor has been reduced by six percent, vehicle delay time has been reduced by 34 percent, and stops have been reduced by 43 percent. The estimated reduction in fuel consumption and emissions is approximately 5 percent, and the estimated annual benefits are $26 million at a cost of $4 million. I think one of the real benefits of the project is that it showed that Dallas County could undertake a multi-jurisdictional effort and that the County and the six cities with differing goals and priorities could work cooperatively. As a result, the next bond election extended the program to other parts of the County and established $4 million in seed funding for an incident response center.[2]

—On minor streets crossing major roadways, using traffic signals activated only when vehicles are waiting on the minor streets to minimize stopping major traffic flows;

—Installing "smart card" systems with fast throughput lanes on major toll roads in order to speed movement of vehicles with "smart cards" through toll gates;

—Using lane control signals to control the direction of traffic flows on reversible lanes that can be altered to suit regular time-of-day shifts in vehicle movements.

Providing Better Information about Current Congestion Conditions

—Creating programmable electronic overhead signs warning motorists of congestion ahead so they can slow down and divert to alternate routes.

—Broadcasting up-to-date bulletins about traffic conditions over radio stations that drivers can listen to while traveling. This requires some real-time means of collecting and analyzing information about current conditions.

—Maintaining Internet sites featuring current congestion conditions and weather conditions that drivers can consult before leaving on commuting or other trips.

—Creating more prominent signs announcing work zones and signals designed to slow traffic going through work zones, which have high worker injury rates.

Conducting Educational Campaigns against Driving under the Influence of Alcohol or Drugs

Education campaigns can be carried out as follows:

—Employing speakers to tour high schools and present realistically graphic views of the results of accidents caused by driving under the influence.

—Adopting relatively stringent laws imposing heavy fines and losses of licenses on drivers who are convicted of driving under the influence.

—Insofar as it is legal, conducting random but well-publicized stop-and-check sweeps on drivers in high-accident corridors to test their sobriety.

—Publishing the names in prominent media of all persons found driving under the influence.

More Rigorously Enforcing Existing Traffic Laws

Traffic laws are probably the most frequently violated ordinances in American society, but they can be enforced by the following strategies:

—Setting speed limits at realistic levels rather than so low that most drivers are sure to ignore them.

—Using recording cameras at major intersections to identify drivers who run red lights and following up by mail with heavy fines and loss of licenses for those who do not pay them. This tactic has been employed successfully in Australia and is beginning to be used in American cities. The Federal Highway Administration has stated that running red lights causes more than 80,000 crashes per year and results in more than 80,000 injuries and nearly 1,000 deaths annually.[3]

—Installing along busy streets speed-limit-reporting signs that show passing vehicles how fast they are going. Experience shows that such signs may reduce driver speeds at least temporarily, especially in school zones.

—Installing "traffic calming" devices on residential streets used as through streets to slow down excessively speeding drivers. These include speed bumps, barriers creating dead ends on residential streets, traffic circles, and narrowed lanes.

—More effectively enforcing speed limits in areas that have given rise to numerous accidents through greater use of patrol cars and frequent arrests. Unfortunately, such higher-intensity enforcement is difficult to sustain. As the Transportation Research Board said in its exhaustive 1998 study:

> The problem with traditional enforcement methods is their short-lived effect in deterring noncompliers. Extending the effect typically requires a level of enforcement intensity that exceeds the resources provided to the police for speed enforcement and other priorities. Policymakers can increase the resources directed toward speed enforcement, but providing adequate enforcement levels is expensive.[4]

Creating Traffic Management Centers

These centers would collect and disseminate information about current traffic conditions and coordinate the dispatch of repair, rescue, and removal vehicles to scenes of traffic accidents.

Creating and Operating Traffic Management Centers

In the past decade, dozens of state and local governments have created formal traffic management centers (TMCs) to help reduce the negative impacts of traffic congestion on safety, environmental pollution, and travel convenience. An excellent example of a TMC is the one operated by the Maryland Coordinated Highways Action Response Team (CHART), which is a joint effort of the Maryland Department of Transportation and the Maryland State Police.[5] The headquarters is located in a large, specially designed building just south of the Baltimore-Washington International Airport. This center is a roomy high-ceiling combat-information-center-type room with five huge television screens and twelve smaller ones deployed on the walls. Eight major and many more minor computer consoles are arranged in a semicircle in front of these screens. The team operates fifty or so closed-circuit television cameras mounted along the major highways within its jurisdiction. These cameras are placed at key points on those highways and can be moved and zoomed from this spot. The real-time pictures from these cameras can be tuned into computer consoles and projected on the wall screens as desired. The center also receives vehicle speed data every five minutes from a large number of electronic detection loops buried at key points along the highways it monitors. Thus operators of the CHART Operations Center can instantly check on current conditions at many points along the roads they are supposed to monitor. Moreover, they are in continual direct radio and telephone contact with all other state and local agencies relevant to traffic flows. The center also controls eight assistance vehicles that roam these highways during peak hours—four in the Washington area and four in the Baltimore area. They assist motorists in trouble and help clear any lane blockages caused by accidents or other incidents.

This center is open twenty-four hours a day. Alvin Marquess, the operations manager as of December 2003, had been with the program from its inception. He was obviously intimately familiar with, and a strong proponent of, its activities. The CHART program was founded in the mid-1980s, opened a Baltimore-oriented branch in 1990, and moved into its present modern quarters in 1994. Its "war room" is most intensively manned during emergency events such as major snowstorms, big athletic events, and other unusual situations. There are two outlying operations centers in police headquarters near the Washington and Baltimore beltways, and smaller branch operations at the two major football stadiums in Washington and Baltimore. In summer 2001, CHART had about fifty persons assigned to it and was under the jurisdiction of the Maryland Highway Department.

The main goals of this operation and almost all others like it are to keep the traffic flowing on major roadways, mainly by removing lane-blocking incidents as quickly as possible, and to promote safer conditions on those roadways. Achieving these goals effectively requires at least five major activities.

The most important TMC activity is arranging for close cooperation and coordination among the many state, local, and private agencies concerned with maintaining efficient traffic flows. Four major types of agencies work with CHART: the state police (and some local police departments), local fire departments, many public and private medical agencies, and state environmental departments. The last are mainly concerned with cleaning up spills of various hazardous substances. Establishing initial liaisons with these agencies, working out protocols for which ones have which responsibilities at the scenes of accidents and other incidents, continuously communicating current conditions and needs to all these agencies, and revising the protocols among them as experience indicates is necessary are crucial ingredients in operating an effective TMC. Maryland's CHART works more closely with the state police than local police departments because its jurisdiction consists mainly of interstate highways under the operational control of the state police.

Sustaining effective coordination of all the relevant agencies over long time periods is particularly difficult for three reasons. First, each of the many agencies involved receives its resources from a different annual budget and must continue to allocate enough of each year's budget to incident management to remain an effective participant—in spite of many competing demands for those limited resources. Second, all agencies experience continual changes in personnel. This causes frequent losses of today's most effective proponents and most experienced practitioners of incident management. Personnel changes also create a recurrent need to persuade newcomers that incident management is an important function for their agency. Third, constant changes in technology—such as increased use of cell phones to report incidents—plus innovations in response procedures, make it necessary to continually revise the basic protocols among agencies about who should do what to whom and when. Yet such negotiations are always delicate because of the inherent tendency among bureaucrats—public and private—to "protect their own turf." Thus the author of an exhaustive analysis of freeway, incident, and emergency management stated, "Incident management's greatest challenge has been in institutional integration (i.e., in integrating incident management into the mainstream transportation planning and programming processes and in integrating incident management programs across jurisdictional boundaries)."[6]

A second critical activity of every TMC is installing, maintaining, and monitoring electronic surveillance devices that provide a continuous picture of conditions on those roads within its jurisdiction. As previously noted, these consist mainly of remote television cameras mounted along these roadways and controlled from the TMC operations center, speed-reporting loop detectors buried in those roadways, cell-phone and telephone "hot lines" on which motorists can report adverse traffic conditions—usually the source of detecting and locating a majority of incidents, and radio and telephone communications with roving assistance vehicles and with the other relevant public and private agencies just described—especially the state or local police patrolling those roads. In some cases, TMCs receive information from airplanes or helicopters used by local radio stations to broadcast traffic reports to motorists. Many TMCs, including Maryland's CHART, have Internet websites on which citizens can monitor real-time motion pictures of traffic flows being transmitted from remote television cameras to the TMC itself. The receipt of accurate data from these sources in a highly timely manner is what makes it possible for TMCs to orchestrate much faster removal of obstacles to traffic flows than would occur without TMC efforts. A major qualitative difference between TMCs in different parts of the nation consists of the amount of resources that their parent governments (usually state highway departments) are willing to spend on these functions.

An exhaustive 1999 examination of all aspects of TMCs concluded that "the most difficult recurring challenges TMCs noted were related to operations and maintenance staffing."[7]

The third crucial activity of TMCs is dispatching appropriate response teams to the scenes of major accidents or other incidents that are blocking traffic flows. This requires deciding which agencies need to be notified and in what order, communicating with them, and following up—visually, if possible—to ensure that they arrive on the scene and perform their functions appropriately and quickly. Normally, the TMC itself directly controls only a small part of the vehicles needed to respond to a major accident—usually only the roaming repair and removal vehicles it operates. All the other required vehicles are controlled by other agencies with many other responsibilities besides responding to such incidents. At many accident scenes, the rescue and repair vehicles block traffic lanes more fully and for longer periods than the vehicles involved in the accident itself—sometimes for much longer than is absolutely necessary. Although this may be unavoidable under some circumstances, one of the functions of a TMC is to minimize this outcome.

A fourth activity of a major TMC concerns diverting traffic to other routes when a road-blocking incident is likely to delay traffic for a very long time. This requires deciding whether the incident is likely to cause unacceptable delays, having preplanned detour routes ready to use in such cases—including appropriate signage to guide diverted motorists—and coordinating the execution of the diversion plans. Past experience can be the basis for deciding what diversion routes should be planned in advance and what signs and other indicators are needed to make them effective.

The fifth essential activity is collecting information about the frequency and nature of the incidents the TMC encounters and responds to, and evaluating the effectiveness of the response efforts of all the agencies concerned, including the TMC itself. This activity is the major TMC responsibility most often neglected by TMCs for three reasons. First, carrying it out diverts the limited resources available to the TMC from directly responding to ongoing traffic problems. In almost all human activities, "putting out today's fires" normally takes resource allocation precedence over "measuring how well yesterday's fires were dealt with." Second, there is a natural human aversion to avoid evaluating just how effective one's own efforts are, compared with their costs or some other standard. Third, such evaluations are not easy, and they require technical capabilities different from those of operating ongoing traffic management activities successfully. Hence many TMCs are not technically qualified to conduct reliable evaluations. That is why such evaluations are often delegated to nearby universities or consulting firms.

The final activity of TMCs is still being developed: integrated management of all aspects of traffic management in an entire metropolitan region into a single advanced traffic management system (ATMS). In most U.S. regions, this is more of a desired futuristic concept than an operating reality. In theory, it involves integrated and computerized coordination of all local traffic signal systems in the region, all freeway ramp metering systems, all TMCs and their complex sensor and communications systems, all programmable electronic roadway signs and radio broadcasts of current conditions to motorists, the scheduling of all road repairs that might impede traffic, and any other devices or programs that could be used to influence and coordinate traffic flows. Clearly, this goal requires a degree of complexity and major funding in organization, design, institutional cooperation, operation, and maintenance that has not been achieved in many, if any, regions. However, it is the avowed goal of many traffic management professionals.

Are Traffic Management Centers Worth Their Costs?

Most evaluations of the costs and benefits produced by TMCs have concluded that their benefits greatly outweigh their costs. The studies identified several major benefits.

—Faster response times of repair and rescue vehicles to the scenes of traffic-blocking incidents. Responses were faster than the ones that occurred before TMCs existed. This result reduces the total amount of time that many vehicles must spend "stuck in traffic," thereby also reducing fuel consumption and air pollution. For example, a 1995 evaluation of the Freeway Service Patrol (FSP)—teams of tow trucks that provided assistance to motorists in Hayward, California—showed that FSP increased the number of assisted incidents and reduced the average response time for vehicle breakdowns assisted by FSP by 57 percent; for all incidents, the response time declined by 35 percent. However, accident and breakdown clearance times remained about the same, as did the duration of incidents.[8] The main reason response times were faster was that assistance vehicles were already cruising the roads concerned.

—Lower accident rates. Accident rates were lower on the roads served by TMCs than occurred before the TMCs existed, or that occur on similar roads not served by TMCs. Presumably, lower accident rates result from faster removal of lane-blocking obstacles than formerly, since such blockages often lead to "secondary crashes."

—Faster freeway traffic flow speeds during peak hours and expanded freeway capacity. Traffic flow is more speedy because lanes are blocked by incidents for shorter periods than before TMCs existed.

Evaluations of TMCs have been conducted in many states and cities, including Maryland, Minnesota, Los Angeles, Houston, Atlanta, Detroit, Long Island, Boston, northern California, Orlando, Chicago, Seattle, Phoenix, San Antonio, and Milwaukee. In all cases that I was able to track down, the evaluators concluded that the TMCs were producing total benefits well in excess of their costs. For example, the Los Angeles automated traffic surveillance and control system (ATSAC) is used to manage surface street traffic. A 1993 evaluation of its results showed that travel time on controlled streets was reduced by 18 percent, stops were reduced by 41 percent, and air emissions were cut by 35 percent. The study estimated that the overall benefit-cost ratio of this system was 23:1.[9] That type of success is why so many other communities have proceeded to create TMCs of their own.

CHAPTER 8

Increasing Road-Carrying Capacity

The most intuitively obvious response to greater congestion is expanding the peak-hour carrying capacity of the
area's transportation system, especially its roads and streets.
This supply-side strategy can be implemented through
many tactics. However, their long-run effects are sometimes
far different from what was intended; so they should be
analyzed carefully before being adopted.

Building More Roads

Among the various supply-side tactics for reducing congestion, building more roads or widening existing ones seems
particularly appropriate in areas that have experienced, or
are now experiencing, rapid population growth. As a community's residents, workers, and vehicles increase in numbers, it becomes more susceptible to traffic congestion.
Between 1980 and 2000, for example, if a community's
population rose 10 percent, the total vehicle miles driven
there typically rose 61.6 percent; so congestion probably
increased too, at least during peak travel periods.[1]

As pointed out earlier, road construction in the United
States in the past two decades has lagged behind most

measures of vehicle and passenger travel. From 1980 to 2001, the total number of lane miles of roads rose only 4.2 percent. Rural lane miles—which constituted 76.2 percent of all lane miles in 2001—actually declined 3.7 percent in that period, whereas urban lane miles increased by 41.0 percent. But the U.S. resident population rose by 25.3 percent, the number of motor vehicles registered rose by 45.7 percent, and the number of vehicle miles traveled soared 82.1 percent. Thus even in urban areas where most new road construction has taken place, the intensity of road use per mile has increased significantly.[2]

As mentioned earlier, rapid population growth can greatly increase traffic loads on arteries throughout a metropolitan area, regardless of where in the region that growth occurs. Hence remedial policies that reduce initial peak-hour traffic volumes by only a few percent—as do many demand-side tactics—can be swamped by further growth in the region. This is why many people think more transportation capacity is an essential response to the recent increases in traffic volumes.

Unfortunately, once heavy peak-hour congestion has appeared in key parts of a region's road network, building new roads or expanding existing ones there does not reduce the intensity of such congestion much in the long run. Once commuters realize the capacity of specific roads has been increased, they will quickly shift their routes, timing, and modes of travel by moving to those roads during peak periods, thereby filling up the expanded capacity.

As explained in chapter 6, the resulting triple convergence will soon bring congestion back to its maximum levels during peak periods. True, because of greater road capacity, peak periods of congestion may be shorter, and more drivers can use the roads during those periods—which are the most convenient times for their travel. Moreover, the overall mobility of the region is increased because more vehicles can use the expanded roads during peak hours and off-peak hours. So expanding existing road capacity does produce significant benefits, even if it does not end or greatly reduce peak-period congestion.

However, if the metropolitan area as a whole is growing rapidly, the traffic added by growth will soon overfill the newly built capacity, and periods of maximum congestion will go back to their prior length. Also, the added travel capacity may help persuade more people and firms to move into the region, or it may cause more residents already living there to buy and use automotive vehicles.

When building more roads is adopted as a tactic, considerable effort must go into planning and administering road construction. As a result, it takes many years to plan and build or expand a major roadway. Since the traffic in metropolitan areas flows over regional networks that go beyond the boundaries of any one community—except perhaps in the largest central cities—regional coordination of road-building plans and financing is particularly important. In fact, most state governments had regional road-building agencies in their own highway departments. However, in 1991, Congress expanded the powers of the metropolitan planning organizations (MPOs) that it had created in the Highway Act of 1962.[3] MPOs were charged with planning the creation of new ground transportation facilities in each metropolitan area. Hence MPOs have taken over that function, as discussed in chapter 17.

Does Expanding Road Capacity Create "Induced Demand"?

Many environmentalists and other opponents of building more roads claim that doing so is a self-defeating tactic because it evokes "induced demand" that offsets any benefits produced by greater road capacity. Induced demand refers to increases in desires to use the expanded road caused by its very expansion. Some observers even claim that induced demand can exceed the increased capacity of the road, causing congestion to become worse after the capacity expansion than it was previously. Is there really such a thing as induced demand, and can it exceed the capacity that induces it?

As just noted, expanding the capacity of a road that is initially plagued by peak-hour congestion can indeed cause more vehicle drivers to shift onto that road precisely because the road now has more capacity. Its expanded capacity is perceived by drivers as increased speed of movement, which is what attracts them. This follows from the principle of triple convergence already described in chapter 6. In the short run, this additional demand for that road is not so much created by expanding its capacity as it is diverted from other routes, times, and modes onto the expanded road. That conclusion follows from defining "the short run" as "the period during which households' residential locations as well as the spatial distribution of economic activity—and thus of employment—remain fixed. . . . Thus, short-run opportunities to economize on travel demand are likely to be limited to linking individual trips into chains, altering usual travel routes, or changing modes of travel."[4]

Another opportunity to economize is to shift the time of day when travel is carried out. Such diverted increases in usage of the road involve travel that would have occurred in that region anyway—but at other times, on other routes, or on other modes. The capacity expansion initially redistributes such pre-existing travel movements, rather than increasing their total quantity. This is not really induced increases in long-run demand but in short-run traffic.[5]

In the short run, such diverted increases in traffic cannot cause congestion on the expanded road to become worse than it was before the capacity expansion took place. Drivers who were already traveling beforehand will converge from other routes, times, and modes onto the expanded road as long as traffic is moving faster on that road than it is from whence they came. When driving times on the expanded road fail to equal those on the alternatives, convergence from those alternatives will stop. But at that equilibrium point, since those alternatives will have lost traffic, travel times on them will be lower than they were before the road was expanded (except on fixed-rail public transit using separate rights of way, where reductions in passenger loads do not normally affect speed of movement). Therefore, congestion on the expanded roadway will surely not be worse than before the expansion and might even be less intense. However, such lower intensity is most likely to express itself as a shorter period of peak congestion intensity than a lower level of such intensity during its worst moments.

In the long run, road expansion could make congestion worse than it was initially. The long run encompasses enough time so that both people and jobs can change locations, households can purchase or sell cars, firms can move into and out of a region, and so on. Therefore, travel demands and behavior can change much more in the long run than in the short run. Expanding any road increases the overall capacity of the region's road network. That has two long-run impacts that can produce induced demand for the expanded road. First, the capacity expansion increases the potential mobility of the region's existing residents; hence it might persuade some of them to travel more than they would have before the expansion occurred. Even more important, more people and firms might be attracted to move into the region—or closer to the expanded road—because of the road's greater capacity. That would add to the overall usage of that road over time. Therefore, it is conceivable that induced demand might add enough traffic to the expanded roadway in the long run so as to raise the intensity of its peak-hour congestion above that which prevailed before the expansion occurred.

However, this increased intensity is likely to take the form of a longer period of very intense congestion, rather than a greater level of intensity at its worst period. That is true because the worst level of intensity prevailing before the expansion occurred could well have been the maximum possible—that is, vehicles just barely moving. The expansion cannot make the worst moments slower than that, though it could create more of them each day.

Unfortunately, it is enormously difficult to determine in advance—or even post facto—to what extent the benefits of expanding a road will be offset by the added demands it induces in the long run. The problem is that while better roads can induce more growth, more growth can also induce authorities to build more and better roads. So causality runs both ways. As Don Pickerell stated,

> It is extremely difficult to disentangle the long-run effect of improved travel speeds and lower generalized prices on transportation system usage from exogenous changes in the demographic and macroeconomic factors that also affect travel demand. Compounding this difficulty is the fact that opportunities to measure the response of demand to generalized price changes [which produce higher movement speeds] arise primarily where investments in expanding network capacity are made, which tend to be exactly where demographic and macroeconomic growth is most rapid and thus most likely to confound measurement of the response to price.[6]

Moreover, the population growth in any region is influenced by myriad factors besides the region's road capacity. Since it takes years to plan and build a major road or road expansion, and more years for that improvement to affect regional growth, many unpredictable forces can influence the growth of the region during the time between planning the road and experiencing its ultimate effects.

Some recent studies have tried to account for this two-way causality by comparing population growth, road capacity, and vehicle miles of travel over long periods of time. Robert Cervero and Mark Hansen studied thirty-four urban counties in California over a twenty-two-year period from 1976 to 1997. They concluded that every 10 percent increase in lane mile capacity was accompanied by an induced 5.6 percent rise in vehicle miles traveled (VMT), other things equal. Conversely, a 10 percent rise in VMT was accompanied by an induced 3.3 percent rise in lane mile capacity, other things equal. In a follow-up study Cervero found that:

Over a six to eight year period following freeway expansion, around twenty percent of added capacity is "preserved," [that is, not offset by induced demand or other growth] and around eighty percent gets absorbed or depleted. Half of this absorption is due to external factors, like growing population and income. The other half is due to induced-demand effects, mostly higher speeds but also increased building activities.[7]

Cervero also found that road expansions did not influence traffic volumes unless they produced at least short-run improvements in traffic speed. For every 100 percent increase in lane capacity, they found a 40 percent rise in travel on the roads involved that was attributable to higher speed and more building along the road—that is, induced demand. What does this analysis imply about the oft-repeated statement "We cannot build our way out of congestion"? If that statement is taken to mean "Building more road capacity cannot *fully eliminate* all peak-hour congestion once such congestion has initially appeared," then that statement is true. If the statement is taken to mean, "When a growing region builds more road capacity, at least some of the benefits are likely to be offset by induced demand in the long run," that statement is also true. But if the statement is taken to mean, "Adding to road capacity cannot possibly reduce the intensity of existing peak-hour congestion in the road network as a whole," then it is false. Or if it is taken to mean, "Adding to road capacity can never improve traffic conditions because all the benefits will always be offset by induced demand," it is also false. In fact, it is important to recognize that induced demand is not just a social cost because it offsets some of any added capacity; it also provides benefits to those responding to the added capacity, since it improves their travel experiences. Even if traffic is not moving any faster on the expanded road during the peak congestion periods than it was formerly, more people are able to use that road and other roads during those most preferred periods. (Whether their gain is worth the costs of expanding the road is another issue that cannot be analyzed here.)

In summary, building more road capacity almost always has some beneficial impacts on initially existing congestion. However, over the long run, those benefits are also normally offset to some degree by induced demand responses. And those benefits could conceivably be fully offset or absorbed under unusual circumstances, especially in rapidly growing regions. Nevertheless, as Don Pickerell concluded:

The potential for expansion of transportation systems [both roads and transit] to induce additional travel demand is *not* a reason to forego investments in physical facilities or new technologies that increase capacity. . . . whether this is the case for specific investment proposals can only be determined by careful analysis. It is not an issue that can or should be settled by a sweeping indictment of expanding transportation capacity that is rooted in some vague conviction that travel is objectionable, no matter how deeply that conviction is held.[8]

Ramp Metering on Expressways and Freeways

One widely used method of increasing the traffic-handling capacity of existing expressways and freeways is ramp metering. It consists of controlling the rate at which vehicles enter major limited-access roads by using signal lights at on-ramps. If entry to such roads is left uncontrolled, vehicles tend to move onto those roads from specific ramps in bunches that slow the existing flow of traffic. To avoid such platooning, ramp meters are used to admit new entrants onto the main road one at a time, with an interval of five to twenty seconds between entries.

Ramp metering can also be used to limit the total number of vehicles using a major expressway or freeway in a given period so as to keep traffic flowing at the high speeds that produce maximum throughputs. As explained in appendix A, the net entry of many vehicles onto such a road (more vehicles entering any given mile than are leaving that mile) during any one hour reduces the average time and space intervals between vehicles.[9] This often causes drivers to slow down for safety purposes. But such slowdowns result in lower hourly flow rates, thereby decreasing the hourly carrying capacity of the road as long as this congestion lasts. To prevent this outcome, ramp metering can limit the total number of vehicles using a main roadway during any one hour by lengthening the interval between individual vehicle entries onto the roadway.

However, if large numbers of people want to enter a roadway during the peak period, such metering may result in a long queue at each entry ramp. In essence, the congestion prevented on the main roadway by ramp metering is transferred to congestion on the entry ramps. In some cases, delays at freeway entry ramps have become as long as twenty minutes.

If the roadway's entry ramps are very long (as in Minneapolis and St. Paul freeways), the queues resulting from such congestion can often be confined to the ramps themselves. But if those ramps are short (as in Dallas and Houston freeways), such queues may spill congestion out onto local streets or arterials near the main roadway. Proponents of ramp metering claim that the resulting peak-hour congestion outside the main roadway is much less inefficient for society than slowing down traffic on that roadway below its optimal speed and flow levels. However, this claim is not easy to prove under all conditions.

Ramp metering has two opposite impacts on the desires of drivers to use metered freeways during peak periods. On one hand, by speeding movement on ramp-metered freeways, metering encourages more people to try to get onto those roads during peak hours than would if the roads were highly congested. In other words, metering increases peak-hour *convergence* on such freeways. On the other hand, by creating congestion at metered ramps, metering motivates some drivers to use other routes or travel outside of peak periods. In this sense, ramp metering is a form of demand management that increases peak-hour *divergence*. It is hard to know in advance which of these contrasting effects will dominate in any particular situation. However, most regions that use ramp metering believe it has a net positive impact on the efficiency of their road systems.

An excellent study of ramp metering was carried out in 2000 by Cambridge Systematics, Inc., for the Twin Cities Ramp Meter Evaluation process.[10] The Minnesota Department of Transportation shut down the extensive system of ramp metering on Twin Cities freeways for a month and a half. It then compared traffic conditions with and without ramp metering in four major freeway corridors. Without ramp meters:

—Freeway volume fell 9 percent, and peak period throughput (VMT) fell 14 percent.

—Freeway travel times were 22 percent longer. The time thus lost more than offset the elimination of delays at the ramp meters when they were operating, according to Minnesota officials.

—Freeway speeds declined 14 percent.

—Systemwide crashes increased 26 percent.

—There was a sizable net annual increase in auto emissions.

—Fuel consumption decreased by 5.5 million gallons because of less waiting at ramps.

The Minnesota Department of Transportation concluded that ramp metering had a high ratio of benefits to costs, and so it restored use of ramp metering throughout the freeway system.

Part of this same study consisted of compiling data on the impacts of ramp metering in other communities. The study's finding of 22 percent savings in travel time with ramp meters compares favorably to the average of 25 percent (in a range of 7 percent to 91 percent) for thirteen other communities. These calculations do not take into account delays at the ramp meters. Freeway traffic volumes and throughputs also averaged 18 percent higher with ramp metering. But areas with more than fifty ramp meters—Long Island, Phoenix, and Portland—had an average throughput increase of 38 percent. All areas showed large and positive benefit-to-cost ratios from ramp metering.

Ramp metering has most often been employed on freeway sections that have peak-period speeds before metering of less than 30 miles per hour, vehicle flows per lane of 1,200 to 1,500 vehicles per hour, relatively high accident rates, and major merging problems. In regions where such conditions are widespread, ramp metering should be seriously considered as a means of increasing the peak-hour capacity of existing freeways without having to build more pavement—unless the ramps need to be lengthened to hold longer queues.[11]

Using High-Occupancy Vehicle (HOV) Lanes

The single greatest cause of peak-hour congestion is the desire of commuters to ride alone in their private vehicles. Peak-hour vehicular traffic volumes could be slashed if a large fraction of such "Lone Rangers" would participate in car pools, thereby reducing the number of vehicles needed to transport any given number of commuters. True, the principle of triple convergence would still operate, so some periods of intense congestion might arise during peak hours. But those periods of intense congestion would be much shorter than the ones prevalent now.

One way to encourage doubling up is to set aside lanes for persons traveling in high-occupancy vehicles (HOVs). "High occupancy" is defined as three or more persons in the Washington, D.C., area, but only two or more in many parts of southern California and in most places where HOV lanes are used. If HOV travelers can move noticeably faster than lone drivers, people will be encouraged to shift to HOV travel.[12]

Many areas have already established HOV lanes for cars and buses. A 1999 study done by Joseph L. Schofer and Edward J. Czepiel counted about 150 HOV existing facilities in North America, with more than 1,200 route miles in service. Many more were then planned that have since come into service.[13] But in most regions, HOVs are still a small fraction of all vehicles moving during peak hours, with the result that these lanes are normally less congested than other lanes and HOV riders are able to move faster and spend less time commuting.

The Seattle region has achieved remarkable success with HOV lanes on interstates 5, 405, and 90, and state routes 520 and 167.[14] The percentage of people in these corridors using shared ride methods (including car pools and public transit) rose notably from 1998 to 2000. "On average, peak-period HOV lane person throughput on the corridors studied grew by roughly 17 percent in two years, and vehicle throughput grew by about 16 percent."[15] By 2000, it appears that about one-third of all peak-period travelers in these corridors used HOVs or public transit using HOV lanes. In ten interstate segments studied, the share of all peak-hour travelers using these means exceeded 30 percent in six segments during the morning rush and in nine segments during the evening rush. The Regional HOV Policy Advisory Committee established a target of having all HOV lanes exhibiting speeds of 45 miles per hour or better, 90 percent of the time. This goal has not been met in all segments. One reason is that HOV drivers tend to slow down when general purpose lanes are experiencing heavy congestion, although the former still maintain a notable speed advantage over the latter. Even so, in nine out of the ten segments analyzed, HOV lanes maintain a considerable speed and travel time advantage over general purpose lanes. In short, this tactic is working well in Seattle.

The Washington, D.C., metropolitan region has also achieved favorable results from its extensive network of HOV lanes on major interstates. Evaluations of HOV performance included the following conclusions. "All of these HOV facilities are currently operating at a high level of service, and providing substantial time savings relative to alternative LOV facilities. Expressed on a per mile basis, the savings range from approximately 0.5 minutes per mile to just over 1.4 minutes per-mile. For travelers making use of the full length of these facilities, the savings range from 5 to 12 minutes on I-270, from 17 to 28 minutes on I-66, and from 34 to 39 minutes on I-95/I-395. . . . In general, the movement of persons per lane per hour is significantly higher in HOV lanes than in non-HOV lanes. HOV lane person movement ranged from 2,200 to 4,700 per lane per hour while non-HOV lane person movement ranged from 1,400 to 2,000 persons per lane per hour."[16]

One purpose of exclusive HOV lanes is to reduce the inherent time-saving advantage of driving alone, which occurs because picking up and discharging multiple passengers increases trip time. Thus people who value time highly are likely to drive alone to save time, even though they might have to pay $1.80 a day in operating costs and $5.00 parking, or $6.80 for both commuting trips combined.[17] This would be relatively more than a bus ride that might cost $2.00 but take twenty minutes longer each way. The commuter is paying a premium of $4.80 to save forty minutes—which puts a value of $7.20 per hour on that individual's time (not taking into account the greater comfort and privacy of driving alone). Commuters who value their time at less than that rate would be economically better off taking the bus. If the time saved by solo driving was reduced to only fifteen minutes, its implicit value would rise to $19.20 per hour. Undoubtedly, fewer people would value their time at more than that.[18] Thus the smaller the time advantage of driving alone, the more commuters are motivated to use ride sharing or buses.

Moreover, when the large numbers of commuters driving alone in an area generates peak-hour congestion, an opportunity arises for creating a driving-time advantage for people who share rides and use HOV lanes, as described above. It makes sense to consider establishing or expanding such lanes only in locations where general traffic lanes have become heavily congested during peak hours. If traffic is then flowing freely in general travel lanes, there is no time-saving advantage of traveling in HOV lanes, though there may be a cost advantage of sharing travel costs.

HOV Lanes Should Be Created by Expanding Overall Road Capacity

Experience already gained with HOV lanes suggests that congestion is not necessarily alleviated by shifting existing lanes from normal to exclusive HOV use. Instead, this reduces the overall peak-hour capacity of the road, because HOV lanes often carry fewer cars per hour—and sometimes even fewer persons per hour—than normal lanes.[19] Congestion on the normal lanes thus intensifies and encourages persons driving alone to cheat by driving in the HOV lanes. It also enrages thousands of lone drivers who find their commuting worse than before. When this tactic was first tried on the busy Santa Monica Freeway in the Los Angeles area, the negative reactions of drivers were so intense that it was canceled within a month.

The best way to create HOV lanes is to add new lanes to existing roads, by pressing former shoulder space into use, or by adding more pavement. Instead of slowing down all other lanes, the new fast-moving HOV lanes will speed up traffic on normal lanes by drawing vehicles away from them.

Thus the most effective means of creating or expanding HOV lanes is a form of adding to an area's road capacity. This fact stimulates support for such a policy among those who believe more road capacity is needed. But it also may arouse opposition for more HOV lanes among those who believe adding to road capacity is undesirable because it generates more traffic, more air pollution, and higher infrastructure costs. Thus environmentalists and those who are upset by additional growth in their communities often oppose the establishment or expansion of HOV lanes through the creation of additional road capacity.

Experience shows that HOV lanes that carry light traffic loads create an *empty lane syndrome*—a feeling among drivers on adjacent crowded general traffic lanes that the HOV lanes are being underutilized at the expense of increasing congestion in the general lanes. When traffic on an HOV lane is fewer than 800 to 1,000 vehicles per hour, resentment among drivers on nearby general traffic lanes frequently rises to levels that stimulate a political reaction removing the HOV designation from that lane. This happened in northern New Jersey for the lightly used HOV lanes on Interstate 287. The negative reaction to those HOV lanes was so great that it also led to the closing of HOV lanes on nearby Interstate 80, even though the latter HOV lanes were being heavily used.[20]

An important aspect of HOV lanes concerns how intensively they are used by transit vehicles such as large buses. When many buses use an HOV lane during peak hours, its volume of persons carried per hour can become substantially higher than the volumes achieved on adjacent general traffic lanes. This occurs because faster traffic flows in the HOV lanes permit more vehicles per hour to pass any given point, and because the number of persons carried per vehicle rises much higher on HOV lanes used by many buses.

Another aspect of HOV lanes is how many persons per vehicle are required to qualify vehicles for using such lanes. Because most drivers are reluctant to share rides with others, the higher the requirement, the smaller the number of drivers willing to meet it. As a result, lowering the HOV requirement can greatly increase the number of vehicles using HOV lanes. On Interstate 66 in northern Virginia, relaxing the HOV requirement from three or more persons to two or more persons in March 1995 resulted in a 60 percent increase in lane utilization to 1,700 vehicles per hour.[21] Some HOV lanes began with restrictions as high as eight or more persons per vehicle—which really means only buses could use them. But today almost none have restrictions higher than three or more persons, and most use two or more persons.

Experience also indicates that HOV lanes need strict policing, at least when they are first created, to reduce cheating. If fines for invading HOV space are high enough and imposed often enough, solo motorists will be more likely to stay out of it. Another finding is that most people who use HOV lanes appear to do so because it saves them money rather than because HOV lanes speed their commuting.[22] This implies that HOV lanes will be used most intensively when many firms along the route are carrying out traffic management programs to persuade their employees to engage in ride sharing.

Since adding HOV lanes is a form of building new roads, its limitations are about the same as those of any road-building tactic. However, HOV lanes can encourage people to ride more than one per car and thus have more potential for reducing traffic congestion than simply adding road capacity. But that potential is likely to be realized only if many people adopt HOV travel. They are most likely to do so if they are participating in ride-sharing programs sponsored by their employers. Otherwise, using additional lanes for exclusive HOV purposes may not expand total peak-hour capacity any more than permitting all drivers to use them. Hence the actual use of HOV lanes should be continually monitored and compared to normal use of the same lanes.

Another aspect of HOV lanes is permitting single-occupancy vehicles (SOVs) to use them during peak periods if SOV drivers pay a variable toll. This toll is set high enough to restrict the total number of vehicles on these lanes sufficiently to permit continuous high-speed traffic flows. These lanes are called high-occupancy toll (HOT) lanes.

Using Ride Sharing

From 1990 to 2000, the total number of U.S. commuters tallied by the Census Bureau rose by 13.2 million, or 11.5 percent, but the number who commuted by ride sharing rose only 256,000, or 1.6 percent. Thus, in spite of greater use of HOV lanes during the 1990s than ever before, the fraction of all commuters who shared rides in privately owned vehicles declined from 13.4 percent in 1990 to 12.2 percent in 2000. It appears that the greater household purchasing power generated by the widespread prosperity of the 1990s enabled more commuters to pass up the economies of sharing rides with others in favor of the powerful attraction of driving alone. The strength of this attraction is further indicated by the fact that the fraction of all commuters riding with other people on public transit also fell from 5.3 percent in 1990 to 4.7 percent in 2000. Both the share and the absolute number of all commuters who walked to work declined slightly.[23]

Unfortunately from the viewpoint of reducing congestion, a host of strong forces in U.S. society are operating to diminish the attractiveness of ride sharing. Among them are the following:

—Ride sharing works best when a lot of commuters share the same points of origin or destination. But both jobs and housing are becoming increasingly dispersed because new growth areas are dominated by low-density settlements.

—Flexible work hours and more people working at home cause fewer workers to share the same arrival and departure times within the same workplace.

—More jobs require workers to visit several locations during the day, making ride sharing impractical.

—More workers are acting as independent contractors, or working part time, with their own schedules different from those of most other workers in the same organization. [24]

—As real incomes rise, time becomes more valuable, and ride sharing takes noticeably more time than driving alone.

To encourage ride sharing, employers who manage large numbers of workers at a single site should institute the same working hours for as many of those workers as possible. However, where many small firms are clustered close together, employers should encourage flexible working hours so persons from different firms can arrange to travel at the same times.

From 1990 to 2000, 97.6 percent of the increase in commuting workers consisted of those who drove to work alone, even though they constituted only 75.7 percent of all commuters in 2000. Thus attempts to increase ride sharing seem likely to be more effective in times of economic adversity when more households need to conserve resources than in times of great prosperity when people feel freer to indulge in the "luxury" of commuting alone. This is partly true because ride sharing is most common among low-wage workers who are less able to afford owning their own vehicles than better-paid workers.

One of the most effective means of encouraging ride sharing is a program of cashing out free parking offered by employers. This creates an economic incentive for solo drivers who get free parking to switch to ride sharing or public transit.

Another set of factors that can increase ride sharing is a combination of intense peak-hour congestion and fast-moving HOV lanes. In the San Francisco Bay area, custom has established at least three "casual car pool" pickup points on the East Bay side and one on the San Francisco side where single drivers can stop and collect two passengers en route to the Bay Bridge. Then they can qualify to use faster free HOV lanes getting to and through the toll collection area westbound, or faster lanes eastbound. Most passengers get dropped off by their spouses at these pickup points, though some ride in from distant transit stops and switch to cars to save on fares. This ploy saved thirty to forty minutes westbound in the morning during the "dot-com boom," though less when the boom ended.[25] This tactic works only if both drivers and passengers believe the persons they ride with are unlikely to pose any personal threat to their safety.

Other Tactics for Making Road Travel More Efficient

Highway engineers have devised many ways of making traffic flow faster and more smoothly over existing roads. These tactics do not alter the total volume of traffic but ameliorate certain problems that keep traffic from moving smoothly. It is not within the scope of this book to analyze these devices in detail. Rather, they are merely listed here as follows:

—Programming repairs and improvements so as to properly maintain existing expressways, highways, and streets, and timing these actions to avoid carrying them out in high-traffic periods.

—Coordinating the timing of traffic signals along arterial streets. Traffic speed can also be improved by replacing older traffic signals with modern computer-controlled signals.

—Using multiple repair vehicles to rove major arteries during peak hours and clear accidents quickly. The nearest such vehicle can be rapidly radio-dispatched to any accident scene.

—Creating television monitoring systems along major roadways to spot accident tie-ups quickly and permit rapid dispatch of accident clearance teams to such sites.

—Upgrading "normal" city streets or major arterials to wider "super-streets" that also have partly limited access.

—Converting streets from two-way to one-way movement.

—Electronically controlling signs above expressways or regular radio announcements to provide real-time information on current traffic conditions for motorists.

—Changing street parking patterns to provide more room for traffic flows or shorter delays while drivers are entering or leaving parking spaces.

Combinations of these tactics can notably affect peak-hour times and speeds on congested expressways. For example, the Washington State Department of Transportation instituted a combination of ramp controls, television monitors, visual signals to motorists, park-and-ride lots, and added high-occupancy vehicle (HOV) lanes to improve traffic flows on Interstate 5 in the Seattle area. After the ramp-metering program was started in 1981, but before the new HOV lanes were opened, peak-hour driving time on the main lanes of a 6.9 mile segment fell from 22.0 minutes to 12.0-13.0 minutes.[26] The average time motorists had to wait at signaled ramps before entering the expressway was less than 3.0 minutes. Over a six-year period, the entire project, including new HOV lanes, further reduced peak-hour driving time on that segment to 9.5 minutes and cut average ramp waiting time to less than 2.0 minutes. Yet total peak-hour traffic handled by all lanes in this part of Interstate 5 increased by 86 percent northbound and 62 percent southbound.[27]

CHAPTER 9

Creating More
Public Transit Capacity

This chapter explores trying to cope with peak-hour traffic congestion by creating additional public transit capacity. This tactic is advocated by many urban planners, transit agencies, manufacturers of transit equipment, environmentalists seeking to limit increased use of automotive vehicles or reduce air pollution, persons unable to own or drive their own private vehicles, and politicians frustrated by their inability to reduce congestion by other means.

Public Transit and Traffic Congestion

Public transit has certain fundamental characteristics that directly affect its ability to help cope with peak-hour traffic congestion. It is necessary to understand the most important ones before analyzing what effects increasing transit capacity might have on congestion.

The forms of public transit dominant in the United States—buses, subways, commuter rail trains, heavy and light rail systems—can function efficiently only when they serve relatively high-density areas at their points of origin or destination or both. Yet the residential settlement patterns dominant in nearly all U.S. metropolitan areas involve

TABLE 9-1. Workers Aged 16 and Over Commuting by Public Transit, 2000

Percent of workers commuting by public transit	Number of areas	Workers aged 16 and over		Public transit commuters	
		Number	Percent of U.S. total	Number	Percent of U.S. total
In metro areas					
10 percent and over	2	13,537,326	10.55	2,804,990	46.23
From 5.0 to 9.99	11	18,596,145	14.50	1,552,299	25.58
From 3.5 to 4.99	12	15,924,316	12.41	684,692	11.28
From 2.0 to 3.49	36	17,747,306	13.83	486,122	8.01
From 1.5 to 1.99	26	11,390,493	8.88	200,011	3.30
From 1.0 to 1.49	52	10,489,431	8.18	133,334	2.20
From 0.5 to 0.99	95	13,415,888	10.46	101,442	1.67
Under 0.5 percent	46	4,076,731	3.18	13,578	0.22
Total	280	105,177,636	81.99	5,976,468	98.50
Outside metro areas[a]		23,101,592	18.01	91,235	1.50
Total[b]		128,279,228	100.00	6,067,703	100.00

Source: U.S. Bureau of the Census, 2000 data, table DP-3, "Profile of Selected Economic Characteristics: 2000, Geographic Areas, Inside Metropolitan Areas," and table P-30, "Means of Transportation to Work for Workers 16 Years and Over."
a. Share of workers commuting on public transit is 0.39 percent.
b. Share of all U.S. workers commuting on public transit is 4.73 percent.

relatively low densities, especially in the suburbs where most Americans live.

As a result of the first trait just mentioned, public transit facilities and services are highly concentrated in a few parts of the nation and largely absent from most parts of many metropolitan areas and nearly all rural areas. Transit facilities are found mainly in large, high-density cities and some of their surrounding suburbs.

In only two metropolitan areas, New York and Chicago, did more than 10 percent of all workers commute by public transit in 2000, as shown in table 9-1. In only 13 such areas (CMSAs or MSAs) out of the 280 in the nation did more than 5 percent of all workers commute by transit. Those 13 areas contained 25 percent of all U.S. workers but provided 72 percent of all U.S. transit commuters. In contrast, in 141 metropolitan areas plus all nonmetropolitan areas combined, less than 1 percent of all workers commuted by transit. Those low-transit-using areas held 32 percent of all U.S. workers but provided only 3.4 percent of all transit commuters.

A regression with the percentage of all MSA commuters using transit in 2000 as the dependent variable and four independent variables had an adjusted r-squared of 0.874, or 0.800 without New York. Central city population density was by far the most powerful independent variable. The total population of the MSA was not statistically significant, with or without New York.[1] However, the total population of the central city was statistically significant when used instead of the total MSA population.

This concentration makes comparisons of nationwide transit data, transit patronage, and private automotive vehicle usage almost meaningless. Residents of much of the nation cannot effectively use public transit for commuting or other travel because it is not available to them. In contrast, residents of almost the entire nation have access to private automotive vehicles and the road systems they use.

Public transit suffers from the same concentration of its patronage during daily peak-travel periods that causes congestion on roads and highways. Therefore, most transit facilities experience peak-hour overcrowding similar to that found on commuter roads and are greatly underutilized—compared with their capacity—much of the rest of each day.

For example, from April 2000 through April 2001, in the Bay Area Rapid Transit system, 54 percent of all weekday exits occurred during the two peak periods of 6:30 to 9:30 a.m. and 4:00 to 7:00 p.m. This is quite similar to the 40.7 percent of all work trips on all modes that the 1995 Nationwide Personal Transportation Survey reported occurred between 6:00 and 9:00 a.m. and 4:00 and 7:00 p.m., compared with only 39.7 percent of all nonwork trips that occurred during those hours.[2]

In October 2002, 47.5 percent of daily ridership on Chicago Transit Authority buses and subway trains occurred during the peak hours of 6:00 to 9:00 a.m. and 4:00 to 7:00 p.m., though they composed only 25 percent of the hours in the day.[3]

Consequently, current users of public transit often have to wait in lines during peak periods or endure very crowded conditions once they enter transit vehicles in such periods.

More than 60 percent of all unlinked transit trips in 2001 were by bus, and buses use the same streets as most private automotive vehicles (except when buses use exclusive bus lanes or HOV lanes).[4] As a result, bus travelers are often caught up in traffic-induced delays that plague drivers of private vehicles. Moreover, buses are relatively large vehicles that make frequent stops. Hence buses themselves are important contributors to general traffic congestion, especially in areas where many are concentrated together, as in large downtowns where many bus routes converge within a few blocks.

Commuting and other trips on transit typically take much more time than similar trips by private automotive vehicles. This is an inherent result of certain basic traits of transit. These include the need to move from one's home to a transit stop or station, often by walking; the need to wait for a bus or train to arrive; the loss of time for each rider when the transit vehicle stops to pick up or discharge other passengers at places other than where that rider is going; and the need to move from the transit exit point to one's final destination, usually again by walking or by transferring to another mode of travel. These time-consuming ingredients are either absent or present to a lesser degree than when one moves by private vehicle.

Consequently, in 2000, the average commuting trip by transit in the United States required 47.7 minutes versus only 24.1 minutes for such trips by private vehicles driven by single occupants and 28.5 minutes for trips in car pools.[5]

Why Reducing Traffic Congestion Is Not a Valid Reason for Expanding Transit Capacity

The most cogent reason to expand public transit capacity is to offer people more choices of travel modes besides private automotive vehicles. Greater numbers of choices are especially important for persons who cannot operate such vehicles themselves, such as the very young, the very old, or those suffering from various disabilities. About 26 percent of all residents in America in 2000 were 16 or under (24.2 percent) or 85 or older (1.5 percent)—a total of 72.3 million persons. Another group consists of persons whose normal daily trips are on heavily congested roadways and therefore include frequent delays. Many such persons would prefer riding on public transit to continuing to drive themselves in frustrating traffic jams. Without question, expanding the travel mode choices available to all these people is often an excellent reason to create more public transit capacity, especially in regions that have very little transit service now.

However, expanding transit capacity rarely reduces existing roadway traffic congestion that has reached high levels of intensity. This conclusion may seem counterintuitive. If all the expressways leading into a major downtown are jammed every day during peak periods, it seems reasonable to assume that building an extensive fixed rail system on separate rights-of-way also serving the downtown will divert thousands of commuters off the roads, thereby relieving congestion.

In fact, such extensive systems have been built since 1950 in San Francisco, Washington, and Atlanta. But peak-hour congestion did not decline in any of these regions; in fact, it got worse. Because of the principle of triple convergence, any initial improvement in speed on the expressways caused by such diversions to the new transit systems did not last. In the short run, all the auto-driving commuters who shifted from expressways to the new rail systems were replaced on those expressways by other auto-driving commuters who had formerly traveled on other routes or at other times or on other modes. In the long run, the expanded overall capacity of each region's transportation network—including more highways built in the same time periods—helped encourage more people and firms to locate in those regions. The resulting "induced demand" for travel soaked up all the additional capacity of all types in each region. This outcome was certainly not caused primarily by transit expansion. But neither did that expansion succeed in reducing rising roadway congestion in any perceptible way.

True, the expanded transit systems surely increased travel choices, thereby producing benefits for those who used them. And they enabled more people to travel during peak hours on transit and roads combined, thereby benefiting many auto-driving commuters too. But they did not reduce the intensity of peak-hour traffic congestion.

Some transit proponents argue that if these transit systems had not been built or expanded, all those using them would now be driving during peak periods—thereby making roadway congestion much worse than it is now. Hence these transit systems must have reduced peak-hour congestion. But this argument is at least partly false. If those transit systems had not been built, the total capacity of each regional transportation system for handling persons wanting to travel during peak hours would have been smaller. Hence many persons now traveling during peak hours by driving on expressways or riding on transit would have taken other routes, shifted to other times of the day, used previously existing buses, or made fewer trips per month. The intensity of congestion at the worst parts of the peak periods would have been the same as it is now—not worse—although the peak periods might have been longer. True, if existing levels of peak-hour congestion in a region are low, then expanding transit capacity there might cause them to fall even lower. In such circumstances, adding transit capacity might be justified as desirable because it might prevent intense peak-hour congestion from ever appearing. But once peak-hour congestion on any major roadway has become chronically severe, with traffic crawling along for a notable period every day, then adding more transit capacity to attract drivers away from that roadway will not eliminate such periods of crawling traffic—though it might shorten them. True, as already noted, more transit capacity will expand the travel choices available to the community, which is a social benefit. But that overall capacity expansion may also induce more travel in the long run, thereby at least partly offsetting its positive impacts on congestion.

In short, there are often valid reasons to expand existing public transit systems or build new ones. But reducing existing intense traffic congestion is not one of those reasons.

How Widely Used Is Public Transit for Commuting Trips?

Traffic congestion is normally heaviest during daily peak periods when most people are traveling to or from work, so public transit's relationship to commuting is crucial to its possible role in alleviating congestion. Aside from several large cities with extensive mass transit systems, public transit is not widely used for work trips in the United States. The major reason is that access to transit is not available in many parts of the nation. Therefore, nationwide data are generally not as useful in understanding transit's true role as more localized regional data.

Nevertheless, a cursory analysis of nationwide data does provide some overall perspective. In the nation as a whole, transit commuting in 2000 was done by only 4.73 percent of all workers over 16; whereas 87.89 percent—18.6 times as many—commuted in privately owned vehicles.[6] Transit commuters declined from 5.27 percent of all workers over 16 in 1990 to 4.73 percent in 2000—even falling in absolute numbers by 1,886. In contrast, the total number of workers rose 13.2 million in that decade, and 99.5 percent of that increase consisted of more workers driving to work, either alone or in car pools.

Transit commuting is concentrated in central cities, especially a few large ones. In 2000, 10.5 percent of all central city workers commuted by public transit, compared with 2.9 percent of all suburban workers and 0.6 percent of all workers living outside metropolitan areas. However, the overall central city percentage is distorted by the immense

TABLE 9-2. Public Transit Commuting in Major Cities, 1990 and 2000

City	Number of public transit commuters			Percent of all city workers	
	1990	2000	Percent change	1990	2000
1. New York	1,701,192	1,684,850	−0.96	53.45	52.78
2. Chicago	351,059	310,924	−11.43	29.71	26.08
3. Philadelphia	183,715	144,936	−21.11	28.68	25.44
4. Los Angeles	171,746	152,435	−11.24	10.54	10.20
5. San Francisco	128,160	130,311	1.68	33.52	31.13
6. Boston	89,096	89,906	0.91	31.54	32.29
7. Washington, D.C.	111,422	86,493	−22.37	36.60	33.15
8. Baltimore	67,817	48,573	−28.38	22.04	19.48
9. Houston	50,359	49,441	−1.82	6.52	5.87
10. Seattle	44,416	55,652	25.30	15.88	17.58
11. Oakland	28,637	29,728	3.81	17.88	17.44
12. Portland	23,672	33,410	41.14	11.05	12.33
13. Atlanta	34,340	26,893	−21.69	19.96	15.03
14. Denver	18,500	23,487	26.96	7.99	8.43
15. Cleveland	24,998	21,092	−15.63	14.06	12.00
16. Dallas	33,349	29,361	−11.96	6.66	5.47
17. San Diego	23,773	24,236	1.95	4.24	4.18
18. Minneapolis	30,214	29,681	−1.76	16.02	14.55
19. San Jose	14,084	17,482	24.13	3.51	4.09
20. Phoenix	15,620	19,564	25.25	3.30	3.26
21. Detroit	34,933	27,634	−20.89	10.75	8.65
22. Miami	19,133	14,382	−24.83	12.93	11.37
23. San Antonio	19,479	18,632	−4.35	4.93	3.79
Total	3,219,714	3,069,103	−4.68		

Source: U.S. Bureau of the Census, 1990 and 2000 data, table DP-1, "Profile of General Demographic Characteristics," and table DP-3, "Profile of Selected Economic Characteristics."

influence of New York City. About 53 percent of its workers use public transit, and they compose 27.8 percent of all U.S. transit commuters and 42.3 percent of all central city transit commuters. In all central cities excluding New York City, transit commuters make up only 6.6 percent of all workers. When New York City is excluded from total national data for 2000, the share of all workers over 16 using public transit declines from 4.7 percent to 3.5 percent.[7]

Significant fractions of workers commute by public transit in several other large cities too. Table 9-2 shows the twenty-three cities with the greatest number of transit commuters in 2000. The sixth column lists the percentages of all city workers commuting by public transit. In six cities, including New York City, that fraction exceeded 20 percent; in nine others, it was between 10 and 20 percent. These twenty-three cities contained 50.6 percent of all U.S. transit commuters in 2000, though they encompassed only 10.3 percent of the total number of U.S. workers. Only five of these twenty-three cities lost population from 1990 to 2000, but the percentage of workers commuting by transit declined in eighteen of them, and the absolute number doing so fell to fourteen. Hence there was a drop of 4.7 percent in their combined transit commuters in the 1990s. Outside of these twenty-three cities, the fraction of all workers commuting by public transit throughout the United States in 2000 was only 2.4 percent.

Data from earlier censuses show that persons most likely to use public transit for work trips are those who have no automotive vehicle available to their household, live in a central city and work in its central business district, and live in a densely settled community. But all three of these factors are becoming less significant because of recent trends in demography and settlement patterns. The absolute number of households without any private vehicles declined from almost 13 million in 1969 to 10.9 million in 2000—or about 10.3 percent of all households in the latter year.[8] The share of jobs in central cities and central city downtowns has declined steadily in the past decade. These trends are highly likely to continue.[9]

How Widely Is Public Transit Used?

The above commuting data from the 2000 Census do not take into account recent increases in the total number of persons using public transit as measured by ridership and mileage information. Figure 9-1 shows that total passenger miles in all public transit modes combined remained relatively constant from 1990 through 1995 at around 40 billion. From 1995 through 2000, such mileage rose steadily to 47.7 billion in 2000, a four-year increase of 19.7 percent.

Figure 9-2 shows that total use of public transit was higher in 1990 than earlier, declined somewhat during and after the recession of 1990–91, then began rising in 1996. By 2001, the number of unlinked transit trips had increased 24.4 percent above its 1995 level and 9.7 percent above its 1990 level.[10]

Figure 9-3 shows the breakdown of all transit passenger miles by mode for the year 2000. This figure also shows that somewhat under half of all transit miles are on buses (44.6 percent in 2000), though fixed-rail mileage has been a rising share in recent years.[11] (Buses pro-

FIGURE 9-1. Total Transit Passenger Miles on Public Transit, by Type of Transit, 1990–2000

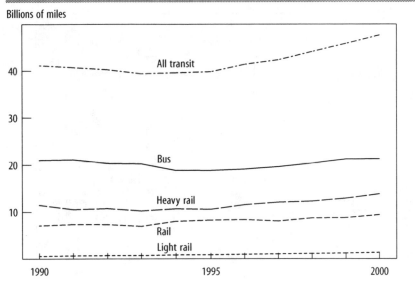

Source: American Public Transportation Association, *APTA Public Transportation Fact Book,* table 8 (www.apta.com [February 2004]).

vided 60 percent of all unlinked transit trips in 2000.) Buses, heavy rail, and commuter rail accounted for 93.3 percent of all such mileage. Light rail provided only 2.8 percent but was rising at a notable rate.

These data plus the census commuting data set forth earlier indicate that increased ridership on public transit apparently does not come primarily from greater transit commuting but from other trip purposes. Examples include tourism, shopping, running errands, obtaining health care, and going to and from school. It is not clear just what fraction of these added trips takes place during peak traffic periods, thereby helping relieve peak-hour congestion. However, traffic congestion in many large metropolitan areas has recently been extending well beyond normal peak periods. Hence transit ridership outside those periods may also affect congestion.

Overall Travel by Public Transit and Travel in Privately Owned Vehicles

As already noted, most American commuters travel in privately owned vehicles (POVs), including cars, light trucks, and sport utility vehicles.

FIGURE 9-2. Total Unlinked Public Transit Trips, 1970–2001

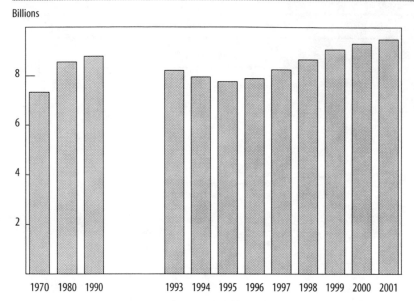

Billions

Source: *APTA Public Transportation Fact Book,* table 5.

FIGURE 9-3. Distribution of Passenger Miles on Public Transit, by Type of Transit, 2000[a]

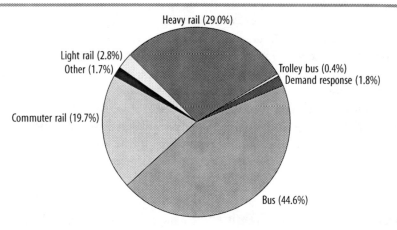

Source: *APTA Public Transportation Fact Book,* table 8.
a. Total miles traveled = 47.7 billion.

The dominance of POVs is even more true of all ground travel than of commuting alone. In every year during the decade 1990–2000, highway passenger miles constituted at least 98.8 percent of both types of travel combined, leaving transit mileage at 1.2 percent or less. From 1990 through 1995, even the percentage increases in highway travel exceeded those in transit travel.[12] However, in 1996 and from 1998 through 2000, percentage gains in transit miles were greater than those on highways. This fact caused some proponents of transit to claim that "growth in public transit exceeds growth in driving."[13] But the absolute gains in highway mileage during those four years combined surpassed those in transit mileage by a ratio of 50 to 1, showing that this claim was exaggerated, to put it mildly.

Why Is Public Transit So Minor in U.S. Ground Transportation?

Americans traveling abroad are often struck by the much larger role that public transit plays in ground transportation everywhere outside the United States. Why are Americans so dependent on POVs for their movements? There are two basic causes.

The most important reason is that most Americans live in low-density settlement patterns, which cannot be efficiently served by the now dominant forms of public transit. Those forms are mainly fixed-rail systems and relatively large buses that need to gather or deliver large numbers of passengers at a few stops or destinations so they can attain economies of scale. But American settlement patterns are dominated by household preferences for low-density housing scattered over wide areas, usually on separate lots, and a similar scatteration of job locations. Hence it is difficult to aggregate a large number of persons at any one point of origin or destination, except the downtown business district.

After an exhaustive study of the relationship between residential density and transit usage, Boris Pushkarev and Jeffrey Zupan concluded that transit usage is minimal at net residential densities less than seven housing units per acre (the equivalent of gross densities of 4,200 to 5,600 persons per square mile), and rises sharply at net densities above seven units per acre. Therefore, "moderate residential densities in the range of 7 to 15 dwellings per acre can support moderately convenient transit service" (by rapid transit, buses, and taxis).[14]

In 2000, only 18 out of 478 urbanized areas had overall densities (including their central cities) of more than 4,000 persons per square mile. Those 18 urbanized areas contained 44.0 million residents, or 15.4

percent of the entire nation. In at least 7 of them, the densities of their fringe portions (outside their central cities)—where most new growth occurs—were well below 4,000 persons per square mile. The average overall density of all 478 urbanized areas was 2,656 persons per square mile. The average overall density of the 460 urbanized areas with densities below 4,000 was 2,051 persons per square mile. Those areas contained 152.0 million residents, or 54.0 percent of the entire nation. Thus, in 2000, less than one-sixth of the U.S. population lived in urbanized areas with overall population densities high enough to sustain economically feasible public transit operations.[15]

Advocates of more transit complain that a major reason more people do not use transit is that it is not easily accessible to them. The Surface Transportation Policy Project states, "Only 4 percent of the nation's 4 million miles of roads are now served by transit, either through buses or parallel train lines . . . Less than half of all Americans (49 percent) report living within one-quarter mile of a transit stop, and only 8.3 percent of households surveyed have subway service available."[16]

This lack of accessibility mainly results from the incompatibility of economical transit operations and America's prevalent low-density settlement patterns, as just noted. Hence it is not really a separate factor from that incompatibility. Proponents of transit recognize this fact by arguing that future settlement patterns should embody much higher average densities than those that have dominated American urban and suburban development for the past fifty years or more.

The second reason for low transit patronage in the United States is that traveling in POVs offers many advantages over doing so in public conveyances.

For one thing, POVs provide more comfort and privacy than many forms of transit, which are often crowded and may require many passengers to stand for long journeys. And of course people traveling by POVs can begin and end their journeys at times most convenient for themselves, without having to adjust their movements to transit schedules. That is why most transit commuting trips take much more time than most driving commuting trips. Figure 9-4 shows a breakdown of commuting trip times into four duration categories for transit and all other modes. The percentage of commuting trips taking an hour or more was five times as great among transit users as among users of all other modes—overwhelmingly POVs.

Persons traveling by POVs also have flexible control over their routes, so they can readily carry out more than one purpose on a trip,

FIGURE 9-4. Average One-Way Commuting Times, 2000

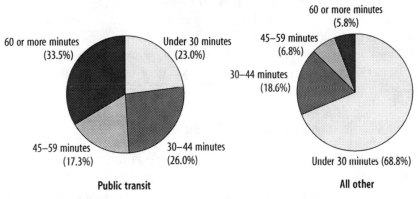

Public transit

Under 30 minutes (23.0%)

30–44 minutes (26.0%)

45–59 minutes (17.3%)

60 or more minutes (33.5%)

All other

Under 30 minutes (68.8%)

30–44 minutes (18.6%)

45–59 minutes (6.8%)

60 or more minutes (5.8%)

Source: 2000 Census.

such as dropping off children or shopping on the way to or from work. Such "trip chaining" would be very difficult on public transit with its fixed routes. An analysis of trip chaining based on the 1995 Nationwide Personal Transportation Survey showed that more than half of all women and nearly half of all men made at least one stop going to or from work.[17]

Importantly, POVs provide many owners with positive senses of freedom of movement and power over their own environments that are lacking for users of public transit. This psychological motive is a key reason why ownership of private automobiles is so avidly pursued throughout the world. And persons traveling by POVs can listen to the radio or records, smoke, and even talk on the telephone without bothering strangers nearby. However, POV drivers cannot read, as many passengers can on public transit.

For commuters provided with free parking by their employers, the operating costs of driving are often less than the costs of taking public transit, especially if the commuters have to own a vehicle for other reasons. Downtown parking often costs $10.00 per day or more; whereas the gasoline cost of driving the average commuting travel of 30 miles per day at 20 miles per gallon and $1.50 per gallon is $2.25. Very few round-trip transit tickets are even close to the resulting driving costs of $12.25 or more when free parking is not available.

Finally, many people enjoy the time they get to spend alone while driving in traffic, even if they have to suffer delays, since they may have few other moments of total privacy in their lives. Patricia Mokhtarian and Ilan Solomon recently surveyed 1,427 commuters in the San Francisco Bay area and discovered that 19 percent positively liked commuting, while 40 percent agreed that "my commute trip is a useful transition between home and work."[18]

These advantages form an immense barrier to convincing most Americans to shift from driving their own POVs or carpooling to using public transit.

Several Reasons to Expand Public Transit

Advocates of expanding transit advance several other arguments not directly related to traffic congestion. These concerns should also influence the allocation of available transportation resources among different modes.

—Demographic changes in American society are causing more households to desire to live in near-downtown neighborhoods best served by transit. These households include immigrants from abroad, "empty nesters" from the baby boom generation, and young professionals. They are supporting new residential construction in close-in neighborhoods that need improved transit service.

—Spending on transportation is the second largest item (after housing) in the budget of most American households. Reducing the dependence of households on using automobiles would help them decrease this budget burden, because transit travel costs are typically lower than automobile travel costs. Seventy-five percent of transportation costs consist of fixed costs like buying a car and insuring it, so there is little incentive for auto owners to cut down on driving to save operating costs. Providing more transit services to more areas would help many low-income households reduce their spending on transportation.

—When both housing and transportation costs are considered together, higher transportation costs in certain regions tend to be offset by lower housing costs in those same regions. Figure 9-5 shows data for twenty-eight metropolitan areas arranged in descending order of the average percentage of household spending on housing and transportation combined.[19] In many regions with a low average percentage of spending on transportation, such as New York City, the percentage spent on housing is high. Therefore, the total percentage spent on housing and transportation combined varies much less among areas than the totals for each component, as figure 9-5 shows. But for low-income

FIGURE 9-5. Consumer Spending on Transportation and Housing, by Metro Area, 2000–01

Average percent of household expenditures

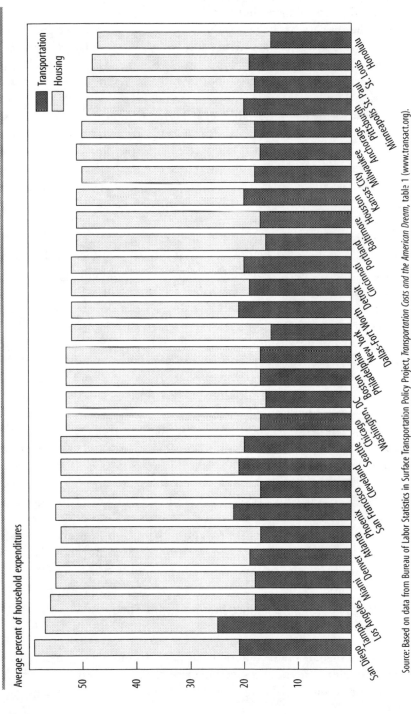

Source: Based on data from Bureau of Labor Statistics in Surface Transportation Policy Project, *Transportation Costs and the American Dream*, table 1 (www.transact.org).

households, spending on housing is more rewarding in the long run than spending on cars (if they own the housing, although most poor households are renters). Cars depreciate in value rapidly while owner-occupied housing normally appreciates over time. Therefore, public policy should help low-income households spend more on ownership housing by providing more transit opportunities.[20]

—Transit-oriented development (TOD) around transit stops—especially on fixed-rail systems—adds to local government property tax revenues and reduces the need for government spending on auto-oriented infrastructures. TOD investments can be privately financed and induced by public spending to expand such transit systems. TOD areas also raise land values in the vicinity of transit stops and can include affordable housing linked to transit use.

Insofar as expanding transit encourages higher-density residential and other development, it reduces the total infrastructure costs that will be generated by future population growth. Therefore, building transit facilities that will attract a higher share of future gains in population will benefit society. This will also reduce driving and thereby cut auto emissions and fuel consumption.

—Most job opportunities for low-income households living in cities are also in cities. Many consist of "replacement jobs" formed by turnover in existing firms, rather than "new jobs" in suburban locations. City workers need adequate public transit to link them to these in-city job opportunities.

—The change in federal legislation making transit allowances for employees tax deductible, along with parking costs for firms, was beneficial in promoting equality of access between transit and highway travel. But this benefit needs to be promoted more widely with federal funds because it is not being used enough to achieve true equality of access between transit and car travel for most employees.

Because this book focuses on the relationship between expanding transit and peak-hour traffic congestion, it does not include any in-depth analysis of these other reasons to expand transit.

Transit Capacity Could Reduce Intense Traffic Congestion in One Situation

In theory, there is one exception to the conclusion that expanding transit capacity cannot reduce existing intensive peak-hour traffic congestion. It was pointed out by Martin J. H. Mogridge. However, his analysis only applies to regions in which the vast majority of peak-hour commuting is done on rapid transit systems with separate rights of way. Central London is an example, since in 2001 around 85 percent of all morning peak-period commuters into that area used public transit (including 77 percent on separate rights of way) and only 11 percent used private cars.[21] When peak-hour travel equilibrium has been reached between the subway system and the major commuting roads, then the travel time required for any given trip is roughly equal on both modes.

That must be the case because travelers can shift modes between transit and roads. If movement on the roads generally takes less time, then people will move from the transit system onto the roads. The added road traffic will slow the average speed on the roads—that is, increase travel times for specific journeys. So roads cannot maintain a travel time superiority over transit very long. Even expanding road capacity does not speed up movement on roads permanently. Rather, doing so simply draws more passengers from transit until the roads become so loaded they slow to the same travel time as transit. Since the percentage of travelers using transit is so great, there are always enough transit passengers willing to shift onto roads to swamp any improvement in speed from building more or wider roads. That is what differentiates this situation from conditions prevailing in every American city except perhaps New York City.

However, if travel time (including getting to the station, waiting, and getting from the station at the other end to the final destination) is less prolonged on transit than on roads, people will move from roads onto the transit system. But unlike roads, fixed-rail transit systems with separate rights of way do not become slower because they have more passengers—they only become more crowded. Transit cars get more and more jammed with standing-room-only crowds, but the trains move just as fast. At some point, the transit system becomes packed to maximum capacity during peak hours. An example is the Tokyo subway system, which becomes so crowded that official "pushers" are used to pack more people into each car. Then people stop moving from roads onto transit because there is no more room. (This occurs after the maximum number of trains have been put into service with the shortest possible headways.) At any passenger loading on transit systems below this maximum, there must be a rough equilibrium with roads and transit or else more people would move off roads onto transit.

If such an equilibrium exists initially, but then some improvement of the transit system decreases the average travel time for movement on that system, that will make transit more attractive than roads. People will move off roads onto transit until transit still has lower travel times than roads but is at maximum capacity or transit and roads are back in rough travel time equilibrium. The improvement in the transit system has to be of a kind that reduces travel times to have this effect. Just increasing the number of passengers that the transit system can carry per hour will not make transit more attractive than roads to current road users, unless transit was previously faster than roads but at maximum load capacity.

Mogridge concluded that, in the long run, the speed of movement on the transit system—that is, its travel times—is the key factor deciding the overall speed of all modes in the city. The other modes have to adjust to come into equilibrium with transit's travel times. But overall travel times on the London transit system had not fallen for roughly a century. Mogridge believed that is why London's road traffic also had not changed in speed for about a century, even though a lot of roads had been built or improved.

Unfortunately, it is extremely difficult to improve a large and extensive regional rail transit system in such a way as to decrease its average travel times. So this analysis may seem largely irrelevant—even in London. However, it does have one key policy implication: that expanding the road system in such a region will not speed up movement either—whether on roads or transit. Road expansion will only affect the percentages of all commuters who use transit and roads. But that conclusion only applies where transit loads are so great and transit routes so extensive that any improvement in roads is shortly offset by a flow of people from transit onto the improved roads, wherever they are. That condition rarely exists in the United States because transit carries such low percentages of all peak-hour commuters in most regions. When major commuting roads are expanded in America, enough people usually do converge on them to offset any initial increases in speed. But most of those convergers come from other roads and streets and other times, not from transit.

Light Rail and Bus Rapid Transit as Transit Alternatives

Additional public transit alternatives to both automobile movements and traditional fixed "heavy" or commuter rail transit systems have been developed largely in the past two decades in the forms of light rail and bus rapid transit systems. Each of these alternatives covers a whole spectrum of possible systems, ranging from slight modifications to trolleys that run on normal streets to completely redesigned vehicles that run on separate, exclusive rights-of-way.

LIGHT RAIL. This form of transit consists of largely electric-powered trams or streetcars that run on tracks on city streets or separate rights-of-way or—most common—some combination of both. Light rail cars are usually smaller and less heavily built than the vehicles used in full subway or metro systems, which the transit industry refers to as "heavy rail." Mike Taplin, the president of the United Kingdom's Light Rail Transit Association (LRTA), differentiated light rail systems from traditional trolleys, streetcars, or trams as follows: "These lines are light rail because they are mostly segregated from other traffic, passengers get on and off at stations rather than in the street, and the cars run faster. However there is no definite border line between streetcar and light rail—they merge gradually from one to another, and as a streetcar system gets upgraded it becomes light rail. A lot of this is to do with planning jargon; streetcars are seen to be old fashioned whereas light rail is trendy!"[22]

According to the LRTA, 82 light rail systems were operating in fifty-eight countries as of January 2004. Japan had 11, Switzerland had 10, Germany had 9, and the United States had 12.[23] Most other nations with such systems had just 1 or 2. Those totals compared with LRTA's counts of 95 heavy rail systems and 365 tramways in operation worldwide at that date.

Proponents extol the following benefits of light rail transit systems:

—Such systems are much less costly to build and operate than heavy rail or metro systems. Because they are electrically powered, light rail vehicles do not emit air pollutants along their routes, and they are relatively quiet compared with heavy or commuter rail systems or heavy motor vehicle traffic.

—Light rail systems are not as affected by congestion as buses or private vehicles because they often run some of their routes off streets and are usually benefited by traffic signal priority where they do run on streets.

—Light rail systems are more permanent than bus routes because they have built-in tracks, so these systems may be more successful in motivating real estate developers to build high-density structures and projects along light rail lines. However, there is little empirical evidence supporting this contention.

—Light rail systems can effectively stimulate downtown prosperity and redevelopment by focusing their trips on service to major downtowns.

According to the American Public Transit Association (APTA), there were 26 light rail systems operating in the United States in 2001. The average trip was 4.3 miles, and the total number of passenger miles in 2001 was 1.437 billion.[24] All U.S. light rail systems combined encompassed 1,078 track miles. Agencies that ran light rail systems with 25.0 or more miles of track were those in Baltimore, Boston, Cleveland, Dallas, Denver, Los Angeles, Newark, Pittsburgh, Philadelphia, Portland, Sacramento, St. Louis, Salt Lake City, San Diego, San Francisco, and San Jose. Among these sixteen U.S. cities with light rail systems, nine had lower percentages of all workers 16 or over commuting by public transit in 2000 than in 1990. The average such percentages in these sixteen cities fell from 15.2 in 1990 to 14.6 percent in 2000. Thus the existence of a light rail system in itself had no perceptible effect in shifting commuters from privately owned vehicles to public transit.

Whether a light rail system reduces previously existing traffic congestion is discussed later in this chapter.

BUS RAPID TRANSIT. Traditional bus systems suffer from several major drawbacks compared with driving in private vehicles. Buses operating on normal city streets are typically much slower than a private car or light truck because buses make many stops to pick up passengers, wait while passengers pay the driver or for handicapped passengers to board, are delayed more by right turns because of their greater length, and are held up longer by traffic lights because of the interaction of all of the above with such signals.

Bus rapid transit systems are becoming more common because they combine various elements designed to reduce buses' sources of delay. These elements may include the following:

—Exclusive bus lanes. Such lanes on existing streets are designated for bus use only.

—Dual exclusive bus lanes. These lanes permit some buses to pass others without stopping at the same locations.

—Skip-stop schedules. These allow some buses to bypass certain stops, especially on express routes.

—Exclusive streets or rights-of-way. In downtown Minneapolis and downtown Denver, whole streets are dedicated to bus and pedestrian use only and called "transit malls." In Houston, many separate rights-of-way similar to HOV lanes have been created for exclusive bus use. This removes buses from congested highways during rush hours. The most extensive such system is in Curitiba, Brazil.

—Traffic signal preference or preemption for buses. In some systems, traffic signals recognize buses as they approach and extend or speed up green lights to give those buses preferential movement treatment.

—Advanced fare payment. Payment is in the form of "smart cards" or segregated entrance areas where passengers pay before boarding the buses to speed up the boarding process. This element is often combined with the next.

—Single-fare collection systems. In these systems all trips cost the same amount, no matter how long the trips are or how many transfers they involve. This speeds up fare collection.

—Special platform and bus boarding designs. Bus floors are placed on the same level as boarding area floors to speed up the boarding process, especially for people with wheelchairs.

—Integration of transit development with land-use policies. This promotes settlement patterns at high enough densities to make transit travel economically feasible. The outstanding example of this element is in Curitiba, Brazil, which has developed several high-density corridors radiating out from its central business district and created bus rapid transit lines on those corridors and as a beltway around the entire region.[25]

These elements can be combined in many ways. They range from barely modifying traditional bus service to creating virtual bus or railroad systems on separate rights-of-way served by specially designed stations.

As an alternative to normal highways, bus rapid transit systems have several advantages over light rail systems. Their vehicles are much more flexible, since all but the largest, specially designed ones can leave dedicated rights-of-way and traverse normal city streets. Hence bus rapid transit systems are more capable of being changed to meet differing conditions over time and conveniently serving many neighborhoods that are away from their fixed rights-of-way. They are also less costly to create because their vehicles are cheaper, and they do not need embedded tracks or sophisticated electronic control systems. According to an excellent study of bus rapid transit systems conducted by the Government Accounting Office, "Adjusting to 2000 dollars, the capital costs for the various types of Bus Rapid Transit systems in cities that we reviewed ranged from a low of $200,000 per mile for an arterial street-

based system to $55 million per mile for a dedicated busway system. . . .
Light rail systems had capital costs that ranged from $12.4 million to
$118.8 million per mile."[26]

Ridership was about equal on light rail and bus transit systems, and
there were no clear differences in operating costs per trip. On one hand,
bus rapid transit systems had slightly faster operating speeds. On the
other hand, bus systems have a poorer public image, partly because bus
patronage is widely associated with low-income persons and traffic congestion. And light rail systems may stimulate more investment along
their rights-of-way if they seem to be more permanent fixtures in the
landscape.

Since the number of regions trying to build light rail systems has
recently exceeded the availability of federal funds for that purpose, more
regions are considering adopting less costly bus transit systems.

Has Expanding Transit Capacity Reduced Traffic Congestion in the Past?

The basic argument for attacking existing traffic congestion by expanding public transit capacity is that doing so would attract commuting and
other peak-hour drivers to shift from POVs to transit. That would
reduce the number of vehicles on roads during peak hours—or at least
slow down future increases in that number. Does past experience show
that expanding transit capacity reduces traffic congestion on a region's
roads?

According to the Texas Transportation Institute (TTI), four of the six
most heavily congested metropolitan areas in 2000 also had among the
largest and most successful public transit systems. They are San Francisco, Chicago, Washington, and Boston, which ranked second, third,
fourth, and fifth in a key measure of congestion—the travel time index.
San Jose and Denver—both of which have light rail systems—both
ranked eighth, and New York City—with by far the nation's most extensive public transit system—ranked tenth in congestion out of the TTI's
total set of seventy-five metropolitan areas. Portland, with its heavily
emphasized light rail system, ranked eleventh.[27] Table 9-3 compares the
following percentages of commuters using transit for seven primary metropolitan statistical areas including some of these regions.

DALLAS. Dallas opened a light rail system in 1996 with 20 miles of
track and 21 stations. The system was expanded in 2002 to 44 miles of

TABLE 9-3. Public Transit Usage and Travel Time Indexes of Commuters
in Seven PMSAs, 2000[a]

Metropolitan area[a]	Travel time index		Public transit usage	
	Score	Rank	Percent of commuters	Rank
San Francisco	1.59	2	18.81	3
Chicago	1.47	3	12.46	5
Seattle	1.45	5	8.01	8
Boston	1.45	5	13.86	4
San Jose	1.42	8	3.51	18
New York	1.41	10	47.03	1
Portland	1.40	11	6.33	9

Source: David Schrank and Tim Lomax, *The 2002 Urban Mobility Report* (College Station, Tex.: Texas Transportation Institute, June 2002); and U.S. Bureau of the Census, table DP-3, "Profile of Selected Economic Characteristics: 2000."
a. Primary metropolitan statistical area.

track and 34 stations. From 1997, the first full year of light rail operation, to 2000, well before the newest section opened, the average number of weekday riders on light rail rose from 34,500 to 38,100, or by 10.4 percent. The average number of daily bus riders (including purchased services) rose 7.4 percent in the same period, but in 2000 was 4.3 times greater than light rail ridership.

However, according to the 2000 Census, the number of transit commuters in the city of Dallas declined 12 percent from 1990 to 2000. The share of all city commuters using transit fell from 6.7 percent to 5.5 percent in 2000. In the entire Dallas MSA, the absolute number of transit commuters declined minutely by 739, but the transit share dropped from 2.4 percent in 1990 to 1.8 percent to 2000. Apparently, in spite of increased ridership on the light rail system and the bus system, there was no net transfer of commuters from private vehicles to transit in the Dallas area.

Moreover, in the Dallas-Fort Worth region, from 1990 to 2000, the TTI travel time index rose by 12.7 percent, and the percentage of travel in congestion rose by 52.6 percent. So traffic congestion in that region worsened in spite of the new light rail system.[28]

PORTLAND. Between 1996 and 2000, the Portland region increased the length of its light rail system from 30.2 to 64.9 miles. Partly as a result, public transit commuting in the entire region (including parts of Vancouver, Washington, as reported by the 2000 Census) rose from 39,259 in 1990 to 60,266 in 2000—a gain of 54 percent. The share of transit commuting also rose from 5.4 to 6.3 percent. Average weekday unlinked trips on the light rail system (which also serves many suburbs) soared from 29,857 in 1996 to 73,562 in 2000, a gain of 146 percent.

However, unlinked bus trips did not increase at all.[29] This implies that many of the additional light rail passengers would otherwise have commuted on buses, not in private vehicles. If the light rail system had not expanded, and unlinked bus trips had therefore increased from 1996 to 2000 in direct proportion to the service area's population increase in those four years (23.6 percent according to the transit authority's own reports to the American Public Transit Association), then bus trips would have risen by 47,574—but they did not rise at all. Thus 100 percent of the increase of 43,705 in light rail trips probably came from buses, leaving a zero net gain from autos. In 2000, in the entire Portland MSA, 804,916 persons commuted in private automotive vehicles, either alone or in car pools. Thus doubling the size of the region's light rail system seems to have had no net impact on reducing the number of private-automotive-vehicle-using commuters. Even if all the light rail trips gained from 1996 to 2000 (divided by two) equaled persons shifted from highways, that would have amounted to a reduction of only 2.6 percent of POV commuters.[30]

Census data for commuting behavior in the Portland region show that the total number of workers in this region rose by about 208,700 in the 1990s.[31] Of that amount, 165,000 were additional persons driving alone or carpooling. That is 79 percent of all the additional commuters in the 1990s. The increase in transit commuters was 20,215, or 9.7 percent of the total gain in commuters. The share of all commuters using transit rose from 5.4 percent in 1990 to 6.3 percent in 2000. Yet, in spite of a doubling of the light rail system, the absolute number of POV-using commuters added from 1990 to 2000 was more than eight times as large as the absolute number of additional transit commuters.

Furthermore, traffic congestion in the Portland region increased dramatically from 1990 to 2000, as indicated by all the measures developed by the Texas Transportation Institute. The Portland region's population grew by 26.6 percent in that decade. According to TTI, the number of freeway and arterial lane miles in the region also grew by 25.5 percent, and the total roadway centerline miles grew by 26.1 percent.[32] But the number of daily vehicle miles traveled on Portland's entire road system rose by 65 percent, the percentage of daily travel in congested conditions rose 52 percent (from 25 percent congested to 38 percent), the total annual delay due to congestion rose by 266 percent, the travel time index increased from 1.16 to 1.40, the road congestion index from 1.02 to 1.27, and the annual delay per peak-period road traveler from sixteen to forty-seven hours—almost tripling. Moreover, the Portland Metro— the regional government in charge of infrastructures—devoted high percentages of all its available transportation funding to improving transit rather than building more roads.

CONCLUSIONS. Portland's experience shows that even greatly expanding a region's transit capacity cannot in itself sufficiently cope with the additional travel demands generated by relatively rapid population growth to prevent rising traffic congestion. This is true even when the transit expansion is large and successful in attracting passengers. Added transit capacity in the form of new light or heavy rail mileage is likely to be partly offset by declines in bus travel (at least compared with what would have happened without the new rail capacity), especially if the transit authority reorganizes its bus routes to feed the new rail systems. More important, experience shows that the vast majority of additional commuters in a growing region will still prefer to travel in private automotive vehicles.

It appears that expanding transit capacity can, at best, achieve two important goals related to traffic congestion. It might offset part—but only part—of the greater ground travel demand by population growth and increasing real incomes. That could slow future increases in traffic congestion. But greater transit capacity probably cannot reduce existing congestion levels once they have become intense, or even stop them from getting worse, except perhaps in very slow-growth regions.

Nevertheless, expanded public transit can also increase the variety of travel and mobility choices available to the population. This is especially important to those people who cannot own or drive private automotive vehicles. These are important benefits from expanding transit capacity. Other benefits for doing so claimed by its proponents—such as reduced air pollution, fuel consumption, and damage from accidents—are surely socially significant too. But they are not directly relevant to traffic congestion itself, so they are not discussed further here.

The Allocation of Public Transportation Funds between Transit and Highways

Advocates of more public transit blame its lack of accessibility to so many Americans in part on what they believe is an imbalance of public funding between transit and highways. They claim highway travel is heavily subsidized by governments, but transit is "unfairly disadvantaged" in funding because it does not face "a level playing field." This section evaluates this claim by examining how much public funding highways and transit receive from all three main levels of government: federal, state, and local. The federal government also collects federal gasoline taxes and then disburses much of them to state and local governments as highway grants. This relationship makes analysis of where transportation funding comes from quite complex.[33]

The following paragraphs set forth principal findings about government funding of public transit and highways.

Total Government Funding

In the 1990s, the relative shares of total government funding of transportation spent for highways and transit remained roughly constant. In 1999, according to the Bureau of Transportation Statistics, total spending on transportation by all three levels of government was $154.8 billion. Of that total, 61.7 percent was spent on highways and roads, and 18.7 percent on public transit. The remaining 19.6 percent was spent on air transport, water transport, rail transport, and pipelines.[34] Transit's share averaged 19.3 percent over the 1990s; the share of highways averaged 60.9 percent.

In the same decade, the absolute amount spent annually on all transportation modes combined (in current dollars) rose from $100.6 billion in 1990 to $154.8 billion 1999. This is shown in figure 9-6. (In constant dollars, the increase was 22 percent.) The amount spent on highways (in current dollars) went up 53 percent, and the amount spent on transit rose 51 percent. Thus, in those fourteen years, transit experienced a slight decline in its relative share of total government transportation spending.

State and Local Funding

State and local governments furnish most of the funding for highways and roads and spend nearly all such funding—including the federal contribution. In 1999, public spending on highways equaled $95.5 billion. About 24.7 percent came from the federal government and 75.3 percent from state and local governments. Almost all of the federal government's spending consisted of grants of various types to state and local governments, which then spent those funds. Consequently, state and

FIGURE 9-6. Government Transportation Spending, 1990–99

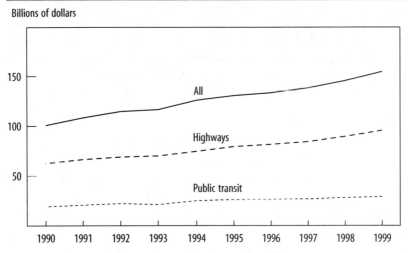

Billions of dollars

Source: Department of Transportation, *National Transportation Statistics 2001*, chap. 3, sec. D, table 3-29a.

local government highway spending constituted almost all publicly funded highway spending. However, the underlying federal contribution to highway and road spending remained about 25 percent throughout the 1990s.

Decline in Federal Spending

The federal government's spending on public transit has declined over time in real terms and as a share of total spending on transit. As a result, state and local governments have been providing an increasing share of transit funding. Total government spending in 1999 on public transit equaled $29.0 billion. About 14.7 percent came from the federal government and 85.3 percent from state and local governments—mostly the latter. However, almost all the federal share consisted of grants to state and local governments. As a result, transit spending by state and local governments—including federal grants—constituted 99.7 percent of all transit spending in the 1990s.

The federal government's share of total public transit spending declined from 36.9 percent in 1980 to 14.7 percent in 1999. This occurred mainly because federal transit grants to state and local governments in current dollars rose 34 percent in that period, but state and local transportation spending on transit in current dollars more than quadrupled, from $5.6 billion to $24.8 billion. In constant 1996 dollars, total federal spending on transit—including grants to state and local governments—actually declined by 32 percent from 1980 to 1999, whereas state and local transit spending—excluding federal grants—rose by 123 percent. Consequently, in constant dollars, the state and local government share of transit funding (excluding federal grants) rose from 64 percent in 1980 to 79 percent in 1990 and 85 percent in 1999.

Federal Subsidy for Public Transit

Public transit's share of total government funding has long been vastly larger than its share of total travel produced, whether measured as trips or passenger miles traveled. Public transit received 20 percent of total federal transportation funding during the 1990s, and an average of 19.3 percent of all government transportation spending, even though it provided less than 2 percent of all passenger mileage traveled in the United States, and less than 5 percent of all commuting trips as of 2000.

By their very nature, almost all public transit systems throughout the world require large public subsidies because they cannot cover their costs through fares or user taxes like the gasoline tax. This is true in part because public transit is inherently a declining-cost industry. That means that, once a transit system has been built and is in operation, the marginal cost of carrying small numbers of additional passengers is almost zero. The socially most efficient way to set fares in such an industry is close to marginal cost. That encourages more patrons to use the capacity already constructed to the maximum degree. But that practice results in revenues insufficient to cover fully either capital or operating costs. Thus it is not surprising that public transit requires large government funding disproportionate to its travel outputs.

Public Funding and Fuel Taxes

The overall public funding of both highways and public transit in the United States is suffering from the increasing inadequacy of current fuel taxes, which appropriately place the main financial burdens of movement on those who move. This is leading to economically and socially inefficient and undesirable results. Fuel taxes are not keeping up with the costs of building, maintaining, and operating the nation's ground transportation for three reasons. First, greater fuel efficiency of vehicle engines allows them to drive more miles per gallon, but taxes are set on a per gallon basis. Second, fuel taxes are not indexed for inflation, but the costs of operating a transportation system rise along with inflation. Third, for political reasons, Congress and state legislatures have repeatedly refused to raise fuel taxes along with inflation, or more, in spite of rising transportation system costs. This situation is pressuring state and local governments to raise more money for transportation services through sales and property taxes, which are regressive (that is, they place heavier relative burdens on low-income households). The result is a socially inefficient shift of transportation funding away from those who use transportation facilities—such as car and truck drivers—to the general public, and especially onto lower-income households.[35] This situation is also "squeezing" interests seeking government funding of transportation into increasingly intense competition for scarce dollars.

Public Transit's Share of Total Government Spending

Some transit advocates are now arguing that transit should receive a much larger share of total government transportation spending than in the past to permit transit to "catch up" with past underfunding in comparison to highways and roads. Examination of actual spending on both modes by all governments during the 1990s, and even back to the 1980s, only partly supports this argument. Transit's relative share in total government transportation spending was only slightly lower in the past than it has been recently. Moreover, transit's percentage share of total government transportation spending has vastly exceeded its percentage share in total travel outputs as far back as 1980.

However, federal spending on public transit in constant dollars actually fell by one-third from 1980 to 1999, and by 14 percent from 1990 to 1999. (In contrast, federal spending on highways rose 17.7 percent in constant dollars from 1990 to 1999.) This has shifted an ever-larger share of the real cost of providing transit from the federal government to state and local governments. A plausible case can be made that federal spending on transit ought to at least remain constant in real terms, and perhaps expand, given the national desirability of making transit available to more people. On one hand, this is one area in which the "catch-up" argument advanced by transit advocates seems to make sense. On the other hand, the public spending done on public transit in region X provides benefits almost entirely for residents of region X. Therefore, why should residents of other regions subsidize transit in region X? Should not residents of region X be responsible for activities that benefit only themselves? The only plausible reason for federal transit aid to region X is that it is a national responsibility to redistribute incomes across the nation to benefit the poorest people in all regions, especially those who live in regions with below-average economic resources. If region X is a particularly poor region, it may be reasonable for the federal government to subsidize services there—such as public transit—that benefit the poorest members of region X. But that means regional wealth should be a major criterion influencing where the federal government spends money aiding public transit. It is not evident that this is now the case.

Federal Funds for More Choice in Modes of Travel

A key point made by transit advocates is that federal spending ought to increase the range of travel choices available to the American public. Thus they applaud the change in federal legislation in the 1991 Intermodal Surface Transportation Efficiency Act (ISTEA) law that permitted states to use Highway Trust Fund money for many other transportation purposes besides roads, such as bike paths, pedestrian walkways, and antipollution and safety projects as well as public transit. This is certainly a reasonable position. The question is: just what share of federal (and state) funds ought to go to such uses, compared with either repairing or building new roads and bridges? There is no scientific or unequivocal way to answer that question.

—Data from the future transportation spending plans of metropolitan planning organizations (MPOs) in the twenty largest metropolitan regions show that transit is scheduled to receive a greatly disproportionate share of planned future spending, compared with its actual share of commuting trips in these regions. "Total spending" is cumulative spending for capacity expansion, operations, and repairs and maintenance in long-range plans that extend outward into the future. In all twenty consolidated metropolitan statistical areas combined, total transportation spending from the long-range plans of their MPOs was $1,100 billion, according to a compilation made by the Federal Highway Administration and the Federal Transit Administration.[36] Of this amount 41 percent was for highways and 57 percent was for transit (the remaining 2 percent share was for other purposes). Yet in only three of these areas was the share of transit in all journey-to-work trips in 2000 over 10 percent. They were New York (24.9 percent), northern New Jersey (also 24.9 percent because those two regions were combined in this calculation), and Chicago (11.5 percent). The average share of transit trips in the other seventeen areas was only 4.3 percent. Moreover, the share of transit is generally much smaller in nonwork trips than in work trips almost everywhere; hence its share of all trips combined is also smaller. Yet the average share of planned transit spending in those seventeen areas was 53 percent. This certainly shows that transit is receiving at least its "fair share" of planned transportation spending in these metropolitan regions, though of course no one can be sure those plans will become realities.

What Changes in the Nature of Public Transit Might Encourage Its Greater Use?

Advocates of expanding public transit concentrate mainly on increasing operations of the types of transit dominant in the United States today. These are heavy buses (those with thirty seats or more), light rail, heavy rail (including subways), and commuter rail. But the biggest single obstacle to greater use of transit is the economic unsuitability of these modes to operating in the low-density areas that dominate American suburbs and new-growth areas. The most prominent existing advocates of expanding transit (such as the Surface Transportation Policy Project) therefore place great emphasis on changing the basic residential settlement patterns that have prevailed in the United States since World War II, and even before that. Hence transit advocates are among the most energetic promoters of "smart growth." That strategy normally stresses shifting new development to much higher densities than in the past and using in-fill development to raise densities in existing built-up areas.

However, as already noted, almost all new development in America, and the vast majority of already developed areas, embodies residential densities far too low to support these types of transit efficiently. A central reason for this fact is that most American households prefer living in low-density settlements versus living in settlements with high enough densities to support transit. The likelihood that transit advocates will succeed in shifting any significant fraction of new development or existing low-density settlements to densities high enough to support these forms of mass transit economically is remote.

An alternative approach to expanding transit is to promote new forms of transit more suitable for operations in low-density environments. However, this approach would require weakening the present dominance over public transit operations of three types of monopolies or quasi-monopolies: regional transportation agencies (RTAs), transit employee unions, and local taxi companies. Therefore, creating new forms of transit is rarely politically acceptable to these monopolies, who are among the main advocates for expanding transit in general.[37] Nevertheless, this approach is worth examining in some detail.

In the past, many private bus companies operated in major metropolitan areas, most serving a relatively small and specialized portion of the region. Over time, these were consolidated into regional transportation agencies (RTAs), partly because rapid expansion of private automobile ownership made many small transit companies economically unfeasible. Gradually, RTAs established virtual monopolies over public transit in their regions, controlling buses, subways, light rail systems, and even commuter rail systems. These monopolists now resist incursion into their markets of private transit operations, such as more luxurious suburban buses. The monopolists fear that individual private operators might "skim the cream" off their various markets by focusing on only those segments of potential transit customers who could generate profitable operations—thereby depriving the RTAs of such customers. This would be similar to what many long-distance telephone companies did to AT&T when long-distance service was deregulated.

Transit employee unions are opposed to forms of transit that might operate without the services of their members, who are relatively well paid. In fact, a substantial fraction of all past federal spending on transit has gone to raising the wages of these workers, rather than to expanding transit services.[38] In many less developed nations, jitney services are operated by individual drivers who own their own cars. They drive up and down major avenues, picking up passengers and delivering them to their destinations or close by, thereby competing with local bus services and formal taxi companies. Jitney service is generally faster than bus service because jitneys do not need to make as many stops. The drivers are also paid much less than unionized bus drivers, which allows them to charge lower fares. True, jitneys do not have to meet the same safety, comfort, and cleanliness standards as major bus companies; hence they can operate at much lower costs.

Established taxi companies are also opposed to legalizing jitney operations, which are now prohibited in most American cities. But jitneys can overcome two of the major obstacles to making public transit accessible in low-density areas. One is the use of large, costly vehicles that run mostly empty in low-density areas—especially outside peak travel hours—but are expensive to buy and operate, mainly because of driver salaries. The second is the employment of well-paid drivers who work full eight-hour days, even though their services are mainly used during morning and evening peak periods. These traits make existing transit operations quite inflexible in relation to the needs of people living in low-density areas.

An example of jitney service occurred in Miami from 1989 to 1991, as described by Dennis Polhill and Matthew Edgar:

> In 1989, the Florida legislature accidentally created a legal loophole that permitted competitive, unregulated services like jitneys. Within months, over 20 jitney firms had emerged to serve the accidentally created market. . . . The new jitney services provided faster trip times, shorter wait times, flexibility in boarding locations and drop-off points, and availability of service in late evening. The largest advantage jitney service had over Metrobus in Miami was trip speed and ease of boarding. In order to board the jitney, the passenger would simply flag down the jitney from any place along the jitney's route—not just bus stops fixed in inconvenient locations. In this sense, it acted much like a taxi service. In addition, the jitneys would run on time in order to satisfy their customers. The irony in Colorado's ban on jitneys is that the largest complaints made by RTD passengers are: trip times are too long; the buses are routinely off schedule; the bus stops are not conveniently located; and, that RTD does not provide late night service. . . .
>
> In the first year, the jitney services attracted 43,000 to 49,000 passengers per weekday. That breaks down to about 110–115 passengers per vehicle per weekday. Most of these passengers said that if not for the jitneys, they would take their own car: a new market was created solely for jitneys in Miami. . . . With no government subsidy, the jitney service was able to charge $1 per passenger, whereas Metrobus charged $1.75. RTD charges $1.75 for peak hour travel, and 75 cents for non-peak travel (to which is added state and federal subsidy worth four times that amount). . . . Despite the benefits . . . Miami ended legal jitney service in 1991. The various jitney services operating without regulations were charged with operating without a license. . . . The reason for ending jitney service was political. The government simply did not feel comfortable allowing the private sector to compete against a public sector monopoly bus system.[39]

Among the innovative forms of public transit that have at least been suggested by one or more experts are the following:

—Jitney services in large cities or moderate-density suburban areas.

—Deregulation of taxi services generally.

—Minibus service, possibly provided on demand. ("On demand" transit is considered a standard category of public service by the American Public Transit Association.) The deregulation of some public transit in the United Kingdom has generated significant increases in the use of minibuses by privately owned transit companies.

—Bus rapid transit.

—Shared rental cars made available on a subscription or at-random basis.

—Commercial passenger van services.

—Leasing vans owned by transit authorities or major employers to individuals at very low cost in return for their using those vans to operate daily car pools during working days—thereby eliminating the wages of a vehicle driver.

—Free or very low-fare shuttle bus services linking commercial districts with rapid transit stations, or providing mobility within large commercial districts like major downtowns or major "edge cities."

—Private express bus services from relatively affluent suburbs to major downtowns or other commercial districts.

—Publicly subsidized shared ownership of private autos by inner-city workers who have jobs in outlying areas. The subsidized owners would have to act as car-pool drivers for a certain minimum number of workers to qualify for this program.

It is not within the scope of this book to describe or evaluate in detail all of these possible alternatives to the major existing forms of public transit. However, a few general observations are relevant.

Most of these tactics would require changes in existing laws and regulations that now provide local or regional monopoly powers over public transit services to RTAs or taxi companies. Some tactics involve substituting unpaid or relatively low-wage labor for currently well-paid unionized drivers of transit vehicles. Transit workers' unions would most likely oppose such tactics on the grounds that implementing them would reduce employment opportunities for union members and reduce passenger security. Thus it may be difficult to create sufficient political support for even experimenting with these tactics enough to discover whether they might be effective in serving low-density areas. Nevertheless, the prospects for greatly expanding public transit through such devices over the long run are, in the author's opinion, better than the chances of persuading Americans to change their preferences for future development from low-density settlement patterns to high-enough-density patterns to support current forms of public transit.

What Would Encourage Greater Use of Present Forms of Public Transit?

The single change in American society that would most encourage major expansion of existing forms of transit would be a change in new development patterns from low density to much higher density.

A second change that might lead to a significant expansion of transit usage would be some very large increase in the costs of operating private automotive vehicles. Even many transit advocates believe that POVs have enormous personal advantages over public transit for most American travelers under most circumstances. Consequently, no feasible improvements in transit services can overcome those advantages. This conclusion has been confirmed by various improvements in transit services over the years that have failed to alter the overwhelming dominance of POVs. Those improvements include shorter intervals between buses or trains, better-located and more routes, air-conditioned vehicles, more comfortable seats and more of them, lower fares, and more convenient transfer arrangements between buses and trains or among buses. None of these costly attempts to increase the attractiveness of public transit is likely to come close to doubling its ridership—especially for work trips. Yet even doubling transit's 2000 share of commuting nationwide from 4.73 to 9.46 percent would reduce POVs' share only from 88.5 percent to 83.2 percent. That would not cause much reduction in peak-hour traffic congestion. Therefore, Boris Pushkarev and Jeffrey Zupan concluded, "From the transit viewpoint, it [would be] much more 'profitable' to gain riders either from restraints on automobile use or from increased density of urban development."[40]

To sum up, specific tactics for raising the cost of driving, especially driving to work alone, include the following:

—Increasing taxes on gasoline;

—Raising the costs of owning private vehicles; and

—Increasing the costs of parking during peak periods.

10

Peak-Hour and
Other Road Pricing

A highly controversial suggestion for attacking traffic congestion is rationing access to major commuter roads by charging variable tolls during peak periods. Those tolls would be set so that the number of drivers willing to pay them would be small enough to permit continuous high-speed driving on the roads involved. As a result, more vehicles would be able to use those roads during peak hours than can now use them under free access but congested conditions. This improves the efficiency of the entire highway system.

Such road pricing is controversial because it disadvantages low-income commuters compared with more affluent ones, and it charges what many people consider an "added tax" for something they can now do free—gain access to major roads during peak hours. Yet public and governmental interest in road pricing is increasing because peak-hour congestion is becoming more intense and more widespread in many regions. There is an acute need to raise more money to pay for ground transportation facilities, some versions of road pricing are already being successfully applied without the drawbacks mentioned above, and a new high-tech method of tracking vehicles and charging tolls could eventually make almost universal road pricing possible with minimum inconvenience to drivers.

As a result, road pricing has begun evolving toward what might become much more widespread application. So understanding the basic nature of road pricing, how it is now evolving, and how it might evolve is an important aspect of understanding how to cope with peak-hour traffic congestion.[1]

The Economic Theory of Peak-Hour Road Pricing

Transportation economists argue that although persons driving onto congested roadways during peak hours are adding to collective costs by increasing delays for others, they are not required to pay the full costs generated by their own behavior.[2] They have to endure their own loss of time from congestion, but they are not charged for the time delays their entry imposes on others. So individual drivers continue to enter a roadway, even when the average total cost of their arrival exceeds the average total benefit of using it.

As a result, peak-hour traffic on some expressways typically rises above the economically optimal level—that is, the level at which the average total cost per driver (including operating costs, time, and any tolls) equals the average total benefit to drivers of using the roadway. When traffic surpasses that level, it slows down even more, so the average total benefit falls further while the average total cost rises higher above it. That misallocates motorists' time and capital invested in road capacity.

The general welfare of all drivers would be greater if traffic could be limited to the lower level at which average total costs equaled average total benefits (see appendix B). This can be achieved by charging each driver a toll for using that road during peak hours. This monetary price should be set to bring the total cost experienced by each person entering a congested roadway up to the average total costs that person is imposing on himself and others. That would be more efficient than the present use of a time price—delay—to ration scarce highway space. If every motorist who now uses those highways during peak hours had to pay a charge for doing so, many would be deterred from driving on them. The higher the charge, the more people would be deterred. In theory, any desired level of peak-hour congestion could be arrived at by setting appropriately high tolls. Then the number of drivers could be kept low

enough to permit continuous high-speed movement on the road—
thereby maximizing the throughput of vehicles per hour.

The reason most transportation economists advocate peak-hour pricing is not to reduce traffic congestion in itself but to maximize the efficient use of society's economic resources.[3] Economists contend that such
resources would be used more efficiently if more motorists could be
induced to shift commuting from peak to nonpeak hours. Less commuter time would be lost through traffic delays, and roads would be
more efficiently used over more of each day. But these changes in commuter behavior recommended by economists would not eliminate traffic
congestion or even reduce it to very low levels. Under these economically optimal peak-hour tolls, traffic volumes would still be greater than
at times when no congestion existed. It would still be worthwhile for
commuters to enter an expressway on which congestion had already
slowed traffic somewhat, since that route would still be superior to others because it is more direct and has no traffic signals. Therefore, even
the imposition of an optimal toll would not end traffic congestion,
though it would in many places reduce congestion well below present
levels.

There is a simpler way to explain why road pricing might be sensible.
Experience proves that the demand for any really desirable good will
exceed its supply if the good is limited in quantity but offered free of
charge. If Super Bowl tickets were free, the number of people wanting
them would vastly exceed the number of seats in the Super Bowl. In
such circumstances, some method must be devised to ration the limited
supply of the good among the large number of people who want it. One
method is to hand the good out on a first-come, first-served basis. Then
long lines will form to get the good until the supply is exhausted. That is
called congestion. Another rationing method commonly used in a free
enterprise society is to charge a money price for the good. If the price is
set just right, the quantity people are willing to consume at that price
will equal the total supply of the good.

Access to freeway space during peak hours is a desirable good definitely in limited supply. When it is free, the number of drivers who want
it greatly exceeds the available space on the roads involved during peak
hours. If that space is handed out on a first-come, first-served basis,
lines will form until the space is fully occupied. That equals traffic congestion. Moreover, since there is no barrier to entering the road, people
will keep doing so until the road becomes so crowded that movement on

it slows to a crawl. It is as though so many people packed themselves into the Super Bowl that they spilled out onto the playing field, thereby ruining the event for everyone else. The alternative of charging a "market clearing" price seems a lot more sensible. By setting the price appropriately, this approach can reduce the number of people willing to pay that price down to a level at which they can all move rapidly on the road. That is the theory of peak-hour road pricing in a nutshell.

Two Different Types of Road Pricing

There are two basically different types of road pricing: area or zone pricing, and roadway facility pricing. In area or zone pricing, transportation authorities select a certain relatively small area in a community which they consider initially plagued by excessive internal congestion. Up to now, this has almost always been a city's downtown. They then establish a cordon line around that area and charge anyone who drives across that line into the designated area a toll designed to discourage such movements. Exemptions are usually granted to residents of the cordoned area and to certain classes of vehicles, such as taxis, buses, police cars and fire trucks, ambulances, and so on. This type of road pricing seeks mainly to reduce congestion on the city streets within the cordoned area. The toll usually does not vary with the time of day, though it could.

The second type of road pricing focuses on the usage of an entire roadway, rather than just a small area. Any vehicles entering this roadway during designated hours are charged a toll that is set high enough to limit the traffic on the roadway to levels that permit high-speed movement. The toll is thus varied over time and may be reduced to zero during periods of relatively low traffic. Roadway facility pricing aims to speed the movement of traffic on the facilities involved by preventing congestion from building up on them. This type of road pricing is what most transportation economists have theorized about for decades.

Although traffic congestion has been intensifying worldwide, no metropolitan area has ever adopted a comprehensive system of road facility pricing to reduce it. Such a system would charge peak-hour tolls for entering every lane in all the major commuter routes in the region and vary the tolls to keep traffic volumes low enough to permit rapid movement on those routes during peak hours. Hong Kong tested a partial system for eight months but then rejected it.

A few cities (Singapore, Oslo, Trondheim, Bergen, and more recently, London) have adopted area or zone peak-hour access tolls aimed at reducing congestion in their downtown areas. However, this approach is suitable only to small, high-density areas in large cities served by extensive public transit networks. Then persons working in the designated areas or visiting there who are discouraged from driving into them by the tolls have the alternative of using public transit. Congestion outside of the designated zones is affected only by a reduction of movements through those outer areas to and from the cordoned zone.

One reason no region anywhere has ever tried a comprehensive system of facility road pricing is that many transportation officials have never been exposed to this concept, and so using it simply does not occur to them.[4] In addition, facility road pricing has been criticized for inequity, inefficiency, and invasion of privacy.

Even though no region has ever tried this approach comprehensively, most of the analysis in this chapter focuses mainly on facility road pricing. That is because only such an approach to road pricing has the potential—at least in theory—of attacking peak-hour congestion throughout a region, rather than just in a relatively small zone. However, since there has been more actual experience with area or zone road pricing, some of this analysis describes just how well that approach has worked.

Hypothetical Case Studies

The pure theory of peak-hour road facility pricing just set forth is quite abstract. Three analyses of a hypothetical commuter freeway can illustrate how the theory would really work.

First, let's make some basic assumptions. Assume there is a four-lane expressway twenty miles long (two lanes in each direction). That is approximately one-third longer than the length of the average commuting trip in 2000. The number of vehicles that wish to use this road in one direction between 6:00 and 9:00 a.m. is 9,000 per lane, which is 3,000 per lane per hour. The drivers of these vehicles have different preferences for speed of travel; some are willing to pay well to move faster, others will pay some but not a lot, and many are not willing to pay any money to travel faster. The average car is 17.0 feet long; the average truck is 50.0 feet long, and 5 percent of the vehicles are trucks, with the rest cars. Therefore, the average vehicle is 18.65 feet long. Vehicles enter this road only at one end and proceed without any possible exits to the other end.

Further assume that the maximum throughput on the road would occur at an unimpeded speed of 60 miles per hour. That would produce an hourly flow of 2,000 vehicles per lane per hour, for a total of 6,000 vehicles per lane in 3.0 hours. (Higher speeds could produce greater throughputs but are considered unsafe. Lower speeds would result in smaller throughputs.) But this would require steady entrance of vehicles throughout the 3.0-hour period, beginning at 6:00 a.m., at 2,000 per lane per hour—one every 1.8 seconds, and permitting no other vehicles to enter. Hence a maximum of 12,000 vehicles would traverse this freeway during the peak period, or 6,000 per lane (the last vehicle to enter would finish its journey at 9:20 a.m.).

Since the vehicles on the road are moving at 60 miles per hour unimpeded, or 88.0 feet per second, there would be an average interval between vehicles (from the back of the first to the front of the second) of 139.7 feet—taking 1.59 seconds to traverse. That is less than the widely recommended 2.0-second interval between speeding vehicles. But since this rate has been repeatedly observed on California freeways, it is used in this analysis. Vehicles would be entering at a rate of one every 1.8 seconds, which is a larger interval than the one extant when they have reached flowing speed, so there is no impediment to their reaching that speed. Table 10-1 displays the quantitative results of these hypothetical cases.

CASE ONE—ROAD PRICING. Case one exists when road pricing is used to prevent more than 2,000 vehicles per lane per hour from entering this freeway. A variable toll for entry is set high enough to keep down the number of entrants to that level. The toll authorities keep track of how many vehicles are entering the road every hour. If more than 2,000 drivers per lane per hour are willing to pay the initial toll, it is raised until the number willing to enter is almost exactly 2,000 per lane per hour. If fewer than 2,000 enter, the toll is reduced until that number are entering. All remaining drivers who are unwilling or unable to pay whatever toll is set must find alternative means of travel during these three peak hours. After some experience, the authorities will have a reasonably accurate idea of how high to set the toll to maintain an even entry rate of 2,000 vehicles per lane per hour, though this may vary somewhat from day to day.

TABLE 10-1. Dynamics of Speed-Flow Relationships, Three Hypothetical Cases

Item	Case number 1	Case number 2	Case number 3
Vehicles trying to enter/lane/hour	2,000	3,000	3,000
Initial time between entering vehicles (seconds)	1.80	1.20	1.20
Initial speed (mph)	60	60	60
Initial space between vehicles (feet)	140	87	87
Adjusted space between vehicles (feet)	140	129	88
Adjusted time between vehicles (seconds)	1.59	1.75	2.02
Adjusted expressway flow-speed (mph)	60	50	30
Adjusted vehicles throughput/lane/hour	2,000	1,800	1,475
Adjusted time between entering vehicles (seconds)	1.80	2.00	2.47
Vehicle throughput in 3-hour peak period/lane	6,000	5,400	4,425
Time to travel 20 miles (minutes)	20	24	40
Time for 6,000 vehicles to enter at adjusted speed (minutes)	180	215	247
Time for 6,000 vehicles to complete route at that speed (minutes)	200	239	287
Time as percent of time under road pricing	100.0	119.5	143.5
Average vehicles within 1 mile at adjusted speed	33.3	36.0	49.5

Source: Author's calculations.

In case one, since 2,000 vehicles enter the roadway per lane per hour for three hours, a total of 6,000 vehicles per lane will pass over the road during this peak period. They will enter 1.8 seconds apart, and each will take 20.0 minutes to traverse the route. At any given instant, there will be an average of 33.3 vehicles on each mile of the road. Those vehicles that enter right at 9:00 a.m. will not finish the trip until 9:20 a.m., so the peak period needed to handle these 6,000 vehicles is actually 3 hours and 20 minutes. The other 3,000 vehicle drivers (per lane) who wanted to use this road from 6:00 to 9:00 a.m. (1,000 in each hour) will be turned away and will have to find alternative times, routes, or modes for their journeys. However, their "being turned away" is a result of their preferences and choice; they simply do not value the time saving as worth the cost of the toll.

CASE TWO—UNRESTRICTED ACCESS TO THE FREEWAY. In case two, there is no barrier to vehicles entering the expressway. The 9,000 vehicles per lane whose drivers want to travel on this road in this period arrive at the same steady pace, but this time at a rate of 3,000 per lane per hour. Each hopes to move at 60 miles per hour in an unimpeded fashion. If 3,000 enter the freeway every hour, that would be 50 vehicles per minute, or one every 1.2 seconds. Allowing for the time it would take for the average vehicle itself to pass by any given point at 60 miles per hour, there would be only 0.99 second of time *between* vehicles. That interval would produce a physical distance between vehicles of only 87 feet if they were moving at 60 miles per hour.

But drivers would quickly perceive this as too close for safety, so they would slow down to lengthen the interval between vehicles. If they dropped their average speed to 50 miles per hour, then data from actual roadway measurements indicate they might lengthen the average interval between vehicles to about 1.75 seconds, or 129 feet. At that speed and those intervals, 1,800 vehicles would be flowing through the expressway per hour.

However, that rate of flow is inconsistent with the assumption that 3,000 vehicles are entering each lane of the road each hour. In fact, as any number of vehicles above 2,000 per lane per hour enter the road, the slowdown in speed necessary to increase the interval between vehicles to a safe size backs up vehicles at the beginning of the freeway, slowing the rate of entry too. So the dynamic result of admitting more than 2,000 vehicles per hour for any significant time period is a feedback that produces a slowdown in the speed of flow on the road, a backup at the entry point, and a reduction of the entry rate below 2,000 per hour. However, if vehicles are flowing onto the road at the entry point at the rate indicated by the on-the-road throughput of 1,800 per hour, they would be entering at a rate of one every 2.00 seconds—a longer interval than occurred when traffic was flowing at 60 miles per hour.

It is difficult to quantify exactly how this dynamic feedback works. There are few reliable data on the time or interval distances between vehicles that can be sustained at each speed. If it is assumed that speed drops to 50 miles per hour, permitting a flow rate of 1,800 vehicles per hour, then in 3 hours, that would produce a total throughput of 5,400 vehicles per lane. It would take each vehicle 24 minutes to traverse the freeway, or 20 percent longer than under road pricing. The total per lane from 6:00 to 9:00 a.m. would be 600 fewer vehicles than in the case of peak-hour tolls. Accommodating the same number of vehicles as entered the road from 6:00 to 9:00 a.m. under road pricing (6,000 per lane) would take 3 hours and 20 minutes for all of them to enter the road, plus 24 more minutes for the last entrants to traverse it. That is 224 minutes versus 200 minutes under road pricing, or an increase in time of 12 percent for the same number of vehicles to make this trip.

CASE THREE—UNRESTRICTED ACCESS BUT SLOWER SPEED. An alternative would be that the drivers dropped their speed further to be consistent with the space interval of 88 feet between vehicles resulting from one entering every 1.2 seconds. Based on empirical observations, the speed associated with that interval would be about 30 miles per hour. At that speed, with that interval, the flow rate would be 1,475 vehicles per hour. Only 4,425 vehicles per lane would get onto the road from 6:00 to 9:00 a.m. It would take each one 40 minutes to traverse the freeway, or twice as long as under road pricing. For 6,000 vehicles per lane to enter the freeway at that speed would require 4 hours and 4 minutes. The last one would finish traversing the road 284 minutes after the first one entered. That is an increase in time of 42 percent over case one. Thus, if the 30-mile-per-hour case is actually the alternative to road pricing, road pricing would save its users 20 minutes of travel time each way. If the toll for using the road were $2.00 each way, the implicit value of time would be $6.00 per hour, since paying it would save one-third of an hour. Importantly, at the slower speeds, there are more vehicles per mile on the road at any given instant because they are closer together than at higher speeds and remain on each mile longer. Thus, if vehicles are moving at 5 miles per hour with 10 feet between them, the throughput rate would be 921 vehicles per lane per hour. There would be 184 vehicles in each mile of road, forming a nearly solid line of creeping machines.

It is not possible to determine a priori at what speed the traffic flow would reach some type of equilibrium. But in any case, for 6,000 vehicles per lane to complete the 20-mile journey would certainly take much more time than under road pricing. When drivers learned from experience how long these delays were, many would choose not to travel on this road during these peak hours. That would reduce the number of cars entering during each hour.

Peak-Hour Travel and Roadway Facility Pricing

This analysis leads to the following conclusions about peak-hour travel.

Whenever the number of vehicles seeking to enter a freeway is larger than the hourly throughput that can be sustained at its designed maximum speed (in this analysis, assumed to be 60 miles per hour), then many of those vehicles desiring to travel on the road during the three-hour peak period will be unable to do so—regardless of whether or not road pricing is used. The basic cause of inability to accommodate all potential users is the excess demand for the road, not the way that demand is handled. In all cases where such excess demand exists, because the capacity of the road is limited, many vehicles seeking entry will be turned away during peak hours.

When excess demand for a road exists, space on the road must be rationed among those seeking to use it, either by charging a price to enter the road (case one) and setting the price to permit maximum speed and throughput, or by allowing vehicles to keep entering until the road is "full" (cases two and three).

If road pricing is used to maintain the speed of flow at the designed maximum, then the number of vehicles that can enter and use this road during the three-hour peak period is significantly larger than if the rationing device is simply letting whoever gets there first enter the roadway until it is "full." Therefore, from the viewpoint of overall efficiency of vehicle movement, road pricing is a much more efficient road-space rationing device than congestion. Permitting more vehicles to enter the road without regard to the impact of such entry on speed will inevitably slow down the flow below the designed maximum, reducing the hourly throughput below the maximum sustainable level.

From the viewpoint of individual drivers, the matchups between individual preferences and actual behavior under road pricing are superior to those under congestion. Drivers who value rapid movement during peak hours highly enough to pay for it—and have the resources—are able to obtain such movement, whereas those who do not value such movement enough to pay for it—or do not have the resources—cannot achieve it—at least not during peak hours. But under congestion, neither group can achieve rapid movement during peak hours, regardless of their desires or resources, though some members of both groups can achieve slow movement during those hours. Which members of those groups get to move during peak hours is a matter of chance or who gets there first, not a matter of the strength of their preferences or the amount of their resources. Under both road pricing and congestion, a lot of people who want to move faster during peak hours are unable to do so. But road pricing enables those who have strong intensity of desire—and the means to pay—to accomplish their goals; whereas congestion prevents everyone from moving rapidly and prevents many drivers from completing their journeys during peak hours.

In short, road pricing is a much more efficient means of rationing scarce road space than congestion—socially and individually— in every respect except distributional equity.

Equity Issues

Charging high enough tolls on major freeways during peak hours to permit continuous high-speed flows would surely disadvantage lower-income travelers versus higher-income ones. Moreover, if the amount of excess demand for peak-hour use of any freeway becomes large, the fraction of potential users of that freeway who are denied access by road pricing could exceed 50 percent. And if all the major commuting freeways in a metropolitan region are subject to similar roadway facility pricing, the alternatives available to those "priced off the major roads" will diminish greatly. True, if the net profits from collecting tolls are sufficient, the "excess" revenues could be used to improve alternative roads or transit facilities. But it is unlikely that such improvements in alternative means of movement will fully offset the inconvenience suffered by persons unable—or unwilling—to drive on the tolled facility during peak hours. This will subject sizable percentages of all commuters to disappointment and frustration.

Of course, almost everyone trying to use such roads during peak periods is already subjected to disappointment and frustration by intensive congestion. But under all-lane road pricing, many will blame their inability to use their preferred roads during peak hours at least partly on the economically discriminatory nature of road pricing. They may conclude that rationing by congestion, though a less efficient use of road resources from society's overall viewpoint, is more likely to give them personally a chance at least some of the time to use the roads they prefer when they want to use them. In a democracy, this situation is likely to lead elected officials to prohibit peak-hour road pricing on all major commuting routes—as has been the case up to now.

Clifford Winston and Chad Shirley argue that this situation shows that major roads should be privatized and thus taken out of the political arena.[5] They contend that shifting such roads into private ownership would permit their nonelected operators to adopt peak-hour road pricing. That would greatly increase the efficiency with which the capital invested in roads is used throughout the economy. However, this view is economically correct but politically naive. Removing major roads from public ownership would by no means remove them from public concern, since they are the backbone of the nation's ground transportation system. As long as the vast majority of American drivers strongly oppose all-lane peak-hour road pricing, American elected officials will never permit its widespread adoption, no matter who owns the roads. According to the 2000 Census, 89.7 percent of all households had at least one private vehicle available to their members. In 1995, about 74 percent of low-income households owned at least one vehicle.[6] Among 1995 workers living in low-income households, 84 percent made work trips by private vehicle.[7] Therefore, the number of persons who believe they might be inconvenienced by all-lane road pricing is much greater than the number who are sure they could afford the price of driving during the most convenient periods—which would presumably have the highest road-usage fees.

In practice, the strength of this objection will depend in part on how high the peak-hour tolls must be to reduce congestion significantly. But tolls might have to be made very large indeed to cut down on peak-hour demands for vital routes. New York City doubled its bridge and tunnel tolls a few years ago without any noticeable drop in cross-river traffic. More recently, New York City has begun charging higher tolls on its Hudson River crossing during peak periods. It raised the cash toll to $6.00 for cars during all hours but gave a $1.00 discount at any hour to users of E-Z Pass "smart cards" to encourage the use of such cards. Another $1.00 discount was given to E-Z Pass users during off-peak hours. This shifted a slight amount of traffic from those periods to other times of the day without greatly affecting daily traffic totals.[8] It has been estimated that effective road pricing in southern California would require peak-period charges of $0.65 per mile in urban areas and $0.21 per mile in suburban areas. Those charges are far larger than the $0.02–0.04 per mile average charged on most existing toll roads.[9] If so, the typical fifteen-mile suburban auto commuting journey would cost $3.15 in tolls each way—or $1,512 per year. Few politicians will be willing to impose such costs on most auto-driving voters.

The second major objection to road pricing is that it is merely a way for the government to tax the citizenry. By charging money for something that was formerly free—travel on highways during peak periods—the government is depriving citizens of income they could otherwise spend themselves. This antagonizes people who believe that the government in our society is already too big and intrusive. How strong this objection will prove depends in part on what is done with the money collected from road-pricing tolls and whether other road charges like gasoline taxes are reduced or eliminated.

The potential revenues from widespread use of peak-hour congestion pricing are huge. Some reports estimate that adopting congestion prices throughout the United States might raise $54 billion per year (in 1981 dollars). In net benefits, that might amount to $20 to $60 billion per year.[10] Even after allowing for the costs of running these systems, this would produce substantial amounts of government funds.

Some defenders of road pricing contend that this money could be redistributed to low-income households or drivers to offset the inequitable impacts of road prices themselves.[11] Patrick DeCorla-Souza has suggested using some of the revenue to subsidize the insurance costs of door-to-door jitney service that could use the fast lanes without tolls. He also recommends giving drivers in the nontolled lanes "toll credits," which they could use to drive on the high-occupancy toll (HOT) lanes about once a week.[12]

The most obvious use of any such "excess" funds would be improving the transportation systems serving the areas that provide the money. That could help finance roads, public transit, and other transportation-related facilities like bike paths and pedestrian sidewalks. Improved transit systems could be substituted for peak-hour private vehicle travel by low-income commuters. However, many commuters cannot use public transit, since their trips do not start or end near public transit routes. Even so, quite plausible uses of funds collected from road pricing, plus time savings from faster movements, could make all income classes of drivers better off, even after taking payment of the road prices into account.[13] The monetary value of the commuting time saved—especially after improving existing transportation systems—would more than outweigh the costs of the peak-hour charges.

Some economists contend it would be more economically efficient to channel the revenues from peak-hour tolls into general government expenditures.[14] But the hostility of those citizens who see these tolls as "just another tax" would be reinforced if most of the funds were added to general revenues. Overall experience with new taxes of all kinds shows that the citizenry usually feels better about paying them when the money raised is spent on the activity from which the taxes are collected. Also peak-hour highway tolls might have a better reception if they are seen as a form of user fee. Moreover, if some of the funds are used to improve public transit, that would provide more travel options for drivers forced off highways by the peak-hour tolls.

Still another answer to the equity objection is that peak-hour traffic is becoming so congested that most people, even poor ones, would be willing to pay some price—including greater inconvenience—to improve it.

Efficiency Issues

It is also said that efficiency would suffer if drivers were charged time-based fees, which would slow traffic to an intolerable level for toll collection or would have to rely on unenforceable collection methods. But technological developments are providing ways to overcome these objections.

An electronic device already used to pay road tolls in many regions is a smart card or E-Z Pass that motorists purchase, containing a prepaid amount of credit. This device is about the size of a deck of cards and is fastened to the top inside of the windshield. As a vehicle with this device approaches the toll booth, electronic equipment in the toll booth reads the amount of credit remaining in the smart card and subtracts the trip's toll from that amount. The equipment also raises the toll gate so the vehicle can pass through at a fairly high speed without stopping. Whenever the total amount of credit in the card falls below a designated level, the system detects that fact and mails a notice to the card owner that more credit needs to be purchased. This system does not record the license or credit card number of each vehicle that passes through it, unless that vehicle's credit total is below the designated level. Hence this approach is less subject to privacy objections than systems that record the identity of each vehicle as it passes through every toll location. Smart card systems also avoid bill collection problems, because card owners who fail to keep their credit amounts current have to stop and pay the toll in cash. So users have to pay in advance to enjoy rapid passage through toll areas.

Another electronic tracking and billing system was operated as a demonstration for eight months in downtown Hong Kong.[15] Careful evaluation proved it works effectively. Yet the Hong Kong government rejected broader use of road pricing, in part because citizens regarded the tolls as "just another tax," despite the government's attempt to explain how the system increased economic efficiency.[16] People also thought that such a tax, once established, would never be abolished and might even be increased to support nontransportation activities. Citizens also believed that the television cameras used to monitor traffic violations could be used to track individuals whom the government wanted to arrest.

Although few cost-benefit analyses have been performed for road pricing, the costs of installing a system could surely be repaid rapidly through peak-hour charges.[17]

HOT Lanes—A Form of Partial Road Pricing

A relatively recent innovation in road pricing has been the development of high-occupancy toll (HOT) lanes, or "value pricing." The original idea was to permit single-occupancy vehicles (SOVs) to use HOV lanes by paying a toll, at least during peak hours. This concept began as a means of increasing the patronage of HOV lanes that were not running close to capacity during peak hours from HOVs alone. Another goal is to provide daily commuters who use highly congested freeways with a choice between moving much faster on separate lanes for a money price, or remaining in slow, congested lanes without paying any money price.

HOT lanes are designated lanes available to HOVs (including buses) for no price or a low toll and to SOVs for a variable money toll. The toll is varied by the HOT lane operators to keep total traffic in those lanes low enough to permit uninterrupted high-speed flow. HOT lanes are always located adjacent to nontolled "normal" freeway lanes so that commuters can continue using the freeway without a toll—if they are willing to endure the congestion.

The most thoroughly studied set of HOT lanes is part of State Route 91 in southern California, a ten-mile east-west freeway between the Riverside area and Orange County.[18] This roadway originally had four lanes in each direction, but two lanes in each direction were added to its median strip in 1995. These lanes are separated from the original lanes by a painted buffer with pylons. They were initially opened to HOVs with three or more riders (HOV 3+) for no charge and to other vehicles that paid a toll. However, after 1998, HOV 3+ users have been charged half the posted toll. The added HOT lanes were privately financed for $134 million through bonds to be repaid from toll revenues. All users of the HOT lanes must purchase a prepaid transponder smart card that permits them to pass through toll gates without stopping. More than 364,000 such transponders have been distributed to local drivers.

The California Department of Transportation has thoroughly evaluated the performance of these express or valued-priced lanes and arrived at the following findings:

—Before the express lanes opened, State Route 91 was a heavily congested expressway on which a typical peak-hour trip took more than one hour. Within six months of opening the new lanes, the typical trip delay for all users of this roadway—including those on the free lanes—dropped from thirty to forty minutes to under ten minutes. This delay has risen notably since then as general levels of congestion in the entire region have increased.

—Total traffic on State Route 91 increased around 17 percent from the opening of the new lanes to one year later. Total traffic was diminished somewhat in late 1998 by the opening of another nearby expressway that siphoned off some drivers from State Route 91.

—In 1999, at the height of peak periods, the express lanes accommodated 1,400 to 1,600 vehicles per lane per hour. That rate is about the same flow volume as occurs on the adjacent free lanes and is a considerably higher rate than those lanes had accommodated before the express lanes opened. Thus the HOT lanes added sufficient overall capacity to the road to reduce congestion substantially on all lanes.

—Use of the express lanes is sensitive to the degree of congestion on the free lanes. During off-peak midday periods, only about 7 percent of all vehicles use express lanes. During the evening peak hours when the free lanes are most congested, about 35 percent of all drivers use the express lanes. Also, as general congestion on this expressway has risen over time, the share of drivers using the express lanes has increased.

—Commuters in high-income groups (incomes greater than $100,000) are twice as likely to use the toll lanes as those in low-income groups (incomes under $25,000)—(23 percent versus 10 percent), and only half as likely to be nonusers (37 percent versus 73 percent). Even so, about half of high-income commuters rarely use the express lanes, and about one-fourth of low-income commuters do so regularly.

—Women are much more likely than men to use the express lanes.

HOT lanes can best be created in two ways. One is building additional capacity and using it for that purpose, as in State Route 91. The second is converting existing HOV lanes to HOT lanes where the HOV lanes are being used below capacity. HOT lanes should not be created by converting existing free lanes because that reduces the capacity of the remaining free lanes. That worsens congestion on the latter and angers their users. HOT lanes will not work effectively unless the adjacent free lanes are heavily congested, since drivers have to have a notable motivation to pay the tolls on the HOT lanes. The worse the congestion is on free lanes, the greater the motivation for drivers to pay to enjoy faster movement on the HOT lanes.

This fact shows that HOT lanes are not designed to eliminate congestion and cannot do so. Rather, they are designed to accomplish two other goals. One is to give those commuters who value rapid movement the choice of achieving such movement by paying a toll. This choice is a potential benefit to commuters in all income groups, not just the most affluent. Even the poorest drivers occasionally have strong needs to travel quickly during peak hours—strong enough needs to make them willing to pay HOT lane tolls. But those needs cannot be met if all the lanes in key freeways are heavily congested in peak hours. The other goal is to expand the overall capacity of the road concerned, thereby making all its users—including those in free lanes—better off.

A major potential advantage of HOT lanes is that they are less vulnerable to being attacked as unfair to low-income drivers than is full use of peak-hour road pricing. Placing all the lanes in a major freeway under peak-hour tolls greatly reduces the ability of low-income drivers to use that road at all during peak periods. In contrast, HOT lanes leave a majority of the lanes on the freeways concerned free of peak-hour tolls and therefore just as available to low-income users as they were formerly. Moreover, as long as HOT lanes are created through new construction or by converting underused existing HOV lanes, their creation adds to the overall capacity of the road, thereby benefiting users of the free lanes too. This could make expanding road capacity through creating HOT lanes far more acceptable to most American drivers than full peak-hour road pricing, thereby reducing the strong existing political pressures to prevent peak-hour tolls of any type. True, some criticism of HOT lanes as "Lexus lanes" favoring the wealthy has arisen. This viewpoint even caused the governor of Maryland to prohibit a HOT lane project in that state. But a far more persuasive case can be made that HOT lanes favor all income groups than can be made for placing peak-hour tolls on all the lanes of major roads.

Because HOT lanes charge tolls, they generate revenues that can be used to finance their creation. Experience with California State Route 91 shows that a private firm can raise enough revenue from HOT lane operations to pay off the bonds needed to build them and to pay their operating expenses. However, that road used land in the publicly owned median strip for the new lanes, which means the land costs were lower than they would be under many other circumstances. Moreover, if the private firm is profit oriented, it may oppose any public policies that reduce congestion in the free lanes, since lower congestion there would reduce the motivation for drivers to pay tolls on the HOT lanes. Publicity about this attitude by the private firm that owned State Route 91 caused a large public outcry. Consequently, the state had to purchase the lanes from their private owner and take over operating them. Thus it might be better to have such projects owned by private non-profit organizations or public agencies than by private profit-making firms.[19]

Kenneth Orski and Robert Poole have proposed creating whole regional networks of HOT lanes, mainly by converting now underutilized HOV lanes to HOT lanes.[20] They recommend using these lanes by combining bus rapid transit vehicles and tolls for single-occupancy vehicles. This approach could open up the choice of using high-speed corridors to drivers all over a region now confronted by intensive congestion on all major routes during peak periods.

A New High-Tech Approach to Road Pricing

A much more radical approach to road pricing is based on global positioning system (GPS) satellites combined with in-vehicle computers and toll schedules for all roads everywhere.[21] The computer in each vehicle would track and record the vehicle's movements using GPS satellites. Whenever the vehicle drove over a road that had a price attached to it, that movement would be measured by the GPS system and its central computer, and the result would be linked to a preset per mile toll for that road in the computer's memory. The resulting charge would be tallied and recorded in the in-vehicle computer and then transferred to a smart card. The in-vehicle computer would keep separate charge records for every jurisdiction through which the vehicle had passed. Every month or so, the vehicle driver would pull up to an uploading terminal, probably located in a gas station. The driver would remove the smart card from the in-vehicle computer and insert it into the uploading terminal. The uploading terminal would transmit the smart card's data to the central computer, which would thereby discover how much the vehicle's owner owed. It would send the owner a bill. The central system computer would then allocate the resulting toll collections to different governmental units and send each the money generated by vehicles driving on its roads, minus a small administrative charge.

This system has several major advantages over currently used road pricing schemes for the following reasons:

—It enables jurisdictions to charge tolls on all their roads in proportion to how much those roads are actually being used by individual vehicles. Thus it has the potential for replacing the gasoline fuel tax as a general means of financing roads and allocating the costs to users in proportion to how much they use each road.

—It does not impede the progress of any vehicles, since no tolls are collected on the ground.

—No toll gates, toll booths, electronic wiring systems, or other toll collection mechanisms need be constructed. Therefore, jurisdictions can collect tolls on any roads anywhere as long as the appropriate data are entered into in-vehicle computers, without the costs or inconvenience of having to build and operate toll-collection facilities on the ground.

—It enables individual jursidictions responsible for creating and maintaining roads to set charges for using those roads that will be applicable to—and collected from—everyone who uses those roads. In practice, this toll-setting power would undoubtedly be subject to some more general governmental regulations.

—It preserves the privacy of individual vehicle owners and users. Exact route information is kept only within on-vehicle computers. Each such computer compiles a separate overall charge for each jurisdiction through which the vehicle has passed and communicates only that overall charge to the central system computer, not the specific route data. Once the monthly charges have been uploaded into the central system computer, they are erased from the on-vehicle computer.

—It permits discriminatory charging schemes for different types of vehicles (such as trucks, buses, and cars) and different types of roads.

—It would allow highway authorities to use variable peak-hour road pricing to combat congestion by posting electronic signs at the entrances to roads subject to such pricing, and communicating pricing data in advance on the Internet, without requiring vehicles to stop and get tickets or pay tolls. (However, the inventors of this system do not recommend this use until this system has been established primarily as a revenue-raising system, in order to keep the system from becoming too complex and therefore less publicly acceptable.)

—Heavy trucks could be charged in a more discriminatory manner because privacy issues are less significant for them. Hence more complex information could be kept and transmitted to central system computers and even linked to on-board weight measurements of individual trucks.

The technology for this system already exists and could be significantly reduced in cost by the mass production needed to supply large numbers of vehicles with the requisite equipment. Similar GPS tracking and centralized information collection systems are already being used in Europe and the United States by private trucking firms.

The proponents of this system believe it will become vital if and when most automotive vehicles shift to fuel cells or other new means of propulsion that will not generate revenues through fuel taxes. However, switching from present means of financing roads to using this system would require an immense change in many long-established institutions and procedures. Even just getting the required equipment installed in most cars would take many years because millions of existing cars would have to be retired and replaced by new ones.

So at this time, widespread use of this system is more a gleam in the eyes of its inventors than a real prospect for the near future. Yet road pricing may eventually evolve in this direction.[22]

Recent Experience with Other Forms of Road Pricing

Besides the HOT lanes just described, other forms of anticongestion road pricing are being used around the world. (All toll roads use road pricing but usually not as an anticongestion tactic.) Area or zone pricing has been in operation for several years in Oslo, Bergen, and Trondheim in Norway and for more than twenty-five years in Singapore and was begun in London early in 2003. Results of the Singapore and London systems are as follows.

SINGAPORE. The area licensing scheme was begun in June 1975 to reduce intensive traffic congestion in the Singapore central business district and the adjacent Chinatown and Orchard Road corridor. All vehicles (except those in exempted categories) were charged $3.00 per day or $60.00 per month if they entered this cordoned area from 7:30 to 9:30 a.m., though that was soon extended to 10:15 a.m. In mid-1975, traffic in the central business district was moving slowly at 12 miles per hour. By the end of 1975, traffic volume entering the restricted zone had fallen by 44 percent, and the number of private cars by 73 percent. By 1988, the total vehicle population of Singapore was 77 percent higher than in 1975, but total traffic entering the restricted zone during peak hours was 31 percent lower than in early 1975. The drop in car traffic was accompanied by large shifts of commuters to public transit and car pooling. In 1989, the charge for entering the restricted zone was extended to the evening peak period from 4:30 to 6:30 p.m.

However, studies in 1992 showed that some traffic was shifting from the restricted hours to other locations and other hours, mainly from noon to 4:00 p.m. Speeds on nineteen roads outside the restricted zone were lower in those hours than during the restricted period. To cope with this diversion, in 1994 another charge was added of $2.00 per day or $40.00 per month for vehicles entering the zone from 10:15 a.m. to 4:30 p.m.; that rate was doubled for company cars. Thus the Singapore system does vary the size of its tolls at different hours in a fixed response to congestion intensity.

This system has been very effective at restricting traffic in the center of the city. However, Singapore has a very extensive public transit system and greatly restricts private ownership of automotive vehicles in general.[23]

LONDON. The cordon zone in London consists of the City district (the financial center) and much of Westminster (an office and government center). This central London zone covers about 8 square miles, or only 1.3 percent of London's 622 square miles. There is a charge of five pounds for entering this zone from 7:00 a.m. to 6:30 p.m. Once the charge has been incurred on any given day, a driver can enter and leave the zone as often as desired without any added charge. Payment can be made at certain shops, by phone, on the Internet, by mail, or through a smart card. Television cameras record all vehicles entering the zone and at midnight computers compare the list of entrants with a list of those who have paid. Those who have not paid are sent violation notices and fined 80 pounds, with a 50 percent reduction for prompt payment. Certain classes of vehicles are exempt from the charge. They include vehicles owned by residents within the cordon area (a 90 percent discount) or disabled persons, buses, alternative fuel vehicles (including electric cars), taxis, motorcycles, and roadside recovery vehicles.

Todd Litman has reported on the results of this system, which began on February 17, 2003.[24] Before congestion pricing, about 1.1 million persons entered the cordon zone each day during the peak period, 84 percent on public transit (42 percent on national rail, 35 percent on subways, and 7 percent on buses) and 12 percent in about 100,000 private vehicles.[25] Another 30,000 private vehicles entered the zone outside of the peak period. Since the charges began, about 110,000 vehicles per day have paid to enter (including those entering outside peak times)—98,000 individual drivers and 12,000 service vehicles. However, there are 20,000 fewer vehicles in the zone each day. Fines have been issued to about 4,000 vehicles per day, though that figure is declining. Average speed of movement within the zone has risen from 8 miles per hour to 11 miles per hour. Peak-period congestion delays fell 30 percent, bus delays fell 50 percent, and taxi fares dropped 20 to 40 percent owing to fewer delays. Bus ridership increased 14 percent and subway ridership went up 1 percent. There is 10 percent more traffic on peripheral roads, but delays there have not risen. Public sentiment has swung from considerable opposition to majority support, although a few business firms in the zone claim sales are down.

In short, this cordon form of congestion pricing has had notable impacts on traffic conditions in the affected zone. Yet the charges are not varied in peak periods or for specific traffic flows or for specific types of vehicles. Total money collections are running at a pace of 68 million pounds per year, lower than originally expected.[26]

This system leaves traffic flows in the vast majority of London largely unchanged, except for lower throughputs aimed at central London. In 2001, London as a whole contained 7.3 million residents and 4.3 million jobs. About 43 percent of all London workers commuted by car, with about 1.4 riders per car. That equals 1.32 million private vehicles per day used by commuters. Since the new central London road-pricing scheme reduced the flow of such vehicles into that area by about 20,000, that is only a 1.5 percent drop in the number of private vehicles used by commuters each day throughout London. Average traffic speeds in noncentral London were about 22 miles per hour in off-peak periods and 16 miles per hour in peak periods.

LEE COUNTY, FLORIDA. This Florida county adopted a variable pricing scheme in 1999 for two bridges that join Fort Myers and Cape Coral.[27] The normal toll over these bridges is $1.00 per passenger car. There are two classes of bridge users: those who use prepaid electronic smart cards and those who pay in cash at toll collection booths. Annual and semiannual smart cards can be purchased for 50 percent discounts. Only drivers using smart cards are eligible for the variable toll discount. Smart card drivers traveling right before and after the peak travel periods are given 50 percent discounts on their tolls. Thus, during these off-peak periods, a traveler without a smart card still pays $1.00, but a smart card traveler pays $0.50, and a discount-eligible smart card traveler pays $0.25. The four off-peak periods during which these discounts apply are 6:30 to 7:00 a.m., 9:00 to 11:00 a.m., 2:00 to 4:00 p.m., and 6:30 to 7:00 p.m.

The basic idea is to motivate persons who would normally cross these bridges during the peak periods of 7:00 to 9:00 a.m. and 4:00 to 6:30 p.m. to shift their travel times slightly to receive lower tolls. The incentive is not very great—either $0.50 or $0.25 per trip—depending on whether the driver is eligible for regular discounts. The practice of discounting the normal toll during off-peak "shoulder" periods, instead of raising the toll during the peak periods, was entirely political. The elected officials who promoted the toll bridge were only able to get enough support for it by promising never to raise the toll above $1.00. So the only way they could use variable pricing aimed at reducing congestion and still keep their promise was to lower the tolls during the "shoulder" periods.

The impact of variable pricing on driver behavior was studied by comparing time flows of vehicles in multiple-month periods before and after the variable-pricing scheme was implemented. As a check, the same measurements were made for non–smart card users of the bridge, who did not receive the variable pricing discount. At both bridges, traffic in the 6:30 to 7:00 a.m. discount period rose sharply after variable pricing began: 22 percent on one bridge and 17.5 percent on the other. Traffic during the peak period of 7:00 to 9:00 a.m. declined on both bridges to the greatest degree from 7:00 to 7:30 a.m.: 10 percent on one bridge and 12 percent on the other. Declines in the last three half-hours during the peak period were smaller. Traffic also rose during the after-peak periods from 9:00 to 11:00 a.m. but much less than in the pre-peak-period shoulder. Impacts during the afternoon and evening periods were noticeable but clearly less significant in both the shoulder and peak periods than in the morning. The control group of drivers not receiving the variable pricing discount showed slight increases in traffic during the morning peak period on one bridge, but very little change at other times, and very little changes at any times on the other bridge. Ironically, total traffic on one bridge rose 1 to 2 percent during morning and evening peak periods after variable pricing was introduced, while it declined slightly during both peaks on the other bridge. (This confirms the concept of driver convergence described in chapter 6.) The number of travelers not eligible for the variable pricing discount increased during the peak periods, replacing some of those who were eligible who shifted their travel to nonpeak times. So the net reduction in peak-period traffic was relatively small or nonexistent.

It is clear that even the small economic incentive provided by this scheme did influence some time-shifting of travel on these bridges. However, surveys of persons using these bridges showed that saving money was not their major incentive for changing travel. When they were asked if variable pricing had ever caused them to change the time of their travel, 92 percent said no. To make variable pricing more effective in influencing driver behavior, the size of the economic benefit of avoiding peak periods should probably be considerably larger than it is on these bridges.

The Need for More Revenues to Support Ground Transportation

As explained in chapter 9, revenues from motor fuel taxes have recently not been keeping up with the costs of expanding and maintaining the nation's ground transportation systems. True, fuel and vehicle taxes combined were a higher percentage of total highway revenues in 2000 (59.3 percent) than in 1990 (55.2 percent).[28] But this resulted mainly from large increases in federal gasoline tax rates in 1983 and the early 1990s. After 1993, federal gas tax revenues plateaued at around $20 billion per year. And from 2000 to 2001, while total highway revenues rose 3.2 percent, fuel and vehicle taxes fell 4.1 percent to only 54.6 of total revenues. But in that one year, bond issue proceeds rose 12.2 percent, other taxes and fees (including sales taxes) rose 37.7 percent, and general fund appropriations rose 18.1 percent. As a result, the share of total revenues provided by the last three categories went from 26.6 percent in 2000 to 30.5 percent in 2001.

Martin Wachs believes this may indicate a trend toward a declining share of total highway funds produced by fuel taxes and rising shares produced by borrowing and sales and property taxes.[29] Governments seem reluctant to raise fuel taxes even though more economical engines mean every mile of driving produces less revenue from such taxes than formerly. Inflation further eats away at the purchasing power of fuel taxes while raising the costs of building and maintaining roads.

These short-run trends are reinforced by the long-run prospect of having to shift sources of automobile energy away from gasoline and fossil fuels to fuel cells and other types that are not well suited to raising funds from fuel taxes. Wachs believes that increasing the flow of funds into ground transportation from road tolls—which produced only 6.6 percent of highway revenues in 2001—would have two positive impacts. It would help improve short-run highway funding and lay the foundation for a long-run move to almost complete funding by user fees collected through the high-tech means discussed earlier. Otherwise state and local governments will continue expanding sales taxes, borrowing, and property taxes to fund ground transportation. This would move the burden of such funding from the users of ground transportation, where it ought to be, to the general public, with the heaviest relative burdens on low-income households. Avoiding that outcome provides an additional incentive for expanding the use of user fees collected through road-pricing schemes of various types.

The Future of Road Pricing

As congestion worsens in many parts of the nation, pressures will rise to combat it with various types of road pricing. The technological means of using road pricing with minimal disruption of traffic flows have now been well developed and tested in practice, as described earlier. The forms most likely to be given serious consideration in the United States are HOT lanes and all-lane use of variable tolls on a few major expressways during peak periods. Those forms are most likely because America's most intense peak-hour congestion is on expressways rather than in downtown areas. Exceptions are in the downtowns of the largest American cities, especially New York, Boston, San Francisco, and Chicago. Area or zone pricing like that used in Singapore, London, and Norway is mainly suitable for the centers of large cities where city streets become clogged with traffic. For all three of these systems, the toll revenues they raise can pay for the costs of implementing them and may also help pay for other transportation improvements. HOT lanes and all-lane variable tolls will reduce congestion by adding to road capacity or speeding the flow of vehicles on existing lanes. Cordon systems do not add to road capacity, but they do result in somewhat faster traffic flows within the target zone.

HOT lanes appear to have the highest probability of public acceptance in the near future. They are self-financing, expand speed of movement choices available to all travelers, add to total road capacity, and thereby even benefit those on the same roads who do not use them, and do not exclude travelers who do not want to pay tolls from using the roads involved during peak periods. Therefore, they are closer to an "everybody wins" tactic than the other two devices. True, they do not eliminate peak-hour congestion on the roads where they are employed; in fact, they rely on the continuance of such congestion for their financial viability. Yet by offering a choice of faster movement to anyone willing to pay for it, they provide an important partial antidote to intensive peak-hour congestion.

Cordon systems have the least powerful impact on congestion throughout a region because they are so tightly focused on small areas. Some American downtowns are already using partial cordon systems by excluding private vehicles from major streets where only buses can travel. Others have blocked all vehicles from pedestrian mall areas. But these systems do not reduce congestion in outlying portions of metropolitan areas where it has become as intense as in most downtowns. And they might negatively affect many merchants in the cordoned zones. So this tactic seems unlikely to become widespread in the United States. And even if it did, that would not remedy most of the congestion in any metropolitan area.

All-lane variable tolls during peak hours on major expressways seem the least likely to be widely adopted because they disadvantage lower-income travelers and would therefore be politically unpopular. Even so, this tactic might be tried on a few heavily congested expressways where nearby alternative routes and off-road transit systems were available for travelers unwilling or unable to pay the tolls. However, regionwide adoption of this tactic on all the major commuter expressways in a metropolitan area simultaneously seems highly unlikely.

Except for privately operated systems used by trucking firms, high-tech GPS systems tying tolls to the behavior of individual travelers through in-vehicle computers will probably occur widely only in the very long run—say by 2015 or later. Such systems might be part of the gradual shift from gasoline engines to fuel cells or electric engines that visionaries foresee at some distant date. But that is a long way off.

In the near future, even though HOT lanes may expand, no applications of road pricing are likely to eliminate peak-hour traffic congestion, especially on roads where such congestion has already become intense.

Other Aspects of Road Pricing

Peak-hour road pricing tactics raise several other issues.

PRIVACY. Some people believe computerized vehicle tracking and toll billing systems would invade their privacy if such systems enabled governments to trace personal movements throughout a metropolitan area. This was one of the main reasons Hong Kong rejected a broad adoption of road pricing. However, there are ways to collect tolls without recording exactly where individual drivers are at any given moment, as noted in the preceding discussion of the high-tech GPS system. Thus this problem can be solved technologically.

DIVERSION OF TRAFFIC. Many drivers not wanting to pay road tolls on either cordon systems or all-lane variable toll systems would shift their travel to nearby streets not subjected to such tolls. This could lead to intensive peak-hour congestion on such streets, including residential streets. That would upset households living there. This problem has already arisen in many large cities because of the diversionary impact of congestion itself, even where no tolls are involved. Local governments have responded with a variety of "traffic calming" devices to slow down vehicle movement on such streets, thus discouraging them from being used as alternative commuting routes. These devices include narrower streets, speed bumps, dead-end streets, center islands, short portions of streets narrowed sharply (chokers), and chicanes (shaping streets in S-curves).[30]

PRIVATELY OWNED TOLL ROADS. Only a few such roads have been built, but many are proposed. However, merely because a road charges tolls does not mean its managers will set those tolls to reduce peak-hour congestion. Nearly all publicly owned toll roads charge flat, nonvarying rates calculated to achieve revenue goals. There is no reason to suppose most private owners of toll roads will behave differently from public owners. So most private toll roads will not have much impact on congestion. However, there is no reason in theory why private operators could not build toll roads with variable peak-hour pricing as long as those roads were paired with, or very nearby, free lanes too. Then the variable peak-hour toll lanes would not be subject to the criticism that they were forcing all low-income drivers off that road entirely.

LAND VALUES. Peak-hour congestion tolls would affect land values, especially along the roads where such tolls were adopted. As Kenneth Small, Clifford Winston, and Carol A. Evans observed, "The burdens of a new tax or user charge are shifted throughout the economy through price adjustments. If congestion pricing were adopted, land values and wages would change as various competitive forces worked themselves out. . . . Owners of urban land are particularly likely to be adversely affected, and this would shift at least part of the burden from road users to landowners, making it even more doubtful that low-income workers will be hurt."[31]

Many of these long-run adjustments are unpredictable, so it is not clear just which social groups would gain or lose. It is doubtful, however, that these impacts would be large enough or clear enough to affect the political acceptability of road pricing.

Would a Regional Authority Be Necessary?

Since the road networks in every metropolitan area transcend the boundaries of any one community, it would be impossible to plan and implement an effective peak-hour congestion pricing system except at a regional level. It is also unlikely that a purely voluntary coalition of local governments could make the tough resource allocation and locational decisions necessary for creating such a regional system. However, the regional metropolitan planning organization could perform this function, as could a state agency, by forming a subgroup assigned to a specific region and working with local authorities there.

Of course, peak-hour congestion pricing could be used in a limited zone entirely within one big city's boundaries, as in London. But this would not reduce congestion throughout the metropolitan area.

CHAPTER 11

Demand-Side
Behavioral Tactics

Several anticongestion tactics try to change the way people behave within existing transportation systems and settlement patterns. Most of these tactics suffer from the same serious drawback: they reduce the number of daily driving commuters by only a small percentage, and so that reduction is likely to be offset by the principle of triple convergence. For every commuter removed from traffic by one of these tactics, another driver who is now using other routes or other modes, or going at other times, will move onto whatever space is vacated by the first one. So the intensity of peak-period congestion will be essentially unchanged, though the time period with the most intense congestion may not last as long, since total travel on the roads will have declined. Nevertheless, these tactics are analyzed because they are so often proposed as a means of combating peak-hour congestion.

Shifting Peak-Hour Trips to Other Times of the Day

Many peak-hour trips could be shifted to other times of the day by staggering work hours among different organizations, adopting flextime policies, or having some organizations adopt four-day weeks. According to the 1995 Nationwide Personal Transportation Survey (NPTS), on an average 1995 weekday, only 17.1 percent of all the day's trips were made in the morning peak period from 6:00 to 9:00 a.m., whereas 23.1 percent were made in the evening peak period from 4:00 to 7:00 pm. (table 11-1).[1] The share of work-related trips differed in these two peak periods, but exactly what that share was in each is not obvious. That is because the 1995 NPTS counted journeys *from home to work* (labeled "journey to work" trips) differently from journeys *from work to home*. The results appear in table 11-2 (derived from table 11-1).

Thus commuting both to and from work constituted only 19.0 percent of all daily trips, but 47.2 percent of all peak-period trips (45.4 percent in the morning peak and 49.0 in the evening peak). All work-related travel—including journey-to-work, work-related business, and home trips combined—made up almost identical shares of about one-half of the total trips within each peak period. So work-related trips formed a very important share of all peak-period road travel in 1995—though about half of such travel was not work related.

If 10 percent of all peak-period trips that were either journeys to work or journeys home from work were shifted to other times by changing work hours, that would reduce current total peak trips by 4.5 percent in the morning and 4.9 percent in the evening. However, this conclusion assumes these reductions would not be offset by the principle of triple convergence. So the potential for reducing congestion by changing work hours is limited. Even so, this tactic might be worth trying as part of a larger strategy that also encouraged car pools and instituted HOV lanes.

Changing work hours would probably not require a single regional authority, because it would be unwise to make such a policy mandatory for all employers. A single private organization could be set up in each metropolitan area to encourage more organizations to adopt varying work hours, but it should operate on a voluntary basis.

Encouraging More People to Work at Home

Many employees who used to spend every weekday in the office are now working at home all or part of the time. This enables them to reduce the number of trips they make between home and the workplace each week. If this trend affected enough workers, it could reduce the

TABLE 11-1. Weekday Trips from the 1995 Nationwide Personal Travel Survey, by Purpose and Time of Day[a]

Period	Total	Journey to work	Work-related business	Work to home	Other
1 a.m. to 6 a.m.					
Number of trips	4,982	2,606	158	1,134	1,082
Percent by purpose	1.88	7.36	1.70	1.31	0.81
Percent of period	100.00	52.31	3.17	22.76	21.72
Percent of daily total	1.88	0.98	0.06	0.43	0.41
6 a.m. to 9 a.m.					
Number of trips	45,292	17,058	1,727	3,509	22,993
Percent by purpose	17.08	48.18	18.61	4.06	17.17
Percent of period	100.00	37.66	3.81	7.75	50.77
Percent of daily total	17.08	6.43	0.65	1.32	8.67
9 a.m. to 1 p.m.					
Number of trips	61,730	7,152	3,594	13,469	37,504
Percent by purpose	23.28	20.20	38.72	15.58	28.00
Percent of period	100.00	11.59	5.82	21.82	60.75
Percent of daily total	23.28	2.70	1.36	5.08	14.15
1 p.m. to 4 p.m.					
Number of trips	59,995	5,770	2,401	22,056	29,761
Percent by purpose	22.63	16.30	25.87	25.52	22.22
Percent of period	100.00	9.62	4.00	36.76	49.61
Percent of daily total	22.63	2.18	0.91	8.32	11.23
4 p.m. to 7 p.m.					
Number of trips	61,281	1,924	1,097	28,111	30,144
Percent by purpose	23.12	5.43	11.82	32.52	22.50
Percent of period	100.00	3.14	1.79	45.87	49.19
Percent of daily total	23.12	0.73	0.41	10.60	11.37
7 p.m. to 10 p.m.					
Number of trips	25,140	514	231	13,704	10,684
Percent by purpose	9.48	1.45	2.49	15.85	7.98
Percent of period	100.00	2.04	0.92	54.51	42.50
Percent of daily total	9.48	0.19	0.09	5.17	4.03
10 p.m. to 1 a.m.					
Number of trips	6,687	381	73	4,457	1,776
Percent by purpose	2.52	1.08	0.79	5.16	1.33
Percent of period	100.00	5.70	1.09	66.65	26.56
Percent of daily total	2.52	0.14	0.03	1.68	0.67
Total					
Number of trips	265,107	35,405	9,281	86,440	133,944
Percent by purpose	100.00	100.00	100.00	100.00	100.00
Percent of period	100.00	13.35	3.50	32.61	50.52
Percent of daily total	100.00	13.35	3.50	32.61	50.52

Source: Federal Highway Administration, *1995 NPTS Data Book*, chap. 6, "Journey to Work," table 6-17, p. 6-30.

a. Totals do not equal sums of individual parts because purposes of some trips are not known.

TABLE 11-2. Purpose and Share of Weekday Trips in Peak Periods
Percent

Trip purpose	6:00 to 9:00 a. m. peak period		4:00 to 7:00 p.m. peak period	
	All daily trips	All trips in this period	All daily trips	All trips in this period
Journey to work	6.4	37.7	0.7	3.1
Home	1.3	7.7	10.6	45.9
Subtotal	7.7	45.4	11.3	49.0
Work-related business	0.7	3.8	0.4	1.8
Subtotal of above three	8.4	49.2	11.7	50.8
Other	8.7	50.8	11.4	49.2
Total	17.1	100.0	23.1	100.0

Source: See table 11-1.

total number of daily work trips appreciably and might thereby help to relieve congestion.

Computers and electronic communications have made working at home more feasible than ever before. They allow employees to transmit work done at home to their offices instantly and receive messages through e-mail, telephone lines, modems, and fax machines. This permits "telecommuting"—acting as though one were at the office when one is working at home.

Despite the advantages of working at home, few people will want to do so all the time. Most people enjoy socializing with their fellow workers and find face-to-face meetings vital to maintain close links with their organizations. And people who want to be promoted need to be readily available to their superiors. Hence widespread home employment is likely to remain mainly a part-time arrangement, particularly because most employers believe they cannot monitor or control people working at home as closely as those working in offices or factories.

In 1992, according to the Federal Transit Administration, about 4 million workers were telecommuting.[2] In 2001, the International Telework Association and Council deduced from a nationwide telephone survey that 28.8 million workers were telecommuting.[3] But that total included those working on the road, in satellite offices, and in telework centers. Since those workers had to commute to the sites of their activities, their telecommuting did not necessarily reduce the number of peak-hour work trips on roads. However, about 6.24 million telecommuters worked at home some of the time—usually one day per week.

TABLE 11-3. Telecommuting and Its Effect on Road Trips
Percent

Nonhome workers telecommuting	Percent of all workers doing so	Work trips as share of all morning peak trips	Reduction in all morning peak-hour trips from staying home	
			One weekday	Half time
10	9.67	37.7	0.73	1.83
15	14.50	37.7	1.10	2.75
20	19.34	37.7	1.46	3.65
25	24.18	37.7	1.83	4.58
30	29.01	37.7	2.19	5.48
35	33.84	37.7	2.55	6.38
40	38.68	37.7	2.92	7.30
45	43.51	37.7	3.29	8.22
50	48.35	37.7	3.65	9.13

Source: Author's calculations; and Federal Highway Administration, *1995 NPTS Data Book*, chap. 6, "Journey to Work," table 6-17, p. 6-30.

Their doing so did reduce the number of peak-hour work trips at least slightly. They composed 4.86 percent of all employed nonagricultural workers.[4]

Suppose, however, that the percentage of all workers who did not work at home in 2000 may eventually be able to spend either one day a week or half time working at home. The percentages of all morning peak-hour trips eliminated by various percentages of all workers telecommuting one day a week or half time are estimated in table 11-3 (based on 2000 Census data). Table 11-3 shows that if 25 percent of all the workers who do not now work at home were to telecommute half the time, the total number of all trips—including nonwork trips—in each daily rush hour on all modes would be cut by about only 4.58 percent. But in 2001, only 4.86 percent of all workers telecommuted by working at home; so a shift to 25 percent more telecommuting half time would be a huge change in behavior.

Thus telecommuting would have to become a lot more common to make any significant impact on initial morning peak-hour traffic. Moreover, if telecommuting did at first cut peak-hour trips, some travelers now avoiding those hours because of congestion would start driving then because of the principle of triple convergence. That would prevent the full initial reduction in peak-hour trips from becoming permanent.

Nevertheless, since telecommuting could reduce the total number of work trips each day, public anticongestion policies should encourage more people to work at home at least some of the time. Such policies could include liberalized tax deductions for expenses incurred working at home, efforts to prevent telephone companies from charging higher-than-usual rates for modems and home data transmission, modified health and worker compensation insurance policies to cover periods of working at home, and an easing of federal regulations that discourage home work to avoid sweatshop conditions.

Any drastic telecommuting policies would have to be administered across all or large portions of a state or metropolitan area, rather than within just one community. Similarly, tax policies encouraging telecommuting could only be adopted by state or federal governments. Therefore, no one metropolitan agency would be needed to encourage effective telecommuting.

Restricting Automobile Travel

Some communities have considered restricting the automobile travel of people on certain days (such as Tuesdays) by ordering those with auto license numbers ending in certain digits (such as 1 or 2) or certain letters (such as A through E) to stay off the street on those days. Violators would be subject to heavy fines.

In theory, by assigning two digits and five letters of the alphabet to each weekday, one-fifth of all cars could be kept idle each weekday. Owners of grounded license plates would have to ride share, use public transit, or stay home. This arbitrary approach does not take into account commuters who cannot easily avoid driving all five days of the week. Hence this tactic is likely to be extremely unpopular among American commuters. Therefore, the political probability of its being adopted is very low.

Encouraging Ride Sharing

The most effective means of reducing peak-hour congestion would be to persuade solo drivers to share vehicles. In 2000, 87.9 percent of all morning peak-hour commuters were in private vehicles, and 75.7 percent were driving alone. Since commuters driving to work constitute 37.7 percent of all morning peak-hour trips, these "lone rangers" were about 28.5 percent of all such trips (or 34.3 percent including commuters driving home from work during the morning peak hours). Convincing large fractions of them to commute in two-person vehicles could reduce morning traffic.

The problem is how to persuade people to double up, since doing so is less convenient than driving alone. The number of workers sharing rides can be increased in several ways. Probably the most effective is by raising the cost of parking for commuters—especially free parking provided by employers. Other tactics too, such as the following, can increase ride sharing.

Obstacles Created by Local Government

One method is to award a building permit for each new commercial building only if its developer agrees to reduce the number of commuting trips generated by that structure to a level below the number of workers it will house. This is furthered if the developer is prohibited from creating large numbers of parking spaces for the building's tenants. Portland, Oregon, has sharply restricted the provision of parking spaces by developers of downtown office buildings, partly to stimulate more patronage for its light rail system. Judy Davis of Parsons, Brinckerhoff points out, "Downtown development projects have had limits on the number of new commuter parking spaces allowed since the mid-1970s. Office buildings on the mall can provide only 0.7 parking spaces for every 1,000 square of office space, while buildings farther away are allowed more, but never more than two spaces per 1,000 square feet. These limits have shrunk the supply of downtown parking from 3.4 parking spaces for every 1,000 square feet of office space in 1973 to 1.5 spaces in 1990."[5]

Employers' Persuasion

Another method of encouraging ride sharing was exemplified by Regulation 15, adopted by the Southern California Air Quality Management District in 1987. It required all employers of 100 or more persons to encourage their workers arriving between 6:00 and 10:00 a.m. to reduce their use of private vehicles. Such employers were supposed to submit trip reduction plans to the Air Quality Management District for approval. Regulation 15 sought to create a regionwide average commuter vehicle ridership of 1.5, with a target of 1.75 for downtown Los Angeles workers. That would have meant 60 percent ride sharing among the latter.[6] However, this regulation aroused so much opposition among both employers and workers that it was soon repealed.

Transportation Management Associations

California also adopted a statewide congestion management requirement applying to all jurisdictions that share in recently increased gas tax revenues. Such policies pressure developers and employers to form transportation management associations (TMAs) aimed at encouraging ride sharing and public transit use among their workers. These associations adopt trip-reducing policies, such as the following.[7]

—Prohibiting free parking for workers driving to work alone.

—Providing free parking for workers using car or van pools.

—Allocating the most conveniently located parking spaces to vans or cars used in van pools or car pools.

—Allowing workers to adopt flextime hours so they can more easily share rides with others in the same building. However, flextime makes ride sharing more difficult overall in that it increases the dispersion of worker hours.

—Providing data centers where prospective carpoolers from different firms can locate others who might drive to work with them.

—Providing vans at company expense for employees who will use them to share rides with other employees.

—Assigning a full-time person to supervise all ride-sharing arrangements and incentives.

—Providing free shuttle buses linking buildings to nearby public transit lines during morning and evening peak hours.

—Subsidizing fares for workers who commute on public transit. Federal legislation has been adopted that allows employers to deduct transit allowances for such employees as a business expense up to $65 per month per employee.

—Persuading public transit suppliers to route buses or other transit services directly to, or adjacent to, a firm's offices or job centers.

A serious drawback of transportation management associations is their bureaucratic intrusion into their member organizations. To be effective, a TMA must pressure those organizations to shift their employees into ride sharing and must also monitor their performances. Up to now, TMAs have mainly been formed where new job centers were being developed. Developers have strong incentives to set up such TMAs if local governments require them before granting building permits.

But what about employers in buildings developed before local governments adopted such regulations? They make up well over 90 percent of all employers in most areas but are under no legal pressure to encourage ride sharing, unless their state or area adopts something like southern California's now-defunct Regulation 15. Even if their state or local governments adopt strong measures to promote ride sharing, it is unclear who will enforce those measures. To do so would require much greater monitoring of private firms by governments. Just getting existing firms to promote ride sharing strongly—when most have done nothing up to now— would require extensive outreach efforts. Who would provide those efforts? How would they influence millions of existing organizations without a huge promotional effort requiring an extensive bureaucracy?

These questions have not yet been answered by the promoters of TMAs. No single TMA could function effectively across an entire metropolitan area. To do so, it would have to interact directly with thousands of immensely diverse organizations. That would require a massive effort almost sure to become bogged down in bureaucratic red tape. Therefore, a regional TMA makes sense only as an umbrella agency, offering resources and encouragement to many smaller TMAs in specific employment centers. Even then, most existing employers probably cannot be brought into local TMAs voluntarily, unless traffic congestion becomes far worse. So effective encouragement of ride sharing seems likely only under two conditions: where new workplaces are being created by developers, local governments can make building permits contingent on the formation and operation of TMAs, and where the firms clustered in a single major suburban employment node tend to generate heavy local congestion and so have a strong incentive to cooperate in reducing it. But these situations cover only a tiny fraction of all workers who now commute by driving alone. Therefore, the potential of TMAs to encourage extensive ride sharing is relatively limited.

Use of High-Occupancy Vehicle Lanes

High-occupancy vehicle (HOV) lanes are separate lanes reserved (at least during peak hours) for vehicles carrying two-or-more or three-or-more persons, including transit buses. The prospect of faster movement on HOV lanes and lower costs because of expense sharing is designed to lure at least some solo drivers into taking on or becoming passengers. The goal is to move more people per vehicle—and therefore more per lane per hour—on these HOV lanes than on "normal" lanes. (How well this works is analyzed in chapter 8.) However, surveys indicate that reducing costs is a stronger motive for ride sharing than saving time by using HOV lanes.

Ride sharing has been found to cut daily work trips by as much as 17 to 40 percent.[8] But those are the greatest decreases on record, and they occurred where public transit services were available nearby. Hence such large trip reductions are not likely to prevail in much of a locality's work force. Gaining a 10 percent reduction in trips throughout an entire metropolitan area by encouraging ride sharing would be a heroic achievement.

As an earlier discussion shows, a 10 percent reduction in lone commuters would cause an initial drop in morning peak-hour trips of all types by 2.8 to 3.4 percent. But this small reduction is likely to be heavily offset by the subsequent convergence of non-peak-hour travelers into that hour. However, ride-sharing programs might cut peak-hour congestion near a specific employment center if the transportation management association there was particularly successful.

Raising the Cost of Driving Alone

Another way to reduce peak-hour congestion is to discourage people from making automotive trips by raising the cost of driving, especially driving alone, in privately owned vehicles. This approach is among those with the greatest potential effectiveness—but it is also the least popular among citizens and therefore among elected officials too.

In a high proportion of all U.S. households, workers drive private vehicles, and the share of their incomes spent on transportation—an average of 18.8 percent in 2002—was second only to that spent for housing. However, the transportation share was actually lower for households with low incomes. Yet increases in driving costs would be absolutely harder for low-income households to bear than for higher-income households.[9] This regressivity could be offset by reducing the auto license fees for low-income households or offering special rebates. Funds for such compensation could be raised from tactics that charge drivers more money—in the form of higher gasoline taxes or peak-hour parking charges. But there is no intrinsic link between such tactics and the way the money is spent, so there is no assurance such compensation would actually be paid. In spite of these drawbacks, the potential effectiveness of this approach makes it worthwhile to consider.

Increased Taxes on Gasoline

The most obvious way to increase the cost of driving is substantially raising taxes on gasoline, as nearly all other developed nations have

TABLE 11-4. Retail Gasoline Price in the United States and
Other Developed Countries (including tax)

Country	Retail gasoline price (U.S. dollars)	Ratio to U.S. price	Percent of distance of 1997 passenger travel in passenger cars
Belgium	4.27	2.56	n.a.
France	4.38	2.62	84.5
Germany	4.79	2.87	82.1
Italy	4.58	2.74	76.1
Netherlands	5.05	3.02	82.0
United Kingdom	4.67	2.80	87.7
United States	1.67	...	98.9

Source: *Weekly Retail Premium Gasoline Prices* (including taxes) (www.eia.doe.gov/emeu/international/gas1.html [January 2004]); and United Kingdom Commission for Integrated Transport, "Published Reports: European Best Practice in Transport—Benchmarking," sec. III, "Inputs and Outputs" (www.cfit.gov.uk/reports/ebptbench/03.htm [January 2004]).
 n.a. Not available.

already done. The retail price of unleaded premium gasoline in seven developed nations, including all taxes, and the percentages of passenger travel by autos as of June 2003 are shown in table 11-4. The nations listed in table 11-4 were ensuring through high taxes that their motorists paid at least 2.56 times as much per gallon for gasoline as did Americans. All had lower percentages of their passenger travel by automobile, though automobiles still dominated overall passenger travel.[10]

What impact would a large increase in gasoline taxes have on commuter driving? The price elasticity of gasoline is the percentage reduction in gasoline consumption that would result from raising its price by 1 percent. Gasoline's price elasticity is higher in the long run than in the short run because it takes time for car drivers to adjust their behavior to any sizable change in costs. Estimates of this elasticity vary widely, but a recent calculation of the long-run price elasticity for work trips is -0.51.[11] If so, a 10 percent rise in the price of gasoline would cause a 5.1 percent drop in gasoline consumption for work trips in the long run, though a much smaller fall in the short run. In late June 2003, unleaded premium gasoline was selling in the United States for an average price of $1.67 per gallon, including all taxes.[12] To get a 10 percent long-run drop in gasoline consumption for work trips, the government would have to raise the tax by 19.6 percent of the total price, or 32.7 cents per gallon. That would still leave the U.S. price far lower than gasoline prices in any of the other developed nations just discussed. If the price of gasoline was doubled to $3.34 per gallon, its consumption would—in theory—eventually drop by about 51 percent.[13] However, that seems to be an implausibly high estimate, given the dependence of American households on automotive vehicles.

Moreover, much higher gasoline prices would soon cause motorists to switch to cars getting better mileage. In the past decade, American consumers have flocked to ownership of gas-guzzling sport utility vehicles (SUVs), which are not subject to the same fuel consumption regulations as traditional passenger cars. In 2002, sales of light trucks (including SUVs) were 51.5 percent of the combined sales of light trucks and cars.[14] This emphasis might change if gasoline prices were much higher. Such a shift to more fuel-economical vehicles would reduce the long-run negative impact of higher gasoline prices on total driving. Even so, large increases in gasoline prices would probably be an effective method of reducing work trips, compared with many alternative policies. Many commuters might have difficulty switching from cars to transit, because the routes they travel are not well served by transit. But much higher gasoline costs might be still the most effective method of greatly increasing commuter ride sharing.

This tactic could not be implemented by a regional or a local agency. Substantial increases in gasoline prices would have to be achieved through higher federal gasoline taxes or increases in world oil prices caused by external factors, such as the Iraq war in 1991. If individual states raised their gas taxes far above those of nearby states, they would encourage large-scale out-of-state buying. Only a uniform national gasoline tax increase could avoid subregional price and market distortions.

However, Congress has decisively rejected all attempts to raise federal gasoline taxes designed to reduce driving, conserve fuel, or improve the environment by cutting air pollution. Powerful resistance from many citizens, the oil industry, the automobile industry, the road-building industry, and the trucking industry has motivated members of Congress to place preservation of low-cost fuel above these other goals. Congress has also refused to raise the fuel economy standards applicable to light trucks and SUVs to make them comparable to those in force for passenger cars, thereby further revealing the low priority Congress places on conserving fuel or reducing air pollution. Congress is not likely to change this behavior unless some type of crisis occurs.

Raising the Cost of Vehicle Ownership

Another tactic would be to increase the cost of owning a vehicle. In some nations, this is done through high sales or import taxes. In 1982, for example, Denmark charged a sales tax on a new midsized passenger car equal to 186 percent of the pretax price of the car.[15] In Singapore, potential car owners must buy an expensive license to purchase a vehicle. It costs 150 percent of the vehicle's open market value and is in addition to paying for the vehicle and for a 45 percent import duty on it. (This combined 200 percent surcharge can be reduced somewhat if the purchaser gets rid of an older existing car.) Furthermore, prospective new car buyers must bid annually for a certificate of entitlement, and it can cost as much as another $50,000.[16] Consequently, only 11 percent of the households there own private vehicles, compared with about 90 percent in the United States. However, Singapore does not permit true competition among its political parties; so its government—though elected—can impose such measures on the population without fear of their being contested by a rival political party.

U.S. authorities could also introduce high annual auto and light truck license fees, say, $500 to $1,000. This tactic would not focus on peak-hour driving alone; it would discourage all automotive vehicle travel. Such high ownership costs would therefore encourage ride sharing. But this tactic would be extremely unpopular in a nation where about 90 percent of all households own at least one car or light truck, and more than 50 percent own two or more. These cost-raising tactics would also require action at least at the state level.

"Cashing Out" Free Parking

Employers' provision of free parking is an enormous subsidy for workers to drive to work alone, especially if their workplaces are located where the market price of parking is high. In downtown districts where parking spaces cost up to $20 per day, free parking is a subsidy that hugely exceeds all the cash costs of driving, including fuel and vehicle expenses. Since American firms provide 84.8 million free parking spaces to their workers, there is a huge potential for reducing commuting by solo drivers through reducing the free parking bonanza.

However, simply prohibiting free parking is probably not politically possible, since it would remove a benefit from millions without providing any compensating gains. The most promising approach is pressuring or persuading employers to use "cash-out" programs. The employer offers employees a choice of receiving a free parking space or a money payment representing the cost of such a space to the employer. Employees who accept "cash outs" can then shift to public transit or car pooling instead of driving to work. This means employees who continue to drive to work are forgoing a cash benefit they could receive. Thus they are paying an implicit charge for formerly free parking. Employers supposedly break even because they have to furnish fewer parking spaces, thereby saving the cash they pay to those who cash out. Society gains from having fewer cars on the road and less air pollution. The California legislature passed a law in 1992 requiring all employers who rented parking spaces from third parties and provided them free to their employees to make such cash-outs available to their workers. This law has not been enforced, but enough experience has been accumulated to evaluate its potential effectiveness.[17]

Eight case studies involving employers in the Los Angeles region showed that, on the average, the number of solo drivers fell from 76 to 63 percent, or by 17 percent. The number of carpoolers rose 64 percent, and the number of public transit riders rose 50 percent. Vehicle miles traveled by private vehicles to the eight firms declined 12 percent. The firms' spending for commuting subsidies rose by $2 a month per employee. This program reduced traffic flows and air pollution and increased employer and employee satisfaction. Moreover, the program benefited the business districts where these firms were located by reducing the demand for parking there without reducing the number of persons commuting there. As Donald Shoup summarized this program, "Employer-paid parking is a matching grant for driving to work, and it stimulates solo driving. By converting this grant for driving into a block grant for commuting [in any form], cashing out employer-paid parking can neutralize a powerful and ubiquitous subsidy for the automobile."[18]

Taxing Parking during Peak Periods

Another method of raising parking costs is to place a surcharge on every vehicle parked during the morning peak hour. Those charges would hit commuting workers but not most shoppers or persons running errands. To be effective, parking surcharges would have to be large, especially on spaces provided free by employers. Otherwise they would not tip the balance of net commuting benefits away from driving alone to ride sharing or using transit. However, such a charge would certainly be viewed by the public and the providers of parking spaces as "another tax." Hence the politics of passing such a charge at the local or state level to reduce congestion is not favorable, given the large number of workers who now drive alone and enjoy free parking.

There are three significant differences between charging peak-hour prices on roads and on parking. First, although in the past it would have been technically easier to collect peak-hour fees on parking than on roads, today—thanks to electronic smart cards—it would probably be easier to collect road tolls. Collecting parking fees on the millions of parking spaces now provided free by employers might generate a whole new bureaucracy that further interfered with the activities of many organizations, especially small firms.

Second, higher parking fees would penalize all peak-hour auto commuters, regardless of their travel routes. In contrast, road pricing would penalize only those commuters who used those roads on which peak-hour tolls were charged. In this respect, parking charges would seemingly be more effective at discouraging peak-hour commuting.

However, parking fees would be levied against only some of the vehicles using formerly congested toll roads during peak hours, whereas road pricing would charge all such vehicles. Parking charges would miss long-distance trucks or other vehicles making trips through a region, plus drivers running errands that did not require long parking. Yet such non-work-oriented trips constitute 50.8 percent of all morning peak period trips. Hence peak-hour parking fees would have no impact on half of morning peak-period traffic. Furthermore, even if parking fees caused some solo drivers to shift to transit or ride sharing, any space they made available on previously congested expressways would soon be filled by other drivers converging from other routes, times, or modes.

Another issue engendered by peak-hour parking fees is what should be done with the money raised. High parking fees would be more politically acceptable if those paying them believed the money would be used to improve transportation systems in the areas where they were collected.

To affect commuting throughout a metropolitan area, such parking charges would have to be implemented everywhere therein. Although the specific surcharges used in different subregions need not be identical, they should bear some rational relationship to one another. Thus parking charges in areas with the greatest congestion should be higher than those in areas with light congestion. But it may be difficult to achieve such coordination without instituting some complex administrative process for dealing with thousands of parking providers throughout the metropolitan area. If the rules, regulations, and general schedules of parking surcharges were uniform over the entire area, however, administration and enforcement could be delegated to local governments. Thus only setting the rules, regulations, and general fee schedules, and supervising their implementation, would require a regional authority.

Because of the coverage inefficiency, administrative complexity, and likely political unpopularity of peak-hour parking fees, they do not represent a very promising way to discourage solo drivers from commuting.

Ending Tax Deductibility

A milder form of reducing free parking for solo-driving commuters would be to end the income tax deductibility of all employer expenses connected with providing such parking. That would include capital and operating expenses for building and maintaining parking spaces used by solo commuters. This change would encourage business firms to reduce free parking for solo drivers.

Greater Use of Transit

Persuading more people to switch from driving to using transit could greatly reduce congestion, even if the transit consisted of buses using now-congested roadways. (This aspect of influencing demand is discussed in chapter 9.)

Intelligent Transportation Systems

Intelligent transportation systems (ITS) comprise several systems of electronic sensing, computing, and communications for managing traffic flows on major highways. Beginning in fiscal year 1991, the Federal Highway Administration has spent more than $1 billion on federal research and development grants for these systems.[19] In July 2002, the Senate Appropriations Committee approved a budget of $232 million for ITS activities in fiscal 2003.[20] One source claims, "Since 1991 when Congress endorsed a drive toward intelligent transportation systems, $8.5 billion has been funneled toward government-backed technology projects, such as toll collection, automated traffic monitoring and computer-assisted dispatch networks for emergency crews."[21]

Clearly, significant amounts have been, and are being, spent on developing various types of ITS. ITS encompasses the following basic high-technology approaches to improving traffic flows.[22]

—Travel and transportation management, as exemplified by the transportation management centers discussed in chapter 7. This includes advanced traffic management systems (ATMS) that gather information electronically on congestion and flow conditions from many points of a highway network. They feed the information to a control center, which analyzes it and adjusts traffic signals, ramp entry controls, and lane direction controls throughout the system to reduce delays.

—Travel demand management is aimed at decreasing travel in single-occupant vehicles and improving travelers' route and timing decisions by providing pretrip and real-time information. Advanced traveler information systems (ATIS) gather traffic data but feed the information to individual drivers before they leave home or as they commute so they can adjust routes and timing to prevailing conditions.

—Public transportation operations provide better information to transit users and transit operators.

—Electronic payment enables people to pay for transportation services, tolls, and facilities through smart cards.

—Commercial vehicle operations facilitate interstate trucking by using electronic data to substitute for paperwork, weighing trucks without slowing them down, and monitoring hazardous materials shipments. This tactic also includes improving communications among drivers and their offices to make truck deliveries more efficient and better adapted to current market conditions.

—Emergency management facilitates quick notification of authorities and rapid responses to emergencies.

—Advanced vehicle control and safety systems increase the throughput capacity of roads by using collision warning devices, automatic braking, and even automated highway systems that control vehicle movements rather than having drivers do so.

The concept underlying advanced traffic management systems and advanced traveler information systems is that better information about current traffic conditions during peak hours will enable traffic managers and individual travelers to make more efficient decisions that will in turn reduce congestion. This concept is probably valid to some extent. Quick responses could help avoid the traffic jams caused by the accidents and other unpredictable incidents that occur every day. But peak-hour traffic congestion is not caused by a lack of information. It is caused by too many people traveling at the same time on the same roads, mainly alone in private vehicles. Most are well aware that they will encounter congestion, but that does not stop them. Improving information about where congestion is worst will not necessarily reduce peak-hour overloading. Drivers informed that route A is unusually crowded will shift to route B, overcrowding it too. All this means that heavy investment in improving drivers' and traffic managers' information is unlikely to reduce overall peak-hour congestion very much.

One exception has been the experience of the Seattle region in combining ramp metering with traveler information and real-time management of freeway signs and nearby traffic lights. Seattle's integrated overall system of managing information and vehicle flows has notably reduced peak-hour commuting times and increased throughputs on several major roadways.

Some experts believe advanced vehicle control systems might prove more useful in the very long run if the systems could enable vehicles moving at high speeds to travel closer together, thus increasing highway capacity. However, unless the capacities of local streets at the exits of such roads were greatly expanded, delivering two or three times as many vehicles per hour to those that exist would simply cause massive traffic backups on both local streets and automated freeways. Yet expanding local street capacities to match the—in theory—increased throughput capacities of automated freeways is virtually impossible in most heavily built-up areas like major downtowns and business districts. Doing so would be too costly and disruptive of existing structures to be feasible. Moreover, if throughputs on freeways were increased from present approximate maximums of 2,000 vehicles per hour to 4,000-6,000 per hour, any major crash might involve hundreds of vehicles and people and cause horrendous damage and injuries. Who would bear the legal liabilities for such events is unclear. But in our litigious society, answering that question to the satisfaction of the major participants, public and private, would be a critical prerequisite to adopting such a technology. Finally, the cost of creating "automated highways" over any significant portion of even just the interstate system would be enormous. These practical objections indicate that advanced vehicle control systems in the form of high-speed automated highways are not likely to be feasible on a large scale for at least several decades, if ever. However, some individual components—such as collision warning devices for individual vehicles—might prove usable much sooner.

These conclusions do not mean that all smart highway systems are useless or not worth supporting. But they do imply that similar amounts of money, or perhaps even less, spent on implementing peak-hour road pricing or parking fees would have much more powerful—and immediate—effects in reducing peak-hour congestion. Because most ITS concepts are still unproven in practice and may take years to establish, they will not be considered further in this book.

Conclusions

Nine demand-side tactics for reducing peak-hour traffic congestion have been analyzed in this chapter. Three are primarily regulatory, four primarily market based, one is informational, and the ninth consists of a bundle of technological tactics. Each regulatory tactic—changing work hours, encouraging telecommuting, and encouraging ride sharing—appears to have only limited potential for reducing peak-hour trips. None is likely to decrease such trips initially by more than 5-7 percent, although together they might cause a 10-15 percent initial decrease. But any initial reductions they caused would soon be partly offset by triple convergence. So their net long-run impacts on peak-hour congestion would be even smaller.

The four market-based tactics would raise the costs of driving during peak hours, either for all drivers—as with higher gasoline taxes or auto license fees—or for all commuting drivers—as with peak-hour parking fees—or for all drivers using toll roads—as with peak-hour road pricing. If these cost increases were big enough, they could make it too expensive for many commuters to continue driving alone during peak hours. That would divert more peak-hour trips to other times or eliminate more trips altogether than could the regulatory tactics. But that effectiveness would also hurt low-income commuters more than high-income ones, unless some compensation were paid to the former. Furthermore, only road pricing would avoid the possibility that some convergence would offset initial traffic-flow gains.

However, all four market-based tactics are politically unacceptable for most citizens and officials, precisely because they would impose large added direct monetary costs on peak-hour travel. The higher those costs, the more effective these tactics and the greater the political resistance to them. So advocates of these tactics face major marketing and persuasion tasks before they can get them adopted.

Two of the market-based tactics would probably require regional legal and administrative authority. Two others, higher gasoline taxes or license fees, could only be achieved through state or federal government action. The regulatory tactics would also need regional authority if they were mandatory throughout a metropolitan area. However, they might be administered by local governments or private firms without becoming completely ineffective, something not true of the market-based tactics.

The last tactic analyzed is intelligent transportation systems, a set of diverse actions aimed mainly at better managing information flows within traffic management systems and between those systems and vehicle drivers. Some of these devices have already proved useful in reducing peak-hour congestion, for example, the information flows used to operate ramp management on commuter freeways. Others have some possibility of marginally aiding in coping with peak-hour congestion. But futuristic visions of automated highways or other purely technological "cures" will most likely retain their present status as utopian urban myths.

CHAPTER 12

Remedies That
Increase Densities

A principal cause of the massive amount of daily travel in nearly every U.S. metropolitan area is the low density of residential and other settlements there. Because housing and jobs are spread over such a broad territory, people have to drive long distances to commute and perform other daily tasks. Therefore, many commentators have suggested combating congestion by increasing densities, especially for housing. Moreover, creating higher densities is a central tenet of the entire "smart growth" movement that has grown up across America as a reaction to the perceived ills of "suburban sprawl." One of the most widely deplored of those ills is rising traffic congestion. Therefore, two crucial questions are as follows: can urban and suburban densities be significantly increased in the future? And if densities could be increased, how might that affect traffic congestion?

Social Benefits of Higher Density in Areas of New Growth

Settling areas of future growth at higher average densities than in the past could produce the following social benefits:
—Reduced total movements required by the population. This could have several ancillary benefits, such as reducing

energy consumption, decreasing air pollution, and lowering traffic congestion. The last two would not necessarily follow from higher density, since they also depend on other conditions.

—Reduced costs of building infrastructure trunk lines. Examples are major sewer, water, highway, and utility lines. Estimates of the trunk-line cost savings from having higher density future development run into billions of dollars per year nationwide.[1]

—Increased feasibility of using public transit for commuting. Greater use of public transit would reduce total energy consumption and air pollution and could reduce traffic congestion under some conditions. It would also offer more travel choices to persons not able to use their own private vehicles.

—Greater feasibility of building relatively low-cost housing. Medium-density housing units (low-rise apartments) are less expensive to develop than high-rise or low-density single-family units.

—An increased sense of community among residents. Many urban theorists believe that if people lived closer together and could more easily interact in public spaces without using automobiles, they would develop much more intensive feelings of social solidarity and of belonging to a community. This is a controversial conclusion difficult to test empirically, but it is an oft-cited justification of the "smart growth" movement.[2]

Only the first three benefits are directly related to traffic congestion, so the last two are not analyzed in this book.

These potential benefits can be assessed by comparing two ways of developing areas of new growth: first, at the average densities now prevailing in the metropolitan areas concerned, and second, at notably higher densities. The term *density* as used here refers to gross residential density. It means the total number of residents per square mile, counting all the land used for any purposes in measuring each territory's area. This is different from net residential density. The latter is the number of dwelling units per acre of land actually used for residential purposes excluding streets and all nonresidential land.[3]

The Marginality Problem

All strategies that raise residential densities suffer from one major drawback: they might influence additional future settlement patterns, but they would leave existing settlements largely unchanged. Because the latter are already in place, it would cost far too much to alter them extensively. Although some demolition of existing structures and subsequent redevelopment on their sites will occur in every metropolitan area, the vast majority of homes and workplaces that will exist ten years from today—perhaps even twenty years—are already there and will not be removed or drastically altered. Most additional housing units and workplaces will be built around the periphery of these existing settlements. It will be difficult for any locational tactics to have much effect on the movement patterns within such existing settlements.

It is especially difficult to change existing *average* residential densities. For example, if a metropolitan area containing 1 million persons has an average current density of 3,000 persons per square mile, it occupies 333.3 square miles. (The average gross population density of the 50 largest urbanized areas in the United States in 2000 was 3,116 persons per square mile.) Of the 335 U.S. metropolitan statistical areas in 2000, the 10 that grew fastest from 1990 to 2000 had an average overall growth of 51.8 percent in that decade, or 4.26 per year compounded.[4] If this hypothetical area grew at the same rapid rate, it would gain 518,000 persons in ten years. Most would settle in newly built communities around the periphery of previously built-up settlements.

If the entire increase in population settled in new growth areas at a density double that of the initial sections (that is, 6,000 persons per square mile), they would occupy 86.3 additional square miles. The entire settlement would then cover 419.6 square miles, with an average overall density of 3,617 persons per square mile. That represents a 21 percent increase in the whole region's average density in a decade from a 51.8 percent increase in its population. What would it take to get a 50 percent increase in regional density (to 4,500 persons per square mile) within ten years with a 5 percent compound annual population growth rate (higher than the growth rate of all but one U.S. metropolitan area in the 1990s), if all population gains were in areas of new growth? All those new areas would have to be settled at a gross density of about 22,000 persons per square mile. That is 83 percent of the average density of New York City as of 2000. That outcome is extremely unlikely.

Why not raise residential densities in existing older areas too? As already mentioned, tearing down existing structures and building new, higher-density ones is very costly. Remodeling is less costly but cannot increase densities as much. And residents of every existing neighborhood nearly always oppose major changes there, of whatever type. Hence they will strongly resist increasing densities in or near them, and they have the political power to do so. Consequently, local governments are not likely to permit substantial increases in density in existing neighborhoods, as proven by experience across the nation. The only exception concerns up-zoning in neighborhoods near downtowns.

What about developing empty in-fill sites? Some studies have estimated that as much as 10 percent of the land within settled portions of metropolitan areas is vacant and might therefore be considered for in-fill construction. If 10 percent of the original 333.3 square miles in this hypothetical community is vacant, that would be a total of 33.3 square miles. Not all that land could be redeveloped with housing; some of it would have to be used for additional streets, schools, and other uses. Other vacant parcels would be unsuitable for residential use because of topographic or other obstacles. If 60 percent of all that vacant land (20.0 square miles)—was developed with housing at a density of 10,000 persons per square mile—more than triple the density in the rest of the region—such in-fill development could accommodate 200,000 additional residents. Such a density would require at least three-to-six-story multifamily structures. Then 1.2 million persons would live in 333.3 square miles, for an average overall density of 3,600 persons per square mile, or 20 percent more than in the original situation. However, this outcome would require residents living near all that vacant land to accept densities next door that were much higher than those in their own neighborhoods. So increases in overall density of this magnitude purely from in-fill development represent a theoretically possible but highly improbable maximum possible attainment. If the same in-fill sites were developed at average densities of 6,000 persons per square mile—double the average density in the rest of the region—the resulting increase in the region's overall density would be from 3,000 to 3,360 persons per square mile, or 12 percent. In neither case would average densities in the whole region even be close to what is required to make public transit economically feasible. However, in some smaller portions of the region, "spot densities" would undoubtedly be high enough that those portions could be feasibly served by public transit.

In short, it is extremely difficult to increase substantially the average density of an entire metropolitan area—including existing settlements—through marginal growth or new in-fill development.

Higher Densities for Future Growth

Higher average densities in new-growth areas help to reduce the need for movement generated by future population growth. They do so by accommodating that growth in a smaller added area than would be possible if development continued at the present average density. Consequently, the new residents would have to travel shorter distances to accomplish their normal tasks of living. That would reduce total energy consumed in traveling. Whether additional benefits from less travel would accrue depends on other factors. Less total travel would clearly reduce the total amount of air pollutants emitted. Whether this would in turn reduce effective air pollution would depend on locally prevailing ambient air conditions in the given area. Similarly, lower total miles driven might reduce traffic congestion under some circumstances.

DIFFERENTIATING BETWEEN REGIONAL AND LOCAL CONGESTION. Both traffic congestion and air pollution in certain neighborhoods would be greater in areas newly settled at high densities than in those settled at lower densities because more vehicles would be owned and used per square mile. However, people living in very high-density settlements typically own fewer vehicles per household, and use transit more often, than those living in low-density settlements. So there is some offset to having more households per square mile. Moreover, under some climatic conditions, air pollutants generated in a small area remain there for considerable periods. It is easy for residents to conclude—erroneously—that regional congestion and air pollution would also be worse with higher average density. This argument is often used by local residents opposing nearby increases in density. But both air pollution and traffic congestion often spread from their points of origin to other parts of a region. Therefore, the regional levels of these maladies are just as important to society as a whole, and perhaps more so, than their local levels.

REDUCING THE COSTS OF BUILDING INFRASTRUCTURE. Higher densities tend to shorten the trunk lines required to supply areas of new growth with major urban infrastructure. Trunk lines are the main channels through which utilities are delivered to each neighborhood from central stations, such as sewer treatment plants, water works, or electric generation plants. Trunk lines also include expressways and other arteries joining the main subregions of the metropolitan area. In each neighborhood, local feeder systems connect trunk lines to individual housing

TABLE 12-1. Traits of New Additions to a Metropolitan Area,
Three Density Assumptions[a]

Traits of the new area	Density of added population per square mile				
	2,000	3,000	5,000	7,500	10,000
Square miles added	140	93	56	37	28
Percent added to original area	42.0	28.0	16.8	11.2	8.4
Total square miles in metropolitan area	473.38	426.70	389.35	370.68	361.34
New radius of metropolitan area (miles)	12.28	11.65	11.13	10.86	10.72
Percentage radius added	19.2	13.15	8.08	5.46	4.12
New average metropolitan density	2,704	3,000	3,288	3,453	3,543
Percent change in average density	−9.9	0.0	9.6	15.1	18.1

Source: Author's calculations based on U.S. Bureau of the Census, 2000 Census, STF3, detailed tables (www.factfinder.census.gov [November 2003]).

a. Assumes initial population of 1 million, average initial density of 3,000 persons per square mile, and an area of 333.3 square miles in a circular shape. See text.

units or commercial facilities. Changes in average population density do not greatly affect the costs per housing unit or commercial square foot of local feeder facilities. But they do reduce the total areas served by trunk lines—and hence the costs of building them.[5]

This benefit arises from the geometry of circles and the fact that many metropolitan areas are roughly circular in shape. The formula relating a circle's area to its radius is: area = pi * (radius)^2. Population density is related to the area of a territory, whereas the length of trunk lines is related to its radius. Therefore, increasing the radius of a circle by any given percentage increases its area by a much larger percentage.

The significance for trunk-line costs can be seen from the same hypothetical metropolitan area initially containing 1 million residents within a circular settlement at an average density of 3,000 persons per square mile. The residents occupy a circle containing 333.3 square miles; its radius is 10.3 miles. If the area's population expands 2.5 percent a year (compounded), in ten years it will have a total population of 1,280,085. Assuming the area contains a circular shape, how big it will become depends on the average density of added development. The greater that density, the smaller the added area. But the length of the radius will increase proportionately less than its total area (table 12-1).

The higher the density of this marginal growth, the shorter the radial trunk lines would have to be. Thus, if the marginal density is established at a low 2,000 persons per square mile, existing trunk lines would have to expand 19.2 percent to reach the outermost regions. But if the density were 10,000 persons per square mile, those lines would have to grow only 4.1 percent.

These hypothetical calculations are admittedly too precise. No metropolitan area is perfectly circular, nor does it expand outward in all directions at exactly the same rate. In fact, many are next to bodies of water or mountains that block all growth in certain directions. Nevertheless, the basic idea that high density permits lower-cost infrastructure trunk lines is valid.

DENSITY OF NEW GROWTH AREAS AND AVERAGE COMMUTING DISTANCES. Appendix D presents a detailed spatial analysis of the relationships between settlement densities and average commuting distances. It leads to the following important conclusions:

One, differing density levels in new growth areas have relatively limited impacts on overall commuting distances because most of every metropolitan area's future settlement has already been built. Unless a metropolitan area grows very rapidly, most of whatever development will be there in twenty years is already there. So influencing the density of the areas added through growth will mainly affect traffic patterns in those new areas, rather than in the entire metropolitan area.

Two, average commuting distances will be much longer within new growth areas built at very low densities than in those built at medium or high densities. This is true even though low-density areas will contain more job sites than higher-density areas, because the former are spread out more. The model in appendix D shows that a large exurban area (defined as an outer suburban area, where new growth takes place) settled at 2,885 residents per square mile generates an average one-way commuting distance for exurban residents alone of 10.94 miles, which is 38 percent shorter than the 17.66 miles generated by a similar exurban settlement having only 312 persons per square mile. Reducing the daily commuting of such residents by 38 percent over a long period would substantially cut the total miles traveled within a major U.S. metropolitan area. This is especially true in areas experiencing rapid population growth. New growth areas there will contain a considerable fraction of the total populations of such regions by the end of the next two decades.

The exact percentage just cited is not important, for it is the result of a hypothetical model based on somewhat arbitrary assumptions. But this general conclusion has important implications for total national energy consumption.

Three, the percentage reduction in average commuting distances achieved by raising residential densities is much smaller than the percentage increases in densities needed to achieve it. The 38 percent reduction in average exurban commuting distance just mentioned resulted from an 825 percent increase in exurban residential density. Another simulation showed that more than tripling exurban densities would cut average exurban commuting distance less than 22 percent. One reason is that low-density settlement patterns also generate more widely dispersed job locations. Those scattered job sites reduce commuting distances for exurban residents, in spite of considerable cross commuting.[6] This means that cutting average commuting distances significantly by changing densities in areas of new growth requires extremely large increases in density there. Small density changes will not have an appreciable effect on average commuting distance—even that of exurban workers alone.

Four, the biggest impacts of changing densities on average commuting distances are caused by moving from very low to medium densities, rather than from medium to very high densities. Thus moving from 1,000 to 5,000 persons per square mile would cut average commuting distances much more than moving from 5,000 to 10,000 persons per square mile, even though the absolute increase in density is greater in the second case. The reason lies in the basic way circular metropolitan areas grow. If 1 million persons resided in a perfectly circular metropolitan area, its radius would be 17.84 miles at a density of 1,000 persons per square mile, 7.98 miles at a density of 5,000 persons, and 5.64 miles at a density of 10,000 persons. The overall radial difference between the lowest-density case and the highest-density one is 12.20 miles. But 81 percent of that difference lies in going from a density of 1,000 to a density of 5,000; only 19 percent lies in going from 5,000 to 10,000. Thus to conserve energy and shorten total travel, it is more important to avoid having new growth occur at very low densities than to have such growth occur at very high densities.

Five, reducing average commuting distances does not necessarily translate into reducing traffic congestion, although it may. Relatively long average commuting distances will not generate intensive traffic congestion if they occur in very low-density areas well served with expressways and other roads, employment sites in those areas are dispersed enough so that many workers do not converge on a few job centers or a few highway bottlenecks, and the absolute number of daily commuters does not greatly exceed the road system's capacity to handle them. Furthermore, since commuting trips constitute less than half of all peak-hour trips in the morning and evening, changes in those trips affect only part of the causes of congestion.

Six, holding residential densities in peripheral areas of new growth above very low levels can contribute significantly to reduced traffic congestion there, but only if certain other conditions are present.

Increasing the Feasibility of Using Mass Transit

Another potential benefit of higher density is that it makes greater use of public transit for commuting more feasible. If more workers shifted from private vehicles to buses or rapid transit systems, peak-hour traffic congestion would decline. An important 1977 study conducted by Boris Pushkarev and Jeffrey Zupan, *Public Transportation and Land Use Policy*, has concluded that the amount of transit patronage generated by the population living in any urban area depends on two sets of factors.[7]

One set concerns the characteristics of the residential area, including population density, incidence of automobile ownership among residents, their income levels, age, and average household size, proximity to the central business district and the nearest other major business district, and absolute size of those districts. The greater all of these variables except automobile ownership and age, the greater the propensity of local residents to use public transit, other things equal.[8]

The second set of factors relates to the public transportation serving the area, including proximity of the nearest rapid transit station, frequency of transit service, per trip price, speed, other amenities it offers, and whether there is commuter rail service to the area. The greater all of these variables except trip cost, the greater the propensity of residents to use public transit, other things equal.[9] Specific quantitative relationships among these many variables are myriad, varied, and complex. Consequently, separate estimates of transit usage must be calculated for each specific area.

A recent study in the St. Louis region compared those census tracts in which transit work trips were made by more than 10 percent of commuting workers with those in which transit work trips were made by fewer than 10 percent.[10] Similar analyses were done for census data from 1990 and 2000. In both years, 86 census tracts had high transit usage; they constituted 19 percent of all tracts in 1990 and 17 percent in 2000. The average density of these high-transit-usage tracts was 4,899 persons per square mile in 1990 and 3,831 in 2000. Those densities were notably greater than the densities of all the tracts composing the region's "core area" containing 78.5 percent of its total population, which were 2,771 persons per square mile in 1990 and 2,564 in 2000.

TABLE 12-2. Public Transit Use and Other Characteristics of Residents of St. Louis Region
Percent unless noted otherwise

Characteristic	High-transit usage tracts	Core-area tracts	Region as a whole
Work trips by public transit	16.9	3.1	2.6
Share of total population (2000)	10.9	78.5	100.0
Share of total area	1.5	16.6	100.0
Resident households with no vehicles	31.7	10.2	9.2
Poverty rate	31.6	10.6	9.9
Unemployment rate	16.2	5.8	5.5
Vacancy rate	20.2	7.4	7.2
Female-headed households	53.2	22.4	20.3
Median value of owner-occupied housing units (dollars)	56,160	116,884	116,864
Median household income (dollars)	22,889	46,573	47,164
Persons per household	2.53	2.47	2.51
Residents 65 and over	12.6	13.3	12.9
Average commuting time in minutes	27.5	24.5	25.4

Source: See table 12-1.

Comparisons of certain other traits as of 2000 among these 86 tracts, the 399 tracts containing the region's core area (which include some of the 86 tracts), and the region as a whole are shown in table 12-2. These data show that the high-transit-usage tracts contained much lower-income households than the region as a whole, with several other traits related to their low-income status. However, they had almost the same average commuting time as the region as a whole.

According to the 1995 *Nationwide Personal Transportation Survey*, the percentage of persons who said there was some form of public transit available near them varied directly with the population density of their communities. That fraction ranged from 24 percent in areas with under 500 persons per square mile to 73 percent where density was 2,000 to 3,999, 88 percent where it was 4,000 to 9,999, and 98 percent where it was 10,000 or more.[11]

As noted in chapter 9, a regression with the percentage of all metropolitan area commuters using transit in 2000 as the dependent variable and four independent variables had an adjusted r-squared of 0.874, or 0.800 without New York. Central city population density was by far the most powerful independent variable.[12]

The earlier study on public transportation and land use policy by Pushkarev and Zupan also arrived at several pertinent conclusions as follows:

ɡ the quality or quantity of public transportation service
tential for reducing traffic congestion, compared with
ᴜomobile usage or changing urban densities.

—Residential densities do affect public transit usage. At residential densities below seven housing units per net acre (or gross densities under 4,200 to 5,600 persons per square mile), public transit use is minimal. It increases sharply at densities above seven units per net acre. Therefore, "moderate residential densities in the range of 7 to 15 dwellings per acre can support moderately convenient transit service" (by rapid transit, buses, and taxis).[13]

—In generating transit usage, the residential density of an area is less significant than its location. Residential areas near large downtown areas generate much higher fractions of transit trips than those with the same densities but farther out. Moreover, areas within 2,000 feet of rapid transit stops exhibit much higher fractions of transit usage than those farther from such stops. Therefore, clustering high-density housing in relatively small areas near downtowns or rapid transit stops is more effective at increasing public transportation usage than raising average residential densities over large areas.

—The density of nonresidential clusters—such as large shopping centers or business districts—is much more important in generating public transportation usage than residential density, other things equal. Hence clustering many nonresidential land uses close together would be more effective at promoting public transportation usage than raising residential densities but keeping commercial space dispersed. However, commercial nodes need 10 million square feet of nonresidential space or more to generate much public transportation usage. Moreover, to make bus service effective there, that space must be concentrated within not much more than a single square mile.

—Sizable outlying shopping centers can support intermediate-quality bus service if the surrounding residential areas have net densities of 7 housing units per acre or higher. "Intermediate service" means one-half mile route spacing and about 40 buses per day, or one at least every half-hour. If 50 percent of the land is used for housing (excluding streets) and the average household size is 2.5 persons, then 7 units per net acre is equivalent to 5,600 persons per square mile.[14]

—"The most important policies necessary to control rapidly rising transit costs are not in the area of land use, but rather in the area of labor relations" by keeping labor costs down. This is true because

70–85 percent of the operating and maintenance costs of public transportation are labor costs.

—Rather general relationships between residential densities and the feasibility of specific types of public transportation can be identified, although they are subject to great individual variation. By and large, these relationships imply that local bus service is feasible in even relatively low-density residential communities, at the "minimum" service level of twenty buses per day at one-half mile route spacing; express buses are feasible in many medium-sized cities if they are linked to park-and-ride facilities; and fixed-rail services of all types are feasible only if they converge on relatively large downtowns. Rapid transit and commuter rail require particularly large downtown business districts.

—At least two major shifts in public policy could enhance the prospects for increasing use of public transportation for commuting. One is to prohibit the spread of new office buildings and multifamily housing through low-density areas. The second is to put more emphasis on taxing land and less on taxing improvements to encourage higher-density development.

CLUSTERING HIGH-DENSITY HOUSING NEAR SUBURBAN TRANSIT STOPS. Clustering high-density housing near rapid transit stops could substantially increase public transportation usage. Many households living within 2,000 feet of a rapid transit stop would be willing to walk to the stop and use the transportation provided there for daily trips, including commuting trips. That would reduce automobile usage by those households. Some urban designers have therefore proposed small, high-density pedestrian-oriented settlements served by fixed-rail transit, called "pedestrian pockets" or "transit-oriented developments."[15]

However, there is an inherent conflict between two methods of increasing transit usage by influencing what is developed around outlying transit stops, especially those on fixed-rail or light-rail systems.[16] On one hand, many transit operators would like to maximize the number of riders who drive to the stop, park there, and ride the transit trains. Since this approach can tap potential riders from a large surrounding territory, it could produce big gains in ridership. But it requires closely surrounding each stop with many parking spaces. On the other hand, urban designers promoting transit-oriented neighborhoods want to create high-density residential and commercial uses within walking distance of the transit stop. This requires surrounding each stop with relatively high-density housing and commercial structures not consistent with open parking lots.

Achieving both these goals simultaneously would be desirable. Doing so would require using the ground floors along walking paths to the station for retail and other interesting activities to maintain an attractive ambience for pedestrians living nearby. Hence the high-density structures for housing or commercial uses would have to be on top of underground parking designed to accommodate drive-in transit users. Or the parking for drive-in transit users could be structured parking above other ground-floor uses. But both those compromises require very costly construction that reduces the economic feasibility of the entire development. This conflict makes creation of effective transit-oriented development much more complex and difficult than pursuing either of these approaches without the other. That is one reason why so few effective transit-oriented developments have been built.

How effective such clustering might be in reducing suburban automotive traffic congestion is discussed in appendix E. The calculations there show that even extremely extensive suburban rapid transit systems serving many high-density housing clusters near their stops would carry only relatively small fractions of all suburban commuters. Creating high-density housing clusters around suburban rapid transit stops would also produce relatively small reductions in traffic congestion, compared with the economic and political efforts required to build and maintain the transit systems and create high-density clusters around each suburban stop.

A REVERSED CAUSALITY RELATIONSHIP BETWEEN TRANSIT USE AND DENSITY. Most of the links just discussed involve the effects of varied residential densities on public transit usage. But causality sometimes flows in the opposite direction. When many commuters into a business district use public transit, developers may be motivated to increase the district's nonresidential density. For example, when a new public transit system is built serving a downtown, more people can commute there without causing any greater peak-hour roadway congestion—hence without raising average commuting times. Yet commuting times influence workers' choices of where to live and work. If more workers can reach downtown in the same commuting time as before, more will want to work there. The suggestion that this may justify developers' building more office space or other facilities there is borne out by the huge expansion of office space in the downtowns of both San

Francisco and Washington after the construction of mass transit serving them.[17]

Consequently, one way to strengthen the market for office and other space within a business center is to build more off-road transit facilities to serve it. That is undoubtedly why downtown business interests so strongly support construction of new fixed-rail transit systems, especially if they can obtain federal subsidies to cover much of the costs. Portland, Oregon, is a striking example of this relationship. Its city officials have deliberately promoted new light rail systems in part to strengthen the region's downtown. This relationship also holds for residential densities, especially in outlying locations. Thus the better the public transit service to a residential neighborhood, the higher the density of housing that can be supported there, other things being equal. That is why high-density housing clusters have appeared around mass transit stops in Toronto and Arlington County, Virginia. Persons living there can commute by transit during peak hours without encountering highway congestion, and more people are encouraged to live near such transit stops than would live in those areas if the stops did not exist. However, for this relationship to bear fruit, local residents must permit previously low-density development near transit stops to be converted to higher-density development.

Existing U.S. Residential Density Variations by Geographic Areas

Whether greater transit usage can realistically be encouraged by raising existing residential densities depends greatly on how high those densities are to start with. Residential densities within U.S. metropolitan areas vary enormously.[18] These variations are partly related to the periods in which various U.S. regions were first settled. Large, older cities established long before automobiles became the dominant form of ground transportation tend to have much higher densities than newer settlements created since that time. Since this chapter focuses on areas of new growth, the data of most concern pertain to suburban areas.

The Census Bureau has delineated 476 urbanized areas as of 2000; each contains at least 50,000 residents in a central city (a few have more than one central city) and in relatively developed "fringe areas" lying outside those cities.[19] Urbanized areas differ from larger metropolitan areas because the former contain only territory settled at relatively high densities, compared with the sparsely settled farmland, rural areas, and mountainous or desert terrain that make up a large part of many metropolitan areas. The fringe portions of urbanized areas are where most population growth and other urban development occurs.

The 50 largest urbanized areas in 2000 contained 127.7 million residents, or 45.4 percent of the entire nation's population. They had a combined overall density (their total population divided by their total area) of 3,307 persons per square mile. About one-third of the total population of these urbanized areas lived in their central cities, although those cities encompassed only 26 percent of the total land area. Thus central cities had a 51 percent higher overall average density (4,305 persons per square mile) than their fringe areas (2,858 persons per square mile).[20]

Fringe-area densities among these 50 urbanized areas range from a high of 7,559 persons per square mile in the San Jose area to a low of 1,133 persons per square mile in the Charlotte area.[21] (Fringe area densities do not go much below 1,000 persons per square mile because the Census Bureau excludes settlements with much lower densities from its definitions of urbanized areas.) However, very few fringe areas have relatively high densities. Only 5 out of these 50 largest areas had fringe densities in 2000 exceeding 5,000 persons per square mile: San Jose, Los Angeles-Long Beach, San Francisco-Oakland, Salt Lake City, and Kansas City.

These 5 urbanized areas contained 18.6 million people, of which 12.4 million lived in their fringe areas. But the other 85 percent of the fringe-area residents of 50 largest urbanized areas lived in fringes with densities less than 5,000 persons per square mile. The overall distribution of fringe-area populations among all of these 50 urbanized areas by gross densities (including the five areas above) is shown in table 12-3.

It is clear from these data that the vast majority of persons living in the fringe areas of these 50 urbanized areas inhabit relatively low-density settlements. More than half are in fringes with densities under 3,000 persons per square mile, which normally means less than 3.75 to 5.00 dwelling units per net residential acre.[22] Three-quarters live in fringe areas with average densities of less than 4,000 persons per square mile, which normally means less than 5.0 to 6.7 dwelling units per net residential acre. Only 10.6 percent live where densities are greater than 5,000 persons per square mile, which normally means more than 6.25 to 8.33 dwelling units per net residential acre. Yet these are the largest urbanized areas in the nation, containing the highest-density central

TABLE 12-3. Distribution of Fringe-Area Populations

Persons per square mile	Number of urbanized areas	Total fringe area population (millions)	Percent of fringe area population
Under 2,000	9	9.3	11.2
2,000 to 2,999	19	34.4	41.6
3,000 to 3,999	8	18.5	22.3
4,000 to 4,999	4	8.1	9.9
5,000 to 5,999	3	3.7	4.4
6,000 to 7,499	1	8.1	9.8
7,500 to 9,999	1	0.6	0.8
10,000 and over	0	0	0
Totals	45	82.7	100.0

Source: See table 12-1.

cities—and most of the highest-density fringe areas. In 2000, 43 U.S. cities containing over 50,000 residents—out of 601 such cities—had gross densities of 10,000 persons per square mile or more; all 43 of those cities are located in these 50 urbanized areas. Thus densities in the remaining 426 urbanized areas in 2000 were, by and large, lower than those shown in table 12-3.

True, even if an entire fringe area has an overall density of under 3,000 persons per square mile, several portions of it may have much higher densities. Many individual suburbs in fringe areas do have higher densities, and many suburbs with low overall densities contain individual high-density neighborhoods. This is clear from data on specific metropolitan areas. The distribution of suburban densities in various urbanized areas is shown in table 12-4. This table breaks down the total suburban population of various urbanized areas by residential density groups, from under 2,000 persons per square mile to 10,000 persons or more per square mile. (The whole population of each municipality is classified in the density group containing that city's average density, even though parts of that city may have densities quite different from its average.) The percentage of each area's total population in each of these density groups is indicated in the last column under each area heading.

Surprisingly, the Los Angeles-Long Beach metropolitan area—consisting of Los Angeles County—has the highest average suburban population density of any U.S. metropolitan area, even though that region is widely perceived as the most "sprawling" of all U.S. regions.[23] Figure 12-1 shows data for the California urbanized areas in graphic form. The differences in density distributions among these California regions are

TABLE 12-4. Suburban Densities in Selected Urbanized Areas, 2000[a]

Region and density (persons/square mile)	Number of cities	Population	
		Total	Percent
Los Angeles County suburbs[b]			
Under 2,000	13	304,926	6.32
2,000 to 2,999	10	225,246	4.67
3,000 to 3,999	7	336,045	6.97
4,000 to 4,999	5	228,467	4.74
5,000 to 5,999	5	366,307	7.59
6,000 to 7,499	10	869,629	18.03
7,500 to 9,999	11	1,034,575	21.45
10,000 and over	25	1,459,120	30.25
Total	86	4,824,315	100.00
Riverside and San Bernardino County municipalities			
Under 2,000	21	554,310	21.61
2,000 to 2,999	9	449,975	17.54
3,000 to 3,999	8	868,800	33.87
4,000 to 4,999	7	593,600	23.14
5,000 to 5,999	1	20,300	0.79
6,000 to 7,499	1	33,500	1.31
7,500 to 9,999	0	0	0.00
10,000 and over	1	44,282	1.73
Total	48	2,564,767	100.00
Orange County municipalities			
Under 2,000	0	0	0
2,000 to 2,999	7	180,359	6.73
3,000 to 3,999	3	237,400	8.86
4,000 to 4,999	2	78,398	2.93
5,000 to 5,999	6	520,572	19.44
6,000 to 7,499	7	852,309	31.82
7,500 to 9,999	4	327,785	12.24
10,000 and over	4	481,301	17.97
Total	33	2,678,124	100.00
San Francisco Bay area suburban municipalities			
Under 2,000	18	208,462	5.22
2,000 to 2,999	15	566,069	14.16
3,000 to 3,999	25	1,191,534	29.81
4,000 to 4,999	16	791,678	19.81
5,000 to 5,999	5	261,843	6.55
6,000 to 7,499	12	573,679	14.35
7,500 to 9,999	4	240,472	6.02
10,000 and over	3	163,342	4.09
Total	98	3,997,079	100.00

continued on next page

TABLE 12-4. Suburban Densities in Selected Urbanized Areas, 2000[a] (continued)

Region and density (persons/square mile)	Number of cities	Population Total	Percent
Chicago suburbs in Illinois[c]			
Under 2,000	74	322,577	6.95
2,000 to 2,999	41	535,687	11.54
3,000 to 3,999	43	879,715	18.96
4,000 to 4,999	54	1,475,251	31.79
5,000 to 5,999	23	627,350	13.52
6,000 to 7,499	14	406,621	8.76
7,500 to 9,999	6	149,326	3.22
10,000 and over	7	244,023	5.26
Total	262	4,640,550	100.00
Atlanta 10-county region, incorporated suburbs			
Under 2,000	38	273,652	38.72
2,000 to 2,999	15	315,322	44.61
3,000 to 3,999	5	85,325	12.07
4,000 to 4,999	2	25,292	3.58
5,000 to 5,999	0	0	0.00
6,000 to 7,499	1	7,231	1.02
7,500 to 9,999	0	0	0.00
10,000 and over	0	0	0.00
Total	61	706,822	100.00

Source: U.S. Bureau of the Census, 2000 (www.census.gov).

a. Average individual densities are as follows: Los Angeles County suburbs, 7,503; Riverside and San Bernardino County municipalities, 2,269; Orange County municipalities, 6,110; San Francisco Bay area suburban municipalities, 4,100; Chicago suburbs in Illinois, 3,812; and Atlanta ten-county region, incorporated suburbs, 1,868 (unincorporated areas contain 2,306,083 residents, with an overall density of 935 persons per square mile).

b. Excludes Malibu.

c. Excludes seven suburbs, with total population of 7,976.

striking. The heavy black line showing Los Angeles County indicates a high percentage of that area's total suburban population lives in relatively high-density communities—51 percent at 7,500 persons per square mile or more, and 30 percent at over 10,000 persons per square mile. Orange County also has high proportions of its residents living in relatively high-density communities. In sharp contrast, residents of all Riverside and San Bernardino municipalities combined live at much lower densities, with more than 70 percent at under 4,000 persons per square mile and only 3 percent at 6,000 per square mile or higher.[24] This is because those two counties act in part as bedroom suburbs to the heavy concentrations of jobs in both Los Angeles and Orange Counties. The San Fran-

FIGURE 12-1. Densities in California Suburban Areas, 2000

Percent of total population

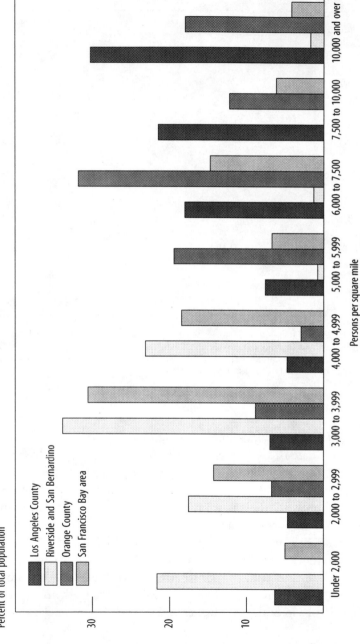

Persons per square mile

Los Angeles County
Riverside and San Bernardino
Orange County
San Francisco Bay area

Under 2,000
2,000 to 2,999
3,000 to 3,999
4,000 to 4,999
5,000 to 5,999
6,000 to 7,500
7,500 to 10,000
10,000 and over

30
20
10

Source: Author's calculations based on 2000 Census.

cisco Bay area's suburban residents live mainly in low-density communities similar to those in Riverside and San Bernardino counties.[25]

Densities for the suburbs in the Chicago and Atlanta urbanized areas are relatively low. Atlanta is unusual because two-thirds of its suburbanites live in unincorporated portions of the 10 counties included in these data. The overall density of those unincorporated areas is only 935 persons per square mile.

Total average densities among all the areas in table 12-4 vary from a low of 1,868 persons per square mile in the incorporated suburbs of Atlanta to a high of 7,503 in the suburban communities in Los Angeles County. Since Los Angeles is the center of the fastest-growing part of the United States in absolute terms, these data seem to contradict the conclusion that new-growth suburbs will not adopt relatively high residential densities.

However, the newer and farther outlying suburbs in the greater Los Angeles area, where the fastest population growth is occurring, are in Riverside and San Bernardino counties. As noted, those suburbs have much lower densities than the older suburbs in Los Angeles County. Similarly, in the San Francisco Bay area, the outlying frontiers of current growth—Napa, Solano, and Sonoma counties—had much lower densities in 2000 than closer-in counties.

Among individual suburban incorporated areas in the regions just discussed, densities vary even more enormously. The highest suburban density was 23,409 persons per square mile in Maywood, a suburb of Los Angeles containing only 1.2 square miles. Los Angeles County contains 25 suburban cities with densities above 10,000 persons per square mile. The lowest suburban density was 19 persons per square mile in Vernon, another Los Angeles suburb. These data indicate that U.S. suburban densities have until now reached relatively high levels only in older, closer-in suburbs, not in the more peripheral areas of new growth. Yet it is in the latter that densities would have to be increased sharply to reduce burgeoning suburban traffic congestion. Hence the previous conclusion that achieving high residential densities there would violate the preferences of the existing residents seems correct.

Are Low-Density Settlements "Socially Sub-Optimal"?

Defendants of suburban sprawl argue that if people want to live in low-density settlements, they should be allowed to do so—as long as they pay the full costs involved. From a welfare theory viewpoint, there is no reason for society to favor any particular suburban residential densities, as long as two conditions hold. One is that citizens choosing to live at low densities pay the full costs of their choice. The second is that those citizens do not create barriers that prevent other citizens from living at higher densities.

DO RESIDENTS OF LOW-DENSITY AREAS PAY THE FULL COSTS OF LIVING THERE? Low-density settlements over large areas cause longer average commuting distances than would higher-density settlements with the same population under conditions widely prevalent in U.S. metropolitan areas. Therefore, low-density settlement generates more total automotive vehicle trip miles per day, which consume more energy and cause greater emission of pollutants. The consumption of more energy does not involve any clear-cut social costs, since those who choose low-density living pay for it themselves by purchasing more fuel for their vehicles.

But the discharge of more air pollutants is ambiguous. Because of variations in ambient air conditions, the emission of more pollutants does not always cause greater effective air pollution. But it can and often does. Insofar as it does, and insofar as such pollution generates more sickness and other negative effects, the persons choosing low-density settlements are imposing a higher cost on society than would arise from higher-density settlements, without paying that cost. Hence the prices of different settlement patterns confronting households in markets will make low-density living seem more favorable than it would if its users had to pay its full social costs. This bias will lead to settlement patterns of lower density than is socially optimal. However, the resulting welfare loss varies greatly from one community to another.

Similarly, low-density settlements can generate more intensive traffic congestion than higher-density settlements under certain conditions. However, the relationship between average settlement density and traffic congestion is even more tenuous than that between density and effective air pollution. Low-density settlement only causes more traffic congestion if the areas concerned are not well served with expressways and other road systems, or job sites where workers from those areas are employed are concentrated in such a way that many workers must converge on either a few job sites or a few highway bottlenecks, or the absolute number of commuters moving in these areas each day greatly exceeds the capacity of the road system. Under any of those conditions, low density is likely to create more traffic congestion than higher density. Then the fact that commuters using the congested roads do not pay for doing so will generate welfare losses that would not arise if densities were higher, or if all drivers had to pay direct tolls for using congested roads during peak hours.

Low-density settlements covering large areas also generate greater infrastructure trunk-line costs than would the same population living at much higher densities. Some of these greater costs can be charged directly to the residents concerned; so they enter into the cost of choosing low-density living. However, most local officials claim that governments cannot fully recover all the costs of the public infrastructures serving new growth areas through charges against the new residents. Some infrastructure improvements benefit newcomers and existing community residents in ways that cannot be disentangled through user charges or impact fees.

DO RESIDENTS OF LOW-DENSITY AREAS BLOCK CHOICES OF HIGHER DENSITIES BY OTHERS? Nearly all suburban communities have zoning ordinances that control the densities at which new homes can be built or existing ones redeveloped. Typically, these ordinances severely restrict the amount of land on which relatively high-density housing can be developed. That includes both multifamily housing and single-family housing on small lots. Analysis of this practice by many urban economists and by the Advisory Commission on Regulatory Barriers to Affordable Housing has clearly shown that suburban zoning often prevents the creation of higher-density—and therefore relatively low-cost—housing.[26] Many suburban governments pass zoning ordinances deliberately designed to prevent lower-cost housing in their communities. Their residents fear lower-cost housing located nearby would reduce the market values of their own homes. They also do not want to live near households of lower socioeconomic status. So they adopt laws that raise the cost of building new units, for example, by requiring relatively low-density housing.

Many residents of such exclusionary communities benefit from restrictions preventing the construction of lower-cost housing and entry of lower-income households because such rulings drive up the market prices of their own homes. In this way, they also attain the kind of local socioeconomic mixtures they prefer. But these policies impose costs on the low- and moderate-income households excluded from such communities. Since the benefited households generally have much higher incomes than the penalized households, this amounts to a regressive redistribution of welfare. In my opinion, it is therefore socially undesirable.

Insofar as low-density settlement is accompanied by the widespread use of such restrictive zoning ordinances, it reduces society's efficiency and welfare by inhibiting the choices of households that would prefer higher-density housing units. Such units could often be relatively inexpensive because units of moderately high density are less costly to build than those of very high density or very low density. Moreover, many low-wage workers employed in communities where housing is too expensive for them must commute from other communities, often driving long distances. Thus restrictive zoning contributes to longer average commuting journeys than would otherwise occur.

THE SOCIAL OPTIMALITY OF LOW-DENSITY SETTLEMENTS. Low-density settlements are not socially suboptimal if their occupants pay the full social costs of living in them and do not prevent the creation of higher-density settlements there. But in most U.S. metropolitan areas, many big low-density settlements do not meet these conditions, for reasons just set forth. Society would be better off if residents of these areas had to bear more fully the costs their low-density choices have created and if their restrictions on the density choices of others were greatly reduced. Under those conditions, average suburban densities would be somewhat higher than they are now. This change would probably involve more clusters of higher-density settlements within basically low-density regions, rather than higher average densities throughout each region. However, the degree to which actual densities would be higher if socially optimal conditions prevailed is extremely difficult to estimate.

IMPLICATIONS FOR REDUCING TRAFFIC CONGESTION. Even if existing U.S. settlements had socially suboptimal densities, raising their densities would not necessarily reduce existing traffic congestion. In fact, Gerald A. Carlino has recently argued that higher-density metropolitan areas have grown more slowly than lower-density ones, partly because the former generate greater congestion.[27] He cites the fact that smaller metropolitan areas, which have lower densities than big ones, have captured an increasing share of total employment in the period 1951 to 1996. He contends that intensifying congestion in higher-density regions may be the key cause of this deconcentration, though he cites no data supporting the conclusion that congestion is higher in more dense regions. To check this argument, I conducted a multiple regression across 351 urbanized areas, using the percentage increase in population from 1990 to 2000, as the dependent variable. The independent variables were the urbanized area population in 1990, the land area of the urbanized area in 1990 in square miles, the absolute increase in urbanized area population from 1990 to 2000, the 1990 density of the urbanized area in persons per square mile, the percentage change in the size of the urbanized area from 1990 to 2000, and the average January temperature of the major city in the urbanized area.[28]

The best regression result was an adjusted r-squared of 0.7415 with five of these variables significant at the .01 level. They were the percentage increase in each urbanized area's land area, because many were expanded from 1990 to 2000 (a strongly positive effect), the absolute change in the urbanized area's population from 1990 to 2000, even though it had a low direct correlation with the percentage change (a positive effect), the land area of the urbanized area in 1990 (a negative effect), the average January temperature (a positive effect), and the urbanized area's 1990 population density (a negative effect). This outcome supports Carlino's claim that higher regional density may contribute to slower regional growth, though it does not show that this occurs through greater congestion. However, the earlier regression on levels of traffic congestion in chapter 3 indicates that urbanized area density had a positive impact on the travel time index that the Texas Transportation Institute uses to measure congestion intensity. Thus increasing residential density across a whole region may worsen traffic congestion rather than improving it.

However, it is plausible that raising densities in the peripheral new-growth portions of a region may at least lead to shorter overall commuting journeys in those portions than would permitting growth to occur there at very low densities. But the difficulties of raising densities are great. In fact, trying to decrease current traffic congestion by raising residential densities in existing suburbs is like trying to improve the position of a painting hung too high on the living room wall by jacking up the ceiling instead of moving the painting. The effort required by the remedy is wholly disproportionate to the severity of the problem, the pain it causes, and the benefits of ending it.

However, trying to reduce future traffic congestion in potential new-growth areas might justify adopting some minimum average density levels to reduce the average length of future commuting trips there.

How Higher Residential Densities Might Be Achieved

In theory, there are three ways to attain higher suburban densities: by demolishing existing structures and redeveloping the cleared land with more intensive uses, or modifying existing structures; by building new structures on vacant, in-fill sites at higher densities than in surrounding development; and by creating new peripheral developments on vacant land at higher densities than the average for regions that are already built up. But only the third method has shown much promise of greatly changing the future overall density of a metropolitan area.

Densities can be raised on vacant peripheral land by using smaller lots for detached single-family homes, allocating a higher percentage of all residentially zoned vacant land to multifamily or attached single-family housing, raising the permissible densities for such housing, and allocating a higher percentage of total land area to residential uses. All of these policies can be legally imposed by local zoning regulations.

However, the first three are normally opposed by existing residents, who tend to believe those tactics undesirably "change the established character" of their communities. They fear greater traffic congestion, shortages of on-street parking, greater noise and air pollution, lower property values of nearby single-family homes, overloading of public facilities such as parks and schools, and the introduction of "undesirable people." Thus higher-density housing is considered a LULU by existing residents, who therefore adopt a not-in-my-backyard (NIMBY) attitude toward it. A LULU is a locally undesirable land use—something that produces benefits for its entire region but has negative effects on its immediate neighborhood. Major airports are considered LULUs because of the noise and traffic they generate for their neighbors. The abbreviation NIMBY expresses the attitude of persons who do not want what they consider LULUs near them, regardless of the social importance of locating those land uses somewhere.

It is hard to overcome this parochial response by persuading local governments to permit higher-density development. Most local governments have strong incentives to support the land-use preferences of their own citizens, while ignoring the needs of the metropolitan area as a whole. Hence the best way to encourage higher-density development in areas of new growth is through policies adopted by territorially broader levels of government—especially the state government. State officials have constituencies that often encompass an entire metropolitan area, including many potential residents of areas of new growth. These persons would benefit from lower-cost housing and other fruits of higher-density development. Sensitive to this fact, officials at broader levels of government are more likely to adopt policies that take into account areawide or societywide interests than officials in fragmented local governments.[29]

One such policy would be to revise property taxes so they fall much more heavily on land than on improvements. This would encourage maximum-intensity development of each site. A second policy would be to greatly increase property taxes on vacant land near the edges of a metropolitan area. In many states, such vacant land is now taxed relatively lightly, especially if classified as agricultural. Higher land taxes would motivate owners of such land to develop it quickly as intensively as possible, rather than hold it vacant while speculating on future value increases.

However, the impacts of these policies would be limited because most suburbs already tightly ration high-intensity land uses through restrictive zoning. This creates a shortage of high-intensity uses and drives up the costs of building high-density developments. Thus the major factor preventing more high-density development in most suburbs is not the lack of tax incentives but the inability to get local permission to build it. Consequently, the way to achieve higher average densities in areas of new growth is to change suburban zoning policies. The details of how that might be done are beyond the scope of this book.

Another way to raise peripheral densities would be to adopt an urban growth boundary. It would force most new development into zones contiguous to territory already built up. Oregon has followed this policy for more than two decades. It has raised average densities in areas of new growth within such boundaries.[30] However, the overall average density of the Portland urbanized area has remained relatively low (3,340 persons per square mile in 2000), and it increased only 10.6 percent from 1990 to 2000. That increase ranked twenty-fourth among the 50 largest urbanized areas; 17 other large urbanized areas had percentage increases in density twice as great, and 14 had increases three times as great. The density of the city of Portland increased 12.3 percent in the 1990s. That was the ninth greatest increase among the 50 largest urbanized areas. But in 2000, the city of Portland still had a relatively low density for a central city (3,939 persons per square mile); that density ranked twenty-sixth among the central cities of the 50 largest urbanized areas. Thus, even though the Portland area has had a strongly enforced urban growth boundary for more than twenty years, its overall density has not increased substantially. Even its central city still has a density much lower than that normally considered the threshold for economically feasible public transit service.

One of the biggest advantages of urban growth boundaries is that they reduce the "leap-frog" development that initially bypasses large vacant sites in mostly developed territory. Leap-frog development raises trunk line infrastructure costs, in comparison with solid, contiguous development. Moreover, when new development is confined to well-defined territories within urban growth boundaries, uncertainties about future growth patterns are reduced. This permits developers and local governments to shorten the time required for planning and gaining government permissions for new projects. The resulting decreases in development costs can offset the higher prices of land within urban growth boundaries.

But reducing leap-frog development also has negative effects. Such development creates pockets of undeveloped land that stand vacant after the frontier of development has passed beyond them. If initial development of those sites is deferred long enough, they will eventually be improved at higher densities than would have prevailed if they had been developed when at the frontier.[31]

Another tactic to help achieve higher densities in areas of new growth is to provide persuasive evidence that well-designed, moderate-density, new multifamily residential developments would not negatively affect the market value of nearby single-family homes. The Advisory Commission on Regulatory Barriers to Affordable Housing found fifteen relevant studies of this topic. Fourteen "reached the conclusion that there are no significant negative effects from locating subsidized, special-purpose, or manufactured housing near market-rate developments."[32] A more recent study by George Galster concluded that the impact of creating new subsidized housing on the market prices of nearby single-family homes was not always negligible; sometimes it was negative, sometimes negligible, and sometimes positive. In effect, that impact was contingent on circumstances that varied widely from one situation to another.[33]

Clearly, overcoming current suburban resistance to higher-density development will not be easy. It can probably be done only if officials at higher levels of government, especially at the state level, become convinced that the benefits of higher density are worth the political costs of achieving it. Moreover, efforts at raising densities in order to reduce traffic congestion are likely to be most successful if they concentrate on raising densities in relatively small areas with excellent access to existing public transit service. These include areas close to subway or commuter train stops or to major downtowns. Residents of such areas are much more likely to shift from auto travel to transit travel for many trips than residents living farther from transit service. Raising the commercial density of downtowns or major commercial districts may also encourage more transit use by concentrating more destinations for many travelers in one spot. These small-area tactics are likely to be much more effective in coping with traffic congestion than trying to raise the overall residential density of large areas, such as whole urbanized area fringes.

13

Changing the
Jobs-Housing Balance

One strategy for reducing congestion focuses on changing
the balance between jobs and housing in each subregion of
a metropolitan area. The basic idea is to encourage people
to live closer to where they work and thereby shorten average commuting journeys.

The Nature of Jobs-Housing Imbalances

Under quite common circumstances, long average commuting journeys generate more traffic congestion than shorter
ones. Long journeys often result from imbalances between
job sites and the places where people reside. Many more
jobs than housing units tend to be concentrated in areas
with a job surplus or a housing shortage. These areas
include most downtown business districts, large retail and
office clusters around big regional shopping centers, and
office and industrial facilities surrounding regional airports.
Many people who work there must commute from relatively long distances.[1]

Areas with a job shortage or a housing surplus tend to
have many more housing units than jobs. They are mainly
outlying suburbs at the frontier of new growth where land

is relatively inexpensive and so housing costs less than in closer-in areas. That attracts low- and moderate-income households or those who want large homes without paying immense prices. Many people living there must commute long distances to reach their jobs.

Even if the number of housing units in an area is exactly the same as that required to shelter everyone who works there, the cost and styles of those housing units may not be appropriate for those workers. For example, low-wage workers employed in a regional shopping center close to the Pacific coast may be unable to afford any nearby housing if exclusionary zoning and above-average amenities keep prices high. Hence an effective jobs-housing balance can only be achieved by closely matching the number of local housing units and the prices and styles of those units to the number and economic capabilities of locally employed workers.

There is little doubt that such jobs-housing imbalances are widespread in large U.S. metropolitan areas. When the ratio of workers employed to workers residing in twenty-two San Francisco Bay area cities was calculated, it was found that the average ratio was 1.05—nearly perfect balance (any ratio between 0.75 and 1.50 was assumed to indicate reasonable local balance). But seven of the twenty-two cities had ratios outside this range.[2] Both results partly reflect the fact that, the smaller the territory surveyed, the greater the probability its jobs and housing will not be balanced. Conversely, over any whole region, jobs and housing are always balanced by definition (except for the few workers who commute in from outside it or who live in it but work outside).

Such imbalances probably do contribute to traffic congestion. However, their mere existence does not prove that they are socially undesirable, could be removed through public policies, or altered to greatly reduce traffic congestion.

Some Undesirable Effects of Imbalances

In theory, if more housing units were located in areas with a job surplus and more jobs in areas with a housing surplus, workers would live closer to their jobs, and total commuting travel would decline. Therefore, one strategy for reducing traffic congestion is to adjust existing or proposed future settlement patterns to approach a jobs-housing balance.

The importance attributed to this strategy can be seen from calculations of future traffic congestion made by the Southern California Association of Governments (SCAG). Projections in 1986 indicated that the population of the six-county SCAG area was likely to increase by 5.9 million, or 47.5 percent, between 1984 and 2010. In that period, the region would add about 3 million jobs—but not where its new housing would be created. As a result, traffic congestion in SCAG's region was projected to increase drastically to near-paralysis levels. In fact, SCAG's population rose from 12.4 million in 1984 to 16.5 million in 2000. At that rate of annual absolute growth, SCAG would contain 19.0 million people by 2010, or about 4 percent more than its staff had predicted in 1984. In fact, SCAG's fears about a worsening jobs-housing balance have certainly come true, as SCAG pointed out in a 2001 report.[3]

One way to mitigate resulting adverse effects would be to build many miles of additional freeways. But SCAG has concluded such action would cost much more than could be financed. Another approach would be to change the projected locations of added jobs and housing units. According to SCAG's calculations in 1986, if 12 percent of the new jobs created by 2010 were shifted from areas of job surplus to areas of housing surplus, and 6 percent of the new housing units from areas of housing surplus to those with a job surplus, the projected increase in traffic congestion would be cut 35 percent. Hence SCAG adopted an official policy of influencing the future location of jobs and housing.[4] The required direct government intervention in the locational choices of private firms and households was a radical departure from past public policies. This policy of locational intervention was ratified again in SCAG's 2001 report and expanded to an even greater variety of public policies. They ranged from changing the curricula in public schools to altering the basic tax structure of the state.[5]

In 2000, the California state legislature passed the Jobs-Housing Balance Incentive Grant Program. It allocated $25 million in grants to communities that submitted promising proposals to improve their jobs-housing balance. However, in 2002, the amount to be spent was reduced somewhat. Since applications were not due until May 2003, it is not possible in this book to evaluate how effective this program might be in achieving its goals.[6] Furthermore, the Inter-Regional Partnership Jobs-Housing Balance Pilot Program has developed a whole package of dozens of policy proposals aimed at improving the jobs-housing balance among several counties in the greater San Francisco Bay region.[7]

The Causes of Imbalances

Jobs-housing imbalances are the result of the inherent dynamics of metropolitan-area growth that probably cannot be changed and specific public policies that could be changed.

—The inherent dynamics of metropolitan growth. When a metropolitan area is first established, jobs cluster near its center. That location provides greater access to all points within the area than any other spot. Such accessibility enables many firms to tap wider markets and bigger labor pools. Moreover, they cluster together to improve the efficiency of their interactions. Thus they can pay higher rents than homeowners can for high-access central land. Consequently, residential uses move to the outer edges of the developed area, where land is less costly. This automatically creates some subregions with a job surplus and others with a housing surplus. Hence significant jobs-housing imbalances are socially and economically efficient results of the "normal" urban development process.

At first, commuting distances between these specialized regions are short. But as the entire area grows, they become longer. Also, many retail and other services closely tied to daily household living move to peripheral sites to get closer to their customers. This often creates new decentralized job centers. In this way, more jobs gradually move out into areas with a housing surplus, reducing initial jobs-housing imbalances there. Some offices and industrial firms also move to where workers reside in order to more easily tap the labor pools there. This process has been furthered by rapid expansion of automotive vehicle ownership and usage since 1970 and recent advances in telecommunications.

This evolution can be observed in Orange County, California, as shown in figure 13-1. In 1950, the county had 61 percent more resident households than local jobs. But in the 1970s, the number of jobs began growing faster than the number of households. By the early 1970s, these two numbers were equal. After that, job growth consistently outpaced household growth, so more and more workers had to commute into Orange County from elsewhere. By 2000, Orange County contained 38 percent more jobs than resident households.[8] Thus a "natural" process tends to reduce initial housing surpluses in once-outlying areas over time as new growth passes beyond them. But it can go too far, creating a local surplus of jobs relative to housing, as happened in Orange County.

FIGURE 13-1. Jobs and Households, Orange County, 1950–2000

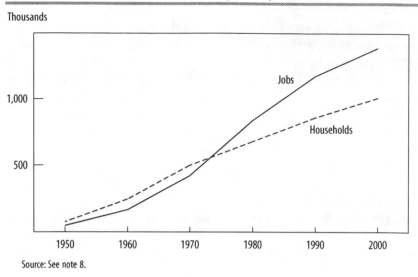

Source: See note 8.

However, in neighboring Riverside and San Bernardino counties, household growth kept up with job growth through these five decades, as shown in figure 13-2. This happened mainly because those two counties had a lot of unsettled space. They were therefore able to provide shelter for workers employed in adjacent Orange and Los Angeles counties, where job growth was exceeding housing construction. So the "natural evolution" of the jobs-housing balance can vary greatly from place to place, depending on particular local conditions.

However, the gradual leveling off of initial jobs-housing imbalances over time is strengthened by individual adjustments to long commuting journeys. As SCAG stated in 2001:

Historically, the geographic imbalance between jobs and housing in the SCAG Region has been a problem that has been largely self-correcting. Jobs have moved from their original centers to housing-rich suburbs to take advantage of lower land and labor costs and provide shorter commute trips for their employees. The end result is the multi-centered urban fabric that characterizes the region today. This phenomenon also explains why average home-to-work commute times in the region have remained relatively constant over the last several decades.[9]

FIGURE 13-2. Jobs and Households, Riverside and San Bernardino Counties, 1950–2000

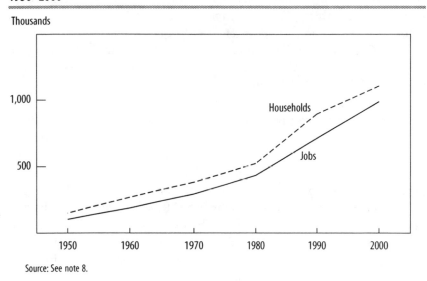

Source: See note 8.

—Travel costs less than land. One factor operating against this equilibrating process is that commuting travel is less costly to many households than land or housing. In 2000, the average U.S. household spent 19.5 percent of its annual income for transportation, not counting the cost of time spent in traveling. But it spent 32 percent for housing.[10] Therefore it can benefit if it can greatly reduce housing costs by increasing its transportation costs somewhat. Commuting farther out can sharply reduce costs because peripheral land is so much less expensive.[11] The main added transportation cost is the value of the additional time required. Traveling 1 mile farther would increase annual work-trip travel by 2 miles per day, or 480 miles per year (2 miles per day on 240 workdays). At $0.10 per mile operating costs, that is only $48.00. If the extra trip distance was traveled at 30 miles per hour (higher than the average speed for the whole trip because it is farther out), then each mile would take two minutes, or 4 minutes more per day. Over 240 days, that is 960 minutes, or 16 hours. If the commuter's time was valued at half the average hourly wage in 2001 of $14.33, or $7.17 per hour, that would add $114.72 more. The total added annual cost would equal $162.53 per additional mile of commuting each way.

What can $162.53 per year in added travel costs buy in less expensive housing? If any home purchase is financed with a 20 percent down payment and a thirty-year mortgage at 7 percent interest, the annual total cost of the monthly payments will equal 6.3869 percent of the home's purchase price. Therefore, $162.53 is equivalent to the mortgage payments on $2,545 of additional home price ($162.53 equals 6.3869 percent of $2,545). So driving out one more mile means the commuter would have $2,545 less to pay for a home. If the price of housing falls more than that amount per mile of added driving, the household would benefit from the longer commute. Earlier investigations have estimated that home prices fall as much as 1.5 percent for every additional mile farther out from the central business district.[12] $2,545 is equal to 1.5 percent of a home priced at $169,649. Therefore, whenever the average or median price of a home in a region is $170,000 or more, it is likely to be worthwhile to drive out farther. The expenses of the added mile of travel every day would be less than the reduction in home prices of housing one mile farther out. In 2002, according to the National Association of Realtors (NAR), the median price of existing single-family homes sold exceeded $170,000 in 36 of the 138 metropolitan areas on which NAR keeps sales records and exceeded $200,000 in 17 of them.[13] These 36 metropolitan areas contained 74.1 million people in 2000, or 26.3 percent of the entire American population. Thus "driving until you qualify" is a sensible strategy in a significant share of American metropolitan areas. This is why so many households are making very long commuting journeys in high-housing-cost metropolitan areas. There is a strong incentive for these households to behave in ways that aggravate jobs-housing imbalances.

—Labor market factors. Because of the long-run increase in the number of women working outside the home, there are now more households with two or more earners. So it has become harder for many households to choose housing that minimizes commuting journeys for all their workers, since the jobs may be far apart. High job turnover rates also make it difficult for households to maintain short commuting distances. Taking a new job may replace an initially short commute with a much longer one. In some industries, movement among jobs occurs at high rates. These factors can both cause and perpetuate jobs-housing imbalance.

—Exclusionary practices of local governments. Many communities near large outlying job clusters seem to have deliberately adopted local ordinances that drive up housing prices. Hence, many people who work in communities with high housing costs cannot afford to live there and must commute long distances to housing they can afford.

Some local governments engage in tactics of raising the cost of housing to improve their fiscal health. Most believe that commercial real estate uses—which entail jobs—produce greater local property or sales tax revenues than they require in local government expenditures; hence they arc fiscal gainers. In contrast, low- and moderate-income residents typically require larger local expenditures than they produce in local tax revenues; hence they are fiscal losers. So such governments adopt zoning and other ordinances that encourage commercial land uses and discourage relatively modest-cost housing. These policies stimulate more local jobs than housing units, thereby contributing to a quantitative jobs-housing imbalance. Such policies also create a qualitative imbalance by preventing local construction of housing affordable to many local workers. Such exclusionary policies include growth moratoriums, downzoning to prohibit even moderate-density housing, restriction of land zoned for multifamily housing, long delays in review and approval of permits, and costly reporting and environmental protection requirements. In essence, fiscal zoning rejects the social need for localities to enable the low-income workers absolutely necessary for their day-to-day operation to live near where they work.

Six Tactics for Changing Existing Imbalances

Reducing existing jobs-housing imbalances in a metropolitan area has often been proposed as a means of cutting traffic congestion. There are six possible ways to achieve a closer jobs-housing balance in each of the various types of imbalanced areas just described:

—Add large numbers of new housing units to areas with job surpluses. In already-well-built-up areas, this may require major in-fill housing development and raising densities in existing neighborhoods—both highly controversial policies.

—Change the quality of new housing units being built in areas that have many low-wage jobs but mainly high-cost housing by creating more housing units suitable for occupancy by low- and moderate-wage workers employed there. In high-housing-cost areas, this is difficult to do without major housing subsidies from the public sector.

—Block the creation of many more jobs in areas with a job surplus. As an example, in 1989, Palo Alto, California, dramatically reduced the amount of its land zoned for commercial development specifically to limit the future growth of traffic from such development. Mainly by lowering permissible floor area ratios (FARs) it cut the potential for future nonresidential development from 25.3 million square feet to 3.3 million. It also adopted a host of related programs shifting the emphasis of future growth from nonresidential to residential.[14] In spite of these steps, traffic congestion has worsened since then, but the local government believes it would have been even worse without these policies.

—Move existing jobs from areas with a job surplus to newer areas with a housing surplus. However, many high-tech firms want to remain close to other high-tech firms and be located in the highest-amenity parts of their region so they can more easily attract skilled professional workers. Hence they often resist moving out of established industry centers to the "boondocks."

—Encourage the formation of most jobs in areas with a housing surplus rather than in those with a job surplus. This policy is subject to the same problem as the preceding one.

—Inhibit the creation of additional housing units in newer areas with a housing surplus.

These tactics are so closely related that several must be carried out simultaneously to create a more balanced jobs-housing situation in an entire metropolitan area. If some are successfully implemented but others are not, the overall housing situation could become worse. For example, if building more housing units in areas with a housing surplus was successfully slowed but no more relatively low-priced units were created in areas with a job surplus, the shortage of affordable housing would increase. If population growth nevertheless continued, the result would be a doubling-up of low-income households in units built for single-family occupancy. This has occurred in many southern California localities during the 1980s and the 1990s.

Thus successfully improving the jobs-housing balance throughout a metropolitan area requires complex coordination of very different policies in its different subregions. But in nearly all U.S. metropolitan areas, control over key land-use policies is divided among dozens or even hundreds of local governments with parochial perspectives. This fragmented structure poses enormous obstacles to carrying out the type of cohesive, integrated strategy necessary to achieve a desirable jobs-housing balance in each part of a large metropolitan area.

Feasibility of Tactics for Changing Balances

Several factors will influence the feasibility of public policies aimed at improving jobs-housing balances.

Workers' Preferences

Most policies seeking to reduce jobs-housing imbalances implicitly assume that most people would like to live as close to their jobs as possible. But experience suggests otherwise, particularly the behavior of people living in large master-planned communities. These communities have been developed to contain jobs and housing affordable to the people that hold those jobs. Moreover, the housing is conveniently accessible to the jobs by car, foot, bicycle, and bus. Yet a study of fifteen matched pairs of planned and unplanned communities showed no significant difference in the work and commuting behavior of their residents.[15] In both types, more than 84 percent of residents chose to work at some distance from their homes; the average commuting time was twenty-five minutes, the average distance was from 9.9 to 10.8 miles, and the shares of workers commuting different distances were similar.

Moreover, in a survey of twenty-two San Francisco Bay area communities, a majority of workers living in most communities were employed elsewhere (the average was 63 percent); and a majority working there lived elsewhere (that average was 62 percent).[16] This strong pattern of cross commuting surely indicates that where workers choose to live is influenced by many factors other than the length of their commuting journeys.

Thus making nearby housing in appropriate price ranges available to workers employed in a job center will not persuade most of them to live there. A great many factors enter into people's residential choices, including where their relatives and friends live, the quality of life in different neighborhoods, the quality of local schools, where jobs of other members of the household are located, and the age, ethnic composition, and socioeconomic status of the local population. Neighborhoods containing a tremendous variety of these traits are found in most metropolitan areas. That is why so many people choose to live far from their jobs even when they can find housing they could afford much closer to those jobs.

Appropriate Geographic Subregions

Balancing jobs and housing must be related to specific subregions in a metropolitan area. In each subregion, the number and types of jobs are supposed to match the number and types of housing units. Hence, an essential part of any balancing strategy is to decide exactly where to draw subregional boundaries.

In theory, such boundaries ought to demarcate so-called commute sheds; that is, areas considered to be within desirable commuting range of major job centers. However, putting this concept into practice is extremely difficult, as the consulting firm of Hamilton, Rabinovitz, and Alschuler pointed out:

> There are often multiple important employment centers (and, therefore, multiple arguable focal points for overlapping commute sheds) within a given subarea of Southern California. And, since most households now involve more than one wage earner, and each wage earner may be involved in an occupation whose practitioners need to be concentrated in a different employment center, a single household may fall within two or more commute sheds separated by 20 miles or more. Because most commute sheds cross municipal lines, and often many of them, there is usually no local government . . . jurisdictionally competent to set or carry out jobs-housing balance policy for the full shed. Finally . . . most municipalities in Los Angeles County contain the workplaces of only a tiny fraction of their residents.[17]

The smaller the share of a total metropolitan area encompassed by any subregion, the more likely that subregion is to contain a disproportionate fraction of jobs or housing compared with the area as a whole—and therefore the more likely it is to be imbalanced. This means the entire balancing act is greatly affected by a purely arbitrary decision concerning how large the subregions are made. Moreover, size is not the only vital dimension. As politicians in charge of electoral districting have long known, there are myriad ways to draw boundaries for subregions of equal population or area within some larger territory. Yet the feasibility of achieving a desired jobs-housing balance depends on exactly how boundaries are drawn for the subregions concerned.

Most subregions will be created by combining smaller communities that already have legally defined boundaries. This makes it easier to collect data and is more acceptable politically than creating wholly new entities. But the people deciding how to define subregions will be tempted to choose boundaries that minimize the difficulties of attaining whatever definition of balance they are using. Thus the definition of subregions will inevitably become semipolitical, rather than purely technical or scientific.

A Qualitative Jobs-Housing Balance in Each Subregion

As just noted, having enough appropriate-quality housing units in each subregion to shelter the number of workers employed there is not sufficient to attain a jobs-housing balance. For one thing, the average distance between the housing units and the jobs in each such subregion would have to be shorter than current average suburban commuting distances (about twelve miles in 2000). That would only be possible if each subregion was small. But the smaller each subregion, the more difficult it is to attain an appropriate balance therein.

Furthermore, even if the jobs and housing units in each small subregion were perfectly balanced quantitatively, they would most likely remain imbalanced qualitatively. Thus thousands of new units could be built in Santa Clara County, California, near Silicon Valley, to offset the large surplus of jobs there. But the cost of existing single-family housing units there averaged more than $400,000 in 2001. If most new units added had similar prices, most workers employed there could not afford them. Experience proves that "natural" forces will not appropriately match local housing prices to the wage levels of locally employed workers in each subregion for two reasons. Both local government policies and strong demands for housing in high-amenity areas by high-income households raise housing prices in many communities. The policies necessary to overcome local regulatory barriers to affordable housing are complex and difficult to get adopted and to implement.

Administrative Difficulties of Achieving a Jobs-Housing Balance

A jobs-housing strategy would require creating a regional agency with strong authority over local government land-use policies. Only such a regional agency could coherently choose the specific boundaries of the subregions within which balancing should occur, determine which communities could use more jobs and housing and where additional jobs and housing should be discouraged, pass regulations aimed at achieving those goals, and monitor the subsequent behavior of the communities involved. But a regional agency that powerful has at least two

serious drawbacks. First, this approach would entail transferring considerable sovereignty over land-use decisions from local governments to a
regional agency. Such a power shift is sure to encounter vehement and
sustained opposition from most local governments and citizens. Second,
such a powerful regional agency would form another layer of government regulation affecting the real estate development process. That
process is already burdened with lengthy delays that greatly increase
development costs.

Policy Time-Lag Problem

Another problem is likely to arise from the inherent dynamism of job
and housing markets. When the regional agency mandated to seek
greater jobs-housing balance is established, it will set targets for each
subregion on the basis of data already several years old, because of the
difficulties of obtaining current information. By the time its policies
become even partly implemented, at least several more years will have
passed. By then, many of the overall and individual adjustments to long
commuting journeys described earlier will have taken place. That will
make the actual relationship between jobs and housing in every community different from what the regional agency first thought it would be.
Hence the policies may no longer be appropriate.

Such policy obsolescence because of informational and implementation time lags is endemic to many government actions in a dynamic society. It is particularly likely to plague any strategy to attain a jobs-
housing balance because of the high mobility of American households.
In 2000, 9 percent of owner-occupant households and 31 percent of
renter-occupants had moved within the previous twelve months. The
overall fraction moving annually was 15 percent, but it was 50 percent
higher in the West (18 percent) than in the Northeast (12 percent).[18]
Thus, even if an appropriate jobs-housing balance is attained at some
moment, it will be difficult to sustain.

"Spontaneous" Achievement of Policy Tactics

Recently major U.S. metropolitan areas have been "spontaneously"
implementing some of the tactics just listed without any explicit public
policies aimed at doing so. For example, more housing has been added
to older, more central areas with a job surplus. But in most metropolitan
areas, these additions have been much smaller than the number of jobs
added through new downtown office space occupancy. Really signifi-

cant housing increases in close-in neighborhoods require raising density, which has encountered severe political opposition. Hence the first tactic listed earlier has not been taken up on any large scale.

In contrast, for the past thirty years there has been a major and nearly universal out-migration of jobs and residents from central cities to suburbs. This has accomplished the second, third, and fourth tactics listed to some degree. It has caused some spontaneous improvement in the jobs-housing balance in areas with a job surplus and those with a housing surplus. Jobs are likely to continue moving into outlying areas with housing surpluses, probably at an accelerating rate. But a lot of new housing has also been built in these peripheral areas, and this trend is likely to continue unless deliberately opposed. Until now, such new homebuilding has more than offset the movement of additional jobs into these areas. Hence most such areas still have large housing surpluses.

Moreover, during the 1980s and the 1990s, many additional jobs were created in downtown areas because so much new office space was built there. This directly contravened the second tactic described and indirectly opposed the third and fourth tactics. In general, then, recent trends are probably worsening the jobs-housing imbalances in most U.S. metropolitan areas.

The Political Asymmetry Problem

A great difficulty in trying to improve subregional jobs-housing balances through public policies is that the six tactics described earlier will meet with varying political responses. Some are almost sure to be rejected, whereas others are quite likely to be adopted. This would cause incomplete and distorted application of the complete set of policies. The net result might increase rather than decrease commuting problems.

The tactics most likely to be rejected are those connected with building more housing for low- and moderate-income households in or near areas with a job surplus. Such areas include downtowns and large outlying nodes containing retail, office, and industrial facilities. Since most such areas contain few vacant parcels, many additional housing units could only be built there if existing structures were razed and the area redeveloped at higher densities. But present residents would strongly resist higher densities.

Local governments would also resist limits on adding more jobs. They want the added local tax revenues such jobs provide. As a result,

.ey ingredients of any overall jobs-housing balancing strategy
.d be extremely difficult to put in place politically.

Uther subregions suffer from the opposite problem: a surplus of
housing units in relation to jobs. There the appropriate balancing policy
would be to inhibit more housing construction. That policy would probably be enthusiastically accepted by many existing residents and local
governments eager to limit further growth. Hence many such communities would adopt growth limits reducing annual additions to the housing
supply. But those communities are also the ones in which the least
expensive new housing in each metropolitan area is being built. Consequently, the policies that are supposed to improve the balance between
jobs and housing might choke off the creation of additional new, relatively low-cost housing in peripheral areas—without adding many new
units in older areas with job surpluses. This outcome would make the
shortage of affordable housing worse and would not shorten average
commuting distances.[19] This description is not far from what has happened in both northern and southern California in the 1990s.

The Jobs-Housing Balance and Traffic Congestion

Even if the jobs-housing balances in a metropolitan area were improved,
how much would that cut traffic congestion? The direct goal of such
changes would be to decrease average commuting distances, though that
would not necessarily reduce traffic congestion. Other conditions are
also required. However, the main issue is, would improving the jobs-
housing balance significantly reduce average commuting distances?

To answer that question, one must first specify just what is meant by
"improving the jobs-housing balance." Public policy cannot and should
not dictate to every worker where he or she must live to reduce traffic
congestion. Therefore, what could public policies on the jobs-housing
balance be expected to achieve? The answer is creation of enough housing near each major job center, at appropriate price levels, to enable, in
theory, every worker in that center to live within a relatively short commuting distance.

Since most workers do not choose their housing solely to minimize
their commuting times, however, even if an adequate supply of appropriately priced housing were created near every job center, many workers in each center would not occupy that housing. Large amounts of
cross commuting would still take place. But would there be much less

cross commuting than there is now? No one knows, nor has much research been done on this subject. Workers employed in large job centers in southern California had longer commutes than those employed outside such centers, except for centers located in exurban parts of the metropolitan area.[20] Data from the 1980 and 1990 censuses also show that the shortest commuting times were among workers who lived and worked outside the central cities. The longest were among those who lived outside central cities but worked downtown. So if many jobs were moved out of the large clusters where they now outnumber nearby housing units, or many new housing units were built near them, the average commuting distances should decline.

The maximum possible reduction in average commuting distances from an improved jobs-housing balance can be estimated from the model metropolitan area set forth in appendix C. In that model, workers both reside and work in three subregions: the central city, older suburbs, and newer exurbs. In the base case, 30 percent of the population lives in the central city, one-half in the older suburbs, and 20 percent in the exurbs. But 40 percent of the jobs are in the central city, 50 percent in the suburbs, and only 10 percent in the exurbs. The ratio of local jobs to locally resident workers is 0.50 for the exurbs, 1.00 for the older suburbs, and 1.33 for the central city, so substantial imbalances exist. About 48.4 percent of all workers commute from one subregion to another. The average commuting distance for all workers is 10.08 miles.

Job locations can be adjusted to cut cross commuting among subregions in half, so that only 24.2 percent of all workers are cross commuting. Then the ratio of local jobs to locally resident workers is 0.75 for the exurbs, 1.01 for the older suburbs, and 1.16 for the central city. All subregions are closer to being balanced. The average commuting distance is 9.12 miles, or 9.5 percent less than in the base case. That is a notable reduction in average commuting distances, but it requires a much larger proportional drop in cross commuting.

These simulations do not take into account the immense real-world obstacles to shifting that many jobs. Nor do they include movements of housing locations. Moreover, reducing average commuting distances does not always alleviate traffic congestion. However, actual declines in average commuting distances of the magnitude derived from the model would probably improve traffic congestion significantly, other things being equal.

Summary

In summary, a jobs-housing balancing strategy is not likely to reduce traffic congestion effectively, even in the long run, for three main reasons. First, deliberately decreasing existing jobs-housing imbalances throughout any large U.S. metropolitan area is extraordinarily difficult. The range of policies required, the depth of institutional change needed, and the extremely strong political resistance that must be overcome are all immense. It is a task akin to moving mountains without using bulldozers or dynamite. Within the fragmented institutional structure of U.S. metropolitan areas, doing so verges on the impossible.

Second, the resulting improvements in traffic congestion are probably not large and would be difficult to sustain. Matching the affordable housing supply in an area with the wage earners who work there would not necessarily persuade the latter to occupy the former. Even if policymakers achieved such a match, many locally employed workers would still choose to live far from their jobs to gain other benefits besides minimizing their commutes.

The final argument against this strategy is that the energy and degree of institutional change it requires would cut traffic congestion much more if used to implement other strategies aimed at the same goal. Examples are adopting peak-hour road pricing or peak-hour parking charges. Such major institutional changes can be achieved only through expenditure of strong personal leadership and energy, plus accumulated political capital. Why focus those scarce resources on altering an area's jobs-housing imbalances when other institutional changes would be much more effective at cutting traffic congestion?

This does not mean that improving the jobs-housing balance in a region is a bad idea or that it would produce no social benefits. If accomplished, it could help provide greater justice and equality of housing and job opportunities for low- and moderate-income households, improve the availability of the local labor force in suburban communities, increase socioeconomic and cultural diversity in such communities, and enable old and young members of families living there to remain residents of those communities. Hence it may be socially desirable to try improving the jobs-housing balances in many communities or even throughout a metropolitan area. But that strategy should not be pursued primarily to reduce traffic congestion.

CHAPTER 14

Concentrating Jobs in Large Clusters

Some advocates of the greater use of public transit to relieve traffic congestion and air pollution propose concentrating more jobs in large clusters outside of downtowns. They believe that common commuting destinations for larger numbers of workers would encourage greater commuting via transit and ride sharing. This tactic is advocated by some proponents of "smart growth" as part of increasing densities in order to combat sprawl. This chapter examines how practical this strategy might be in U.S. metropolitan areas.

Background Analysis

There are two types of advantages from concentrating jobs in clusters within a metropolitan area. One type involves productive efficiency and stems from the economics of agglomerating related economic activities. The other type involves transportation and stems from the greater efficiency of public transit in serving high-density clusters at points of origin and destination.

The Economics of Agglomeration

Economists and geographers have long agreed that two basic reasons exist for cities to have arisen and prospered over many centuries. One, placing people and activities closer together reduces transportation costs among them. Two, related productive activities are more innovative and more efficient when they are clustered relatively close together, enabling an easy exchange of ideas, materials, and workers. Cities also arose as centers of security against attack, centers of religious worship, centers of trade at points where travelers had to shift from one mode to another, and locations adjacent to key raw materials like coal and iron. For most of human history, all these reasons for people and activities to cluster together were intimately connected with the high costs and great difficulties of moving people and goods over long distances, especially on land.

However, since the advent of railroads in the early nineteenth century, technological innovations in transportation have radically reduced the costs of moving people and goods over land. At first, these changes led to greater centralization and spatial clustering of activities. Railroads are efficient transporters mainly over relatively long distances. So the economic advantages of being close together remained strong within each region. As a result, the industrialization of the American economy in the nineteenth and early twentieth centuries generated ever-larger urban concentrations of jobs and people in cities. This concentration led to increasing congestion of vehicles in the central parts of those cities. It started with horse-drawn vehicles but continued after motorized vehicles were introduced.

But the widespread use of automotive vehicles in the twentieth century—especially after World War II—changed that situation immensely. Automobiles and trucks made it possible to move rapidly and conveniently over relatively short distances. Hence activities and workers could spread out much more than before *within each region* and still interact efficiently. Such spreading out was one way to avoid the intense congestion at the heart of each metropolitan area. This factor, and the sheer population growth in most American metropolitan regions after World War II, caused rapid outward expansion of settled areas. First, residents moved outward seeking less costly land, then retail facilities followed the residents, then wholesale and distribution facilities and many industrial plants moved away from central congestion, and finally office activities followed. The resulting outward movement involved not only peripheral growth but also true deconcentration and dispersion of activities. This occurred in part because of the diseconomies of agglomeration—mainly increasing congestion of all types in high-density areas, especially in and around central business districts.

This trend toward dispersing activities into lower-density settlements was further accelerated by developments in communications. They included telephones, fax machines, television, computers, fiber optics, satellites, cell phones, and the Internet. All made it easier, faster, cheaper, and more convenient to communicate over space, further reducing the need for activities to remain clustered together. True, many economists believe the clustering of firms in related industries in a single region—such as the computer industry in the Silicon Valley south of San Francisco—still provides important economies of production and innovation. But this centripetal force pulling firms closer together is being increasingly weakened by the centrifugal forces tending to disperse them in space.

The Economics of Density in Transportation

As discussed earlier, high-density settlements have two opposite impacts on the efficiency of different modes of transportation. For public transit, relatively high density is a prerequisite for efficient operations. Each transit vehicle needs to carry many persons to spread the high costs of operating relatively large vehicles with paid drivers. That means transit works best when its origin points or destination points—preferably both—have high densities that can generate such large loads. Moreover, increasing the overall load on transit systems with off-road rights of way does not slow down their speed; it just makes each vehicle or car more crowded.

In contrast, high-density settlements cause automotive vehicles to become less efficient because such settlements generate more and more vehicles moving per square mile. But the speed of movement on roads, unlike that on separate transit rights of way, slows down the more vehicles travel on those roads (see appendix A). Hence greater settlement densities lead to more intensive congestion and less efficient movement on roads—unless many travelers switch to off-road public transit. This is evident from levels of automotive traffic congestion in and near huge downtowns like those in Tokyo, London, New York, and Bombay. Conversely, regions heavily dependent on automotive vehicles for movement—as are almost all American metropolitan areas—tend to spread out in lower-density settlements, partly to avoid the intensive congestion found in very high-density areas.

Conflicting Trends and the Smart-Growth Movement

The preceding analysis shows that the deconcentration into low-density settlements generated in part by automotive vehicles is in direct conflict with the concentration in higher-density settlements needed to make public transit efficient. In the recent past, a whole movement on metropolitan planning and development—the "smart growth" movement—has sprung up because of this conflict.[1]

Advocates of smart growth deplore the spreading out of regional settlements in low-density patterns in "suburban sprawl." They claim that sprawl has several socially adverse effects. For instance, it reduces the amount of available open land by converting it to urban uses and in this process destroys many environmentally sensitive sites and agriculturally rich farmlands. It also generates excessive amounts of automotive travel, which spawns too much air pollution and petroleum consumption, as well as wasteful traffic congestion. It also neglects and weakens inner-city areas by shifting too many jobs to far-out regions that unemployed inner-city workers cannot reach and causes underinvesting in maintaining older city and inner-ring suburban neighborhoods. Critics say that sprawl compels society to spend too much on extending infrastructures like roads, utility systems, and sewer systems far into peripheral areas, instead of using existing infrastructure systems closer in. Finally, it weakens the sense of community in neighborhoods and cities and whole regions that is necessary for a politically and socially healthy society.

One of the remedies for these ills proposed by advocates of smart growth is clustering relatively high-density settlements close to public transit stops. This will help slow down the outward movement of population, permit people to walk instead of drive for many of their daily activities, and create nodes where public transit can operate efficiently. These are called transit-oriented developments and are exemplified by such neighborhoods as the Ballston area in Arlington County, Virginia, and Walnut Creek in California.

The remainder of this chapter explores the feasibility and desirability of clustering jobs together in concentrations large enough to make public transit within a region more efficient.[2]

The Job-Concentration Strategy

If many jobs were concentrated in each of one or more small areas, then enough workers could ride the same transit vehicles to and from work to reduce substantially the subsidies inherent in the operation of such vehicles. If a much larger fraction of all workers commuted by mass transit, then the total number of vehicles on the roads would decline enough to reduce peak-hour congestion. That is the justification for a job-concentration strategy relevant to this book.

Large job centers thus formed might be linked by fixed-rail mass transit, as in many European metropolitan areas. That arrangement is clearly most feasible in areas that already have extensive mass transit systems. An optimal system would permit workers located in any part of the metropolitan area to commute to any job center with no more than one transfer. But even areas without fixed-rail systems could connect major job concentrations with buses operating on exclusive busways or in high-occupancy (HOV) lanes.

In the 1980s, a job-concentration strategy was proposed for the greater Toronto area that would bring many jobs together in a few big clusters.[3] This "nodal" strategy would presumably reduce the need for automobile commuting and encourage greater use of public transportation. It was visualized as lying somewhere along a continuum between two other strategies also proposed: the "spread" strategy, which promotes continued low-density sprawl supported by massive new freeway construction; and the "central" strategy, which concentrates most future population and job growth within the inner parts of the metropolitan area, relies heavily on public transit, and calls for only minimal freeway expansion. In 1998, the city of Toronto merged with several other major jurisdictions in its metropolitan area, and the combined community began working on a new plan. In 2002, that new plan was completed, embodying a combination of the strategies just described with growth focused along major transportation corridors.[4]

The other reason for adopting a job-concentration strategy is similar but involves ride sharing. Since many workers will have the same points of departure and commuting destinations, more will find it easier to share rides in their own cars or in vans provided by their employers. And clustering many firms together makes it easier to create strong transportation management associations (TMAs) through which employers can jointly urge workers to share rides. Experience shows that ride sharing increases notably when employers put great pressure on their workers to use it and reward those who do.

Job concentrations also allow TMAs to provide certain direct services for workers more efficiently than if firms were scattered widely. For example, TMAs can provide shuttle buses or shuttle vans linking different parts of the job-concentration area for a low fee or even free. This would make it easier for employees to visit one another, lunch together, or shop during lunch breaks without using their cars, thereby reducing local congestion.

Once employers in a cluster started working together to promote ride sharing, they could more easily undertake other tactics for reducing congestion. For example, they might stagger their work hours. They could also agree not to provide free parking to their employees. They could do that without becoming noncompetitive with employers at other locations by providing commuting allowances to all their workers and by charging those who drove alone for parking spaces, or by adopting cashing-out programs for free parking as described earlier.

If large job concentrations could feasibly be created in suburbs or large cities, there is little doubt that they could more easily generate additional ride sharing, and perhaps more use of mass transit than now occurs. However, this strategy would not reduce average commuting distances unless the housing locations of workers also changed. Moreover, job concentration is somewhat in conflict with achieving a better jobs-housing balance. In theory, the latter would be better served by scattering jobs widely, closer to housing.

Feasibility of Job Concentration

In assessing this strategy for American metropolitan areas, several factors should be taken into account.

—Existing jobs are now widely scattered, especially in suburbs. Hence concentrating significant fractions of them in big centers would require major relocations. Job dispersal has been encouraged by suburban zoning ordinances that prohibit high-density commercial construction. These regulations mandate low-rise, well-landscaped workplaces served by their own parking lots, or they locate businesses in elongated ribbons along major commercial streets. This pattern is strikingly illustrated by 1980 data from the five-county Los Angeles area for nineteen large activity centers covering 23,980 acres and containing 821,700 jobs. The biggest was the downtown Los Angeles core, which held 373,300 jobs in 6,737 acres. But all nineteen centers combined accounted for only 17.5 percent of the 4.7 million jobs in the five-county area. The remaining 82.5 percent were scattered outside these centers. Thus job concentration in the Los Angeles area is best described as dispersed rather than polycentric.[5]

Robert Lang analyzed the spatial locations of office jobs in thirteen of the largest United States metropolitan areas in 1999. He classified locations into four categories: primary downtowns, secondary downtowns, edge cities (large suburban nodes), and "edgeless cities" (that is, widely dispersed). Only in the New York and Chicago areas were there more office jobs in primary downtowns than in dispersed locations, which were mainly in the suburbs. In the other eleven regions, dispersed locations contained more office jobs than any other part of the region.[6] Yet office jobs are generally considered more concentrated in downtowns—both primary and secondary—than any other types of jobs. Hence it is reasonable to conclude that most other jobs are at least just as dispersed as office jobs and probably more dispersed.

Edward L. Glaeser, Matthew Kahn, and Chenghuan Chu examined the spatial distribution of all types of jobs in the one hundred largest American metropolitan areas, using 1996 data.[7] They found that, among all jobs within thirty-five miles from the central city center, an average of only 22 percent were within three miles. About 35 percent were from ten to thirty-five miles out, and 43 percent were from three to ten miles out. Among the eleven largest metropolitan areas in the United States, which together contained about one-third of the nation's total population, 19.7 percent of these jobs were within three miles, 27.3 percent were from three to ten miles, and 53.05 percent were from ten to thirty-five miles. Thus extensive job dispersal is a widespread phenomenon.

As a result, concentrating much greater fractions of existing jobs in activity centers would require a massive relocation of existing employers. This strategy can be much more effectively applied to the initial settlement of areas of new growth than to the rearrangement of areas already settled. It would have to be adopted by planners and governments of areas of new growth before those areas were settled and used to influence where future jobs were located therein.

—Each large metropolitan area already contains several major outlying employment centers, but most people who work there do not commute by public transit. Most such centers are clusters of employers around regional shopping malls. Examples are Tyson's Corner outside of Washington, D.C., Oakbrook outside of Chicago, the South Coast Plaza in Orange County, California, and the Galleria in Houston. These edge cities contain thousands of jobs in retail, office, service, light industrial, and warehouse structures.[8]

However, these structures are not right next to one another, as are downtown buildings. Rather, each building is normally surrounded by its own parking lots—sometimes decked ones, which isolate it from other structures. This makes pedestrian movement aesthetically unattractive and inefficient and encourages the use of cars to commute and to move between buildings. Higher fractions of workers commute by automotive vehicles to these outlying centers than to downtowns, which are better served by transit. The 1980 data on the Los Angeles area cited above showed that only 8.3 percent of workers in the eighteen largest activity centers outside of the downtown commuted by public transit, compared with 20.7 percent of downtown workers and 3.5 percent of all workers not employed in any of the nineteen largest centers. Therefore, outlying centers generate more automotive traffic per 1,000 workers than downtowns—especially around noontime. This often gives rise to three rush hours, rather than just those in the morning and evening.

Thus the mere existence of large job concentrations does not create conditions conducive to greater transit commuting. The concentrations must be compact enough so that most workers can easily walk to one or a few transit stops, and transit service must be frequent. Both conditions are rare in existing outlying activity centers.

—Most suburban communities would oppose concentrating jobs in just a few large centers. They seek to capture as many jobs as they can within their boundaries to maximize local tax revenues. The fragmented structure of local governments in most U.S. metropolitan areas causes intense competition for commercial "ratables." Large job concentrations would undoubtedly be located in a relatively small fraction of all the local communities within a metropolitan area. The only exception would be areas such as the one around Washington, D.C., where entire large counties make up the main local governments. The few communities containing large job concentrations would benefit greatly from the tax revenues generated there. But surrounding communities would suffer from having lower tax bases and would try to prevent jobs from moving into these few centers by offering employers more advantageous tax and benefit packages. Therefore, in most metropolitan areas, local governments would be likely to oppose a job-concentration strategy—unless some new method of funding local governments were adopted.[9]

—This strategy would not by itself reduce traffic congestion; it would have to be accompanied by substantial changes in transportation arrangements. Most workers in large suburban job centers drive to work alone. Concentrating many jobs in a few big centers would initially increase congestion there because so many more auto-driving commuters would converge on them each day. This means that the job-concentration strategy can decrease congestion only if it is accompanied by one or both of two other actions. One is the provision of greatly expanded and improved public transit facilities and service. The other is the vigorous promotion of private ride-sharing programs by key private and public employers there.

—Getting any sizable fraction of American workers outside of New York City and a few other densely populated cities to commute by public transit would require extensive changes in their behavior that they now strongly resist. In twenty-three of the nation's largest metropolitan areas in 2000, the proportion of workers commuting in private vehicles was 89.0 percent among suburban-resident workers, versus 66.0 percent among those living in central cities.[10] The proportion of suburban-resident workers using public transit was only 4.34 percent, and the proportion using car pools was 11.40 percent. Both these fractions declined from 1990 to 2000. There is little evidence that concentrating jobs in big suburban clusters would produce big changes in commuting behavior. Surveys in Walnut Creek, California, on how workers commute to offices in large job clusters next to fixed-rail mass transit stops indicate that less than 2 percent use mass transit. However, 2000 Census data for the census tract containing the Ballston metro stop in Arlington, Virginia, showed that 42 percent of workers living in that tract commuted by transit.[11]

—Even if this strategy succeeded in changing commuter behavior, it would impose heavy financial burdens on governments. Fixed-rail public transit systems are costly to build, and almost all public transit systems in developed nations—including buses—incur large operating losses. Except in some Asian nations, most public transit systems throughout the world lose money on their construction costs and current operations.[12] Raising fares on fixed-rail systems to cover their full costs is politically unacceptable or would reduce their patronage to unfeasibly low levels, or both. Consequently, few metropolitan areas anywhere will build fixed-rail transit systems without substantial subsidies from their national governments. And extensive public transit systems can only rarely be operated without large ongoing subsidies. Because the job-concentration strategy requires greater use of public transit to reduce congestion, it would need massive subsidies not now available.

—If job concentration led to development of an effective ride-sharing program, it could reduce traffic congestion to some extent without undue public expense. Employers could more easily cooperate to promote ride sharing among their workers if jobs were clustered in a sizable activity center than if they were widely scattered. Moreover, many more workers would have access to a bigger group of possible riders from which to form car or van pools. Ride sharing can be carried out without much public expense. It would be even more encouraged by the creation of HOV lanes on nearby expressways, although that might involve heavy public expenditures. Furthermore, once employer associations were formed to promote ride sharing, they could more effectively implement other tactics aimed at reducing traffic congestion, as noted earlier.

Administrative Problems

Concentrating most new suburban jobs in a few outlying centers would require two institutional changes in most U.S. metropolitan areas. One would permit many communities to share in the tax revenues generated by those centers. The only nonconsolidated U.S. metropolitan area that now has such an arrangement is Minnesota's Twin Cities area, which uses tax-base sharing. The second institutional change would give a regional agency the power to encourage job concentration, perhaps by prohibiting added jobs in certain areas. Otherwise, competition among individual communities would continue the broad scattering of jobs.

Thus a job-concentration strategy would require regulatory intervention into current land-use decisionmaking. It would probably create another layer of regulation that would control, or at least strongly influence, where potential employers could locate their jobs. Many employers, except perhaps the smallest, might have to obtain permission from a regional job control agency when they were deciding where to locate or expand. This would be a radical departure from the universal and traditional U.S. practice of permitting individual employers to enjoy freedom of locational choice.

The only alternative would be some market-oriented incentive structure that motivated individual employers to locate in key job centers and avoid other sites. For example, property tax rates could be made much lower in such centers and higher elsewhere. However, most firms do not base their locational decisions primarily on property taxes. Or a special worker surtax might be imposed on all firms that newly locate outside selected job centers, but not on those that move inside those centers. This would at least leave locational decisions up to individual employers. But it would require discriminatory taxes or fees that might be found illegal. Such incentives would still require a powerful role by a regional or state agency. Only such an agency could decide which parts of the metropolitan area would be favored with positive inducements and which would suffer from negative ones.

Furthermore, a job-concentration strategy would confer a quasi-monopoly position on the owners of land within the selected job clusters. Unless there were so many designated job centers that competition among them restrained land prices in all of them, they would be able to charge exorbitantly high prices or rents for their land. This could only be avoided through commercial rent controls or land-price controls, or by government acquisition and administration of all the land within the job-concentration zones. Neither is compatible with normal free enterprise behavior. Conversely, a job-concentration policy would deprive many owners of land outside the selected centers of all chances to gain high property values or rents from commercial land uses. Those landowners would fiercely oppose this strategy, and they would vastly outnumber landowners benefited by it. This stacks the deck politically against the adoption of such a scheme in a democracy.

In fact, this situation illustrates a general difficulty with policies designed to curb purely individualistic behavior to achieve community goals. There is an inescapable conflict between unconstrained individual freedoms long traditional among Americans and certain widely desired community objectives they now seek. As noted earlier, this conflict is inherent in many policies aimed at reducing traffic congestion.

Good Locations for a Job-Concentration Strategy

A few metropolitan areas are dominated by geographically large local governments, such as the county governments around Washington, D.C. These governments encompass huge territories that already contain major job centers. So they could steer at least some additional jobs into those few centers without creating another layer of government, particularly by pressuring owners of currently developed sites in such centers to fill in those sites with more structures. New commercial buildings could be placed in present parking or landscaped areas, and more parking could be provided by decking other parking lots. This would convert now sprawling but inefficient offices in these centers into more compact, downtown-like districts, permit more efficient pedestrian interchanges, and encourage more ride sharing, and—if these centers were served by rapid transit—more commuting off the highways.

Since these governments already contain the areas that would lose potential jobs under such a policy and the centers that would gain jobs, they would not have to adopt new tax-sharing arrangements. And they could use their existing development permission powers to steer new jobs into these centers, thereby avoiding two serious obstacles to the job-concentration strategy.

Achieving an Effective Job-Concentration Strategy

A deliberate strategy of suburban job concentration is not likely to play a significant role in reducing future traffic congestion in American metropolitan areas. One reason is that it would force long-established behavior patterns of workers and employers to change. However, that is true of almost any strategy likely to reduce future traffic congestion.

More important, in a world of fragmented local governments, a job-concentration strategy would require regional bureaucratic control over job locations. That would add another layer to the already complex real estate development process. Moreover, the fiscal system that now finances most local governments would have to be greatly modified so that those communities containing big job clusters would not capture unfair shares of property tax revenue. The required legal and institutional changes would be extremely unpopular among local governments and employers. One result would be increased monopoly power over land prices by those fortunate enough to own property within the chosen concentration areas.

Furthermore, for maximum effectiveness, this strategy must be linked to extensive public transit facilities. Metropolitan areas that already have fixed-rail systems could tie additional job centers into those systems or just expand the job centers they now contain. But most U.S. metropolitan areas do not have off-road mass transit systems and would require huge public investments in building them to link job centers.

This would be necessary even to serve such centers only with bus transit. Buses would need exclusive busways or HOV lanes for maximum effectiveness. And all additional transit facilities would require continuous subsidies to help pay for their operating costs. Such added spending is not likely to be forthcoming from governments at any level.

Nevertheless, metropolitan areas with four specific traits might at least consider adopting some elements of a job-concentration strategy. Such areas should have more than 1.2 million residents, suffer from severe traffic congestion, contain a few, geographically large suburban governments, and already have fixed-rail mass transit systems. Because of their large suburban political jurisdictions, they could avoid some of the most controversial intergovernmental power struggles that would otherwise accompany this strategy. But smaller metropolitan areas, or those with highly fragmented local government structures, or those without extensive existing public transit systems, are not likely to find this strategy very effective. That group includes the vast majority of U.S. metropolitan areas.

CHAPTER 15

Local Growth Management Policies

Many local governments have reacted to rapid growth in general and traffic congestion in particular by adopting ordinances that limit future development within their boundaries. The nature and impact of such ordinances and their likely effectiveness in reducing congestion are important subjects for analysis.[1]

Some Basic Definitions

The types of policies that local governments adopt in response to the pressures of growth are often characterized by three different terms. These terms do not have universally accepted definitions, but this analysis assumes they are defined as follows.

GROWTH CONTROLS. These policies are aimed at limiting or reducing the amount of growth that a community will permit within its borders compared to what has occurred there in the recent past. Examples are caps on the number of housing units that can be built in the community each year and moratoriums halting all new housing construction for a given period. Growth controls generally have more drastic impacts on where future growth occurs than growth management policies.

GROWTH MANAGEMENT POLICIES. These policies are not aimed at reducing or halting growth but at directing future growth into forms that local residents consider most desirable. Examples are zoning regulations aimed at maximizing land uses that produce net fiscal benefits to the local government and minimizing uses that produce net fiscal losses to that government. However, such policies can have the same effects as growth controls under certain conditions.

SMART GROWTH. This type of strategy consists of a set of both goals and specific policies aimed at reducing those effects of sprawl development in an entire region that sprawl's opponents consider undesirable. However, smart growth usually encompasses the following goals:

—Preserving open space and agricultural lands by slowing down the outward expansion of urban development beyond the currently developed periphery. This goal may be pursued by adopting urban growth boundaries or special utility districts.

—Reducing the dependence of resident ground transportation on private automotive vehicles by increasing the use of public transit, bicycling, and walking.

—Permitting the mixing of different land uses—such as housing and retail—in the same areas, rather than entirely segregating them into different zones.

—Encouraging higher density and more compact development than in the past through developing in-fill sites, raising densities in existing neighborhoods, and requiring higher average densities in new neighborhoods.

—Revitalizing older existing neighborhoods.

Other elements, such as promoting more affordable housing, are advocated by some smart-growth proponents but are less prevalent. Several smart growth elements can also be considered forms of either growth controls or growth management, depending on how they are applied. The preceding definitions are used in this analysis unless otherwise noted. For convenience, all three types of policies or actions are referred to collectively as growth-related actions or policies.

Why Local Governments Adopt Growth Management or Controls to Reduce Traffic Congestion

Local growth-related laws can focus on commercial development, residential development, or both. At least forty-one types of such policies have been identified in past studies.[2] These include caps on the number of housing units or square feet of commercial space that can be built annually, height limits on commercial buildings, down zoning of vacant parcels to reduce the density at which they can be developed, and many others. This book cannot go into the details of such policies, but it assumes many of these policies would decrease the amount of future growth in the adopting community. But how effective could growth control or growth management policies be in reducing traffic - congestion?

At first glance, since traffic flows are generated by commercial and residential developments, decreasing the future amount of such development within the community seems likely to reduce the traffic flows arising there. Local governments have often used this argument to restrict commercial development and multifamily housing projects. For example, Walnut Creek, California, in response to increasing traffic congestion in its downtown area, prohibited office developments above a certain height and building size. Palo Alto, California, down zoned its commercially zoned land by reducing the amount of development permitted on that land from 25 million square feet to 3 million. The explicit purpose of this change was to decrease future increases in traffic.[3] Other relevant growth-related policies force developers to bear some of the costs of the roads necessary to handle traffic generated by their projects. This can be done through impact fees or exactions required before awarding permission to build new projects. Or a community may adopt some form of "concurrency" policy. That means it will not grant permission for new developments until the infrastructures needed to serve them are already built or at least planned and paid for. Florida has adopted such a policy statewide.[4]

In the late 1980s, local growth-management and growth control policies became widespread local government responses to rapid population increases, often aimed in part at rising traffic congestion. In California, in particular, hundreds of communities adopted such laws.[5] Three traffic-related factors influenced these decisions.

First, traffic congestion was growing much worse, and local politicians and government leaders wanted to appear to be "doing something" in response. Since the basic causes of congestion are regionwide in nature, local leaders cannot directly control the true causes of congestion unless they carry out highly controversial policies throughout the region. Not only would that daunting task take years, but it would also run counter to their strong desire to preserve their own local sovereignty.

Second, local officials can readily pass purely local ordinances, often without much controversy. In contrast, they cannot easily pass region-wide ordinances, nor do most officials want to do so. Hence they pass local laws to appear responsive to their constituents' concerns about this problem, even if those laws will not work well. Such laws need not be entirely symbolic, although they usually do not affect many fundamental causes of congestion.

Third, most social costs likely to result from local growth-related laws are not borne mainly by residents in the adopting communities but by potential future residents and people living elsewhere. The largest such likely cost is higher future housing prices that might be faced by persons seeking to move into the community. But those higher housing prices also benefit existing homeowners, who usually account for a majority of the local electorate.[6] Hence there is a strong political incentive for local officials to adopt such policies.

Can Local Growth Controls Affect Traffic Congestion?

In reality, locally adopted growth-related policies can have little, if any, impact on existing traffic congestion levels in the communities that pass them. Almost all new local growth-related policies regulate future growth. But today's traffic is generated by past and current growth that is already in place.

Whether a community's policies can affect its future traffic congestion levels depends on three main factors. The first is whether most of its traffic is generated locally or somewhere else. If locally, then local ordinances may be able to keep future traffic flows from rising as much as they would if growth proceeded unchecked. But if most local traffic arises elsewhere and passes through the adopting community, its own laws may not affect its future traffic flows at all. Then the key factor is how much additional future development will occur where most of its traffic is being generated, which is presumably beyond the locality's control.

The second key factor is whether the adopting community contains much available land on which developers could build more traffic-generating uses. Such land could be vacant sites or sites improved with structures that could be replaced by or renovated into higher-intensity uses. If the community contains little such land, its future growth will be limited, regardless of the policies it adopts. Hence growth-related policies would not greatly affect its future traffic flows. However, communities with very little developable land are not likely to adopt such policies anyway.

The third important factor to consider is to what extent any growth diverted from the adopting community by its growth-related policies will relocate to areas where it still generates traffic passing through that community. As noted in chapter 6, no one suburb can influence the overall growth of its entire metropolitan area by adopting local growth-related policies. Even if such policies succeed in limiting a locality's future growth, those policies will simply shift that growth from the adopting community to others nearby. Some of the added traffic generated by this diverted growth may still pass through the adopting community. However, since the growth diverted away from any one community is likely to spread over many others, it is highly improbable that all the traffic generated by this displaced growth will still flow through the community from which it was diverted.

All three of these conditions are most likely to prevail in new-growth suburbs on the edges of metropolitan areas. Those suburbs not only contain the largest amounts of vacant land but also have the fewest other communities lying beyond them that might generate traffic flowing back through them. These three conditions are necessary but not sufficient to ensure that local ordinances will actually influence the community's future traffic congestion. Whether that happens depends on the policies adopted.

Direct Effects on Local Land Uses

Local growth-related policies can affect local land use in at least four ways. They can influence the specific uses carried out on particular sites. This is done by prohibiting certain uses that developers would otherwise pursue because of their high profitability, such as multifamily housing in neighborhoods occupied primarily by single-family homes. Such policies can also limit annual additions to the local supply of property, for example, by putting a cap on the number of additional housing units that developers are allowed to build each year. They can raise private development costs by adding directly to costs, increasing the time required to complete any project, or reducing the density of development permitted on a given site. And they can increase public sector costs by requiring construction of certain public improvements before private development is permitted.

Effects on the Community and Its Metropolitan Area

Growth-related policies also affect the community adopting them and its metropolitan area. Many growth control policies are designed to slow the pace of new development in the adopting locality. Such policies often raise the market prices of new and existing housing and other properties in the adopting community by restricting supplies there. This also causes higher rents because land values increase and rental units are in scarcer supply than they would otherwise be. Most empirical studies indicate a housing price increase in the adopting community of 5–10 percent, although one study showed a 17–38 percent increase.[7]

Higher housing prices and rents make the adopting community more socially exclusionary by shifting its composition to a higher income group than it would otherwise have contained. However, this change takes a long time, unless the community's total population is growing rapidly. If many communities in a metropolitan area adopt growth-control policies, low- and moderate-income households will find it harder to become homeowners, or even to find rental accommodations they can afford.

But higher housing prices also increase the wealth of the community's existing homeowners, who usually form a majority of its households. This positive effect generates strong political support for such policies. It also means that higher housing prices in themselves cannot be judged as unequivocally harmful to society, even though they make it harder for low- and moderate-income households to become homeowners or to rent decent-quality shelter.[8] However, the losers from higher home prices are generally poorer than the gainers. So the widespread adoption of growth-control policies has a regressive net impact on the distribution of incomes and wealth in the general metropolitan area.

Some local growth-related policies may increase the demand for housing within the adopting communities. When a community adopts exclusionary policies, the price of homes there may initially rise because of smaller additions to supply. Higher prices would normally reduce the demand for housing there. But if many households within the metropolitan area value exclusivity for its own sake, the community's increased exclusivity may increase demand for housing there, in spite of the higher prices.[9] That would drive housing prices there still higher, with all the effects just described.

Growth-control policies tend also to spread the ultimate growth of the metropolitan area over a larger space than it would otherwise have occupied. Such policies generally reduce the fully built-out density of the communities that adopt them, compared with what those densities would have been. Therefore, the more communities adopt growth control policies, the lower the average density of the metropolitan area, and the larger the territory its built-up areas must occupy to accommodate any given total population. Growth management and smart growth policies do not necessarily have this impact.

Effects on Traffic Congestion

By slowing the pace of new development in the communities that adopt them, local growth controls can reduce future increases in locally generated traffic—if these communities have the three traits mentioned earlier.

If such policies force developers to build or pay for more roads and other traffic-handling facilities than would otherwise have been built, they may increase the traffic-handling capacity of the locality's road system. This could also reduce future traffic congestion there. However, developers are generally required to build intersections, exit and entry lanes, parking areas, and other spot traffic-handling facilities, rather than add to the general capacity of the community's road system.

By diverting future growth to other communities, growth control policies shift future traffic there, too. Finally, by spreading future development of the entire metropolitan area during any given period over a larger territory than it would otherwise have occupied, growth control policies require households to drive longer distances. That adds to the metropolitan area's total traffic flows, probably increasing future traffic congestion.

In sum, growth control laws can reduce future peak-hour traffic congestion in the communities passing them under some circumstances. But they do so only at the expense of increasing future congestion in the rest of their metropolitan area. Hence their net impact on traffic congestion can hardly be considered desirable for society as a whole. Although the congestion costs that such laws impose on nonresidents are not large, and may even be smaller than the benefits provided to local residents, those costs are likely to be distributed regressively. Therefore, concerning their impacts on traffic congestion, local growth control ordinances are essentially beggar-thy-neighbor devices. As already noted, this conclusion does not necessarily apply to growth management or smart growth policies that do not limit or reduce future growth in a locality.

Are Smart Growth Policies More Likely to Have Socially Beneficial Effects on Traffic Congestion?

In the 1990s and more recently, many persons and groups dismayed by rising traffic congestion and other alleged ills of "suburban sprawl" have proposed a set of policies known as "smart growth."[10] Several quite different viewpoints exist on just what those policies should be, though proponents of all these viewpoints refer to their favorite policies as smart growth. At least four different groups with differing perspectives claim they are advocating smart growth. They are many environmentalists and other persons advocating slower overall growth; real estate developers, homebuilders, and other progrowth advocates; mayors and other civic leaders in big cities; and persons who do not want to affect the total amount of future growth in their region but want that growth to occupy less total land area than continuation of current growth trends would produce. In this analysis, members of the fourth group will be referred to as *advocates of compact growth*.[11] The goals—and recommended policies—of each group diverge significantly in at least several dimensions from the goals and policies of the other three groups.

Policies proposed by all these groups cover fourteen different elements, each of which can take several forms. For example, a key element is "urban containment" involving some limits on the outward extension of new development beyond existing built-up areas. Such containment can be attempted at the regional or local level, or both. Some advocates of smart growth favor strong urban growth boundaries to check outward growth; others favor weaker utility service districts; still others oppose any constraints on outward growth. Yet all refer to their stands on this issue as appropriate to smart growth as they visualize it.

These fourteen elements are shown in table 15-1. The first column lists the fourteen elements (with the first element subdivided into regional and local forms). The next four columns indicate the attitudes toward each element typically expressed by the four major advocacy

TABLE 15-1. Fourteen Potential Elements of Smart Growth

Smart growth element	Views of advocate groups				Prevalence	Areas where currently exists
	Antigrowth	Progrowth	Inner-city	Compact growth		
1. Limit outward extension of growth						
a. At the regional level	Strongly favor	Strongly oppose	Favor	Favor	Rare at regional level	Portland, Lexington, Seattle
b. At the local government level	Strongly favor	Strongly oppose	Favor	May favor	Common at local level	Boulder, many California cities
2. Finance new infrastructures by loading costs onto new developments	Strongly favor	Strongly oppose	Favor	Usually favor	Widespread practice	Many California cities
3. Reduce auto dependence by increasing emphasis on transit	Strongly favor	Oppose	Strongly favor	Strongly favor	Widespread attempts	Portland, San Diego, Atlanta
4. Promote compact, mixed-use development	Strongly favor	Oppose	Strongly favor	Strongly favor	Moderately frequent	Portland, Seattle, Maryland
5. Create financial incentives for local governments to designate growth areas	Favor	Oppose	Neutral	Strongly favor	Rare	Maryland
6. Adopt fiscal resource sharing	Favor	Oppose	Favor	Favor	Very rare	Twin Cities
7. Choose some form of regional governance or planning coordination	Oppose	Strongly oppose	Oppose	Often favor	Rare	Portland, Twin Cities, Atlanta
8. Adopt faster and more certain development permissions processes	Oppose	Strongly favor	Neutral	May favor	Rare	Portland
9. Create widespread affordable housing	Oppose	Favor	Favor	Favor	Rare	Montgomery County (Md.)
10. Develop consensus-building process	Favor	Oppose	Favor	Favor	Rare	Seattle
11. Preserve open space and environment	Strongly favor	Favor	Favor	Strongly favor	Widespread practice	Boulder, Lexington
12. Redevelop inner-core areas and encourage development on in-fill sites	Strongly favor	Favor	Strongly favor	Strongly favor	Widespread attempts	Denver, Seattle, Portland
13. Encourage new forms of urban design	Strongly favor	Strongly favor	Favor	Strongly favor	Widespread practice	Seaside
14. Create stronger sense of community	Strongly favor	Favor	Strongly favor	Strongly favor	Rare	Portland

groups just mentioned. The attitudes shown represent the author's best judgment about what each type of group favors on the average, but there are numerous exceptions in particular communities. The sixth column shows how widespread that element is in the United States as of 2002. The last column indicates some metropolitan areas where that element can be found. This matrix indicates that all four groups favor four smart growth elements. They are preserving open space, redeveloping inner-core areas, encouraging new forms of urban design, and creating a stronger sense of community. Three groups—all but the progrowth group—favor seven other elements: limiting outward extension of development at regional and at local levels, financing infrastructure by loading costs onto new developments, reducing transportation auto dependence by encouraging more public transit and walking, promoting compact mixed-use development, adopting fiscal resource sharing, and developing a consensus-building process. However, three groups—all but the compact development group—oppose choosing some form of regional governance or planning. The progrowth group exhibits the greatest opposition to smart growth elements, opposing nine of the fifteen shown in table 15-1. The compact development group favors all fifteen elements; its members are the "purest" supporters of smart growth.

A key issue about these elements is, at what level of government should they be controlled—local, state, or regional? Most smart growth advocates from the first three viewpoints believe local governments are the appropriate controllers of all these elements. They think so even though growth itself and many of its constituent parts—including traffic congestion—are really regionwide phenomena. (Whether traffic-oriented policies should be controlled by local or regional bodies is the subject of chapter 17.) Therefore, this chapter on local growth management policies focuses on how local government control of such policies might affect traffic congestion. The fourth advocacy group is more likely to support regionwide policies, which are analyzed in chapter 17.

The first four elements in table 15-1 probably have the greatest potential relationship to the increasing traffic congestion that has recently been generated by population and other growth in U.S. metropolitan areas. Elements 9, 11, and 12 also might affect traffic congestion.

Limiting Outward Extension of Growth

At the purely local government level, limiting outward extension cannot stop overall outward movement of a region's growth, unless all the local governments in a region voluntarily adopt a highly coordinated and integrated set of policies. This has never happened in any U.S. region. Up to now, when growth limitations have been controlled entirely by individual communities, each community using such a policy has applied limits only to growth within its own boundaries. This has been done by setting aside certain parts of the community—usually those lying farthest away from the region's downtown—as appropriate only for very large-lot development. This essentially preserves those parts as open space. This has happened in Montgomery County, Maryland, and Loudoun County, Virginia. Unless this type of limitation is accompanied by policies that raise existing residential densities in the remainder of the community, this policy essentially shifts regional growth away from the adopting communities to other places within the region. This has the ironic aggregate effect of increasing the outward movement of growth in the region as a whole, as explained earlier. An example of this result is in Contra Costa County in the San Francisco Bay region. Several communities there have adopted local growth boundaries, with the result that the region's growth has "skipped" farther east into the Central Valley. Households seeking lower-cost housing thus have to commute farther to reach more centrally located employment areas. This raises the total amount of automotive travel in the region, compared to what would have occurred if no local growth limits had been adopted. Whether greater total travel causes more intense traffic congestion depends on the exact travel patterns concerned, the amount of additional roads built to accommodate that travel, and whether specific "bottleneck" points are involved—such as the Bay Bridge leading into San Francisco. In general, use of local growth limits worsens overall traffic congestion.

If outward limits on growth are applied at the regional level, as in Portland, Oregon, the outcome could conceivably be different. Then the total amount of automotive travel may be lower than it would have been without such limits, assuming residential development densities within the limits rise. To ensure that outcome, the state government that passes regional growth boundaries must prohibit or drastically limit development outside those boundaries in each region, as Oregon has done. Otherwise, a lot of growth will jump to locations outside the boundaries, as has happened in the Twin Cities region of Minnesota. If densities within the regional growth boundary rise high enough, greater use of public transit may become feasible, further reducing automotive travel. However, the evidence from the Portland region does not indicate that its urban growth boundary has notably reduced traffic congestion, as discussed in chapter 12.

Financing Added Infrastructures by Loading Costs onto New Developments

Loading costs onto new developments tends to raise the cost of housing in the new developments, compared to what it would have been if those infrastructure costs had been spread across the entire community. How this affects traffic congestion depends on whether the infrastructures added to support the new developments are adequate to do so without heavy congestion. However, when the larger existing community does not bear much of the costs of these added infrastructures, the new infrastructures will probably not include much additional capacity lying within the already-built-up parts of the region. This may cause the additional traffic flowing from the new outer developments inward to established job centers to intensify congestion in already-built-up areas. However, if the new infrastructures include expanded capacity in already-built-up areas, congestion there need not worsen. Because of political resistance by existing residents to paying for such improvements, the expectation would be that a policy of loading new infrastructure costs onto new developments would cause heavier traffic congestion in earlier-built-up areas.

Increasing Emphasis on Use of Public Transit

More emphasis on public transit would, if successful, reduce traffic congestion compared to what it would be without such a change in emphasis. However, achieving any significant increase in public transit usage is very difficult through entirely local government policies, except perhaps in very large cities. A regionwide approach would have a much better chance of success—but still not a very good chance.[12]

Promoting Compact, Mixed-Use Development

Mixed-use development presumably would involve raising residential densities at least in new-growth areas, and in some existing areas, higher than they would have been without such a policy.[13] Under some circumstances, higher density can reduce traffic congestion. However, densities have to be raised by enormous percentages to reduce travel—and therefore, presumably, congestion—by relatively small percentages. Moreover, raising densities only in new-growth areas—even if successful—is not likely to affect the overall density of an entire region for a long time, except in very rapidly growing regions, because much of the region is already built up.

Creating Widespread Affordable Housing

Widespread affordable housing is an element of smart growth that has been talked about a lot but not significantly achieved except in a few places that have adopted inclusionary zoning laws. Examples are Montgomery County, Maryland, and the state of New Jersey. If more affordable housing were created throughout suburban portions of U.S. metropolitan regions, relatively low-wage workers could more easily live in the communities where they are employed. This would reduce the necessity of their making long commuting trips from far-out residential areas, where housing is less expensive, to where their jobs are located. Hence achievement of this element would reduce traffic congestion, compared to what it would be without such achievement. But up to now, this has not happened in more than a tiny number of regions.

Preserving Open Space and the Environment

Preserving the environment normally includes setting aside significant tracts of now-undeveloped land (including farmland) in preserves that would prevent that land from being developed for future urban uses. At a small scale, this element would have little effect on traffic congestion. But at a very large scale, it might remove so much land from urban development that additional development would be forced to "leap-frog" out beyond such preserves. That would expand the total automotive travel required to accommodate a given population, thereby worsening traffic congestion. On a limited scale, this has happened in Boulder, Colorado, where the local government adopted a strong open-space-preservation policy accompanied by stringent limits on new housing construction.

Redeveloping Inner-Core Areas and Encouraging Development on In-Fill Sites

Redeveloping the inner core and developing on in-fill sites would have the same relationship to traffic congestion as promoting compact, mixed-use development.

Summary

Altogether, the smart growth policies advocated by environmentalists and others who favor slower growth are not likely to have much impact on rising traffic congestion in the short run. Over the long run, the smart growth policies of raising densities by making growth more compact, shifting more emphasis to public transit, preventing very low-density development in far-out locations, and creating widespread affordable housing could at least slow down the rate at which future traffic congestion intensifies. However, doing so would require much more comprehensive and effective application of these policies than has yet been achieved in any U.S. metropolitan area.

CHAPTER 16

Traffic Congestion around the World

Worsening traffic congestion is a severe problem in almost all large and growing metropolitan areas across the globe. It is found from Calcutta to London, from Caracas to Tokyo, from Cairo to Moscow. In fact, worsening traffic congestion seems to be an endemic quality of life in any large and growing urbanized settlement worldwide, in industrialized and developing nations. In many metropolitan areas outside the United States, traffic congestion is much more intense than in even the largest American regions. Consequently, leaders of most American regions do not have to worry that their economic competitiveness against foreign regions is being undermined by rising traffic congestion in their own regions.[1]

Why Congestion Is Worsening in Large, Growing Metropolitan Areas

The shift from earlier modes of ground transportation to the use of automotive vehicles is a key part of economic modernization everywhere. Where roads are available, automotive vehicles provide faster, more powerful, more efficient, and more flexible means of moving people and goods than their predecessors—which are mainly animal-driven vehicles, trolley cars, railroads, bicycles, and walking. Therefore, as societies raise their average income levels, their members increasingly use automotive vehicles for major mobility tasks. But making the transition from earlier modes of ground travel to automotive vehicles creates several inherent difficulties.

One problem is that older, established cities were laid out physically in preautomotive eras; hence they lack streets and roads suitable for handling automobiles, trucks, and buses. In European villages and cities, for example, narrow streets meander through blocks of long-established stone houses and other structures. Widening and straightening these streets to make them capable of handling large volumes of automotive traffic would require tearing down large sections of the dwellings and other structures in these communities. Hence such "modernizing" of street patterns is vehemently resisted by local residents. As a result, many large European cities in even wealthy countries do not have major traffic arteries or expressways running into their downtown areas comparable to those in the United States. Moreover, parking in these communities is often extremely scarce. There are few vacant lots and no room to store cars along the narrow streets. Hence drivers park their cars in almost any available spaces. These include median strips of roads, parks, sidewalks, and in front of fire hydrants. Lack of parking is a much more severe constraint on the use of vehicles in many older cities than traffic congestion.

Another cause of congestion in developing nations is the mingling of many different modes of movement on the same roads. In parts of South Korea, a typical road accommodates several "bands" of travelers: pedestrians, horse- or bullock-drawn carts, bicyclists, motorcyclists, buses, trucks, and passenger cars. Where these different modes are not physically separated, they interfere with one another's efficiency of movement, especially at intersections. Beijing became so crammed with bicyclists that its government outlawed bicycles on one of its main streets. In Bangkok, motorcycles and mopeds snake their way through cars and trucks up to the front of the line at every red stoplight, then take off in a cloud of exhaust smoke when the light changes. In cities where buses transport the majority of urban travelers, streets may become clogged with buses that make frequent stops for passengers, slowing accompanying traffic.

A further cause of congestion in some developing nations is flagrant disregard for the "rules of the road" among vehicle drivers. Many run through red lights and stop signs, drive on shoulders, follow too closely, turn without signaling, make left turns by cutting across flowing traffic, and ignore speed limits. This behavior causes much higher accident rates in many developing nations than in developed ones, and accidents slow down traffic flows.

Finally, because of the low incomes prevalent in developing nations, many of the automotive vehicles there are old and undermaintained. Hence they break down frequently, disrupting traffic, and are more prone to accidents.

All of these factors contribute to intensifying traffic congestion in large and growing metropolitan areas around the world, especially in developing nations.

The Concept of a "Travel-Time Budget"

Throughout the world, as the incomes of households rise, people shift to faster and more comfortable modes of travel. Some transportation economists theorize that people everywhere have a rough travel time "budget" of about 1.0 to 1.5 hours per day, whether they are poor pedestrians or wealthy car owners.[2] Andreas Schafer and D. Victor surveyed residents of two African villages, thirty-six cities in Europe, Asia, and Latin America, and twenty developed nations to discover how much time those residents spent, on the average, in travel each day. The average results from these groups ranged from slightly under 1.0 hour to slightly over 1.5 hours. Those are remarkably similar results, considering the variety of income levels, travel modes, cultures, ethnic groups, and stages of economic development.[3]

As their incomes rise, people apparently want to increase their mobility during that travel budget time by raising their average travel speed and range. So they shift to costlier but faster means of movement. Those that start by walking eventually acquire bicycles or animal-driven conveyances. As their incomes rise, they shift to public transports like buses or trolleys. But in many poor nations, buses are uncomfortably packed with passengers during peak hours. Hence, as soon as they can afford it, many travelers buy motorcycles or mopeds, which are more private, faster, and more flexible than public transit. The last stage is purchasing a car or truck, which conveys the ultimate feeling of independent ground mobility. This analysis implies that the worldwide demand for

FIGURE 16-1. Income and Vehicles, Twenty-Two Countries, 2000

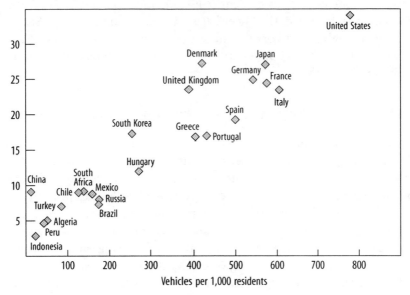

GNP per capita (thousands of U.S. dollars)

Vehicles per 1,000 residents

Source: Author's calculations based on U.S. Bureau of the Census, *Statistical Abstract of the United States: 2002* (2002).

privately owned automotive vehicles will rise sharply in the future if modernization raises incomes in many societies that are now very poor.

Even if there is no one universal travel time budget shared by most people all over the world, the conclusion that rising real incomes will generate widespread desires for greater mobility—and thus for more speed of movement—can still be valid. As long as nearly every individual has some personal concept of a "target" amount of time to spend traveling each day, rising incomes will generate more demands for faster modes of travel—even if the specific travel-time targets of individuals vary greatly in each society. Each person will want to experience the greatest choice of routes and destinations possible within his or her "target" travel time as a means of raising his or her "real travel income." This is especially true if many people like to travel for its own sake, as some recent research suggests.[4] Thus the rising real incomes associated with economic modernization are highly likely to generate demands for more ownership and use of private automotive vehicles.

This relationship can be seen in figure 16-1. It shows verhicles per thousand residents on the X axis and income (gross national product per capita in 2000 in U.S. dollars) on the Y axis for twenty-two nations. As a nation's per capita income rises, so does its number of vehicles per thousand residents. This is evident from the upward slope of the data points, from Indonesia in the lower left-hand corner to the United States in the upper right-hand corner. The simple correlation between these two variables is a positive 0.934, and each is strongly statistically significant in relation to the other.[5]

Behavior toward Automotive Vehicles in Public and Private Sectors

Another key cause of traffic congestion in economically developing nations is a disparity between the speeds at which the public and private sectors adapt to the use of automotive vehicles. The governments there typically have not established effective means of collecting taxes from their citizens, particularly the wealthiest. Hence the financial resources available to the public sector lag behind those available in the private sector. Yet in most of the world, the planning, financing, and construction of streets and roads is the responsibility of the public sector—either local, regional, or national governments. In contrast, the ownership and use of automotive vehicles are largely carried out—and financed—in the private sector. As a result, large numbers of private citizens and firms have the resources to buy and use automotive vehicles. Moreover, they are motivated to do so not only by the efficiency of such vehicles but by the prestige and feelings of personal freedom conferred by owning cars and trucks.

In addition, the production of motor vehicles is conducted almost everywhere by private firms motivated to maximize their profits—mainly by expanding their output. Their major constraint on production volume is the strength of the demand for their vehicles. As that demand increases with rising average incomes in developing societies, these firms increase their production—almost regardless of the road network's capacity for handling the resulting vehicle population. True, the world's major automotive manufacturing firms lobby their governments to build more roads to accommodate greater vehicle populations. But these firms do not hold back on production because of inadequate roads, as long as there are buyers willing and able to absorb their outputs.

As a result of this disparity between the public and private sectors, the number of cars and trucks put into use by the private sector tends to outpace the public sector's ability to finance and build the roads to accommodate those vehicles. This results in continuously overloading existing streets and highways with burgeoning traffic congestion. This problem is especially evident in mostly poor societies where sizable segments of the population achieve rapidly increasing incomes. For example, Calcutta's streets occupy only about 6 percent of the city's land area, compared with as much as 25 percent in some American cities. Consequently, the streets are jammed with all of the many types of travel modes already described for South Korea.

One tactic to reduce this disparity is financing new roads through tolls, preferably in the private sector, thereby avoiding the political costs of shifting taxpayer funds from other possible uses. However, no developing nation has been able to meet enough of its road-building responsibilities through tolls to avoid the disparity just described. One reason is that most residents of these nations are too poor to pay the tolls needed to finance new roads.

Some nations have deliberately adopted severe restraints on the ownership and use of private automotive vehicles in order to restrain traffic congestion. In Singapore—a relatively affluent nation—owning a car requires paying several times as much as the car itself costs. This has kept the number of vehicles per 1,000 inhabitants at 95 in Singapore, compared with 572 in Japan and 779 in the United States. Denmark imposes a 173 percent import tax on new cars. Since no cars are manufactured in Denmark, that means a tax on all cars initially purchased.

The Global Population of Vehicles

The International Road Federation (IRF) publishes surveys on the number of automotive vehicles extant in most of the world's nations, the miles of roads of different types in each nation, and the number of vehicles produced each year throughout the world. Its latest compilation covers the years 1996 through 2000. In some of those years, only part of the data sought has been attained. The following discussion is based on the one most complete annual set of data for each nation during the period 1996 to 2000 published by the IRF.[6] Hence the exact years vary somewhat from one nation to another. Nevertheless, these data are the most comprehensive that the author was able to discover. Hence all the data used will be referred to as for the year 2000, although in many cases they are for 1996, 1997, 1998, or 1999.

In 2000, the IRF reported that there were about 759.1 million cars, trucks, and buses in 164 nations, including all of the largest nations on earth as measured by area or population. Besides those four-or-more-wheeled vehicles, there were many millions of road tractors, motorcycles, and mopeds, but data concerning their number were too incomplete to be analyzed. The 759.1 million vehicles consisted of 566.2 million passenger cars (74.6 percent), 182.8 million trucks and lorries (24.1 percent), and 10.1 million buses and coaches (1.3 percent). The inventories of vehicles in each nation have been aggregated into totals for eight global zones, as shown in table 16-1.

The largest inventory (250.8 million, or 33.0 percent) is in North America (which includes the United States, Canada, and Mexico), closely followed by that in Europe (237.0 million, or 31.2 percent), with northern Asia third (including both Japan and China) (117.6 million, or 15.5 percent).

According to *Automotive World*, the world vehicle population was about 100 million in 1960, rose to 400 million in 1980 (a compound annual growth rate of 7.2 percent), and then to around 780 million in 2000 (a compound annual growth rate of 3.4 percent).[7] These figures imply annual net absolute growth rates of 15 million vehicles from 1960 to 1980 and 19 million from 1980 to 2000. The overall share of vehicles in developing nations was negligible in 1960 but was 30 percent in 2000. The same source estimated that the global vehicle population would reach 1.1 billion by 2020. That implies a future annual net growth rate of 16 million from 2000 to 2020 (a compound annual growth rate of 1.7 percent).

A measure of automotive usage intensity is the number of vehicles per 1,000 inhabitants, shown in table 16-1. Over all 164 nations, this number is 134 vehicles per 1,000 people. This ratio is highest in North America (621.9), with Oceania a close second (611.1) because of the influence of Australia. This ratio is lowest in South Asia (15.4) and Africa (27.7). Thus the region with the highest intensity of automotive vehicle ownership has a ratio forty times greater than the region with the least intensity.

Table 16-2 shows the 50 nations with the largest number of vehicles per nation, ranked in order of the number per nation. The United States contains by far the largest number—214.8 million, which is 28 percent of the total in all 164 nations in this tabulation. The nations with the next largest vehicle populations—exceeding 20 million per nation—are Japan, Germany, Italy, France, Brazil, Russia, and the United Kingdom, in that order. Combined, these eight nations contain 63 percent of the total in all 164 nations. The top 25 nations contain 84.5 percent of the

TABLE 16-1. World Vehicle Population, 1996–2000

Zone (number of nations)	Four-wheeled vehicles					Human population[a]		Vehicles per 1,000 inhabitants	Road network		
	Passenger cars	Buses and coaches	Trucks and vans	Total	Percent of world total	Total (thousands)	Percent of world total		Total (km)	Percent of world total	Vehicles per km of road
Africa (52)	11,556,661	1,349,114	6,256,432	19,162,207	2.52	692,332	12.22	27.7	1,835,618	6.68	10.4
South America (27)	38,510,106	907,659	10,031,288	49,449,053	6.51	406,084	7.17	121.8	2,674,332	9.74	18.5
North America (3)	156,762,803	908,840	93,171,499	250,843,142	33.04	403,345	7.12	621.9	7,535,628	27.44	33.3
South Asia (10)	13,871,008	2,759,153	5,600,998	22,231,159	2.93	1,451,655	25.62	15.4	4,471,005	16.28	5.0
North Asia (8)	84,927,278	1,876,132	30,780,263	117,583,673	15.49	1,604,929	28.33	67.1	2,970,296	10.81	39.6
Former Soviet Union (9)	28,818,026	734,428	4,768,025	34,320,479	4.52	244,102	4.31	140.6	1,052,501	3.83	32.6
Europe (35)	209,679,266	1,208,379	26,148,133	237,035,778	31.22	580,525	10.25	408.3	5,364,014	19.53	44.2
Middle East (15)	10,258,115	260,363	3,502,744	14,021,222	1.85	258,456	4.56	54.2	629,988	2.29	22.3
Oceania (5)	11,817,398	77,756	2,584,646	14,479,800	1.91	23,694	0.42	611.1	931,544	3.39	15.5
Total (164)	566,200,661	10,081,824	182,844,028	759,126,513	100.00	5,665,122	100.00	134.0	27,464,926	100.00	27.6

Source: International Road Federation, World Road Statistics 2002.
a. As of December 31, 2000.

TABLE 16-2. Nations with the Greatest Number of Vehicles

Country	Year	Four- or more wheeled vehicles						Population			Road network (km)			
		Cars	Buses and coaches	Trucks and vans	Total	Percent of world total	Cumulative percent of total	Total (thousands)	Percent of world total	Total vehicles per 1,000 inhabitants	Total	Roads per 1,000 inhabitants	Total vehicles per km of road	Cars per 1,000 inhabitants
United States	1999	132,432,044	728,777	81,614,091	214,774,912	28.29	28.29	275,562	4.86	779.4	6,304,193	22.9	34.1	480.6
Japan	2000	62,438,083	235,483	19,979,360	72,652,926	9.57	37.86	126,919	2.24	572.4	1,161,894	9.2	62.5	492.0
Germany	1999	42,323,672	84,687	2,465,535	44,873,894	5.91	43.77	82,797	1.46	542.0	230,735	2.8	194.5	511.2
Italy	1999	31,416,686	87,039	3,639,103	35,142,828	4.63	48.40	58,000	1.02	605.9	479,688	8.3	73.3	541.7
France	2000	28,060,000	80,000	5,673,000	33,813,000	4.45	52.86	58,800	1.04	575.1	811,603	13.8	41.7	477.2
Brazil	2000	23,241,966	427,213	5,306,130	28,975,309	3.82	56.67	166,113	2.93	174.4	1,724,929	10.4	16.8	139.9
Russian Federation	2000	20,353,000	640,100	4,400,600	25,393,700	3.35	60.02	144,800	2.56	175.4	532,393	3.7	47.7	140.6
United Kingdom	1999	22,785,000	84,000	289,900	23,158,900	3.05	63.07	59,511	1.05	389.2	371,913	6.2	62.3	382.9
Spain	1998	16,100,000	51,800	3,393,000	19,544,800	2.57	65.65	39,134	0.69	499.4	663,795	17.0	29.4	411.4
Canada	1998	13,887,270	68,307	3,625,818	17,581,395	2.32	67.96	30,300	0.53	580.2	901,903	29.8	19.5	458.3
China	2000	8,537,333	...	7,163,201	15,760,534	2.08	70.04	1,265,830	22.34	12.5	1,402,698	1.1	11.2	6.7
Mexico	2000	10,443,489	111,756	7,931,590	15,486,835	2.04	72.08	97,483	1.72	158.9	329,532	3.4	47.0	107.1
South Korea	2000	8,084,005	1,427,663	2,528,527	12,040,195	1.59	73.66	47,275	0.83	254.7	86,990	1.8	138.4	171.0
Poland	2000	9,991,260	82,356	1,783,008	11,856,624	1.56	75.23	38,580	0.68	307.3	364,656	9.5	32.5	259.0
Australia	1998	9,560,600	64,000	2,113,300	11,737,900	1.55	76.77	18,571	0.33	632.1	811,603	43.7	14.5	514.8
India	1998	5,056,000	535,000	2,529,000	8,120,000	1.07	77.84	971,832	17.15	8.4	3,319,644	3.4	2.4	5.2
Netherlands	1999	6,051,000	11,000	684,000	6,746,000	0.89	78.73	15,760	0.28	428.0	116,500	7.4	57.9	383.9
Argentina	1998	5,047,630	43,232	1,453,335	6,544,197	0.86	79.59	36,125	0.64	181.2	215,471	6.0	30.4	139.7
South Africa	1999	3,966,252	164,665	1,904,871	6,035,788	0.80	80.39	43,421	0.77	139.0	362,099	8.3	16.7	91.3
Turkey	1999	4,073,022	333,802	1,071,824	5,478,648	0.72	81.11	64,385	1.14	85.1	385,960	6.0	14.2	63.3
Taiwan	2000	4,716,217	23,923	652,963	5,393,103	0.71	81.82	22,218	0.39	242.7	35,931	1.6	150.1	212.3
Ukraine	2000	5,250,129	...	...	5,250,129	0.69	82.51	49,037	0.87	107.1	169,491	3.5	31.0	107.1
Belgium	2000	4,628,949	14,555	507,910	5,151,414	0.68	83.19	10,245	0.18	502.8	148,216	14.5	34.8	451.8

Indonesia	1998	2,772,531	627,969	1,592,572	4,993,072	0.66	83.85	212,942	3.76	23.4	342,700	1.6	14.6	13.0
Malaysia	2000	4,212,567	48,662	665,284	4,926,513	0.65	84.50	22,600	0.40	218.0	65,877	2.9	74.8	186.4
Sweden	2000	3,999,268	14,432	374,331	4,388,031	0.58	85.07	8,883	0.16	494.0	212,402	23.9	20.7	450.2
Austria	1999	4,009,604	9,834	318,757	4,338,195	0.57	85.65	8,094	0.14	536.0	200,000	24.7	21.7	495.4
Portugal	1998	3,200,000	17,000	1,080,000	4,297,000	0.57	86.21	9,979	0.18	430.6	68,732	6.9	62.5	320.7
Greece	2000	3,195,065	27,037	1,057,422	4,279,524	0.56	86.78	10,600	0.19	403.7	117,000	11.0	36.6	301.4
Switzerland	2000	3,545,247	16,269	278,518	3,840,034	0.51	87.28	7,190	0.13	534.1	71,011	9.9	54.1	493.1
Czech Republic	2000	3,438,870	18,259	275,617	3,732,746	0.49	87.77	10,267	0.18	363.6	55,408	5.4	67.4	334.9
Romania	2000	3,128,782	48,142	413,493	3,590,417	0.47	88.25	22,430	0.40	160.1	198,603	8.9	18.1	139.5
Saudi Arabia	1996	1,744,000	23,040	1,169,000	2,935,000	0.39	88.63	17,820	0.31	164.7	151,470	8.5	19.4	97.9
Hungary	1999	2,400,000	19,100	324,000	2,743,000	0.36	88.99	10,100	0.18	271.5	188,203	18.6	14.6	237.6
Nigeria	1996	885,080	903,449	912,579	2,701,108	0.36	89.35	103,175	1.82	26.2	194,394	1.9	13.9	8.6
New Zealand	2000	2,221,658	13,716	439,606	2,674,980	0.35	89.70	3,843	0.07	696.1	92,053	24.0	29.1	578.1
Iran	1996	1,793,000	55,457	180,154	2,484,000	0.33	90.03	70,290	1.24	35.3	167,157	2.4	14.9	25.5
Philippines	2000	767,948	1,422,003	248,369	2,438,320	0.32	90.35	76,498	1.35	31.9	201,994	2.6	12.1	10.0
Finland	1999	2,082,580	9,487	293,707	2,385,774	0.31	90.66	5,171	0.09	461.4	77,900	15.1	30.6	402.7
Norway	2000	1,851,929	36,686	409,040	2,302,955	0.30	90.97	4,503	0.08	511.4	91,454	20.3	25.2	411.3
Denmark	2000	1,907,879	13,909	308,633	2,230,421	0.29	91.26	5,314	0.09	419.7	71,591	13.5	31.2	359.0
Bulgaria	2000	1,908,392	41,971	271,463	2,221,826	0.29	91.55	8,149	0.14	272.7	37,286.0	4.6	59.6	234.2
Colombia	1999	1,803,201	134,799	134,495	2,122,495	0.28	91.83	41,589	0.73	51.0	112,988.0	2.7	18.8	43.4
Chile	2000	1,320,519	69,578	628,308	2,018,405	0.27	92.10	15,211	0.27	132.7	79,814.0	5.2	25.3	86.8
Venezuela	1996	1,520,000	...	434,000	1,954,000	0.26	92.36	22,000	0.39	88.8	96,155.0	4.4	20.3	69.1
Egypt	1996	1,354,000	37,620	397,000	1,787,000	0.24	92.59	60,390	1.07	29.6	64,000.0	1.1	27.9	22.4
Israel	2000	1,422,032	18,046	309,938	1,750,016	0.23	92.82	6,369	0.11	274.8	16,281.0	2.6	107.5	223.3
Yugoslavia	1999	1,593,183	11,181	130,026	1,734,390	0.23	93.05	10,629	0.19	163.2	49,805.0	4.7	34.8	149.9
Ireland	2000	1,322,887	8,247	205,575	1,546,709	0.20	93.26	3,790	0.07	408.1	92,500.0	24.4	16.7	349.0
Algeria	1996	725,000	...	780,000	1,505,000	0.20	93.45	29,400	0.52	51.2	104,000.0	3.5	14.5	24.7

Source: International Road Federation, *World Road Statistics 2002*.

164-nation total. Thus vehicle populations are heavily concentrated, mainly in developed countries (13 of the top 25).

Global Road Networks

International Road Federation (IRF) data on road networks are less internally consistent than those on vehicle populations, but they are the best available on a global scale.

The 185 nations covered by IRF's road network survey contained 27.465 million kilometers of roads of all types, which is equivalent to 17.061 million miles. For 8.2 percent of this total, the degree of paving is unknown. Of the other 91.8 percent, half is paved.

Note that IRF's survey of nations' roads covered 185 nations, whereas its survey for vehicle populations covered only 164 nations. The nations omitted from the vehicle population data are all very small and do not significantly affect the overall results. Hence this discrepancy is ignored in the remaining analysis, which focuses mainly on entire regions rather than on individual nations.[8]

According to the data in table 16-1 North America contains just over one-fourth of the world's roads and one-third of the world's motor vehicles, though it has only 7 percent of the world's population. Europe similarly has one-fifth of the roads, just under one-third of the vehicles, and only 10 percent of the population. The richest areas have the largest numbers of vehicles per kilometer of road. In contrast, the poorest areas have the greatest amount of road per vehicle, though many of their roads are not paved.

Surprisingly, Oceania has by far the greatest number of miles of road per 1,000 inhabitants, almost entirely because of Australia. North America has 18.7 kilometers of road (11.6 miles) per 1,000 inhabitants, with Europe at about half that level. The rest of the world has much smaller lengths of roads per 1,000 residents, reflecting its lower vehicle populations and lower incomes.

These data show that developing nations will face great infrastructure challenges as the incomes of their populations rise. More and more citizens will buy automotive vehicles and demand more and better roads. At least initially, the number of vehicles per 1,000 inhabitants is likely to rise much faster than road mileage. That is clearly what has happened to the "newly emerging nations" in Asia, which as a continent has large populations but relatively small road networks. This disparity between

TABLE 16-3. Leading Producers of Vehicles

Rank and country		Year	Passenger cars	Buses	Trucks	All four or more wheeled vehicles
1.	United States	1999	5,637,806	27,000	7,387,029	13,051,835
2.	Japan	1999	8,100,169	48,395	1,746,912	9,895,476
3.	Germany	1998	5,348,000	...	379,000	5,727,000
4.	France	2000	4,542,000	3,000	753,000	5,298,000
5.	South Korea	2000	2,602,008	246,288	265,055	3,113,351
6.	Spain	1999	2,281,617	1,588	161,716	2,444,921
7.	Canada	2000	1,359,656	...	791,042	2,150,698
8.	United Kingdom	1998	1,748,000	2,136	224,923	1,975,059
9.	Italy	1999	1,410,317	3,070	287,727	1,701,114
10.	Brazil	2000	1,347,923	24,782	275,415	1,648,120
11.	China	1999	984,377	...	581,990	1,566,367
12.	Mexico	1999	993,772	1,378	499,894	1,495,044
13.	Russia	1999	954,000	50,000	175,000	1,179,000
14.	Belgium	2000	912,233	1,499	110,100	1,023,832
15.	India	2000	701,550	...	173,521	875,071
16.	Poland	2000	532,427	2,015	58,112	592,554
17.	Sweden	2000	404,276	15,428	110,020	529,724
18.	Czech Republic	1998	399,480	1,216	5,399	406,095
19.	Taiwan Province	2000	263,244	399	104,481	368,124
20.	Netherlands	1999	310,000	...	17,000	327,000
21.	Argentina	1999	224,733	1,177	78,899	304,809
22.	Turkey	1999	215,923	31,564	42,892	290,379
23.	South Africa	1999	159,944	6,059	105,405	271,408
24.	Portugal	1999	186,996	146	65,148	252,290
Total			41,620,451	467,140	14,399,680	56,487,271

Source: International Road Federation, *World Road Statistics 2002.*

likely future growth rates in the number of vehicles and in the amount of roads will surely intensify traffic congestion as these nations modernize. That is why traffic congestion is likely to remain worse in much of the developing world than in the United States, in spite of the greater number of vehicles in the United States.

Global Automotive Vehicle Production

Table 16-3 shows the 24 nations that produced the greatest number of new vehicles per year in the years 1998–2000. The United States was by far the biggest, with 13.0 million cars, buses, and trucks. Japan was second with 9.9 million, Germany third with 5.7 million, and France fourth with 5.3 million. Total production for all 24 nations was 56.5 million

FIGURE 16-2. World Vehicle Production, by Region, 1990–2000

Vehicles produced/year (millions)

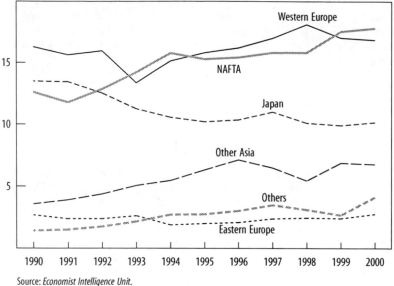

Source: *Economist Intelligence Unit.*

units. If the actual productive capacity of the world at full operation was 60 million vehicles, that represents 8 percent of the world's total vehicle inventory in 2000 (excluding motorcycles, tractors, and motorbikes).

World automotive production for the years 1990 to 2000 by major regions was estimated by the Economist Intelligence Unit as shown in figure 16-2. The figure shows that total production rose irregularly during the decade by 16.8 percent. The amount produced by western Europe remained flat after the recession in the early 1990s; the North American Free Trade Area's (NAFTA's) production rose steadily by 41.3 percent; and Japan's production declined 25 percent (partly because many Japanese firms are building vehicles in the United States, thus raising NAFTA's share). The total share of these three economically developed regions went from 84.6 percent in 1990 to 89.5 percent in 2000. Hence developing nations were not capturing an increasing share of world vehicle production during the 1990s.[9]

As for the future, *Automotive World* recently estimated that world new vehicle sales would rise from 59 million in 2000 to 110 million in 2020.[10]

Implications for Future Vehicle Production and Use

As more nations become modernized and wealthier, vehicle ownership and use are almost certain to rise. That has immense implications for future levels of traffic congestion around the world. For example, China is one of the economically fastest-growing nations in the world. Its gross domestic product expanded 7 to 8 percent annually in the late 1990s and early 2000s. As of 2000, China contained about 15.7 million automotive vehicles, or 12.4 for every 1,000 inhabitants. China's population was 1.265 billion—the world's largest—but was not growing rapidly because of the government's policy of limiting each family to one child. If China's population remained unchanged but its vehicle population rose to 250 per 1,000 inhabitants—about the same as in South Korea or Taiwan in 2000—the number of automotive vehicles in China would rise from 15.7 million to 316.5 million. That is an increase of 301 million vehicles—almost one-third more than the total in the United States today! Yet even then the number of vehicles in China per 1,000 residents would be less than one-third of that in the United States and less than half of that in most developed European nations. Thus the potential impact of further economic modernization on traffic congestion in Chinese cities is staggering.

Similar calculations for other developing nations suggest that the governments of those nations will face enormous future challenges in coping with rising traffic congestion. True, economic modernization will also increase the resource capacity of such nations to build more streets, roads, and expressways. But current experience in many economically emerging nations far more developed than China indicates that public sectors may have great difficulty expanding their road networks enough to keep pace with private production, purchase, and use of automotive vehicles as incomes rise.

Potential implications for future modernization concerning the emission of pollutants from automotive vehicles are also sobering. In 2000, there were 95 nations with fewer than 100 vehicles per 1,000 inhabitants. These nations (including China) contained 3.99 billion people and 69.9 million cars, trucks, and buses, or 17.5 such vehicles per 1,000 inhabitants. If modernization raised the average ratio of vehicles per 1,000 inhabitants in these nations to 100—slightly less than that in Ukraine in 2000—there would then be about 400 million vehicles in those nations—or 330 million more than there are now. That represents an increase of 43 percent over the total world vehicle population in 2000. Yet that estimate does not take into account what would also be happening in the 25 nations that had from 100 to 250 vehicles per 1,000 residents as of 2000, or those that had even higher ratios.

If the world's 120 nations with fewer than 250 vehicles per 1,000 residents raised their vehicle populations to that ratio—similar to that in South Korea in 2000—those nations (including China) would contain 1.167 billion automotive vehicles, or more than 1.5 times the total world vehicle population in 2000. Even if the rest of the world did not increase its vehicle population, the world's total vehicle population would then be 1.74 billion, or 2.3 times as large as it was in 2000.

These admittedly speculative calculations emphasize the need for the world to change its automotive vehicle engines to forms that do not emit nearly as much pollution as gasoline-powered internal combustion engines do now. Hydrogen-powered fuel cells are one possible alternative that would meet that criterion. True, it will be a colossal task to change the huge present logistical infrastructure that supplies gasoline at millions of gas stations around the world to a system suited to some other fuel. But the potential increases in air pollution likely to occur from future modernization if no such change occurs are surely threatening to health and climatic conditions.

Regional Mobility in America and in Economically Competitive Nations

Many Americans are concerned that rising inefficiencies caused by traffic congestion in the United States will make metropolitan areas economically less competitive with those in other nations. These worriers cite extensive use of public transit in many other world cities, inferring that mobility there is superior to mobility in our auto-dominated system.

Contrary to widespread opinion, travel by private automotive vehicles dominates overall ground passenger movement in most western European nations, though total use of public transit there is higher than in the United States. Table 16-4 shows the percentage of passenger miles traveled by specific modes in 1997 for 7 European nations individually and 15 European nations combined.

Thus passenger cars account for 81.8 percent of all person miles traveled in 15 European nations and over 80 percent in 5 of 7 major nations there. True, all forms of public transit combined provide 15.6 percent of passenger ground travel in Europe versus less than 2 percent in the United

TABLE 16-4. Share of Annual Passenger Kilometers Traveled, by Mode, Europe, 1997

Percent

Nation	Passenger cars	Powered two-wheelers	Buses	Urban rail[a]	Railway	Total public transit
Denmark	79	1	13.7	0	6.3	20
Germany	82.1	1.6	7.5	1.6	7.1	16.2
Spain	81.4	3.2	10.2	1.1	1.24	15.3
France	84.5	1.5	5.2	1.2	7.6	14
Italy	76.1	6.4	10.6	0.6	6.3	17.5
Netherlands	82	1.6	7.9	0.8	7.8	16.5
United Kingdom	87.7	0.6	6	0.9	4.8	11.7
15 EU nations	81.8	2.6	8.5	1	6.1	15.6

Source: U.K. Commission for Integrated Transport, "European Best Practice in Transport—Benchmarking," part 3: "Inputs and Outputs" (www.cfit.gov.uk/reports [January 2004]).

a. For example, train or metro.

States. One result is that commuting times in these nations are longer, on the average, than in the United States. Across 15 European nations, the average one-way commuting time in 1996 was 38 minutes versus 22 in the United States in 1995. Denmark, which had the highest percentage of total public transit travel, also had the longest average commuting time of 43 minutes; Italy had the shortest time of 23 minutes.[11]

Congestion around the World

The following examples illustrate how widespread traffic congestion has become in large and growing metropolitan areas all over the world.

ROME, ITALY. Rome has experienced a tripling of passenger kilometers traveled (VKT) in the past thirty-five years because of longer trips and a 650 percent increase in the number of circulating vehicles. This expansion of VKT has not been matched by corresponding increases in public transit usage, which has gone up only 90 percent in that period. Hence the public transit modal share has declined from 56 percent of total motorized trips in 1964 to 34 percent today. Consequently, traffic congestion has increased significantly.

CALCUTTA, INDIA. The city grew from 3.30 million people living in 40.1 square miles in 1981 to 4.39 million living in 72.3 square miles in 1991. Thus the city's overall density was 82,200 persons per square mile in 1981 and 60,700 per square mile in 1991. (In comparison, Manhattan's density in 2000 was about 55,000 persons per square mile.) It is estimated that 600,000 persons live on the streets of Calcutta, and that the density in some neighborhoods exceeds 200,000 persons per square mile.

Roads in this dense city cover only 5.8 percent of the land area, compared with as much as 25 percent in cities in economically developed nations. This causes severe overloading of the limited existing roadways each day. In 1981, there were 150,000 vehicles in Calcutta; in 1991, there were 850,000. That is an average of 70,000 more vehicles per year. The resulting crowding is intensified by the presence in the streets of pedestrians, cows, bullock carts, rickshaws, motorbikes, buses, bicycles, trams, trucks, and cars.[12]

In 1991, an estimated 750,000 persons commuted daily on buses and trams that were designed with a capacity of less than 300,000. This caused extreme crowding on public transit vehicles.

The addition of 15,000 auto rickshaws to the streets, on top of some 30,000 trucks that enter the city daily, has increased congestion, pollution, and accidents. And because street hawkers use sidewalks, many pedestrians must walk in the streets, adding to traffic congestion.[13]

JAKARTA, INDONESIA. In the 1990s, downtown area streets were so crowded and parking was so scarce that many business executives hired chauffeured cars to drop them off at their destinations. They then sent the drivers to circle around or go some distance away and wait until called by cell phone to come back and pick them up.

BANGKOK, THAILAND. Traffic congestion is legendary. There are 540 vehicles owned in that city for every 1,000 residents—100 more than in Tokyo. In 1990, vehicle registrations (including motorbikes) rose 341,275 in a single year.[14] It may take as much as six hours to move between downtown and the airport. The average speed on a main commercial street in rush hours is less than two miles per hour. Trucks from elsewhere are prohibited from entering the city until after 10:00 a.m. to relieve rush-hour traffic jams, so they line up along roads just outside the city limits each morning. It is difficult to schedule more than two business appointments per day if they are not located very close together because of the delays inherent in moving from one part of the metropolitan area to another. Thomas Friedman has reported that people have stopped inviting friends over on weekday evenings because of uncertainty that they will ever arrive.[15]

LONDON. Area workers employed outside of central and inner London are more likely to commute by private vehicles than by transit, as shown in table 16-5. Because the number of commuters rises as the dis-

TABLE 16-5. Mode of Commuting and Job Location, London

Job location	Modal share in 1995 by job location (percent)				
	Private vehicle	Bus/rail	Walk/bike	Other	Number of workers
Central London	17	75	5	2	972,000
Rest of inner London	40	41	16	2	738,000
Outer London	67	18	13	1	1,315,000
Rest of region	76	7	17	1	4,030,000

Source: Genevieve Giuliano, "Urban Travel Patterns," in B. Hoyle and R. Knowles, eds., *Modern Transport Geography*, 2d ed. (John Wiley and Sons, 1998).

tance of their jobs from central London increases, the overall share of the 7.0 million total commuters working in the London area using private vehicles is 62.4 percent. However, that share is only 26.9 percent for jobs in central and inner London combined.[16]

According to French transportation expert Christian Gerondeau, the average automobile commute in most of Europe is about 19 minutes each way. (In the Paris area, it is about 25 minutes.) In contrast, the average transit commute is 49 minutes each way. That is why about 70 percent of European commuters use private cars versus about 15 percent by public transit. He believes only people who do not have a choice of using cars are riding on transit.[17]

In the United Kingdom, the whole approach to road building has changed from "predict traffic demand and then build roads to accommodate it" to "try to limit the growth of traffic demand to levels we can cope with." This change has been described by P. B. Goodwin as a combination of diverse policies from road pricing to expanding public transit alternatives. However, whether this new approach can successfully cope with rising traffic congestion has yet to be demonstrated.[18]

TOKYO. More than 30 million persons ride mass transit daily. But the trains are often overloaded, typically carrying 200 percent of designed capacity. They are so crowded that the subway operators employ "pushers" at each major station to shove more and more passengers into each car. Passengers are jammed together, mostly standing, so they can hardly move. At least they cannot fall over, since there is no place to land! The average one-way commuting trip is one hour, for a daily total of two hours or more.[19] Thus traffic congestion is not confined to roads but also exists in public transit vehicles.

However, even extreme crowding does not slow down the speed of transit vehicles (unless it takes longer to load and unload them at station stops). Thus congestion does not have the same impact on transit commuters as on automobile commuters. On transit, congestion makes passengers personally less comfortable but no slower; in cars, congestion does not change passengers' personal comfort but slows them down.

BEIJING, CHINA. The number of registered automotive vehicles rose from 600,000 in 1990 to 1.6 million in 2000, a gain of 100,000 per year. Although a lot of road building has occurred, it has not kept pace with this huge rise in vehicle ownership and use. Hence traffic jams are a daily occurrence. In 1998, Beijing banned bicycles on a 300-meter stretch of Xisidong Street from 7:00 a.m. to 8:00 p.m. because they were clogging this major street. However, there are still several million bicycles in use every day in Beijing.[20]

SAO PAOLO, BRAZIL. In 1992 about 28 kilometers of the main road network experienced acute congestion in the mornings, and 39 kilometers in the afternoons. By 1996, the distances thus affected had increased to 80 kilometers and 122 kilometers respectively. Those are gains of 39 and 52 percent in just four years.[21]

Strategies Used to Combat Traffic Congestion in Other Nations

Since peak-hour and general traffic congestion are intensifying in almost all large and growing metropolitan areas in the world, authorities in other nations have devised and tried a number of ways to cope with it. This section explores their five main approaches.

Discouraging People from Using Private Vehicles

Use of private vehicles can be discouraged by increasing the costs of owning and driving them. Probably the most widespread tactic of this type is adopting high taxes on the sale of gasoline and other vehicle fuels. As discussed elsewhere in this book, taxes on gasoline create a per mile driving cost in most other developed nations several times as great as that in the United States. And most European governments do not allocate the resulting gasoline tax receipts to improving roads or other forms of transportation. Instead, they "divert" significant fractions of these tax revenues to general governments coffers. In some countries, gas tax revenues are used for transportation, but mainly to subsidize railroads and public transit—not to build more or better roads. This is also a form of penalizing the use of private automotive vehicles.

Another antiautomobile tactic is imposing high taxes on the ownership and use of cars, as in Singapore and Denmark.

Charging Variable Peak-Hour Tolls on Major Commuting Roads

Charging peak-hour tolls on major commuting roads is another tactic to reduce demand and increase average speeds thereon. (This is really another cost-raising tactic, but it deserves separate consideration.) Trondheim, Norway, in 1991 set up a cordon around the city center and charges drivers a fee to enter from 6:00 a.m. to 6:00 p.m. each weekday. The peak rate is about $1.40 charged from 6:00 to 10:00 a.m.; the rate from 10:00 a.m. to 5:00 p.m. is about half that. Transit vehicles pass free; trucks pay double. Polls in Trondheim showed that 72 percent of randomly selected respondents were opposed to the idea before it was adopted. But opposition fell to 48 percent two months after the scheme started and is now at 36 percent. There has been a 10 percent decline in traffic during toll-charging hours and an 8 percent rise during nontoll hours. Hence the main effect has been redistributing trips away from peak hours.

The French government has used similar peak-hour tolls on major roads connecting Paris with southern France to discourage drivers from returning from weekends in the country on Sunday evenings. The result was a 13 percent reduction in such peak-hour traffic. In Seoul, Korea, the government introduced peak-hour tolls in 1996 on two tunnels that had already had flat tolls. Peak-hour traffic fell 24 percent, and the average speed in the tunnels was doubled.

However, up to now, no political leaders anywhere in the world have been willing to install and retain a large-scale peak-hour pricing system, even though economists have been promoting it for decades. A full-blown approach was tried in Hong Kong for six months and worked rather well technically. But it was then rejected by the authorities for several reasons, including fears that the privacy of the drivers could be excessively invaded using data collected by the system.

Promoting Public Transit

Another widely used means of attacking traffic congestion is promoting more extensive use of public transit. Many European and Japanese cities have comprehensive public transit networks consisting of buses, subways, surface railways, and trolleys or trams. In Europe, almost all of these systems lose money and must be heavily subsidized from public funds, sometimes including gasoline tax revenues. In Asia, some public transit systems are so heavily patronized that their fare revenues exceed their operating costs. Even so, transit carries about 15 percent of commuters in 15 western European nations combined, whereas 81 percent of workers commute in private vehicles.

Transportation authorities in many European nations—as in the United States—devote much higher fractions of their total transportation spending to supporting transit than the share of trips or passenger miles provided by transit. Conversely, they focus lower fractions of their total transportation spending on building or improving roads than the overall share of movements provided by automotive vehicles using those roads. This disparity is rationalized by their desire to attack the traffic congestion that has arisen in the past in spite of heavy spending on roads. They reason that building more roads cannot overcome congestion because doing so apparently encourages more driving; hence society cannot build its way out of congestion. Therefore, resources should be devoted to the alternatives to roads—mainly public transit—even though there is little evidence that this approach will reduce congestion much either.

The specific public transit schemes financed for this purpose include modernizing older stations and tracks, buying new buses and rail transit cars, increasing the frequency of service, building more park-and-ride parking facilities, extending existing lines into new territories, modernizing cars and stations, reducing fares, building bicycle lanes and paths, and creating light rail systems.

In Europe, high-speed trains have also been advanced as alternatives to longer intercity driving trips and airplane flights. Such train service works well but is rather expensive for passengers, in spite of massive subsidies from governments. Hence this train service essentially redistributes resources from low- and middle-income taxpayers (including those who pay gasoline taxes) to higher-income train riders. Governments rationalize this regressive situation by claiming trains are less polluting than autos. High-speed trains are really effective only for moderate distances; really long trips take much longer even by fast trains than by airplanes and thus do not attract much patronage.

Employing Land-Use Planning to Reduce Demand

Transportation planners in many nations have long argued that the best way to cope with traffic congestion in the long run is to influence future urban growth patterns and perhaps modify some existing ones. The basic goal would be to shift from sprawling low-density settlement patterns to much higher-density patterns clustered along major transit corridors. Such higher-density settlements could be more feasibly served by public transit, thereby reducing the need for commuters and others to drive.

Some foreign nations have long practiced this approach to some degree. Others have adopted policies that embody that approach in very specific forms.

For example, Curitiba, Brazil, has achieved the most spectacular example of land-use planning aimed at reducing use of private automotive vehicles. In the 1950s, Curitiba contained 150,000 persons. In the early 1970s, it adopted its present combination land-use and transportation plan. It consists of building high-density housing along five-radial transportation corridors extending outward from its downtown. These corridors were served by bus rapid transit vehicles moving between special stops designed to make getting on and off as fast as possible. At these stops, passengers pay before boarding vehicles and walk onto the buses from platforms at the same height as bus floors to minimize time boarding. Each bus is a triple-bodied vehicle that can hold up to 300 passengers. The buses move in designated lanes that keep them unimpeded by other vehicle traffic. They move as fast as subway cars but at a fraction of the cost. The radial lines are joined at various distances from downtown by circular bus rapid transit lines using the same principles. Thus commuters can conveniently move from almost any part of the urbanized area to any other part using bus rapid transit.

Curitiba has grown rapidly and by 1995 contained 1.6 million residents—ten times as many as in 1950. Therefore, it was able to channel most of its present settlements—which were built during this growth period—into the planned high-density pattern along transportation corridors. The result is that about 80 percent of daily commuting transit occurs on bus rapid transit. This illustrates what can be done in a city experiencing rapid growth if its land-use and transportation policies are closely integrated by the area's government.[22]

Stockholm, Sweden, is another example of land-use planning as a tactic. In the 1960s the city extended its rapid transit lines out into vacant land around it and created a series of "new towns" around new transit stops built in then-empty territory. The city government, which controlled land-use zoning throughout its region and owned much of the land therein, then encouraged creation of high-density housing and commercial improvements close to those outlying transit stops. This enabled many persons working downtown to walk to transit stations and commute without using private automotive vehicles.

In England, a similar new towns policy was followed in the 1950s and 1960s and more recently. After the New Towns Planning Act of 1946, the government created half a dozen planned communities on vacant land significantly outside the then-settlement-edge of the London area. By 1990, twenty-eight new towns had been created as far north as Glasgow, each separated from a nearby large city by a "greenbelt" of open country. Each of these communities was designed to contain all types of housing and enough jobs so that its residents could, in theory, all work and live in the same community. For example, the city of Milton Keynes, located thirty miles north of London, by 1999 contained 207,000 residents, including 157,000 workers, and had an unemployment rate of only 1.5 percent. It is located on the M1 expressway joining it to London.[23]

Reducing traffic congestion was not one of the motivating goals of establishing these new communities; they were designed primarily to decentralize population growth away from large cities in a more "rational" settlement pattern marked by large open spaces. Nevertheless, these communities have two relevancies to traffic congestion. First, congestion is typically much less intense in small relatively isolated communities than in very large metropolitan areas. Therefore, locating as much growth as possible in such new towns results in low congestion levels for their residents. Second, by diverting growth from large metropolitan cities, new towns reduce the amount of traffic in them.

However, the vast majority of population growth in the United Kingdom during the past fifty years has *not* occurred in these new towns. Rather, it has taken place through gradual growth in previously existing small communities in each region, or outward from the periphery of a big city's main previously built-up areas. Hence the new town strategy has had only limited impacts on levels of congestion in large metropolitan areas, though it does result in relatively high mobility in the new towns themselves.

Using Intelligent Transportation Systems

Another tactic to combat congestion is the use of intelligent transportation systems. Up to 2002, the most advanced thinking, experimenting, and actual using of ITS methods to combat traffic congestion have been largely carried out in the United States, rather than abroad. However, some other nations are using ITS to cope with congestion and other traffic problems.

In Europe there is a multination ITS cooperative project called TRI-DENT, which stands for transport intermodality data sharing and exchange networks. Until 2002, this approach was largely in experimental stages. Among its goals are accurate travel information to enable fleet managers to control trucks and buses more efficiently, information about congestion, bottlenecks, and road conditions to enable travelers to make better routing and timing decisions "on the fly," and real-time data about trains and buses to help travelers avoid the frustration of waiting for conveyances that are not on time.

In Umea, Sweden, the government has developed an "intelligent speed adaptation" device that combines small receivers in cars with radio beacons mounted on roadside speed limit signs. As a vehicle passes each speed limit sign, the beacon transmits the required limit to the in-car device, which compares that limit to the car's actual speed. If the driver is exceeding the limit, the in-car device warns the driver of that fact. This approach has proved successful at slowing down drivers at less public expense than other traffic calming devices like speed bumps.[24]

In France, the regulatory body in charge of radio broadcasting has dedicated a specific FM frequency all over the nation to traffic information. One implementation is on the A6 and A5 expressways linking Paris to the south, on which traffic bulletins are broadcast interspersed with music. Hence drivers can learn of current traffic conditions while they are traveling on these roads.[25]

In Tokyo, an intelligent traffic guidance system has been developed using geographic positioning satellites (GPS), location devices placed in individual vehicles and equipped with software that issues driving directions to destinations selected by the operators. This system is connected to a current traffic information service run by the Tokyo police that broadcasts real-time data on traffic accidents and congestion to operators of all vehicles in the affected areas.[26]

In Bologna, Italy, an on-demand bus service with variable routes has been developed for areas where normal demand for transit is too low to make regularly scheduled service economically feasible. Users call into a central station and make a reservation. If enough requests are made to justify serving a route, a trip is scheduled and users are notified. Persons without reservations can board if there is room, but those who have called in advance have priority.[27]

In Stockholm, Sweden, a motorway control system has been installed along highly traveled highway E4 north of the city. It consists of electronic signs over each traffic lane at 500- to 800-foot intervals. Signals on these signs indicate proper speed, show when lane changes are necessary, and transmit other information about congestion and possible delays. These signals are transmitted from a traffic control center operated twenty-four hours per day and linked to various in-road speed sensors and television cameras along the highway.[28]

These examples—and others that could be recounted—show that ITS tactics are being used outside the United States to mitigate traffic congestion. However, there are very few, if any, instances where those tactics have notably succeeded in reducing congestion. In most cases, ITS tactics abroad are still in the initial stages of development or deployment, and they have not yet been installed throughout the road system of any large metropolitan area.

Implications of Global Efforts to Combat Traffic Congestion for American Policy

Examination of the evidence about traffic congestion around the globe, and efforts there to reduce it, reveals the following conclusions:

—Peak-hour traffic congestion—in fact, congestion generally—is intensifying in almost all large and growing metropolitan areas throughout the world. Congestion is especially acute in growing cities within developing nations.

A few large cities do not have intensive traffic congestion, but they are mainly not growing in population; suffering from recessions or slow economic growth; or undemocratically imposing very high costs on the use of automotive vehicles. For example, Berlin, Germany, has a population of more than 3 million but experiences relatively mild traffic congestion. It has a grid pattern of very wide streets and an extensive public transit system, including an efficient subway network. But the Berlin region's population is declining, and its economy was seriously suffering as of 2002.

—Once serious peak-hour congestion has appeared in a large and growing region, no such regions appear to have devised successful strategies for significantly reducing that congestion—with the sole exception of Curitiba, Brazil. Many cities have employed tactics drawn from combinations of the five basic anticongestion strategies just described. In many cases, these tactics have reduced congestion levels below what they would have been in the absence of such tactics. But no combination of the tactics has enabled any large foreign city I know about (except Curitiba) to reduce notably its absolute levels of peak-hour or even general congestion.

—Many foreign cities have very extensive public transit systems that provide much higher fractions of total travel then transit does in the United States. But in most cases, the shares of total travel being furnished by public transit are declining and the shares being furnished by private automotive vehicles are rising. This is causing peak-hour traffic congestion to intensify in those cities in spite of their massive transit systems.

—More closely integrated planning and control over land-use policies and transportation policies could help reduce the future growth of traffic congestion in the long run. But such a reduction could occur only if more Americans can be persuaded to live in higher densities than the present averages in U.S. new-growth areas, accept higher-density improvements in existing neighborhoods, and make more use of public transit and walking.

—Other specific anticongestion tactics adopted abroad could be usefully employed in many American regions, but they are not likely to cause absolute reductions in future levels of traffic congestion there.

CHAPTER 17

Regional Anticongestion Policies

Many tactics that would be effective in reducing peak-hour traffic congestion cannot be carried out by individual local governments. These tactics require regional design, implementation, or administration, where "regional" refers to an entire metropolitan area. In most U.S. metropolitan areas, however, no effective regional governmental agencies exist. Moreover, nearly all local governments bitterly oppose creation of such agencies.

Yet in the Intermodal Surface Transportation Efficiency Act of 1991 (ISTEA), Congress strengthened the powers of the metropolitan planning organizations (MPOs) that it had brought into being in 1962. It charged such MPOs with developing coordinated plans for uses of federal and other ground transportation funds in that region, and for overseeing what happened to those plans. However, the powers to implement those plans were left in the hands of other agencies. The mandate given to MPOs was renewed and expanded in the 1997 Transportation Equity Act for the Twenty-First Century (TEA 21) and is likely to be continued when this law is reenacted in 2004. Most large regions and many small ones have created MPOs. Each MPO has in turn launched a regionally coordinated ground transportation investment planning process. This process is designed to formulate, evaluate, develop consensus for, and adopt plans for constructing or modifying specific ground transportation projects throughout its region. Since many of those projects will have crucial impacts on future levels of traffic congestion in the region, MPOs are a vital part of creating effective anticongestion policies at the regional level. Therefore, this chapter includes an extensive discussion of MPOs and their effectiveness.

But effective anticongestion policies involve many elements other than the planning and creation of new infrastructure elements. Examples are converting two-way streets into a system of one-way streets, coordinating traffic signals, using ramp metering to control vehicle flows onto expressways, adopting taxes or other regulations for parking during peak hours, changing residential density patterns in new-growth areas, adopting tax breaks that encourage high-density in-fill development or redevelopment of older neighborhoods, and managing a system of roving patrols on expressways that quickly remove accidents or stalled vehicles from traffic lanes. Other forms of regional organizations besides MPOs are necessary to establish and manage these and other similar tactics aimed at reducing traffic congestion across a region. Hence part of this chapter will explore other institutional forms besides MPOs for carrying out such tactics.

Why Regional Approaches Are Necessary to Reduce Peak-Hour Congestion

As mentioned earlier, anticongestion policies adopted by only one community are not likely to be very effective—even within its boundaries—unless they are closely coordinated with similar policies adopted in most other communities nearby. The main exception pertains to some policies adopted by very large central cities. Regional implementation is particularly important for policies on peak-hour road pricing. No local governments could reduce congestion throughout a region by adopting peak-hour road pricing solely within their own boundaries. Regional implementation would also be vital in establishing a network of high-occupancy vehicle (HOV) lanes, keeping average settlement densities in areas of new growth above some minimal level, building new roads or expanding existing ones, raising gasoline taxes (which requires nationwide action to be most effective), and creating cash-out programs for employers who provide free employee parking.[1]

True, a few remedies could be effectively carried out by individual local governments acting alone. For example, a single local government can coordinate traffic signals on its main streets, institute systems of one-way streets, pressure developers and employers in large job centers to establish traffic management associations, and create roving response teams to clear roadways quickly after traffic accidents (if its territory is large enough to make doing so feasible within its boundaries). But all these tactics would be much more effective if implemented consistently throughout a metropolitan area.

Furthermore, as noted earlier, peak-hour congestion could best be attacked by using several complementary tactics simultaneously. For example, improved traffic signal coordination could be linked to peak-hour road pricing so that traffic diverted from new toll roads would flow efficiently on nearby free-access roads.

A Basic Paradox of Regional Remedies in General

Across America, interest in possible regional remedies to various problems has risen sharply in the past decade. Besides traffic congestion, these problems include air pollution, a widespread shortage of affordable housing, lack of open space, rising infrastructure costs and higher taxes to pay them, inadequate public schools in many large cities, and continuing isolation of the poorest households in deteriorating inner-city neighborhoods. More and more citizens, government officials, and other observers are becoming convinced that the predominant governance system in American regions of many small, highly fragmented local governments is not capable of dealing with these problems effectively. The problems are too spread over each region as a whole, and interconnected across too many localities in each region, to be effectively dealt with by individual governments acting separately. Since the dominant system is not working well, perhaps it is time to explore some other system. The major alternative is some type of "regionalism"—so interest in regional remedies has blossomed.

However, although it is clear that the present fragmented powers system is not working well, it is not yet clear that regional remedies will work any better. Experience with regional remedies is extremely limited because certain aspects of such remedies arouse strong opposition to their enaction. Therefore, few places have adopted them long enough to test whether they are in fact superior to fragmented governance.

Moreover, tackling these problems at the regional level in a democracy involves extremely complex and difficult activities—more difficult than those required to operate our present fragmented governance system. Many more divergent interests must be consulted and persuaded to cooperate than is the case with local governments acting separately. So the politics of achieving consensus on effective policies is much more complex and time consuming at the regional level. Coping with problems at the regional level also involves technically more complex policies than those confined to the local level. Hence the personal and leadership skills and technical abilities required to make regionalism work are hard to find.

Kathryn Foster summarizes what has been learned so far about the effectiveness of regional arrangements of all types as follows:

> Governance systems based on many local governments tend to promote participation and have lower service costs than do regionalized systems. Evidence remains inconclusive that regionalized governance systems are necessarily superior to localized ones in achieving equity or economic growth, although conventional wisdom and perception favor regional arrangements.[2]

Martin Wachs and Jennifer Dill have pointed out that regionally developed transportation plans do not necessarily result in socially equitable allocations of costs and benefits. Wachs and Dill noted that suburbs often have transportation needs different from those of central cities: "Over the past twenty or thirty years, most of the need for new capacity in the form of roads or transit routes is in suburban areas, while there is a growing need in the central cities for maintenance and renewal of existing facilities."[3]

But suburban portions of most metropolitan areas have larger representation on regional bodies because they contain more residents than big cities. Moreover, it is easier to obtain federal and state funding for new facilities than for maintenance and operations. As a result, Wachs and Dill believe that:

> Transportation funds have almost always been more available from both state and federal sources for capital investments—new roads and transit lines—than for maintenance, repair, or system operations. Thus, we believe that the transportation system has been "overcapitalized." More money has been spent on new facili-

ties and equipment than would have been the case had monies been fungible between capital, operations, and maintenance applications.[4]

The main beneficiaries of new roads and transit lines have been suburbanites, who have higher average incomes than city dwellers, who are the main users—and fare payers—on public transit systems. After examining the redistributive impacts of state gas tax funds used for transit operations in the San Francisco Bay area, Brian Taylor found that:

> The larger, inner-city transit operators in the Bay Area carried the overwhelmingly largest share of the passengers and received a dramatically smaller share of the program's resources. Conversely, smaller, more localized suburban transit operators received a far larger proportion of the subsidy dollars under this program than their regional share of transit ridership might suggest they ought to receive.[5]

Nevertheless, Wachs and Dill conclude that most past studies about the redistributive impacts of transportation systems have concluded that such systems tend to use funds collected mainly from white suburbanites to subsidize transit used mainly by minority city dwellers. Yet there is no certain way to be sure that regional bodies (such as MPOs) consisting of representatives from specific parts of each region will usually arrive at socially equitable distributions of the funds they are responsible for allocating. Just because a person living in one part of a region, and chosen to represent that part on a regional agency, is now serving an agency with regionwide responsibilities is no guarantee that this person will actually adopt a truly regional perspective, rather than narrowly representing the parochial interests of his or her own district.

This situation means that creating effective regional remedies for traffic congestion and other urban ills is still an emerging process, with uncertain prospects about which remedies to which problems will prove definitely superior to existing fragmented governance. Right now, the situation is analogous to a mythical kingdom's singing contest that had been narrowed down to two final contestants. The king was to make the final judgment about who would win. Immediately after hearing the first contestant sing, the king awarded the prize to the second contestant—without hearing the latter! Many citizens contemplating existing regional problems are similarly concluding that present fragmented remedies are so bad that regional ones are bound to be better—without yet having tried them. Therefore, although this book recommends trying many regional traffic-congestion remedies for the same reason, the author recognizes the somewhat tentative and experimental nature of those recommendations. Regional remedies are worth trying, but there is no guarantee how effectively they can be made to work. This is evident from experiences with the MPOs created by Congress in 1962 and given greater powers in the 1990s.

MPOs and Implications for Congestion

The need to coordinate the planning and construction of new ground transportation facilities at the regional level is blatantly obvious because so many personal and vehicle movements in each region cross individual community boundaries. In the past, state government highway departments acted as the main regional coordinators in the absence of other formal integration mechanisms. But that approach suffered from serious drawbacks. It focused almost entirely on roads, usually ignoring public transit, walking, and bicycles. It often failed to include any systematic way to receive or evaluate requests from individual localities for projects within their boundaries. It also frequently did not take into account the reactions of localities to proposed projects that would pass through their territories. It had no effective means of coordinating new transportation infrastructures with proposed new land-use developments or future growth areas, or with local growth-control policies. It often lacked formal mechanisms for soliciting and responding to citizen views about proposed projects. It rarely had any formal mechanisms for coordinating the policies of highway departments in adjoining states when a region encompassed land in more than one state.

In recognition of these shortcomings, Congress expanded previously created MPOs and charged them with creating regionally integrated plans for future ground transportation infrastructure projects. This goal seems clear, but achieving it effectively is extremely difficult. As urban economist George Sternlieb was fond of saying, "The words drip easily from the lip, but putting them into practice is something else."[6] Regional intermodal planning of such a multifaceted activity as ground transportation is an extraordinarily complicated and difficult process, especially in a democracy that emphasizes citizen participation. Making that process work effectively will take many years of experience, flexible experimentation, and outstanding leadership—if it can be done even then.

The difficulty of this process is clear from the requirements Congress established for MPOs. Congress declared that each MPO must do as follows:

—Create a long-range, twenty-year strategic plan for regional transportation investment, taking into account all modes of ground movement—roads, transit, walking, and bicycles—and including passenger and freight movements.

—Create a short-range, current program of specific transportation improvement projects (TIP) that has been evaluated as the best feasible alternative and subjected to a process of citizen participation.

—Create widespread regional consensus supporting the long-range plan and the current program among citizens, local governments and elected officials, and business and other private sector leaders. This requires ongoing collaborative planning and close partnerships between the MPO and these other elements of society.

—Coordinate the MPO's planning with the planning of all affected state and local government agencies, especially the state's department of transportation and environmental protection agency.

—Create a sense of regionwide responsibility—a "regional ethos"—among MPO members, even though most of them are political representatives of specific local governments in the region.

—Take full account of the likely effects of all planned projects on air quality in accordance with the 1990 Clean Air Act Amendments (CAAA).

—Develop systems for managing congestion, intermodal relations, transit maintenance, safety, bridge maintenance, and pavement maintenance.

—Use the latest techniques of analysis, evaluation, and behavioral modeling in carrying out all the other steps just set forth.

—Follow all existing regulations for funding requests of the Federal Highway Administration and the Federal Transit Administration, even though they are quite different from each other.

—Do all this within limited budgets for capital (paying for the infrastructure projects) and operations (hiring and running the necessary staff), and without any direct powers to implement the plans it creates, since implementation is left to other agencies.

Carrying out these tasks has proved to be a tremendous challenge to the officials running MPOs, as indicated by several evaluations of their activities conducted by outside observers.[7] The main members of each MPO are primarily representatives of local governments. And several key committees handle various facets of the MPO's responsibilities. All the evaluators agree that no MPO has successfully completed all of these tasks. One evaluation of the Denver region MPO concluded that only 26 percent of the participants in the MPO process surveyed thought that the planning process "was meeting the long-term transportation needs of the region either very well or adequately well with qualifiers."[8] However, the same evaluation found that 77 percent of those surveyed about the Dallas-Ft. Worth MPO thought it was meeting those needs. The Seattle MPO was given a similarly positive evaluation. But both the Dallas-Ft. Worth and Seattle MPO planning processes had taken a long time to develop "and required a great deal of effort from the leadership of the MPO to develop a truly collaborative process."[9]

Another finding of most evaluations was that MPOs are very different from one another and operate under very different regional conditions; hence they should not be expected to behave in the same manner. Nevertheless, the main ingredients to relatively successful MPO performance are similar to those needed to make any complex organization work well. One evaluation enumerated them as follows:

—Effective leadership;

—Staff competence and credibility;

—Regional ethos—a desire to work for the welfare of the entire region, not just the one part of it from which a participant comes;

—Active public involvement;

—Cooperative relationship with the State Department of Transportation;

—Streamlined, efficient processes;

—Close cooperation with land-use authorities; and

—Accountability to elected officials.[10]

The same evaluation stated that "fewer than half the respondents we surveyed believe their MPO is able to meet rapidly changing transportation needs." The major problems encountered by MPOs were inadequate funding, excessively long and complex procedures for arriving at final action plans, inability to coordinate transportation planning with land-use decisions made by local governments and private parties, excessive and duplicative regulatory requirements by state and federal agencies, including the Federal Highway Administration, the Federal Transit Administration, and the Environmental Protection Agency, overly demanding time requirements for participating local officials and private citizens, and inadequately skilled or trained staffs. All the MPOs studied needed—and had requested—additional assistance from the federal government on almost every aspect of their activities.

A major recommendation of several MPO evaluations was that the Department of Transportation should establish, fund, and proactively promote a much more extensive program for expanding the technical and other capabilities of existing MPOs. This program should be aimed at MPO staffs and other participants in the MPO planning process. Moreover, the Department of Transportation needs to better integrate its own agencies' relationships to MPOs. At the time of these evaluations, the Federal Highway Administration, Federal Transit Administration, and Federal Aviation Administration—which have never fully coordinated their own overall approaches to individual metropolitan areas—had disparate, unnecessarily duplicative, and poorly coordinated procedures for relating to and assisting MPOs.

In response to these recommendations, the Department of Transportation in November 2001 established a Metropolitan Capacity Building Program (MCB). Its mission is stated on its website as follows: "To help decision-makers, transportation officials, and staff resolve the increasingly complex issues they face when addressing transportation needs in their communities. This comprehensive program for training, technical assistance, and support is targeted to State, local, regional, and tribal governments, transit operators, and community leaders."[11] This program is surely a step in the right direction, but how well it will work remains to be seen.

These critical comments certainly do not mean that the MPO planning process should be abandoned. Rather, they indicate that achieving the multiple goals of that process is extremely difficult, and will therefore take a long period of experience and experimentation. It will also take willingness by Congress and the federal agencies concerned to adapt current regulations to the lessons that emerge from experience. But even still-developing regional transportation planning will, in the long run, most likely prove superior to continued fragmentation of such planning among uncoordinated local governments.

Other Possible Institutional Arrangements

MPOs deal mainly with building new transportation infrastructures; hence they are not the only organizations necessary to carry out effective anticongestion policies at the regional level. Many such policies involve changing the behavior of existing governmental agencies, private bodies, or individual drivers. Examples are encouraging more ride sharing and transit ridership, adopting zoning laws that prevent very low-density development in outlying areas, providing subsidies for high-density in-fill development, and creating high-density development zones around transit stops. These tactics would also be most effective if planned and managed at the regional level, but they are not within the purview of MPOs. So other institutional forms are needed to carry out such tactics throughout an entire metropolitan area.

These regional anticongestion tactics are of two basic types: those concerned primarily with transportation itself (such as ramp metering or taxing parking facilities), and those concerned primarily with land use as it affects transportation (such as promoting high-density development around transit stops). Most American citizens have quite different attitudes toward these two types of tactics. As Kathryn A. Foster said in her excellent study *Regionalism on Purpose*, "Americans generally embrace regionalism when it promises material gains through improved service delivery or tax-reducing mergers, but reject it when it redistributes resources, promotes racial and class mixing, or jeopardizes local land-use prerogatives."[12]

To put it another way, Americans will accept relatively strong regional arrangements for primarily physical or economic activities much more readily than for social ones—including control over land uses. Therefore, the type of regional arrangement most appropriate for any anticongestion tactic depends on whether that tactic is transportation oriented or land use oriented. Relatively strong regional institutions—such as formal legal structures like metropolitanwide general, multipurpose, or single-purpose government entities—can be used for mainly transportation-oriented tactics. Weaker forms—such as voluntary associations, contracts among local governments, civic collaborations, and private-public partnerships—have less power to compel their participants to change cherished behavior. Therefore, these forms are more likely to be acceptable for mainly land-use-oriented tactics.

Kathryn Foster divided all regional arrangements into two major categories: structural arrangements and nonstructural ones.[13] Table 17-1 depicts arrangements relevant to regional anticongestion policies. It is modeled after the earlier edition of *Stuck in Traffic* and a chart in Foster's *Regionalism on Purpose*.[14]

TABLE 17-1. Institutional Forms of Regional Arrangements

Type	Example
Structural	
Full metropolitan governments	Jacksonville, Indianapolis, Louisville
Multipurpose regional entities	Portland Metro
Single-purpose regional entities	N.Y. Port Authority
State government agencies	Highway departments
Federal or federally mandated agencies	MPOs, air quality management districts
Nonstructural	
Voluntary cooperation among separate governments	Councils of government
Contractual arrangements among local governments	Phoenix Fire Department
Comprehensive local plans under state government mandates and state coordinating agencies	Oregon, New Jersey
Privately run civic organizations	Visioning groups, N.Y. Regional Plan Association

Source: Based on Kathryn A. Foster, *Regionalism on Purpose* (Cambridge: Lincoln Institute of Land Policy, 2001), p. 1; and Anthony Downs, *Stuck in Traffic: Coping with Rush-Hour Traffic Congestion* (Brookings and Lincoln Institute of Land Policy, 1992).

Advantages and Disadvantages

The following five structural arrangements are analyzed according to their advantages and disadvantages.

FULL METROPOLITAN GOVERNMENTS. These arrangements include city-county mergers and "pure" metropolitan governments. On the plus side, they provide true regional-level control over all basic local governmental functions. However, this form has a fatal drawback: it has virtually no political support because it involves regional control over all land uses. Such control is strongly opposed by most suburban residents and by most central city elected officials. That leaves almost no one in favor of these arrangements. Hence only a handful of the more than 300 metropolitan areas in the United States have adopted full metropolitan governance, and none have done so in the past decade. Few are likely to do so in the future either.

MULTIPURPOSE REGIONAL ENTITIES. These arrangements typically combine regional control over major physical infrastructures, such as transportation, sewer systems, and water systems, in one organization. Since these activities are closely interrelated functionally, managing them within a single organization makes sense. Moreover, these elements can strongly affect where new housing and other developments will be created. Therefore, a single institution controlling these elements can significantly influence land-use decisions relevant to transportation without removing formal control over land-use decisions from local governments. So such an institution is politically far less threatening to suburban communities than full metropolitan governance.

SINGLE-PURPOSE REGIONAL ENTITIES. In some U.S. metropolitan areas, all public transit has been turned over to special regional agencies. They now run the bus lines, commuter rail lines, and fixed-rail mass transit systems. In other areas, regional agencies are responsible for key highway-oriented facilities, such as bridges and tunnels. In the New York City area, the regional Port Authority operates bridges, tunnels, bus terminals and bus lines, port facilities, and the main airports. Where such specialized regional agencies already exist, they can under some circumstances carry out regional anticongestion policies.

For example, regional agencies that run rapid transit and bus systems could improve the service and facilities of those systems to divert traffic from highways. Such agencies could also try to encourage high-density residential and commercial development in the vicinity of their major stations. These tactics are not in themselves likely to reduce congestion significantly, but they might be useful as parts of a larger and more comprehensive set of tactics.

Where a regional highway agency already exists, its scope for carrying out congestion-reducing tactics is even greater. For example, the agency that operates the Golden Gate and Bay bridges leading into San Francisco could employ peak-hour tolls on both places. However, this tactic assumes the agency has sufficient political courage to raise peak-hour tolls high enough to dissuade many auto commuters from using the bridges. That proviso emphasizes again the importance of creating widespread public support for regional anticongestion policies among citizens and political leaders. It will not do any good to establish the institutional mechanisms to effect those policies unless such support has been generated in advance.

In most U.S. metropolitan areas, no such specialized transportation agency now exists. However, it is certainly easier to create such an agency to attack congestion than to create a general regional government to achieve the same goal. For one thing, the regional nature of transportation problems is so obvious that hardly anyone can dispute it. Moreover, local governments feel much less threatened by regional transportation-oriented agencies than by more general regional governments.

Therefore, persons promoting regional anticongestion strategies should seriously consider setting up some type of regional transportation agency with responsibilities going beyond the planning responsibilities of an MPO. Creating such an agency would require action by the state government concerned. The agency's jurisdiction should ideally include the planning, construction, and operation of the area's principal highways, bridges and tunnels, mass transit systems, and regional parking regulations. Hence this agency could be the regional MPO and have additional powers. Such an agency is easiest to create when the entire metropolitan area lies within one state. If regional public agencies with the genuine power to affect traffic congestion are ever to be created, this is probably the form most will take.

STATE TRANSPORTATION OR HIGHWAY DEPARTMENTS. State transportation or highway departments have long been responsible for much transportation facility planning, financing, construction, and operation throughout many metropolitan areas. They had three huge advantages in carrying out regional anticongestion policies: their jurisdictional territory encompasses the entire metropolitan area, unless it includes parts of more than one state; they already possess established capabilities and channels of finance, information, and political influence; and their agencies have access to large continuing flows of money to finance transportation activities and investments.

Therefore such agencies could improve highway maintenance, build new roads or expand existing ones, add HOV lanes to existing roads, coordinate traffic signals, and install ramp signals on expressways and arterials. Some state agencies could even install areawide peak-hour road pricing systems—if the federal government removed current restrictions on charging peak-hour tolls on interstate highways.[15]

However, many of these activities—such as building new roads—now come under the planning jurisdiction of the area's MPO. So the state government could no longer act alone on those activities. Moreover, state agencies are poor vehicles for instituting new policies that require citizens and officials to change their long-established behavior. Leadership in creating such change rarely comes from public officials in a democracy because they are essentially followers of public opinion. In fact, this characteristic is one of democracy's greatest strengths. But it means that adopting new methods—especially controversial ones—requires some other source of change.[16]

FEDERAL OR FEDERALLY MANDATED REGIONAL AGENCIES OTHER THAN MPOS. The federal Clean Air Act provides a potentially powerful regional force that might affect traffic congestion. That law established air quality standards for all U.S. metropolitan areas. The federal Environmental Protection Agency (EPA) requires state governments to create plans for cleaning up the air in "non-attainment areas" where air pollution exceeds acceptable levels. Nonattainment areas have boundaries identical with those of metropolitan areas and consolidated metropolitan areas. Therefore, a state can set up a regional organization to coordinate air quality improvement throughout an entire metropolitan area. Moreover, acting through such state-created agencies, the federal government can override or preempt certain local ordinances related to air quality. However, part of this function has now been delegated to MPOs, which are charged with taking into account the possible air pollution impacts of any transportation facilities they propose, and conforming to the requirements of the Clean Air Act Amendments of 1990.

Emissions from automotive vehicles are a primary cause of air pollution. Long average commuting trips in general, and traffic congestion in particular, increase the emissions discharged into the atmosphere. So air quality improvement agencies have become concerned with traffic flows, especially in California. Consequently, the California Air Resources Board has drawn up proposed regulations that would require major changes in driving and commuting behavior over large territories. For example, it has proposed that a significant fraction of all automotive vehicles be powered by fuels other than gasoline by the year 2010. Achieving that goal would require enormous changes in the automobile and petroleum industries and in household behavior. There are thirty-six air districts in California charged with carrying out these regulations in collaboration with their local MPOs.

Such federally empowered agencies could in theory implement many of the potentially most effective anticongestion tactics at regional levels. For example, they could impose peak-hour road pricing and parking charges throughout a metropolitan area. Therefore, federally rooted antipollution agencies represent one of the potentially strongest instruments for carrying out regional anticongestion tactics. In November 1998, the California Air Resources Board amended existing low-emission vehicle regulations to extend passenger car emission standards to light trucks and sport utility vehicles, starting in the year 2004.[17]

Such agencies could adopt and carry out regional anticongestion tactics effectively only if two conditions prevail. First, each agency's leaders must be convinced that certain regional anticongestion tactics are absolutely necessary to reduce their air pollution to acceptable levels. This is not a foregone conclusion. There has been so little experience with regional application of these tactics that no one can be sure just how they would affect air quality. Moreover, there is always a lot of resistance to regional approaches, and so a strong case must be made that these tactics would greatly reduce air pollution before any regional air quality improvement agency will adopt them. Developing such a case is an important task for proponents of anticongestion tactics.

Second, most of the citizenry must voluntarily accept and follow these regulations. Past U.S. experience has repeatedly shown that strong and widespread citizen rejection of laws that require major behavioral changes may severely undermine their effectiveness. This can occur even if the agencies concerned have unchallenged legal authority to pass and enforce such laws. If many citizens ignore or flout such laws, it may be impossible for these agencies to enforce them. That happened in connection with the prohibition of alcoholic beverages during the 1920s and early 1930s. It is now happening in the importation and use of illegal drugs. Even massive federally financed efforts to prevent illegal drug distribution and use have not come close to stopping either one. A similar defiance of laws governing vehicle speed limits occurs throughout the nation every day.

Thus widespread citizen opposition to severe limitations on the design, purchase, and use of cars and trucks could well undermine the effectiveness of federal efforts to impose those limitations. Such opposition would soon be communicated to elected officials, who could restrict the powers of air quality improvement agencies to pass and enforce those laws. Exactly that happened when HOV lanes were first opened on the Santa Monica freeway in Los Angeles, as pointed out earlier. However, it is too soon to predict that this will happen if a regional air-quality improvement agency tries to carry out unpopular anticongestion tactics. In spite of potential citizen resistance, the already legally established powers of such agencies to act across an entire metropolitan area provide a potentially effective means of carrying out regional anticongestion tactics.

The following three nonstructural arrangements are analyzed according to their advantages and disadvantages.

VOLUNTARY COOPERATION AMONG AUTONOMOUS LOCAL GOVERNMENTS. This is the least satisfactory type of arrangement, with the fewest applications to fighting congestion, because it cannot compel local governments to coordinate their behavior closely or to monitor and adjust that behavior. Yet voluntary cooperation could coordinate the upgrading of local streets, timing of traffic signals, conversion of local streets to one-way flows, and creation of roving teams to handle traffic accidents quickly. However, where anticongestion policies require controversial decisions—for example, benefits and costs often have to be allocated across many communities—this arrangement does not work well.

COMPREHENSIVE PLAN PREPARATION AS PART OF A STATE-MANDATED PLANNING PROCESS. Several states require all their local governments to draw up comprehensive land-use plans as parts of their statewide planning systems. These systems are designed to achieve state goals pertaining to the environment, transportation, open space, and housing. The state legislature first establishes broad goals. It then directs all local, county, or regional governments to draw up comprehensive plans pursuing those goals within their own boundaries. This process is normally managed by a state-level agency. It has final coordination and approval power over the plans drawn up by lower-level bodies. By combining state-level goal setting and coordination with detailed local or regional-level planning, this process uses the best traits of governmental bodies at each level. By late 2000, such processes had been adopted by Hawaii, Maine, Oregon, Florida, New Jersey, Maryland, Pennsylvania (at the county level), Rhode Island, Tennessee, and Washington.[18] It is separate from the MPO processes in these states but may be coordinated with the MPO process.

Such a comprehensive planning process could be used to carry out regional anticongestion policies under some circumstances. One such policy is confining all future urban development to average gross residential densities above some minimum level, say, 2,500 persons per square mile. This would shorten average commuting journeys, compared with those in areas with much lower densities. A state could adopt such a minimum-density policy for all its metropolitan areas. Other anticongestion policies this process might entail are clustering high-density housing near rapid transit and commuter rail stations, stimulating formation of transportation management associations, encouraging more people to work at home, and instituting an areawide cash-out program related to free parking provided by employers.

JOINT PUBLIC-PRIVATE COORDINATION, PLANNING, AND POLICY-PROMOTION AGENCIES. Americans have long been noted for forming associations to achieve joint purposes. As Alexis de Tocqueville pointed out: "In no country in the world has the principle of association been more successfully used or applied to a greater multitude of objects than in America."[19] One type especially important in changing public policy has been the public-private organization that transcends individual community boundaries. One example is the United Way organizations that raise and distribute charitable contributions across the nation.

This type of organization has three principal advantages in creating a regional basis for anticongestion policies. First, it can draw together members of private and public organizations, including business firms, labor unions, nonprofit associations, universities, government agencies, and public legislatures and executives. That is to say, it can give members a forum for coming together and discussing joint concerns outside their official organizations.

Second, the agency can establish any geographic jurisdiction its members desire, including entire metropolitan areas. This can be done by a mere declaration of purpose; it requires no official approval by anyone else.

Third, such an agency can take controversial stands without making individual members commit themselves to those stands. Each member can blame all the other members for the position or claim that "the organization" did it. This enables such an organization to take much more controversial collective positions than many of its members would be willing to endorse in public. Hence such an organization is an ideal vehicle for changing public opinion to support some controversial new policy. It can adopt innovative positions ahead of existing public opinion, without exposing individual members to accusations of ignoring that opinion. That is why so many regions have adopted this form for conducting a "visioning" process to formulate very long-range plans for future growth and development.[20]

The two main disadvantages of such organizations are that they have little or no money and that they have no governmental powers. Hence they have almost no ability to carry out whatever public policies they support, and their roles are confined to influencing public opinion and persuading those who do have money and power to adopt the policies they favor. They can therefore become vehicles for persuading the public and its leaders that some problem is serious enough to demand concerted action; formulating, analyzing, and discussing possible means of remedying that problem; and promoting the remedies they believe would be most effective.

These three functions are all vital in securing the adoption of regional approaches to attacking traffic congestion. It is crucial to have some type of public-private regional association outside of government strongly supporting such strategies if they are to be adopted anywhere. If such a regionwide organization already exists to deal with other issues, perhaps it can expand its functions to cope with traffic congestion too. Or else a new organization should be formed for this purpose. The membership should consist of top-level officials in large establishments and other citizens' groups in the metropolitan area concerned, plus governmental leaders who can influence key transportation and land-use policies.

Private sector and public sector leaders should be involved from the start. Such an organization needs an initial convener to interview relevant stakeholders to decide who should be involved in deliberations. After an "inner circle" of possible participants has been identified, there needs to be a preliminary written statement of the problems on which to focus and possible selection of a professional facilitator. If the consensus-building process is carried out skillfully within clearly defined written rules, the participants will become unified by sharing in the deliberative analysis of congestion problems, examination of possible solutions, and arrival at final recommendations. The whole process should be oriented toward creating a consensus across several issues and subissues (dealing with more than one provides more opportunities for different participants to achieve positive gains from the joint result) in which all—or nearly all—participants see themselves as better off than without any agreement. Their common experience in the process, plus the benefits they gain from the final agreement, will secure their emotional commitment to carrying out their final recommendations in the face of the strong resistance sure to arise. Then there should be one or more rounds of having the participants review the consensus with their separate organizations and possibly modifying it to take account of suggested changes. Finally, the organization should launch a concerted campaign of information and political pressure urging the adoption of the regional approaches it has recommended. Examples of such organizations are the San Francisco Bay Area Council and the greater New York Regional Planning Association.[21]

Unfortunately, at the time of writing, no privately sponsored campaigns favoring regional approaches to combat traffic congestion had been successfully carried out anywhere in the United States. One reason is that the creation and empowerment of MPOs have shifted some of the responsibility for dealing with traffic congestion to those agencies. And when private-public coalitions are formed to consider a region's future, they typically define their subject matter more broadly than just traffic congestion, including land-use and environmental issues. This shifts the focus of their deliberations away from traffic congestion to broader issues, and it is much more difficult to gain public support for regional policies than for those pertaining to traffic congestion alone. This analysis of how to organize regional anticongestion policies does not imply that congestion can best be attacked by creating a single regional agency as the czar of all anticongestion policies. Instead, it might be desirable to have different congestion-reducing policies run by different local and regional agencies that organized themselves in ways best suited to their individual tasks. But if several anticongestion agencies are created at the regional level, they should certainly be linked through formal and informal coordination.

Likely Opposition to Regional Anticongestion Agencies

In almost every U.S. metropolitan area, attempts to carry out effective regional anticongestion tactics will be met by strong resistance. Any organizations created for this purpose could work well only if they exercised authority and powers now divided among many local and state government agencies, but most officials in those existing agencies strongly oppose any reduction in their present powers. Local governments are loath to yield any control over their land uses to outsiders. Indeed, the main function of many U.S. local governments is to control land-use patterns to benefit their existing homeowning residents by maintaining or increasing the market values of local homes.[22] Yet many tactics for reducing peak-hour congestion would require shifting at least some local power over land uses to a regional agency.

The MPO structure has accomplished this goal to a great extent concerning the planning and construction of major infrastructure investments. But, as noted earlier, the authority of MPOs does not extend to operating those investments, or to controlling other types of anticongestion policies. Hence additional regional efforts are necessary to make use of all potentially effective anticongestion tactics.

Although most local governments will resist the creation of effective regional agencies, state governments would normally not be expected to do so. State governments encompass entire metropolitan areas or large parts of them; hence they should not exhibit the same narrow parochialism as local governments. In most metropolitan areas, the territory of regional agencies would lie entirely in a single state.[23] And only state governments have the constitutional authority to create such regional agencies. Yet most state governments have been unwilling to create such regional agencies to combat traffic congestion.

One problem is that each agency would most likely be given powers now in part exercised by other state agencies. Officials in those other agencies would be unhappy about giving up any of their present powers. Second, no state legislature is willing to incur the wrath of most local governments unless the legislators have strong incentives to do so. State legislators are elected from local districts. They are often linked personally and politically to local governments. Moreover, since state representatives are seldom elected from districts large enough to encompass an entire metropolitan area, their viewpoints are also parochial.

At the same time, certain positive gains might motivate state legislators to establish regional anticongestion agencies over the objections of local governments. The main gain would be in reducing traffic congestion in the long run, but that gain would be spread over residents and firms in all parts of the metropolitan area. For each beneficiary, it would be only a small part of the general benefits received from all state government actions. Hence few beneficiaries would decide how to vote among state legislative candidates on the basis of this issue alone.

In contrast, the potential loss of local sovereignty from the creation of such regional agencies would be seen by many local officials as a major threat to their welfare. So how each state legislator voted on this issue would heavily influence the support he or she received at the next election from local officials. In the minds of most state legislators, the potential loss of support caused by their favoring creation of strong regional agencies would outweigh the gains from reducing traffic congestion.

This does not mean states will never create effective regional anticongestion agencies, simply that such actions will be rare. Even when they occur, some resistance will persist within state and local governments. Underlying that resistance is the fundamental belief among many citizens that reducing traffic congestion is far less important than pursuing other social or personal goals. Therefore, if reducing congestion means they must change behavior they have cherished for other reasons, they may prefer to endure congestion—while, of course, still complaining loudly about it.

Conditions of Political Support

What would cause the relevant public officials to adopt regional tactics in spite of the above drawbacks? First, traffic congestion must become so widespread and intolerable that a large share of the metropolitan area's citizenry sees it as a crisis. Second, key state and local officials—especially the governor—must believe that carrying out regional anti-congestion tactics is essential to remedying this crisis. Third, credible institutional structures must be available through which to accomplish those regional tactics.

Crisis

In a few metropolitan areas, peak-hour congestion is so bad that reducing it is widely perceived as the central issue facing local governments. Hence the governor and state legislators are strongly motivated to appear to be doing something about this problem in order to be reelected.[24] Otherwise, they are unlikely to act effectively, since the political leaders in a democracy fear asking the citizenry to make fundamental changes in established institutions or behavior. People can be induced to do so without enormous resistance only if they believe they must to alleviate a crisis that is already present or imminent. Elected officials are in turn unwilling to ask the public to make basic changes unless they believe the public thinks itself threatened by such a crisis.

Most such crises involve some sudden disruption of normal life. They must pose serious, obvious, and immediate threats to the welfare of a large percentage of the population. But peak-hour traffic congestion does not change dramatically overnight; rather, it gets a little worse each day. Since each commuter's route differs from those traveled by most others, people do not all encounter the same degree of congestion simultaneously. So there is no widespread common perception about just how bad traffic congestion has become as of any particular date.

Without any sudden crisis to galvanize public officials into action, they are reluctant to ask citizens to make the painful changes necessary to alleviate peak-hour congestion. True, after congestion has become bad enough long enough, more and more citizens and their political leaders may decide it has passed some invisible threshold of acceptability. If enough citizens do, some elected officials will propose the kinds of actions described in this book.

Belief in Regional Remedies

Even if citizens rally, key officials must be convinced that strong regional agencies are essential to cutting traffic congestion. Otherwise they will prefer other remedies not requiring such drastic behavioral changes. But the belief that regional remedies are essential is not widespread. A critical function of public-private anticongestion groups is to nurture and strengthen this belief in the minds of relevant public and private leaders.

Credible Regional Institutions

Even if the first two conditions exist, one or more credible institutional structures for implementing regional congestion remedies must also be available in the metropolitan area concerned. This condition implies that all key segments of the metropolitan area must lie in a single state, because almost all regional bodies with effective action powers can only be created by state legislatures. If a metropolitan area is in two or more states, it will be extremely difficult to create any institutional structures able to carry out anticongestion tactics throughout the region. Rivalries among political leaders and agencies in different states and the legal difficulties of creating interstate compacts will greatly complicate that task.

This condition also implies that regional structures and the widespread belief that they are essential should be in place before traffic congestion produces a crisis. Then when a crisis appears, regional policy responses can be launched immediately. That will permit effective action to start before public concern wanes. This is critical, because the public's attention rarely remains focused on any one issue very long.[25] Persons promoting effective anticongestion tactics must start building a foundation for regional responses well before congestion reaches maximum intensity.

Summary: Irrational Persistence Needed

In the long run, severe peak-hour traffic congestion can only be effectively combated with the aid of at least some regional anticongestion tactics. But it is extremely difficult to create the political support and institutional structures necessary for such tactics. To do so, proponents of these tactics will have to overcome massive resistance from local governments, existing state agencies, and a majority of citizens who do not want to stop commuting alone in their cars.

To accomplish this task they will have to act in advance of any widely perceived congestion crises. Achieving success also demands persisting—perhaps for many years—in spite of continual failure. After all, not one of the more than 340 metropolitan areas in the United States has yet adopted a comprehensive, regionally based strategy for attacking traffic congestion, insofar as I know. This does not mean that all efforts to achieve a regional approach should be abandoned as hopeless. But it does mean that persons attempting such efforts must be prepared to endure failure for a long time. Their motto must be, "Never give up!"

18

Summary and Conclusions

During the 1980s and 1990s, peak-hour traffic congestion became widespread in many U.S. suburban areas. Congestion is especially prevalent in the largest metropolitan areas and in absolutely fast-growing ones. Yet traffic congestion is not much of a concern in smaller metropolitan areas and other regions containing more than one-third of the U.S. population. Reducing congestion is worth doing because traffic jams cost Americans billions of dollars in wasted time and fuel each year and contribute to air pollution. The failure to confront commuters with the true social costs of their driving alone during congested periods has two other ill effects. It understates the cost of living in low-density patterns and may lead to an overinvestment in highways. Both outcomes contribute to an excessive spreading out of American metropolitan areas. That raises energy costs, increases infrastructure costs, increases vehicle miles traveled, and worsens air pollution.

Traffic Congestion: Not All Bad

Although no one likes traffic congestion, the truth is that peak-hour congestion performs an important—and positive—social function. In every modern or modernizing society, more people have good reasons to travel on roads and streets during peak hours than can possibly be accommodated during those same hours by the limited supply of such facilities. That is because modern societies are organized to permit most people to work at the same time, or go to school at the same time, for efficiency purposes. Therefore, each society needs some way to allocate its limited supply of road space among the many people trying to use it during those "rush" periods.

There are—in theory—four ways to cope with the conflict resulting from great demands for road space during morning and evening peak periods and the limited supply available. One is to build enough roads to handle all the demands for them during those periods. But no society can afford to do that, either financially or by enduring the destruction of existing property that would be necessary. Moreover, doing so would be extremely inefficient, since much of the vastly expanded and costly road space would be unused most of the time.

The second approach would be charging motorists money tolls to enter all major roadways during peak hours—"road pricing." If the tolls were set high enough, traffic on those roads could be restrained enough so those on them could move at high speed, without congestion. That would permit more people to make commuting journeys during peak periods than do now. Even so, not everyone seeking to move then could do so. The rest of the people who wanted to travel then would have to shift to other times, other routes, or other modes. Up to now, democracies have universally rejected this approach for two reasons. One is that road pricing gives a big advantage to high-income drivers versus lower-income ones; the former could afford the tolls daily, but the latter would have to travel in less convenient ways. In America, where more than 90 percent of all households own vehicles, most people feel they would be unfairly disadvantaged by this arrangement, so they oppose it. Road pricing also appears to be "just another tax" on a privilege that Americans have always enjoyed without charge—the ability to drive when they want to. Some forms of road pricing—so-called high-occupancy toll (HOT) lanes—would work well, but they would not eliminate peak-hour congestion.

The third way to cope with "excessive" peak-hour demand for road space is to build enough public transit facilities to shift all the "excess" peak-hour demand to transit. Some societies like Japan have done this. The result is tremendous peak-hour overcrowding of transit vehicles, and average commuting times (in the Tokyo area) are more than double those in the United States. Moreover, the transit facilities required are huge money losers subsidized by taxpayers. In America, the low-density settlement patterns dominant in almost all regions cannot be efficiently served by public transit, so little is provided in many regions. Furthermore, since nearly 90 percent of all commuters normally use private vehicles, and less than 5 percent use transit, moving enough peak-hour travelers from cars to transit to eliminate peak-hour road congestion would require colossally costly expansion of transit facilities. So this approach would not end or even substantially reduce peak-hour congestion in America, even though some expansion of transit is surely desirable.

That leaves the fourth approach: waiting in line to use the roads until your turn comes up. That is what congestion is—first-come, first-served access to our limited road space. It is the only method of coping with "excessive" peak-hour demands for limited road space that is politically acceptable to most Americans and economically feasible. True, many economists consider congestion terribly inefficient because road pricing would permit more people to complete commuting journeys during peak periods, congestion does not allocate scarce road space to those willing to pay most to get it, and congestion forces millions of people to "waste time" moving very slowly during those periods. But economists do not run America's democracy, and most Americans prefer congestion to its alternatives, even though they complain about it a lot.

This means that, once demands for peak-hour travel have risen enough in a region to generate serious traffic congestion there, such congestion will remain an inescapable condition of its ground transportation system indefinitely—especially if the region has a fast-growing population. Effective anticongestion tactics may reduce the rate at which peak-hour congestion gets worse, but they will not eliminate it and often will not even prevent it from intensifying at least somewhat.

In essence, congestion is the balancing mechanism we use to cope with the many demands for peak-hour travel we generate by pursuing goals other than minimizing travel time. It is a worldwide urban phenomenon, an inherent part of any region's process of modernization and growth. Drivers should keep that in mind when they become frustrated by being stuck in traffic.

Immediate Causes of Intensifying Peak-Hour Congestion

The most obvious immediate cause is rapid growth in a metropolitan area's population and employment. Equally important has been a remarkable increase in the ownership and use of automotive vehicles. From 1980 to 2000, the total number of cars and trucks registered throughout the United States rose by 65.7 million, or 42.2 percent, compared with an increase of 54.9 million, or 24.3 percent, in the nation's human population. Hence the number of automotive vehicles per 1,000 persons escalated from 688 in 1980 to 787 in 2000.

Contributing to increased congestion has been the declining real cost of driving per mile. This has resulted from slightly lower real costs of gasoline, greatly increased fuel efficiency of passenger cars, and lower real costs of buying vehicles—adjusted for their increases in quality. The inflation-adjusted per mile fuel cost of driving cars (including light trucks and sport utility vehicles) fell by more than 50 percent from 1980 to 2000. That is one reason the number of miles driven per vehicle rose 28 percent from 1980 to 2000.

As a result of more vehicle ownership, lower operating costs, and more intensive usage of vehicles, total vehicle miles traveled each year in the United States soared 80 percent from 1980 to 2000. In the latter year, American privately owned vehicles traveled 2.5 trillion miles, providing 3.9 trillion passenger miles of movement (not counting travel in buses).

Another immediate cause of peak-hour congestion has been the reluctance of U.S. public authorities to build additional roads during the past two decades. Total highway mileage only rose by 2.4 percent from 1980 to 2000. However, urban road mileage increased by 37 percent, as did the number of lane miles in urban areas. Yet those increases did not keep up with an 80 percent rise in vehicle miles traveled.

Another significant creator of congestion consists of accidents and incidents that block lanes and cause traffic pile-ups. Some experts believe accidents and incidents together cause more than half of all traffic congestion. From 1988 to 2000, the annual number of vehicle crashes of all types has been relatively stable at between 6.1 and 6.9 million, involving 10 to 12 million vehicles per year. Therefore, accidents do not seem to be causing congestion to get worse—except that roads are more crowded, so each blockage may affect more vehicles. But other types of incidents—such as stalled engines, flat tires, cars out of gas, lanes blocked by road construction, and bad weather—are far more numerous than accidents. Records of how many such incidents occur are sparse. Yet it is likely that there are ten times as many incidents as accidents, though incidents usually do not block as many lanes or last as long. Moreover, the absolute number of incidents seems likely to rise along with total vehicle miles traveled, rather than remaining stable, as has the number of accidents.

The final immediate cause of congestion has been the perennial failure of society to force vehicle drivers to confront the full costs of their travel during peak hours. Each entrant onto crowded roads adds to traffic congestion, thereby imposing nontrivial losses of time on other drivers there. But each such entrant pays nothing directly for loading that cost onto others. This disparity between individual and collective costs leads to greater congestion than would otherwise occur and decreases national efficiency.

Underlying Causes of Peak-Hour Congestion

Peak-hour traffic congestion is deeply rooted in behavior patterns that reflect certain cherished goals held by most Americans. To reduce congestion, changing some of those fundamental behavior patterns is essential, which is a tall order. Most Americans are not even aware of the strong link between traffic congestion—which they hate—and these ingrained behavior patterns—which they love. This book is meant to foster a better understanding of this connection.

The principal long-term cause of congestion is that so many people want to move during the same few hours each day. A major reason is the concentration of commuting trips between home and work during those hours. This is efficient for employers because it permits workers in many organizations to interact during shared business hours. In 1995, trips to and from work constituted 45 percent of all trips made during the morning rush hours (6:00 to 9:00 a.m.) and 49 percent of all those made during the evening rush hours (4:00 to 7:00 p.m.). School-related trips were a big share of remaining morning rush-hour travel because schools, too, can be run more efficiently when nearly all students attend at the same time.

Another underlying cause is workers' desire to enjoy a wide range of choices of where to live and where to work. The average one-way commuting trip in the United States in 2000 took 25.5 minutes, an increase of 3.1 minutes since 1990, or 14 percent longer. People select home and job locations for many reasons besides minimizing commuting travel. Long commutes have been encouraged by the entry of more women into the formal work force. It is not easy for households with two or more workers to choose a home close to all of its members' jobs.

Equally important is the strong desire of most Americans to live in relatively low-density settlements, dominated by detached single-family homes. This desire is a central part of "the American dream" of success. Moreover, the nation's population has steadily shifted toward the South and the West and more heavily into suburbs. A rising fraction of all U.S. residents now lives in relatively new urban areas, designed and built during the automobile era. These newer areas have lower residential densities than older urban areas, and most of the newer areas can be efficiently served only by individual automotive transportation rather than mass transit. Furthermore, the residents must travel greater distances to conduct their daily lives.

Regional congestion has been greatly affected by the spreading out of workplaces among scattered, low-density establishments, which many suburban zoning ordinances have promoted in recent years. Ironically, such laws are often adopted to limit local traffic congestion generated by high density, but it is much more difficult for workers to use ride sharing or mass transit to reach widely scattered jobs than jobs densely concentrated in a few central nodes.

Most Americans cherish their right to travel in their own private vehicles, usually alone. Ownership of one's car is a deeply ingrained mark of status. Driving alone also provides a much more convenient, faster, and more comfortable means of commuting than ride sharing, buses, or rapid transit, yet it is also the single biggest cause of peak-hour congestion. In 2000, 75.7 percent of all morning commuters drove alone in automotive vehicles—in comparison with 60 percent in 1977 and 73.2 percent in 1990.

The problem is that most Americans do not realize that in pursuing these cherished goals they generate myriad individual vehicle movements during peak hours, thereby producing the congestion they abhor. A main cause of peak-hour congestion lies at the door of American suburban development, which has been so successful in achieving its residents' desires. Until more Americans recognize this linkage, it will be impossible to alter their behavior and reduce traffic congestion to any significant degree.

Proposed Tactics for Coping with Peak-Hour Congestion

There are two basic kinds of tactics for reducing peak-hour congestion. Supply-side tactics expand the carrying capacity of an area's transportation system. Examples are building more roads and improving the service and amenities of public transit. Demand-side tactics reduce the number of trips made on an area's roads during peak hours. Examples are imposing higher gasoline taxes, charging high tolls for travel on major roads during peak hours, and clustering high-density housing around transit stops.

Some tactics of both types are primarily market based. They put various monetary prices on different types of behavior and permit each individual to choose whatever behavior he or she is willing to pay for. An example is charging peak-hour tolls on major roadways. Other tactics are primarily regulatory. They mandate certain types of behavior and forbid others, without regard to individual preferences. An example would be prohibiting employers from offering free parking to their employees. Market-based approaches have the advantage of maximizing individual choice but the disadvantage of favoring high-income households over poorer ones. Many tactics combine market-based and regulatory elements.

As an economist, I favor market-based approaches whenever possible. However, their political feasibility has been restricted by the egalitarian American desire not to provide any relative advantage to high-income travelers versus low- or moderate-income ones. This desire is politically potent because of the high rate of automotive vehicle ownership in America. Moreover, households considering themselves in the low- and moderate-income category vastly outnumber those considering themselves to have high incomes.

Four Essential Principles of Traffic

To determine how proposed anticongestion tactics might work, it is necessary to understand four basic principles of traffic.

The *principle of triple convergence* states that any large initial reduction of peak-hour travel times on an already congested major limited-access roadway will soon be offset by the subsequent convergence on that roadway of drivers who formerly used alternative routes, traveled at other times, or used public transit. Thus even greatly widening any major commuter expressway cannot long reduce peak-hour congestion there. Additional drivers will shift onto that improved road from other routes, other times, and other modes (such as walking or public transit) until movement on it is just as slow as the movement on alternative routes. Since those other routes are less direct than the expressway, such equalization means expressway traffic is usually crawling at the peak hour. Even most wholly new roads will soon fill up during peak hours. The triple convergence principle reduces the long-run effectiveness of many other anticongestion tactics often proposed and therefore should be taken into account in evaluating those tactics. Examples are more telecommmuting, staggered work hours, widening crowded roads, building new roads, expanding transit systems, and prohibiting people with certain license numbers from commuting on given days. All of these tactics might slightly reduce peak-hour traffic when first tried. But whatever reductions they produce will speedily be offset by triple convergence onto any roads where traffic is perceived to be moving faster than on alternative routes. True, such tactics that expand road capacity would permit more people to move during peak hours, but those tactics would not make congestion less intense.

The *principle of the swamping effect* of rapid growth states that relatively small reductions in initial traffic congestion in a rapidly growing metropolitan area will be fully offset within a few years by the arrival of more people, jobs, and vehicles there. As already noted, several proposed anticongestion tactics can produce only small initial reductions. Such small improvements will be fleeting if the areas where they occur are growing rapidly.

The *imperviousness principle* states that no one suburb can adopt policies that will substantially affect the overall population or job growth of its metropolitan area as a whole. Therefore, if any one suburb limits growth within its own boundaries, the growth prevented there will simply move elsewhere in or near its metropolitan area. But since traffic congestion arises because of movements throughout each metropolitan area, individual communities, except for a few large central cities, cannot greatly affect the total amount of traffic in their metropolitan area by means of their local policies alone. If all local communities acted together to limit their growth, they might affect the expansion of the entire metropolitan area. But such concerted action is extremely difficult to arrange in America's fragmented system of local government. Moreover, even then, more people would keep moving into the region if it offered attractive job opportunities. As historic experience shows, inmigrants would overcrowd existing housing and create new substandard units even if local laws prohibited more new home construction.

These three principles help explain why it is extremely difficult to reduce peak-hour traffic congestion permanently. That probably cannot be done by adopting any one tactic alone, even at a very large scale.[1] Hence the *principle of one-hundred small cuts* states that, just as a woodsman with a small axe can only chop down a large tree with many small blows struck over a long time, a region can reduce its peak-hour traffic congestion—or at least slow such congestion's rate of increase— only by applying many different tactics simultaneously in a coordinated manner.

The Global Nature of Rising Traffic Congestion

Many Americans think rising U.S. traffic congestion is making our metropolitan regions economically less competitive with those elsewhere in the world. But this is not the case for one reason: congestion is even worse in large and growing metropolitan regions almost everywhere else. True, reliably accurate measures of congestion are not available for most cities in the world. But eyewitness reports of the intensity of urban peak-hour congestion from all over the globe indicate that most other big metropolitan regions have less mobility and more traffic delays than in the United States. This is true of regions in long-industrialized societies like France, the United Kingdom, and Japan, and in economically still developing societies like India, China, Indonesia, and Brazil.

A major cause of intensive worldwide traffic congestion is that people tend to buy and use more automotive vehicles as their real incomes rise. The desire for the personal freedom and faster mobility that such vehicles provide is almost universal. Moreover, as societies modernize, incomes in the private sector—at least in the wealthiest groups—rise much faster than do taxes collected by the public sector. Hence large numbers of private households and firms switch from cheaper but slower means of movement to privately owned automotive vehicles. But government resources available to build roads and public transit do not increase nearly as fast, especially in developing nations. Hence a disparity arises between the private sector's adoption of automotive vehicles and the public sector's ability to build the roads and bridges those vehicles need for uncongested movement.

Moreover, the basic asymmetry that plagues America between the huge number of people who want to move during peak hours and the limited supply of roads to accommodate them is found everywhere else too. And most other societies do not have the resources to build and maintain as many roads as the United States does. Hence peak-hour congestion builds up everywhere for the same fundamental reasons as it does in America.

True, many other societies—both highly developed and developing— make far more use of public transit to move people than does the United States. This puts fewer vehicles per 1,000 residents on their roads than in America. But most have far fewer roads per 1,000 residents too.[2] And in almost all highly developed nations except Japan, travel by private automotive vehicles far outweighs that by public transit and all other means, and the share of transit in total travel has recently been falling. Furthermore, in developing societies, rapid increases in real income are stimulating immense gains in private vehicle usage.

As a result, future traffic congestion is likely to become much worse in many developing nations. For example, many of China's big cities now have crawling traffic during much of the day. China had about 12.5 vehicles per 1,000 inhabitants in 2000, compared with 779 in the United States. If China's ratio increased to 250—the same as that of South Korea today but only one-third that of the United States—its total vehicle population would rise from 15.7 million to 316.5 million. That population would soar by twenty times to a number 47 percent larger than the total U.S. vehicle population in 2000! So traffic congestion is not only already worse than ours in much of the world today but is likely to become even more intensive in the future.

Many officials in American regions also worry about traffic congestion's impact on the competitiveness of their regions versus other American regions. However, an analysis of relations between regional population growth rates and congestion intensity shows that the fastest growing regions tend to have worse congestion than slow-growing ones. Congestion is apparently in part a sign of prosperity and growth, rather than an obstacle to it.

An Important Behavioral Policy Objective

No one remedial tactic is likely to reduce peak-hour congestion substantially, but one behavioral change could do so: persuading more commuters now driving alone to share rides with others. This tactic would be effective because the overwhelming majority of daily commuters are persons driving alone. Any sizable doubling up of these Lone Rangers would reduce the number of daily commuting trips far more than any other single change. Moreover, such doubling up could occur almost overnight if commuters were motivated strongly enough. This has been shown by sharp shifts in individual travel behavior in Los Angeles during the 1976 Olympic games, in San Francisco right after the 1989 earthquake, and in Atlanta during the 1996 Olympic games. This change cannot be achieved on a big enough scale to cut peak-hour congestion appreciably unless many different tactics are used simultaneously.

Data from 1995 indicate that about 45 percent of all trips in the morning rush hour are to or from work, and data from the 2000 Census show that about three-fourths of all persons commuting to work drive alone. Hence one-third of all morning rush-hour trips involve lone drivers. In the evening rush hour, 49 percent of all trips are to or from work. Thus about 37 percent of all trips then involve lone drivers. Persuading just one-third of these people to share rides would cut the number of peak-hour trips by 11 percent in the morning and 12 percent in the evening. These reductions could produce dramatic effects on the levels of delay and congestion during peak periods. Moreover, these are much larger trip reductions than those likely to result from any attempts to get more people to use mass transit.

Several different anticongestion tactics could effectively influence more people to share commuting trips in private vehicles. They are peak-hour road pricing (including building new high-occupancy toll [HOT] lanes), collecting a surcharge for long-term parking during morning peak hours, raising gasoline taxes, prohibiting employers from providing free parking to their workers, cashing out free parking provided by employers, and creating more high-occupancy vehicle (HOV) lanes adjacent to expressways with heavy congestion during rush hours. What makes all of these tactics except the last two effective is that they greatly increase the costs of driving alone during peak hours. This is unfortunate because it confronts solo-driving commuters with a dilemma of choosing between two costs, both of which they vehemently oppose. One cost is giving up the benefits of driving alone, which the vast majority of commuters prefer. The second cost is suddenly having to start paying a substantial cash charge for continuing the formerly "free" privilege of driving alone.

This is like telling someone who for years has enjoyed drinking clear water without charge from a local spring that she must start either drinking castor oil or paying a hefty price for the water. Neither alternative seems palatable. Nor will most commuters accept the cost until they become absolutely convinced that present congestion is unbearable and there are no other feasible ways to reduce it.

True, reducing the costs of ride sharing might increase its extent without compelling solo commuters to face the unpleasant choice just described. That could be done through greater availability of HOV lanes and employers' provision of benefits to ride-sharing workers. However, these tactics will not cause nearly as many lone drivers to change their ways as forcing them to pay high costs for continuing to commute solo. Hence the best medicines for traffic congestion are also the most difficult to get most commuters to swallow. People resist such tactics partly because most do not realize that their driving alone is the primary cause of peak-hour congestion. Nevertheless, one of the best litmus tests for the potential effectiveness of a proposed tactic against peak-hour congestion is to what extent it would cause greater ride sharing by persons now driving to work alone.

The difficulty of getting more commuters to share rides is revealed by what happened to ride sharing during the 1990s. Although the total number of workers over 16 commuting daily rose 11.5 percent from 1990 to 2000, the number that were ride sharing rose only 1.67 percent. Consequently, the fraction sharing rides fell from 13.4 to 12.2 percent. In contrast, the number driving alone rose 15.3 percent—increasing the share of Lone Rangers from 73.2 to 75.7 percent. The number of commuters using public transit declined slightly, reducing transit's share from 5.3 to 4.7 percent. These data show how strongly Americans want to travel alone.

Rating the Desirability of Anticongestion Tactics

This book analyzes thirty-three different anticongestion tactics to determine their likely effectiveness and social desirability.[3] Because both these qualities have several dimensions, it is not easy to summarize the results. But some method of comparing tactics is necessary to help policymakers choose which ones to pursue most vigorously. Therefore, a rating system has been designed that evaluates each tactic in relation to nine basic criteria of desirability. Box 18-1 displays these traits and some comments on how they are used in this system. These ratings are admittedly subjective rather than scientific; they represent my best judgments. That is inescapable: no "purely scientific" method of evaluating such policies can be devised, because doing so inherently requires value judgments.

Box 18-1. Evaluation Criteria for Anticongestion Tactics

Effectiveness

Extent. How much of the congestion situation in a region is addressed by this tactic? Ratings: narrow (not much addressed), broad (a great deal addressed), and variable (could be narrow, broad, or in between, depending upon particular circumstances).

Impact. How great an impact would this tactic have within its breadth of effectiveness in reducing existing congestion levels? Ratings: great, moderate, or minor.

Weakened by triple convergence? Is any initial impact of this tactic likely to be offset over the intermediate and long terms by triple convergence on the roads involved? Ratings: yes (it will be seriously weakened), no (it will not be seriously weakened), or somewhat (it will be weakened, but not always seriously).

Cost

Direct to commuters. To what extent will this tactic impose costs (financial or in time) on commuters? Ratings: none, minor, moderate, or great.

To society. To what extent will this tactic impose costs (financial or in time) on society as a whole? Ratings: none, minor, moderate, or great.

Implementation

Institutional change. Would this tactic require institutional changes from currently dominant fragmentalized local government control over land uses? Ratings: none, major, or regional (requiring some type of regionwide agency), or cooperative (achievable through purely voluntary coordination among local and other governments).

Ease of administration. Would carrying out the required institutional changes, or simply putting this tactic into practice, be difficult administratively? Ratings: easy, moderate, or hard.

Political Acceptability

How acceptable is this tactic likely to be to the American public and elected officials responsive to public opinion? Ratings: poor, moderate, or good.

Significant Spillover Effects on Nontransport Sectors

What kind of significant spillover effects will this tactic have on nontransportation sectors of the American economy or society? Ratings: none, positive, or negative.

These ratings are not entirely arbitrary, however, since they have been based on the analysis presented earlier. Moreover, by breaking down the rating of each tactic into several categories, this system enables readers to develop their own ratings for specific tactics, which they can do based on reading earlier chapters and their own knowledge and experience.

Table 18-1 shows this rating system applied to all thirty-three anticongestion tactics. The thirty-three tactics have been divided into fifteen supply-side policies and eighteen demand-side.

General Conclusions Derived from the Ratings Table

One of the most important conclusions about anticongestion tactics derived from the ratings shown in table 18-1 and prior analysis is that very few tactics could greatly reduce traffic congestion by themselves, even if they were widely applied. A few others would moderately reduce congestion. But most would have fairly minor effects—if applied alone. That is why a multifaceted approach is so important in attacking congestion.

Many often-recommended supply-side tactics are much more costly to society as a whole than most demand-side tactics. The latter impose most of their costs directly onto commuters to get them to change their behavior. In contrast, several major supply-side tactics cost commuters little directly but require substantial social investments. They involve big public spending on facilities like more roads, improved highway maintenance, new HOV lanes, the upgrading of streets, or construction of more transit facilities. Such tactics receive strong political support from industry groups that would benefit from these investments. They include the automobile, road building, and public transit industries. This is one reason that such tactics have moderately favorable political acceptability. Yet none of the costliest supply-side tactics would greatly reduce congestion; all would have only moderate or minor impacts. One reason is that the initial effects of many of them would soon be offset by the principle of triple convergence.

Demand-side tactics generally have broader effects than most supply-side tactics. That is, they would affect a higher percentage of all commuters to some degree. Yet demand-side tactics are less costly to society as a whole, although they impose more direct costs on commuters. Moreover, some major demand-side tactics would raise large sums that could be used to pay for their implementation; examples are peak-hour road pricing, peak-hour parking surcharges, and higher gasoline taxes.

As a group, the most effective supply-side tactics would require less traumatic institutional change than the most effective demand-side tactics. Several of the latter require regional administration or much greater intergovernmental cooperation than now exists. Most supply-side tactics could be carried out without much change in existing institutional arrangements. That is one reason why they are more politically acceptable than the most effective demand-side tactics.

Demand-side tactics—including the potentially most effective ones— have poor political acceptability at present, whereas supply-side tactics have much better political prospects. The principal reason is that key demand-side tactics work by imposing high costs on solo commuting by private car—and that is how most Americans prefer getting to and from work. These tactics would be extremely unpopular if people knew more about them—although right now, most Americans have never heard of them. And supply-side tactics are politically supported by strong interest groups, whereas demand-side tactics are not.

Four of the five tactics that involve changing the existing or potential location of jobs or housing would have only small effects on traffic congestion. Yet they would require difficult institutional changes and take many years to bear even limited fruits. Only clustering high-density housing near transit stops might have more than a minor impact on congestion—and it could increase congestion in the vicinity of the transit stops themselves.

The above conclusions imply that—in general—demand-side tactics would be much more effective at reducing congestion, and less costly to society in general, than supply-side tactics. (There are some exceptions, such as removing vehicles quickly from blocked lanes and creating traffic management centers.) Nevertheless, demand-side tactics will be much harder to get adopted than supply-side tactics. In fact, political probabilities alone suggest that society is much more likely to attack congestion with supply-side tactics. With a few exceptions, such a strategy would produce relatively few results at great cost, compared with demand-side tactics.

The Potentially Most Comprehensive and Effective Tactics

In reality, only four of these thirty-three anticongestion tactics could produce a significant reduction in peak-hour traffic congestion unaided. That is, each could do so by itself—if applied throughout a metropolitan area. These are peak-hour road pricing on major traffic arteries using

Table 18-1. Tactics for Reducing Traffic Congestion

Tactic	Effectiveness			Costs		Implementation			Significant spillover effects on nontransport sectors
	Extent	Impact	Weakened by triple convergence?	Direct to commuters	To society	Institutional change	Ease of administration	Political acceptability	
Supply side									
1. Rapidly removing accidents from traffic lanes	Variable	Great	No	None	Minor	None	Easy	Good	None
2. Creating traffic management centers	Variable	Great	No	None	Minor	Cooperative	Easy	Good	None
3. Increasing the capabilities of MPOs	Variable	Moderate	No	None	Minor	None	Moderate	Good	Positive
4. Adding HOT lanes to existing freeways	Narrow	Moderate	No	Small	Moderate	None	Moderate	Moderate	None
5. Improving highway maintenance	Broad	Moderate	No	None	Great	None	Moderate	Good	None
6. Building added HOV lanes	Variable	Moderate	No	None	Great	None	Hard	Moderate	None
7. Building new roads without HOV lanes	Variable	Moderate	Somewhat	None	Great	Cooperative	Moderate	Poor	Negative
8. Building separate roads for trucks only	Narrow	Great	No	None	Great	Cooperative	Moderate	Poor	Positive
9. Ramp metering vehicle flows onto freeways	Variable	Moderate	Somewhat	None	Moderate	Regional	Moderate	Moderate	None
10. Developing effective means of providing transit services to low-density areas	Variable	Moderate	No	None	Moderate	Cooperative	Hard	Moderate	Positive
11. Deregulating public transit services to reduce monopolistic powers of administrators and unions	Major	Moderate	No	None	Minor	Major	Hard	Poor	Positive
12. Coordinating traffic signals, electronic signs for drivers, making streets one way	Narrow	Moderate	No	None	Minor	None	Moderate	Good	None
13. Upgrading city streets	Variable	Moderate	No	None	Moderate	None	Easy	Moderate	Positive
14. Building or expanding off-road transit systems	Narrow	Moderate	Somewhat	Minor	Great	Cooperative	Hard	Poor	Positive
15. Increasing public transit usage by improving service or amenities	Narrow	Minor	Somewhat	None	Great	None	Hard	Moderate	Positive
Demand side									
16. Instituting peak-hour tolls on all lanes of main commuting roads	Broad	Great	No	Great	None	Regional	Moderate	Poor	None

17. Using GPS satellites to track vehicles and vary tolls with roads traveled	Broad	Great	No	Great	Moderate	Regional or national	Hard to start up	Poor now	Positive
18. Levying parking tax on peak-hour arrivals	Broad	Great	No	Great	None	Regional	Hard	Poor	None
19. Eliminating business income tax deductibility for employee parking	Broad	Great	Yes	Great	None	Cooperative	Moderate	Poor	None
20. Providing income tax deductibility for commuting allowance for all workers	Variable	Great	Yes	None	Minor	None	Easy	Poor	None
21. "Cashing out" free parking provided by employers by offering daily payment instead	Broad	Great	Somewhat	None	Minor	None	Hard	Moderate	None
22. Substantially increasing gasoline taxes	Broad	Moderate	No	Great	Moderate	None	Easy	Poor	Positive, negative
23. Keeping densities in new-growth areas above minimum levels	Broad	Great	Somewhat	None	Minor	Regional	Hard	Poor	Positive
24. Encouraging formation of TMAs that promote more ride sharing	Narrow	Small	Yes	None	Minor	Cooperative	Hard	Moderate	None
25. Encouraging more people to work at home	Broad	Minor	Yes	None	None	None	Moderate	Good	Positive
26. Changing federal work laws that discourage working at home	Broad	Minor	Yes	None	Minor	None	Moderate	Moderate	Positive
27. Staggering working hours	Broad	Minor	Yes	None	Minor	None	Moderate	Moderate	None
28. Clustering high-density housing at transit stops, creating transit-oriented developments	Variable	Moderate	Somewhat	None	None	Cooperative	Moderate	Moderate	Positive
29. Concentrating jobs in big clusters in areas of new growth	Narrow	Minor	Somewhat	None	Moderate	Cooperative, regional	Hard	Moderate	Positive
30. Increasing automobile license fees, sales taxes	Broad	Minor	No	None	Great	Regional	Easy	Poor	Negative
31. Improving the jobs-housing balance	Broad	Minor	Yes	None	Minor	None	Hard	Poor	Positive
32. Adopting local growth limits	Narrow	Minor	No	None	Minor	Regional	Easy	Good	Negative
33. Requiring commuters not to drive one day per week, based on license plate number	Broad	Great	Yes	Great	Moderate	Little	Hard	Poor	Negative

smart card devices, use of global positioning system (GPS) satellite devices to charge individual vehicles with variable tolls depending on where they travel—a tactic that would take many years to introduce, higher gasoline taxes, and charging a sizable special fee for all parking during morning peak hours. A fifth tactic—creating extensive HOT lanes—would not greatly reduce peak-hour congestion but would give many commuters the option of moving rapidly during peak hours if they were willing to pay a toll.

ROAD PRICING. Peak-hour road pricing with smart card devices has four main advantages over most other tactics. First, it could be fully applied—at least technically, if not politically—within a relatively short time, say, no more than five years. None of the tactics involving changes in residential or job density or location have that trait. Second, it would immediately affect all peak-hour movements on main arteries, not just work-related trips or local trips. Third, and most important, its initial congestion-reducing effects would not be offset by triple convergence of drivers from other roads, time periods, and modes—because all users of those roads would have to pay peak-hour tolls. Fourth, road pricing would produce significant revenues from the tolls collected—revenues usable to finance the tactic itself and perhaps other transportation improvements. These traits apply to placing tolls on all lanes of major commuting expressways and adding HOT lanes to such expressways.

For all other equally comprehensive tactics except parking fees and higher gasoline taxes, such as changing job and housing locations or increasing residential densities, perceptible reductions in congestion would not emerge for many years, if ever. Moreover, their effects would mainly reduce potential future increases in congestion, rather than existing levels.

Peak-hour road pricing on all major commuting expressway lanes with smart card devices would not be a fault-free tactic however. It would be difficult to collect tolls on every street, so some traffic trying to avoid arteries with tolls might cause congestion on nonpriced local streets. Moreover, enforcing the system could heavily burden police departments and courts. Most significant, the political resistance to creating appropriate regional agencies to run such systems is extremely strong.

Even so, the potential advantages of peak-hour road pricing, including the large sums of money gained that could be used to improve local transportation systems—are so great that it really should be tried somewhere. The HOT lanes version is already in operation in two or more locations, but the all-lane version has never been tried anywhere. For several years, the Department of Transportation has attempted to finance experiments with road pricing, but it has been unable to persuade any region to take on the political risks involved. Nevertheless, it should keep promoting an areawide experiment with peak-hour road pricing in some moderate-sized but heavily congested metropolitan area. That effort could be similar to the federally funded metropolitan-area housing allowance experiments of the 1970s. Lessons learned from them greatly affected later federal housing policies.

HIGHER TAXES ON GASOLINE. Another tactic sharing the traits of road pricing to a lesser degree would be placing relatively high taxes on gasoline. That could not be done by individual metropolitan areas; it would require action by states or preferably the federal government. Moreover, its driving-reduction effects would apply to all automotive travel, not just peak-hour trips. This would benefit society as a whole by conserving energy, reducing oil imports, and decreasing air pollution, as well as cutting traffic congestion throughout the day. The money thus raised could be used to improve transportation facilities. The main disadvantage of this tactic is that it would harm low-income households more than middle- and upper-income households.

Higher gasoline taxes would not immediately reduce peak-hour travel much, because it takes time for people to adjust their travel behavior and locational choices to reflect a big shift in costs. But in the long run, a really large increase in gasoline costs—including taxes—could significantly affect all travel behavior. Some scheme to redistribute some of the revenues thus collected to low-income households would help offset the regressive nature of this tactic.

SURCHARGE ON LONG-TERM PARKING DURING THE MORNING PEAK PERIOD. A surcharge on parking would have to cover all employees parking in spaces now provided free by employers. If the charge was large enough, many workers would not be able to afford to continue commuting alone.

This tactic would not affect peak-hour trips that did not end in long-term parking. Examples are interregional truck trips, truck deliveries, local errands, and dropping children at school or with babysitters. These trips constitute a substantial majority of all vehicle movements during morning and evening peak periods, so many drivers who would be affected by peak-hour tolls would escape peak-hour parking charges. To that extent, parking surcharges would be less effective in reducing total peak-hour traffic.

If peak-hour long-term parking surcharges were collected everywhere in a metropolitan area, however, auto-driving commuters could not escape by changing to nonpriced routes, as they could escape peak-hour roadway tolls.

Peak-hour parking surcharges are open to the same four criticisms that have been leveled at peak-hour road pricing. First, they would harm the poor more than the nonpoor. Second, using such a surcharge amounts to taxing something that is now provided free to millions of American workers. Third, this surcharge would raise a lot of money that would have to be spent on something.[4] Fourth, equitable administration of such a surcharge would require regionwide management under uniform regulations.

But other criticisms of peak-hour road pricing do not apply to parking surcharges. The latter do not pose great administrative difficulties, since most parking facilities are already taxed by state or local governments (although parking provided free by employers is not). Nor would this surcharge invade individual privacy. Furthermore, a peak-hour parking surcharge could be implemented quickly without any public investment in new equipment or roadway redesign.

The Heart of the Problem

The two main drawbacks of a peak-hour parking surcharge are the same as those of peak-hour road pricing. Americans do not want to pay a monetary price for what they now seem to be getting free—even though in reality they are paying the high price of time lost in congestion. And most commuters do not want to give up driving to and from work alone—even though their doing so is the central cause of peak-hour congestion. As Hamlet might have put it if he were a commuter today:

> To drive alone, or to ride share,
> That is the question.
> Whether 'tis nobler in the mind to bear
> The jams and delays of outrageous congestion,
> Or to take passengers against a sea of traffic,
> And by ride sharing, end it.

Up to now, most American commuters still seem to prefer driving alone through a "sea of congestion" to putting up with the policies necessary to decrease it.

Other Relatively Effective Tactics

Several other anticongestion tactics promise more limited but still significant reductions in existing peak-hour congestion. They could have a considerable joint impact if coordinated with other tactics in a metropolitan area. These tactics are as follows:

—Using roving response teams to speed up the removal of accidents and other incidents blocking roadways. Because multiple traffic accidents and incidents happen daily in every large metropolitan area, they cause immense total peak-hour delays over the course of a year. Hence this simple tactic can have a substantial impact on average travel time. It could be carried out through existing state highway or transportation departments or some cooperative arrangement among local governments.

—Establishing traffic management centers to manage the roving response teams and coordinate other congestion-reducing activities by public and private agencies. Cost-benefit analyses of the time and fuel-cost savings to vehicle drivers and passengers achieved by those traffic management centers already operating show clearly that such centers provide great net benefits to society. Several dozen are already operating, and more should be built.

—Adding HOT lanes to existing congested expressways. This tactic cannot eliminate peak-hour congestion altogether on those expressways, but it can offer all users of those roads the choice of moving rapidly whenever they are willing to pay a toll. Yet this tactic does not prevent solo drivers who are unwilling or unable to pay the toll from using those roads during peak periods. In fact, it may reduce congestion for them, too, by increasing the overall capacity of the roadways involved. Therefore, adding HOT lanes is politically much more acceptable than placing peak-hour tolls on all lanes of major expressways. Moreover, it will pay for itself in the long run because the tolls it generates can be used to finance the lanes added. Hence this tactic should be seriously considered for any heavily congested expressways with rights of way that have room for additional lanes, or could be expanded to accommodate such lanes.

—Ramp metering vehicle flows onto existing expressways during peak hours. Experience in the Seattle and Twin Cities regions shows that ramp metering can notably speed up vehicle flows and reduce driver delays during rush hours. This tactic is not nearly as costly as building additional lanes—of whatever type—onto existing expressways. It should be integrated with coordinating traffic signals and operating electronic signs to help drivers choose routes.

—Coordinating traffic signals, creating and using electronic signs to inform drivers of road conditions, and converting streets to one-way. Except for electronic signs, these tactics are aimed mainly at improving traffic flows on city streets rather than expressways. Experience shows that they can be effective in speeding traffic movements.

—Increasing the capabilities of metropolitan planning organizations (MPOs). Regional planning of transportation investments and improvements is a complex, difficult process that requires high levels of skill, capability, experience, and leadership. Yet it is vital to achieving the most efficient use of resources in creating and modifying any region's ground transportation systems. The Department of Transportation has recognized the need for increasing the capabilities of MPOs by creating a special program for that purpose. But individual regions should be willing to devote added resources to this goal too.

—Keeping residential densities in areas of new growth above certain minimum levels. This tactic would only affect future congestion levels over a long period, since it can be applied mainly to now-vacant areas as they develop. For that reason, it would not be very expensive in money costs but could have significant effects over the long run. However, it would require major changes in current planning and governance institutions. This tactic would not work well unless all very low-density development around the periphery of a growing region was prohibited through use of an urban growth boundary and very large-lot zoning or other land-use controls outside that boundary.

Moderately Effective Low-Cost Tactics

Two tactics would produce only moderate reductions in traffic congestion but have the advantage of low costs to society in general. However, these tactics would require major shifts in current institutional and legal arrangements and considerable technical innovation.

—Developing means of providing effective public transit service in low-density areas. This suggestion is more of an undeveloped concept than a ready-to-go tactic. If public transit advocates could develop some means of feasibly providing collective services in low-density residential and commercial areas, they would open up huge new markets, because there are so many such areas in the nation. Those areas are precisely where choices of alternative means of movement are most lacking; so this tactic could greatly benefit society as a whole. Possible forms are van pools in which drivers maintain custody of and operate collectively owned vehicles (thereby eliminating driver payrolls), jitney services, on-demand services, and private bus companies operating specialized routes.

—Encouraging development of such new forms of transit could probably best be accomplished by substantially deregulating public transit in general. Opening up mobility markets to private experimentation with absolutely minimal regulation would permit individual entrepreneurs to try out new methods of serving low-density areas, including methods that have not yet been demonstrated to be economically feasible. The risks involved would fall on those entrepreneurs, not on the public sector. Service problems could be remedied over time, rather than having to be demonstrated as minimal before new methods were tried. This would be a version of the legendary Jesuit principle: "It is better to ask for forgiveness than for permission."

Tactics with Small Effects but Low Cost

Most anticongestion tactics would have only a small effect on existing congestion levels. Nevertheless, those neither costly to society nor terribly hard to implement might be worth carrying out—especially if they were combined in a comprehensive anticongestion strategy. Nearly every one of them could be accomplished by action at a single level of government, either local, state, or federal. However, the short-run benefits of all these tactics are subject to relatively rapid erosion over time by the principle of triple convergence. Such tactics are as follows:

—Encouraging more people to work at home. Employers would have to be persuaded to promote more telecommuting among their workers, which could benefit the employers as well as society in general.

—Changing federal work laws that discourage working at home. This is an adjunct to the preceding tactic but is separable from it.

—Staggering working hours. This tactic can be accomplished within each large job center by privately coordinated action among key employers.

—Eliminating the income tax deductibility of providing free parking for employees. This policy could be carried out by Congress with one change in the tax laws. Because of interstate competition for business, states are not likely to change their tax laws in this manner unless Congress provides an umbrella. If employers stopped providing free parking, a prime incentive for driving alone would be removed at one stroke.

—Encouraging development of cashing-out programs for workers who are now provided with free parking by their employers. The employers would offer to pay workers a monthly fee in lieu of providing a free parking space if the workers use car pools or transit. Recent experience shows this tactic can significantly reduce single-occupancy commuting in such firms.

—Providing income tax deductibility for public transit commuting allowances paid to workers. Congress now permits employers to pay workers commuting allowances they can use for public transit and allows the employers to deduct those allowances as part of wages. If Congress also permitted employees to deduct those allowances from their taxable incomes, that would encourage more workers to seek such allowances from their employers and use them to commute by public transit.

—Clustering high-density housing near transit or commuter rail station stops. This tactic could increase transit usage appreciably if done by enough communities in a metropolitan area. That could shift many commuters from driving to work to public transit. However, it might also increase local congestion in the vicinity of the transit stops affected.

—Encouraging the formation of transportation management associations (TMAs). This tactic could be focused on all newly developing businesses and applied in large established job centers. TMAs can be moderately effective at increasing employee ride sharing. The tactic incurs little public expense and does not need to be implemented by public sector regional agencies.

Moderately Effective Tactics Costly to Society as a Whole

Some tactics would produce only moderate reductions in traffic congestion but would be costly to society in general because they consist of building expensive additional transportation facilities. They are strongly supported by industrial groups that stand to benefit from such investments. Most would not be hard to implement, because they could be carried out through existing institutions, although they would take considerable time to bear fruit. Furthermore, they would be less upsetting to commuters in general than the primary demand-side tactics.

For these reasons, elected officials will be tempted to adopt these tactics rather than the potentially more effective and less costly demand-side tactics that their constituents dislike. However, most of these tactics are also subject to being heavily offset by the principle of triple convergence. These tactics include the following:

—Improving highway maintenance. Road maintenance already absorbs the majority of federal funding for roads. That outcome is inherent in the large size of the existing road network, which needs constant repairing and upgrading.

—Upgrading major city streets. This tactic expands flow capacity without the great costs of land acquisition required when building wholly new roads or expanding existing ones.

—Building additional HOV lanes to encourage more ride sharing. It is more expensive but also more effective to build added lanes and make them HOV lanes than to convert existing lanes to HOV use. This tactic is superior to expanding existing roads because it persuades drivers to shift from solo commuting to ride sharing.

—Building new roads—including separate roadways for trucks—or expanding existing roads, without HOV lanes. This tactic is among the most widely used, but its effectiveness is weakened by the principle of triple convergence, except in the case of building separate roadways for trucks. This tactic does not pressure solo commuters to shift to ride sharing. However, by expanding the capacity of the overall road network, this tactic certainly at least reduces the rate at which congestion will increase in the future, compared with what would happen if no more road capacity were created. Moreover, some new road building is essential to cope with population growth, much of which will take place at the periphery of built-up portions of each metropolitan area.

—Increasing public transit usage by improving services and amenities. This tactic could become expensive. It would work best where existing transit systems serve large job concentrations or housing clusters near their stations. However, its potential for reducing suburban traffic congestion is extremely limited even under favorable conditions.

—Building new off-road transit systems or expanding existing ones. Such systems are costly but appear glamorous to local chambers of commerce and elected officials. However, these systems divert relatively few commuters off roadways, especially in fast-growing areas. Yet many metropolitan areas have proposed or are building such systems. They are often persuaded by the argument that "every world-class area ought to have one," rather than by cogent analysis of how these systems will actually work. The costliness of this tactic, and its futility at reducing congestion, are illustrated by the Los Angeles subway built during the 1990s.

Ineffective Tactics

Although some may disagree that the tactics in this strategy are ineffective, the analysis in this book suggests they are just not worth doing under most circumstances.

—Concentrating jobs in big clusters in areas of new growth. This tactic poses almost insuperable political obstacles. It would require major changes in existing property tax systems, insert a whole new layer of bureaucratic regulation into real estate development and the choosing of business locations, and require massive public spending except where fixed-rail systems already exist. It would have little effect on congestion. It could be applied, however, to increase job site densities in large existing suburban activity centers to encourage more transit commuting or more ride sharing among the persons working there.

—Requiring drivers with certain license plates not to drive on specific days of the week. The difficulty with this tactic is that many workers have no available means of getting to their jobs other than driving themselves. Their homes are not close enough to existing public transit to make that mode a feasible alternative, and no other workers living near them also work near enough to their jobs to make car pools practical. If they cannot drive their own cars one day a week, how will they commute on that day? This tactic thus imposes too heavy a cost on this group of workers. Hence they are likely to raise vehement objections to it that will cause elected officials to prevent this tactic from being adopted.

—Improving the jobs-housing balance. This tactic probably cannot be achieved through feasible public policies. Trying to apply it might reduce the potential supply of affordable housing in a metropolitan area because its major parts—which need to be carried out simultaneously— have different political acceptability ratings. Some would be adopted and some rejected, with a likely negative overall result. Moreover, some of its most sensible goals will be attained through "natural" forces and adaptations over time.

—Increasing automobile license fees. Politicians in a democracy where more than 90 percent of all households own private vehicles will never increase license fees to high enough levels to deter vehicle usage. Singapore does so, but it is not a true multiparty democracy in which members of competing parties offer alternative programs to voters. If adopted, this tactic would impose heavier burdens on low-income households than higher-income ones without causing either to change their commuting behavior.

—Placing limits on local growth. This tactic benefits the residents of the communities that adopt such limits but harms all other communities in the metropolitan area.

For convenience of reference, the thirty-three tactics just analyzed are displayed in figure 18-1, which shows how they have been classified according to their potential effectiveness at counteracting peak-hour congestion and their possible costs to society.

Tactics That Require Regional Action

Several of the potentially most effective tactics attacking peak-hour congestion, such as peak-hour road pricing, must be planned and administered across an entire metropolitan area. If peak-hour tolls were placed only on the roads passing through a single community, even a big one, they would not be able to reduce congestion throughout the entire metropolitan area.

Similar regional or even broader planning and administration would be necessary to construct or set aside a network of HOV lanes, eliminate free employee parking, impose a surcharge on peak-hour long-term parking, build separate truck roadways, expand existing road capacity, build new roads, change tax laws to encourage ride sharing, maintain gross residential densities in areas of new growth above some minimum level, and cluster high-density housing near transit or commuter rail stations.

Unfortunately, few U.S. metropolitan areas had effective governmental institutions at the regional level before the creation of metropolitan planning organizations. Even so, six different organizational arrangements could be used to carry out regionwide anticongestion tactics, depending on the situation.

FIGURE 18-1. Classification of Anticongestion Tactics by Effectiveness and Cost to Society

High degree	Effectiveness in counteracting congestion	Low degree
Potentially most effective at directly reducing peak-hour congestion	**Moderately effective, not costly to society**	**Low effectiveness, but relatively low cost**
—Peak-hour road pricing of all major commuting roads	—Developing means of making public transit feasible in low-density areas	—Encouraging more people to work at home (telecommuting)
—Higher taxes on gasoline	—Deregulating public transit markets by ending administrative and union monopolies	—Changing federal work laws that discourage people from working at home
—Creating new high-occupancy toll (HOT) lanes next to congested expressways		—Cashing out free parking provided by employers by providing payment if they stop using free spaces
—Surcharges on long-term parking during morning	**Moderately effective, costly to society**	—Staggering working hours for more workers
—GPS satellite tracking of vehicles and charging variable tolls (long-term future possibility)	—Improving highway maintenance	—Eliminating income-tax deductibility of free parking
	—Upgrading major city streets	—Providing income-tax deductibility for commuting allowances paid to workers
Relatively effective	—Adding new HOV lanes to freeways	—Encouraging formation of transportation management associations among employers
—Roving response teams to remove accidents and incidents	—Building and expanding roads without HOV lanes	—Clustering high-density housing near transit stops in transit-oriented developments
—Traffic management centers	—Building separate roadways for truck traffic	
—Ramp metering peak-hour in-flows onto expressways	—Improving public transit service and amenities	**Very ineffective tactics**
—Improving traffic flows through ITS applications, such as coordinating stoplights, broadcasting current traffic conditions, electronic signs, and one-way streets	—Building and expanding off-road transit systems	—Concentrating jobs in large clusters in new-growth areas
—Increasing the capabilities of metropolitan planning organizations		—Requiring drivers not to drive one day a week, based on their license plate numbers
—Keeping densities in new-growth areas above certain minimum levels		—Trying to improve the jobs-housing balance
		—Increasing automobile licensing fees
		—Placing limits on population and other growth within individual localities

—Metropolitan planning organizations (MPOs). These organizations were initially created by Congress in 1962 but given expanded powers in 1998 to coordinate ground transportation planning and facilities construction in each metropolitan area. They have substantial powers to decide what transportation improvements will be given federal and other funding priority in each region. Hence they are appropriate for such tactics as building more roads, building or expanding HOV lanes and HOT lanes, and building new transit lines or facilities or expanding existing ones. However, they have no powers over land uses. So they cannot effectively manage such tactics as creating transit-oriented developments, preventing very low-density development in outlying areas, clustering jobs together in a few large nodes, or changing the jobs-housing balance.

Because of the complexity of the responsibilities entrusted to MPOs, it would be desirable to expand the capabilities of their staffs and other participants through constant training and education. With some aid from the federal government, each region should devote significant resources to such capacity building for its MPO.

—Voluntary cooperation among autonomous local governments. This would work only for tactics that did not involve controversial decisions or the allocation of costs and benefits among many communities. An example is coordinating traffic signals and systems of one-way streets.

—State transportation or highway departments. In metropolitan areas lying in a single state, these agencies were formerly able to carry out the regional administration of several anticongestion tactics: building roads, adding new HOV lanes to existing roads, improving highway maintenance, and helping localities coordinate small-scale traffic flow devices. In some cases, these agencies could administer the construction of new off-road transit systems or the expansion of existing ones. However, these functions are now supposed to be carried out under the direction of regional MPOs in cooperation with state transportation or highway departments, rather than by the latter alone. Such state departments still have important roles to play, and in some areas they dominate regional MPOs. But the shift of authority to MPOs should broaden the use of public funds beyond focusing solely on highways and increased public participation.

—State and local planning agencies acting under state comprehensive planning systems. A few states have adopted comprehensive planning systems that require each local government to draw up a land-use plan serving goals established at the state level. A state agency has final coordinating and approval powers over all locally prepared plans. This system could be used to carry out such tactics as keeping residential densities in areas of new growth above some minimum level, clustering high-density housing near transit stops, concentrating jobs in nodes, and improving the jobs-housing balance. Unfortunately, most of these land-use tactics can do little to reduce existing congestion, especially in the short run.

—Private coordination, planning, and policy-promotion organizations. In many metropolitan areas, private sector leaders have formed umbrella organizations to study the future problems likely to be caused by regional growth. Members include leaders from private firms, nonprofit entities, civic groups, unions, universities, and public agencies. These organizations have little money and no governmental powers. But they can act as a forum for joint deliberations among their members about what regional problems will emerge and what to do about them. Such organizations can adopt much more controversial stands on issues than their members could individually. They can therefore perform important functions in designing regional policies and helping garner public support for such policies. Examples are the Regional Planning Association in New York, the Bay Area Forum in the San Francisco area, Los Angeles 2020, and Metropolis 2020 in Chicago. Strong leadership from such organizations is probably essential to getting innovative and controversial policies like peak-hour road pricing adopted in any area.

—Specialized regional government agencies. These groups are usually transportation-oriented organizations, such as the New York and New Jersey Port Authority. They have regional powers over varied sets of transportation or infrastructure functions; hence they are often designated as regional MPOs. Where they now exist, they could carry out several types of regional anticongestion policies. And in some metropolitan areas, new agencies of this type could be formed to concentrate on reducing traffic congestion.

—Federally rooted regional agencies. In southern California, the need to carry out the federal Clean Air Act has generated regional air quality management districts connected to the Environmental Protection Agency through the state government. Because of the sweeping powers granted to EPA under that law and the close connection between vehicle usage and air pollution, such agencies could carry out certain anticongestion tactics over entire metropolitan areas. This provides a potentially powerful vehicle for achieving regional anticongestion tactics without the need to gain the approval of a host of local governments. However, MPOs have also been charged to take account of air quality in their planning, development, and implementation of ground transportation investments within each region. Hence MPOs and air quality management districts should work closely together.

These organizational forms present many channels through which regional anticongestion tactics might be carried out. However, there must be widespread political support for these tactics if they are to be effective. Even federally mandated policies to improve air quality will not work if they encounter massive public resistance.

Unfortunately, resistance to effective regional administration of anticongestion tactics—or any other policies—is extremely strong in most metropolitan areas. A primary goal of almost all U.S. local governments is to control land-use patterns to serve the interests of their existing residents—especially homeowners, who are usually more numerous and more politically active than renters. Yet many tactics for reducing peak-hour traffic congestion would require shifting at least some power over local land uses to a regional agency. Even anticongestion policies not directly controlling land uses could have an immense impact on just what land uses would develop in each part of a region. Hence local governments are reluctant to yield any power of approval over transportation facilities within their boundaries to a regional agency with broad goals. Since state legislators and administrators also have strong roots in local governments, they hesitate to create strong regional agencies, even though they have the legal power to do so. Therefore, up to now, few regional anticongestion tactics have been effectively carried out anywhere in the United States. The creation of regional MPOs was a step toward generating the type of powers necessary to achieve regional application of anticongestion tactics. But there is still a long way to go before that application becomes widespread and effective.

Conditions of Political Support

Public officials might adopt regional tactics, in spite of the likely resistance, in certain circumstances. First, traffic congestion must become so widespread and so intolerable that a large fraction of the metropolitan area's citizenry sees it as a crisis. Elected officials in our democracy almost never have the courage to ask citizens to change cherished behavior unless there is an obvious and compelling need to do so. However, traffic congestion does not normally generate crises. The intensity of congestion changes too slowly and varies too greatly among individuals to create a widespread public belief that congestion has suddenly become a disaster threatening society. Even though many citizens complain bitterly about congestion, it has not yet become intolerable enough to create this condition—at least not in most parts of the nation.

However, one type of regional congestion crisis can arise if excessive air pollution generated to a great extent by vehicle traffic causes the Environmental Protection Agency (EPA) to ban any further federal funding of road construction in that region. The EPA threatened to do just that in the Atlanta region. That threat stimulated Georgia's governor and legislature to establish a powerful regional agency to oversee transportation activity in that region. Up to now, that agency has been given very limited powers over land uses; hence its ability to influence traffic congestion in the long run is severely handicapped. What will happen in the future remains to be seen. Similar creation of powerful regional agencies might happen in many other U.S. metropolitan regions in the future.

Second, important state and local officials—especially the governor—must believe that carrying out regional anticongestion tactics is absolutely essential to dealing with this crisis. Otherwise, they will first pursue other tactics less upsetting to their constituents but also much less likely to reduce congestion. Few really understand what causes congestion and what tactics might alleviate it.

Third, there must be some credible institutional structure available through which to implement those regional tactics. In practice, two conditions must be fulfilled.

First, the entire metropolitan area must lie in a single state; then a single state legislature can form new regional organizations to carry out the required anticongestion tactics or give the necessary powers to one or more existing organizations. Metropolitan areas that encompass parts of several states pose extreme legal and administrative difficulties for any such cohesive regional approach. Yet many of the nation's largest metropolitan regions cross state borders, including New York, Chicago, Philadelphia, Boston, Washington, Minneapolis-St. Paul, and Portland.

Second, the groundwork for effective implementation of this type should be established before a congestion crisis occurs. Leaders in the community, and the public in general, should have become persuaded that curing traffic congestion does indeed require regional tactics. Moreover, it would also be desirable to have the proper institutions legally established in advance. A strong MPO is a good start, but it does not have sufficient powers over land uses or facilities operations to do the entire job itself. Then, when congestion approaches the crisis level, regional anticongestion actions can be launched almost immediately. Otherwise it may take so long to get them started that the public will have shifted its concern to other matters, and political support for regional attention will no longer exist. Given the tendency of public and media attention to shift rapidly from one subject to another, this is a serious problem.[5]

Conclusion

In many U.S. metropolitan areas, peak-hour traffic congestion is a socially suboptimal condition that wastes billions of dollars' worth of time and fuel each year and surely adds to air pollution. Its causes are rooted in several long-established goals and cherished behavior patterns of Americans. Yet most citizens do not realize these prized elements of their lives are generating the traffic congestion they hate. The behavior they value that is most to blame for peak-hour congestion is driving to work alone. Any effective tactics must change that behavior among thousands of commuters. That means getting more of them to share rides, use transit, or travel at nonpeak hours. All the workable means of accomplishing these objectives would raise the costs of solo commuting during peak hours. These means include peak-hour road pricing, surcharges on peak-hour long-term parking, and abolishing the free parking benefit for employees.

Naturally, the patient does not enjoy the prospect of taking such bitter medicine. In fact, the patient regards driving to work alone without paying any fee as an established right and views any interference with it as an uncalled-for blow to his or her welfare. Thus whether peak-hour congestion can be significantly reduced boils down to three questions:

—Is traffic congestion widely perceived as being bad enough for most commuters to accept this medicine?

—Do they understand that only this rather painful cure will work—less painful ones will not help much?

—Will their anticongestion feelings be strong enough to cause elected politicians to overcome the entrenched resistance of local governments to regional and other anticongestion tactics?

Up to now, the answer to all these questions throughout the United States has clearly been no. However, the strength of anticongestion sentiments is rising rapidly in many areas, and the opportunities for change are greater than ever before. Moreover, rising air pollution from expanding use of vehicles may cause EPA to threaten more regions with cutting off federal funding for road construction. Nevertheless, considerable peak-hour congestion is almost sure to persist throughout the foreseeable future in all metropolitan areas already experiencing it. That is likely even if the most effective anticongestion tactics are launched there. In fact, because of substantial future population growth throughout the nation, traffic congestion is likely to get worse almost everywhere—no matter what tactics are employed against it. This is true throughout the world. Those tactics may reduce congestion significantly, compared with what it would have been without them, but they will probably fail to eradicate it anywhere soon, if ever.

Therefore, my advice to American drivers stuck in peak-hour traffic is not just to become politically involved but also to learn to enjoy congestion. Get accustomed to it! Get a comfortable, air-conditioned car with a stereo radio, a tape player, a CD player, a hands-free telephone, perhaps a fax machine and a microwave oven, and commute with someone you really like. Then regard the moments spent stuck in traffic simply as an addition to your leisure time.

The Dynamics of Traffic Congestion

Traffic congestion is a complex phenomenon that few people thoroughly understand. This appendix sets forth a simplified description of its fundamental dynamics and mechanics.

Two Basic Types of Congestion

There are two basic types of peak-hour or other traffic congestion: *recurrent congestion* caused by high volumes of vehicles trying to use the roads at the same time during most days, and *incident-caused congestion* arising from specific obstacles to vehicle movement that occur randomly in time and space. As the name "recurrent congestion" suggests, this type happens almost every day in many communities. It arises because of the fundamental nature of traffic flows on overloaded roads. Incident-caused congestion arises "spontaneously" at unpredictable times and places because of specific, nonrecurring events. Examples are a particular motorist's motor failing, obstacles created by road repair crews, and inclement weather conditions. This appendix focuses solely on the dynamics of recurrent congestion.

Vehicle Speeds and Vehicle Flow Volumes on Major Roads

The detailed relationships between vehicle speeds and flow volumes on major expressways have been explored by at least three freeway studies conducted in California. Although these studies came to partially conflicting conclusions, they all help illuminate the nature of traffic congestion on freeways. Therefore, each is briefly explored here.

The 1993 Northern California Study

This analysis is based on data collected on a nine-mile section of Interstate 880 in Hayward, California.[1] The study was conducted by "probe" vehicles driving at seven-minute headways during the study periods. Those periods were twenty-four weekdays in the spring of 1993 before the freeway service patrol (FSP) was put into operation, and twenty-two weekdays in the fall after the FSP was in operation. The purposes were to record data on the number and nature of incidents and accidents, and compare how they were handled without and with the services of the FSP. Speeds and flows were tracked at one-second intervals by loop detectors about one-third of a mile apart on the main freeway and all the ramps.[2]

Three plots of speed versus volume were derived from individual lanes on Interstate 880. One plot is shown in figure A-1, on which an approximate "median line" among all the observations for that lane has been drawn for convenience. The diagram shows speeds on the left side along the Y axis and vehicle volumes per lane per hour on the bottom along the X axis. This lane plot was quite similar to the plot for a second lane. The third lane had somewhat higher maximum flow volumes in the speed range from 50 to 55 miles per hour. Table A-1 presents data taken from the Lane 2 plot in this study and simplified to illustrate the basic relationships between speed and flow volumes that the study revealed.[3]

Analysis of all three plots reveals the following traits:

—The highest flow volumes occurred in only a small percentage of all observations. In two lanes, the highest volumes were slightly more than 2,000 vehicles per lane per hour; in the third lane, the highest volumes were slightly more than 2,500 vehicles per lane per hour.

—In the highest-volume observations, speeds were almost entirely between 40 and 60 miles per hour, mainly in the low 50s. Apparently, the highest volumes on this road could be attained when speeds were

FIGURE A-1. Speed versus Flow

Speed (mph)

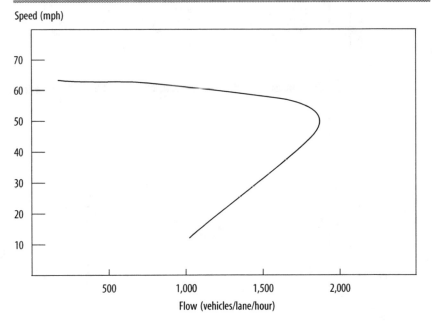

Flow (vehicles/lane/hour)

Source: See note 1.

between about 50 and 55 miles per hour. None of the highest-volume observations had speeds greater than 60 miles per hour, and only one had a speed less than 40 miles per hour. These high volumes implied no interference from congestion or incidents or accidents.

—Many observations clustered around the speed of 60 miles per hour, with flow volumes varying from very low (under 500 vehicles per lane per hour) to just above 1,500 in two lanes and just above 2,000 in the third lane. This shows that vehicles were going about 60 when traffic was very light and were able to maintain that speed to around 1,750 vehicles per lane per hour in "normal" conditions—that is, if not adversely affected by incidents or accidents.

—In the parts of the flow diagrams showing "normal" flows as just described, increases in flow volume were accompanied by a gradual decline in speed. This is shown by a slight downward slope in the median line as flow volumes rose from the lowest levels of about 250 vehicles per lane per hour to around 1,750 in two lanes and to around 2,250 in the third lane.

TABLE A-1. Observed Speed-Flow Combinations, 1993 California Study, Lane 2[a]

Speed (mph)	Vehicles/lane/hour	Speed (feet/second)	Seconds for 1 vehicle to pass a given point	Seconds for hourly flow of vehicles to pass given point	Total passing time of hourly flow (minutes)	Implied interval between vehicles[b]	
						Seconds	Feet
63	500	92.40	0.20	100.92	1.68	7.00	646.63
61	1,000	89.47	0.21	208.46	3.47	3.39	303.43
60	1,125	88.00	0.21	238.42	3.97	2.99	262.95
59	1,250	86.53	0.22	269.40	4.49	2.66	230.57
58	1,500	85.07	0.22	328.86	5.48	2.18	185.51
55	1,750	80.67	0.23	404.60	6.74	1.83	147.29
50	1,800	73.33	0.25	457.77	7.63	1.75	128.02
45	1,750	66.00	0.28	494.51	8.24	1.77	117.12
40	1,700	58.67	0.32	540.43	9.01	1.80	105.59
35	1,600	51.33	0.36	581.30	9.69	1.89	96.85
30	1,475	44.00	0.42	625.20	10.42	2.02	88.74
25	1,300	36.67	0.51	661.23	11.02	2.26	82.89
20	1,250	29.33	0.64	794.74	13.25	2.24	65.83
15	1,200	22.00	0.85	1,017.27	16.95	2.15	47.35
10	1,000	14.67	1.27	1,271.59	21.19	2.33	34.15
5	750	7.33	2.54	1,907.39	31.79	2.26	16.55

Source: Based on data from Caltrans Performance Measuring System (PeMS), http://paleale.eecs.berkeley.edu/FSP/Data/index.html, (June 19, 2002), Chart for Speed versus Flow for Lane 2.
a. Average vehicle length is estimated at 18.65 feet.
b. Back of first vehicle to front of next vehicle.

—After reaching maximum flow levels as noted above at speeds in the low 50s, the median line among observations curved downward sharply and began moving back to the left. As speeds fell because of congestion or incidents, volumes per lane per hour also declined. The line has a much steeper downward slope in this area than it exhibits in the "normal" traffic area. When speeds fell as low as 10 miles per hour, flow volume was about 1,000 vehicles per lane per hour. When flows were at about 1,500 vehicles, speeds were between 20 and 30 miles per hour. At 40 miles per hour, flows were 1,750 to 2,000 vehicles per hour. *Thus congestion not only reduces average speeds but also sharply cuts flow levels of vehicles per lane per hour.*

Factors other than speed and congestion also affect the relationship between speeds and flow volumes. For example, the number of large trucks in the mixture of vehicles can markedly influence this relationship, as can the weather. Kara Kockelman has done research that shows speed-flow relations are also affected by the sex and age of the drivers, what types of vehicles they are driving, and whether it is raining.[4] Thus speed-flow relationships can change markedly from one situation to another. Nevertheless, they tend to exhibit certain basic traits discussed here.

The 1998 Southern California Study

This analysis is based on data collected from PeMS—the Performance Measuring System—created by Caltrans—the California Department of Transportation. PeMS makes use of thousands of 30-second loop detectors placed along California freeways that transmit their observations to a centralized computer system. Data from a 7-mile section of Interstate 405N in the Los Angeles area were collected from 5:00 a.m. to 10:00 a.m. over twenty-two weekdays in June 1998. The following conclusions were derived from these data by the study's authors.[5]

—Recurrent congestion in any one segment of a freeway does not occur in exactly the same manner every weekday but varies considerably from day to day. However, this variation has a roughly normal distribution with a relatively stable mean over time for each road section. But that mean can vary notably among sections of the same freeway, depending on each section's relationships with other sections and with the surrounding community. Thus there is a stochastic (random) element even in daily recurring congestion on a single road segment caused by overloading a freeway.

—The variation in travel times along a single freeway is significant, even at the same times of the day. The study calculated the length of time required for a 78-mile trip between 5:00 and 8:00 a.m. on Interstate 5N in Los Angeles for twenty weekdays in July 2000 and found significant differences. The authors did not indicate to what extent this variance was caused by incidents or only by differences in daily recurrent congestion.

The authors concluded that the maximum number of vehicles per hour could be accommodated at a free-flow speed of 60 miles per hour. Therefore, they argued that any delays resulting from speeds less than 60 miles per hour were caused by congestion. This is a very different standard from that used by Caltrans, which the authors stated were any delays from moving less than 35 miles per hour.

—The exact number of vehicles that could be accommodated *per lane* at 60 miles per hour was not clear from this study. However, a telephone conversation with author Pravin Varaiya held on July 1, 2002, revealed that maximum flows ranged from 2,000 to 2,800 vehicles per lane per hour in southern California. This conclusion was drawn from another study of freeway congestion that did record vehicle flows for each lane separately.

—When vehicles are moving at 60 miles per hour, maximum flows per lane per hour of 2,000 vehicles or more reduce the average amount of space and time between vehicles to very low levels. Assuming the average car is 17 feet long and the average truck is 50 feet long, and that trucks compose 5 percent of all vehicles with cars composing the rest, then the average vehicle length is 18.65 feet. Hence, when the flow is 2,000 vehicles per lane per hour, the average interval between vehicles is 137 feet, or 1.58 seconds (measured from the back of the first vehicle to the front of the trailing vehicle).[6] Under the same assumptions, an hourly flow of 2,800 vehicles produces an average interval of only 93 feet, or 1.07 seconds! (Measured from the front of the first vehicle to the front of the second, that interval would be 111.65 feet, or 1.27 seconds.) That is a time interval much shorter than the long-established "two-second rule" for spacing between vehicles, and a space interval far below that required to stop at that speed. Yet flows of those magnitudes have been observed on southern California freeways.[7]

—However, a speed of 60 miles per hour could be maintained throughout peak periods only by preventing many drivers who want to enter the freeways then from doing so, presumably through ramp metering. The authors of the study believe all ramp meters should be set to keep vehicle flow levels below maximum capacity in order to maintain a free-flowing speed of 60 miles per hour.

—The overall effectiveness of a freeway system at moving traffic would be much greater if vehicle speeds could be kept close to 60 miles per hour than if congestion were permitted to slow those flows substantially.

The 2000 Southern California Study

The same group of authors who performed the 1998 study just described also analyzed data from 3,363 loop detectors in the Los Angeles and Ventura county freeways (Caltrans District 7) from midnight to noon on September 1, 2000. The authors reached the following notable conclusions.[8]

—Maximum flows of vehicles per lane per hour varied substantially across these detectors, which were mainly on four-lane highways. Half had a maximum flow between 1,500 and 2,200 vehicles per hour, one-quarter were below 1,500, and another quarter had maximum flows higher than 2,200. Based on these numbers, the median flow was around 1,850 vehicles per hour (halfway between 1,500 and 2,200).

—About 85 percent of the detectors showed that the speed of flow at the point of maximum volume was between 50 and 70 miles per hour. The occupancy percentage (the percentage of the time that loop detectors were interrupted by a vehicle passing over them) at the point of maximum volume varied between 8 and 15 percent. But this variation is probably affected by the way individual detectors are tuned.

—The most desirable speed to maintain on these freeways is 60 miles per hour, because that permits the maximum volume of flow per hour in most cases. Assume that at a typical location, if traffic is flowing at 60 miles per hour, the maximum possible volume without congestion is 2,000 vehicles per lane per hour. If the road becomes overcrowded, flow speed may drop as low as 15 miles per hour, at which speed the flow may be only 1,200 vehicles per lane per hour. Then 800 fewer vehicles per lane per hour will be able to pass this location than if the traffic were moving at 60 miles per hour. That is a drop in effectiveness of 40 percent.

—What is not yet known clearly is how many drivers who want to enter that road during the peak period would have to be prevented from doing so in order to maintain an average speed of 60 miles per hour.

That depends on the level of congestion initially prevailing at any given moment. As long as there is no real congestion, everyone who wants to enter can be admitted—until congestion appears. The greater the intensity of congestion initially existing, and the greater the number of additional drivers who want to enter the road per hour, the higher the percentage that would have to be prevented in order to re-establish and maintain free flow at 60 miles per hour. Some experts estimate that only 5 to 15 percent of the drivers who want to enter the road then would have to be deflected by ramp metering or other means to maintain a 60-mile-per-hour flow. If the fraction to be deflected is 10 percent, then by preventing 200 drivers from entering the road during the peak hour, the carrying capacity of that road could be expanded from 1,200 to 2,000 vehicles per hour. Four times as many drivers would benefit as were penalized by being prevented from using the road in that period. However, exactly what fraction needs to be deflected from using the road cannot be determined on any general basis.

—Ramp metering to keep fewer drivers from entering a freeway during the peak period than actually want to do so in effect shifts congestion from the freeway to the on-ramps. The speed and volume of flows on the freeway are maintained at near-maximum levels by causing a build-up of congestion at the entry ramps. If the ramps do not have a holding capacity large enough to accommodate all the drivers who must be diverted, then the remainder are shunted onto nearby city streets and arterials, raising congestion on those roadways.

The Dynamics of Recurrent Congestion: The 1993 Study

On a major freeway carrying little traffic, drivers can move relatively unimpeded by other vehicles. So they tend to drive at or somewhat above the posted speed limit, as shown by the top left-hand portion of the median line on the speed-flow chart shown earlier (figure A-1). There is then plenty of room between vehicles. At an average speed of 63 miles per hour with a low average vehicle flow of only 500 vehicles per lane per hour—typical of very early morning traffic—the average time interval between vehicles passing a given point on a specific lane is about 7 seconds. That represents a distance of 637 feet (assuming the average car is 17 feet long, the average truck is 50 feet long, and only 5 percent of the vehicles are trucks). A driver moving 60 miles per hour can stop her car within about 300 feet under good driving conditions.[9]

Therefore, that large average distance between vehicles permits drivers to move at this speed without any discomfort from feeling too close to the next vehicle.

As more vehicles enter the road, the average interval between vehicles in the same lane diminishes, as measured in time and distance. When there are 1,000 vehicles per lane per hour, driving at 63 miles per hour (under the same assumptions as above) reduces the interval between vehicles to 3.4 seconds, or about 308 feet. This interval is getting close to the distance within which a car driver can readily stop in case of problems. At 1,250 vehicles per lane per hour and a speed of 63 miles per hour, the average interval between vehicles is only 2.68 seconds, or 243 feet—less than the interval needed for a car driver to stop in an emergency.

This closeness normally causes many drivers to slow down to increase their safety by raising the average interval between vehicles. Such a slowdown is reflected in the median line on figure A-1. It shows that when there were 1,250 vehicles per lane per hour, the average speed was 59 miles per hour. That produced an average interval between vehicles of 2.66 seconds, or 227 feet—still below the estimated space needed to stop in an emergency.

If even more vehicles enter each lane, average speeds slow down, but total vehicle flow rises until the per hour flow equals about 1,800 vehicles per lane. This was the maximum hourly flow observed in this particular lane. At that point, average speed was 50 miles per hour, and the average interval (under the assumed conditions) was only 1.75 seconds, or 126 feet. This interval has fallen well below the widely known two-second rule of safe driving, which states that each driver should maintain a distance of two seconds of movement between herself and the vehicle just ahead of her.

As the number of vehicles on the road rises still further, the interval between them gets even smaller in space and time unless they reduce their speed considerably. But such reductions in speed decrease the number of vehicles in each lane that can pass by a given point in an hour. Thus, the median curve begins to move back to the left in terms of flow volumes as speeds drop. The resulting combinations of speed and flow volume are shown in table A-1, derived from the scatter plot shown in figure A-1. When the flow volume has fallen to 1,700 vehicles per lane per hour, the average speed is 40 miles per hour, which produces an average interval of 1.79 seconds, or only 103 feet. This causes further declines in speed, which further reduces the hourly flow volume. Gradually, as speeds fall, the average time interval between vehicles in each lane begins to increase, although the space between them gets smaller. At 30 miles per hour with a flow volume of 1,475 vehicles per lane per hour, the time interval has expanded to pass two seconds, though the space interval is down to 87 feet. But at that speed, a car driver can stop within just about that distance under good driving conditions. So safety has been improved at the expense of the ability of the road to carry traffic.

This analysis shows how increasing the number of vehicles allowed to enter a road in any given period can gradually lead to slowing speeds and eventually to lower traffic volumes per lane per hour. That is how recurrent traffic congestion is generated.

The Dynamics of Recurrent Congestion: The 1998 and 2000 Studies

A similar explanation of the dynamics of traffic congestion can be derived from the 1998 and 2000 studies just described. On the average freeway segment, maximum capacity throughput occurs when vehicles are flowing freely at 60 miles per hour. Under average conditions, this situation generates a maximum hourly flow of about 2,000 vehicles per lane per hour. At that speed and volume, the average one-mile segment would contain 33.85 vehicles at any given moment (assuming vehicle lengths and mixtures as mentioned above). Now assume that an increase in vehicles on each segment occurs as more vehicles enter, and that expands the number of vehicles in each one-mile segment by 15 percent to 38.92 vehicles. Those vehicles take up more space in each mile, reducing the average interval between vehicles from 139.75 feet to 117 feet. If all vehicles continue moving at 60 miles per hour, that reduces the time interval between vehicles from an initial 1.59 seconds to 1.35 seconds and the space interval from 140 feet to 119 feet. It also raises the volume of flow by 15 percent to 2,300 vehicles per lane per hour.

If 15 percent more vehicles per hour enter the road so that each one-mile segment contains 44.766 vehicles, those vehicles occupy 18.65 feet times 44.766, or 834.7 feet. That leaves 4,445 feet in the one-mile segment for space between vehicles, or 99.3 feet between each two vehicles, on the average. At 60 miles per hour or 88 feet per second, that is only 1.13 seconds between vehicles. True, the flow rate has risen to 2,690 vehicles per hour, or 17 percent higher than before these added vehicles per mile entered the road. But drivers are almost sure to become uncomfortable with the resulting much smaller intervals between vehicles, so they slow down to lengthen those intervals. How much they slow down depends on how much they want to change the average interval between vehicles. If they change the *time interval* back to 1.59 seconds, then the average speed drops to 51.24 miles per hour, and the volume of flow drops only 1.8 percent to 1,964 vehicles per hour. But the *space interval* between vehicles is still lower than initially—119 feet versus 140 feet— because each vehicle moves less distance in 1.59 seconds at the lower average speed. So drivers tend to slow down further to regain the same space interval between vehicles as before, or at least to increase the smaller interval they now confront. But that means the new larger number of vehicles per mile can no longer be contained within 1 mile, because there is a bigger space between each two following vehicles. In fact, it takes a 15 percent larger road segment to accommodate that larger number of vehicles—because they are maintaining the same space interval with 15 percent more vehicles. The time interval between vehicles is also necessarily larger than it was before because drivers are holding the same space interval at a lower speed.

Both that speed, and the hourly flow volume, depend on how big a time interval drivers decide to maintain, on the average. If they choose to hold a 2.00 second time interval, the average speed will be 47.65 miles per hour, and the volume flow rate will be 1,588 vehicles per lane per hour. That is a drop of 20.6 percent below the initial flow rate of 2,000 vehicles per lane per hour. In that case, an initial increase of 15 percent in the number of vehicles per mile on a road with an average speed of 60 miles per hour and a maximum flow of 2,000 vehicles per lane per hour, followed by a second increase to a flow rate of 2,690 vehicles per hour, eventually causes a 21 percent drop in average speed and flow volume per lane per hour below the initial situation before more vehicles entered. However, these results are variable, depending on the drivers' average choices of space and time intervals between vehicles after the in-flow of additional traffic. And those choices depend on such other variable factors as the weather, the age and sex of the drivers, and the mix of vehicles traveling at any specific time.

The Dynamics of Recovery from Congested Periods

The process of recovering from congested periods is essentially the reverse of the process through which congestion arises, as described above. Once traffic on an expressway segment has slowed to speeds far below those at which maximum capacity flows occur, both speeds and flow rates remain low until many more vehicles move out of the congested road segment than are moving into it. Vehicles may do so either by using exit ramps onto nearby streets and arteries, or by moving ahead into uncongested segments of the same major road. As the number of vehicles per mile on any such congested segment declines, it is possible for drivers to attain larger average spatial intervals between vehicles. That allows them to speed up without reducing the time intervals between vehicles to dangerously low levels. As more and more vehicles exit this segment, and fewer enter it, this process gradually accelerates because larger and larger spatial intervals between vehicles open up. Hence drivers gradually speed up and yet maintain larger spatial and longer time intervals between vehicles. Eventually, drivers return to "optimal"speeds—that is, those at which the largest possible number of vehicles per hour can flow past any one point. These analyses indicate that this speed averages about 60 miles per hour on California expressways, though it varies substantially from one road segment to another, and from time to time on any one segment.

The basic cause of recovery from recurrent congestion is that, as time passes, the periods during which the greatest number of drivers seek to travel also pass. Therefore, the number of vehicles entering the road system declines sharply, and the number leaving it rises. These peak periods are generally from about 6:00 to 9:00 or 9:30 a.m., and from about 4:00 to 7:00 or 7:30 p.m., though they vary from place to place.

Recovery from congestion caused by incidents generally occurs some time after the incident has ceased to block travel lanes, as discussed in detail in chapter 5.

Why Not Limit Traffic Volumes on Key Expressways during Peak Hours?

One seemingly obvious conclusion from the above analysis is that if society wants to maintain high speeds and maximum throughput flows on major roadways, it should limit the number of vehicles permitted to enter those roadways each hour. However, as shown in earlier chapters, many more drivers want to travel during peak periods than the roads available can simultaneously accommodate at those times. Therefore, limiting the number who can enter key roads during peak periods in order to maintain high average speeds would prevent a large number of persons who want to drive during those periods from doing so—probably even a majority. This makes such limitation politically unpopular in a democracy where more than 90 percent of all households have access to their own private automotive vehicles.

Nevertheless, traffic analysts have considered at least the following means of limiting the number of vehicles permitted on expressways during peak hours: peak-hour tolls on all lanes of major commuter roads (chapter 10), ramp metering, which feeds vehicles onto such expressways slowly enough to permit high-speed flows on those roads (chapter 8), high-occupancy vehicle lanes, which permit only vehicles with at least two or perhaps three passengers to use them (chapter 10), high-occupancy toll lanes, which permit only high-occupancy vehicles or single-occupant vehicles that pay tolls to use them (chapter 8), and prohibition of travel on certain days for vehicles with license numbers ending in particular digits—such as no "5s" on Fridays (chapter 11).

Graphic Analysis of Peak-Hour Road Pricing

How congestion tolls increase economic efficiency is depicted in figure B-1. The solid line *PB* is the demand curve for the use of a commuter expressway. It shows the average monetary amount (measured on the vertical axis) that motorists would pay to travel on a highway at any given number of vehicles per lane per hour (measured on the horizontal axis). *PB* is a monetary measure of the average private benefit motorists receive from using the highway. As traffic on the highway rises to more vehicles per lane, this average benefit declines because of increased congestion.

The solid line *MC* shows the private costs incurred by one additional driver at each level of traffic per lane per hour. These costs include auto operating costs plus a monetary value on the time required. As long as the number of vehicles per lane remains below *OQ*, this cost remains constant. That means adding more vehicles in the range *OQ* does not slow the flow of traffic. But when the number of vehicles per lane per hour passes *Q*, congestion begins to reduce average speed. That adds to the time required by the

This appendix has benefited greatly from comments on an earlier draft by Kenneth A. Small, Herbert Mohring, and Clifford Winston.

FIGURE B-1. Economics of Peak-Hour Road Pricing, Welfare, and
Traffic Effects of Tolls

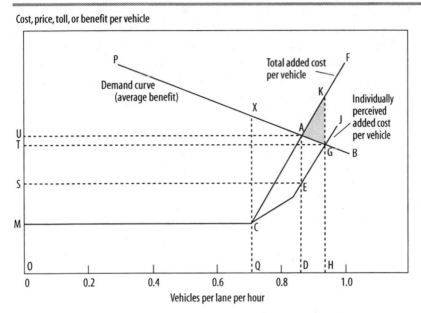

trip, so the cost borne by each added driver rises along the solid curve
MCEJ. The entry of every additional driver also adds to the delays of all
other drivers; so the average total additional cost for all drivers from
entry of one additional driver is greater than the cost borne by the
added driver (when no peak-hour tolls are charged). This marginal cost
of adding another commuter is shown by the curve *MCAF*. These two
costs were identical along the curve *MC* but diverge beyond traffic volume *OQ*.

The inefficiency of no-fee driving on congested roads arises because
each driver does not have to pay the total costs his or her arrival adds to
the overall situation. Guided only by the costs they must bear directly,
drivers keep entering the road as long as that cost—shown by the curve
MCEJ—is below the demand curve, *PB*. traffic per lane keeps rising up
to level *OH*. But it would be socially more efficient for traffic to be limited to the level *OD*. There the total added cost per vehicle—measured
by *MCAF*—crosses the demand curve *PB* at *A*. At that level of traffic,
the average total costs imposed by each additional driver—line *MCAF*—
are equal to the average total benefit received by all drivers—line *PB*.

Higher traffic volumes cause more costs per driver than the benefits they provide per driver; hence they are not socially efficient.

This inefficiency can be measured on the graph. Every added vehicle from traffic level *OD* to traffic level *OH* causes a total added vehicle cost lying along the line segment *AK* (part of curve *MCAF*). Those added costs all exceed the benefits provided by such travel, which are measured by the line segment *AG* (part of curve *PB*). For example, at traffic level *OH*, the total added cost per vehicle is *HK*. That cost exceeds the added benefit per vehicle, *HG*, by the amount indicated by *GK*. Thus the shaded area lying within the triangle connecting points *A, K,* and *G* is a geometric measure of the net collective welfare loss because traffic rises all the way to level *OH*, instead of stabilizing at level *OD*.

To stop traffic volume from rising beyond level *OD*, it is necessary to raise the cost borne by an additional driver at that traffic level, *DE*, to the level *DA*. This cost increase can be achieved by charging a peak-hour toll for entering or using the roadway. That toll should equal the difference between *DA* and *DE*, or the amount *AE*. On the left-hand axis, this equals the price *SU*. If toll *SU* (or *AE*) is added onto the individually borne costs *DE*, then the total cost faced by each additional driver equals *DA* (or *OU*). Then individual drivers will stop entering the expressway at traffic volume *OD*, since the costs they would bear by doing so at higher volumes—to the right of point *A* on *MCAF*—are higher than the benefits they would receive—points on curve *PB* to the right of *A*. Thus the economically optimal toll is *EA* or *SU*, and the economically optimal traffic volume is *OD*.

This traffic volume is not the same as the volume with the lowest level of congestion. That would be any traffic volume up to *OQ*. After that volume level, rising congestion slows down traffic—but not enough to offset the advantages to drivers of using this more direct route.[1]

Translating Gross Residential Densities into Net Residential Densities

Chapter 12 discusses mainly gross residential densities, that is, thousands of total residents per overall square mile of land. This definition includes all land within the community, regardless of its uses, as part of the area concerned. But most Americans who deal with land-use policies conceive of densities in terms of net residential densities, that is, numbers of dwelling units per net residential acre. This definition includes only residential land in its base; it excludes even local streets and parks in residential neighborhoods and all land used for nonresidential purposes.

Unfortunately, there is no simple or well-established way to relate these two different density measures, because circumstances vary widely from one location to another. For convenience, this appendix presents a method of converting either of these measures into the other.

Two variables are especially crucial in these computations. One is the number of residents per dwelling unit, roughly equivalent to persons per household. The other is the proportion of total land area in a community devoted to residential use, as opposed to streets, highways, parks, open space, commercial uses, and public buildings.

The number of persons per dwelling unit is normally smallest in high-density neighborhoods in large cities, such as New York City. It rises in suburban communities where families with children are more concentrated. Similarly, the percentage of total land area devoted to housing is lowest in big-city neighborhoods that feature mixed-use development. It is highest in the peripheral fringe areas where large-lot zoning is dominant. This variation can be shown from data describing average residential densities in the New York region taken from *Public Transportation and Land Use Policy*, by Boris S. Pushkarev and Jeffrey M. Zupan.[1] They list thirty-five communities in descending order of average dwellings per acre of residential land in 1990. The highest was 210.7 in Manhattan, the lowest was 1.28 in Sussex County.

Pushkarev and Zupan translate these net residential densities into gross persons per square mile, derived from actual data. For example, the Manhattan gross density was 69,333 persons per square mile of total land area. If every household contains 2.0 persons, then this link of 210.7 dwellings per net residential area and 69,333 persons per gross square mile implies that 25.8 percent of the land is devoted to residential uses.[2]

A similar calculation concerning Sussex County's 1.28 dwellings per net residential acre and 147 persons per gross square mile—but using 3.5 persons per dwelling—implies a residential land percentage of 50.15 percent. Other areas between these net density extremes imply even higher residential land coverage ratios, as high as 63 percent. So their calculations imply that the percentage of all land devoted to residential uses varies from a low of 25 percent in highly dense urban areas to a high of over 60 percent in some low-density outlying areas.[3]

For purposes of this analysis, an average household size of 2.5 persons is used, since that is close to the 2000 U.S. average household size of about 2.62.[4] Also, a variable residential land coverage factor is employed: 25 percent for relatively high gross densities (usually 15,000 persons per square mile or higher), 37.5 percent for moderate gross densities (about 5,000 to 14,999 persons per square mile), and 50 percent for relatively low gross densities (usually under 5,000 per square mile).

Table C-1 shows conversions from gross to net densities in the first four columns. The next four columns convert back from net to gross densities, using values derived from the first two columns. Each conversion table employs three different fractions of total land area devoted to residential use, for high-, moderate-, and low-density ranges. Multiple values are computed for densities that might be considered in more than

TABLE C-1. Residential Density Conversion[a]

	High density[b]	Moderate density[c]	Low density[d]
	Gross to net conversion		
Residents/gross square mile	Dwellings/net residential acre		
80,000	200.00	...	...
60,000	150.00	...	...
50,000	125.00	...	...
40,000	100.00	...	...
25,000	62.50	...	...
20,000	50.00	33.33	...
15,000	37.50	25.00	...
12,500	31.25	20.83	...
10,000	25.00	16.67	...
7,500	...	12.50	...
6,000	...	10.00	7.50
5,000	...	8.33	6.25
4,000	...	6.67	5.00
3,000	...	5.00	3.75
2,500	...	...	3.13
2,000	...	...	2.50
1,500	...	...	1.88
1,000	...	...	1.25
500	...	...	0.63
	Net to gross conversion		
Dwellings/net residential acre	Residents/gross square mile		
200	80,000	...	...
150	60,000	...	...
100	40,000	...	...
75	30,000	...	...
50	20,000	...	...
40	16,000	...	...
35	14,000	...	...
30	12,000	...	...
25	10,000	...	...
20	8,000	12,000	...
15	6,000	9,000	...
10	4,000	6,000	...
7.5	...	4,500	...
7	...	4,200	...
6	...	3,600	4,800
5	...	3,000	4,000
4	...	2,400	3,200
3	...	...	2,400
2	...	...	1,600
1	...	...	800
0.5	...	...	400
0.25	...	...	200

Source: Author's calculations.

a. Table assumes an average of 2.5 persons per dwelling unit. Conversions are computed from gross to net, then extrapolated back from net to gross. More than one value has been calculated in adjacent columns for net densities near the transition points between the three levels of neighborhood density.

b. 25 percent of land is residential.

c. 37.5 percent of land is residential.

d. 50 percent of land is residential.

one of these three categories, thus permitting readers to use their own discretion in those overlapping ranges. This table may be referred to in order to clarify parts of the book that refer mostly to gross residential densities. However, the data in this table represent an approximation, not a rigid rule.

A Spatial Model for Simulating Changes

The potential impacts on commuting travel of changing the location of jobs or housing can be grasped intuitively without detailed quantitative analysis, as discussed in chapters 12 and 13. But logical proof for the resulting conclusions, and assessing their sensitivity to specific changes in variables, requires detailed quantitative analysis. This can be accomplished by using a spatial model of a typical metropolitan area for simulating various situations.

The Basic Model

The model employed in this book consists of a variable-sized square metropolitan area measuring a maximum of 50 miles on each side, as shown in figure D-1. A square is used instead of a circle to simplify calculations of commuting distances. The base case model has 40 miles on each side. Its total area (1,600 square miles) is divided into an inner central city square measuring 12 miles by 12 miles, older suburbs extending outward from the city's boundary to a square 24 miles on each side, and newer suburbs—exurbs—extending outward from the boundary of the older suburbs to a square with variable boundaries but a maximum of 50

FIGURE D-1. Region Used for Commuting Distance Simulations

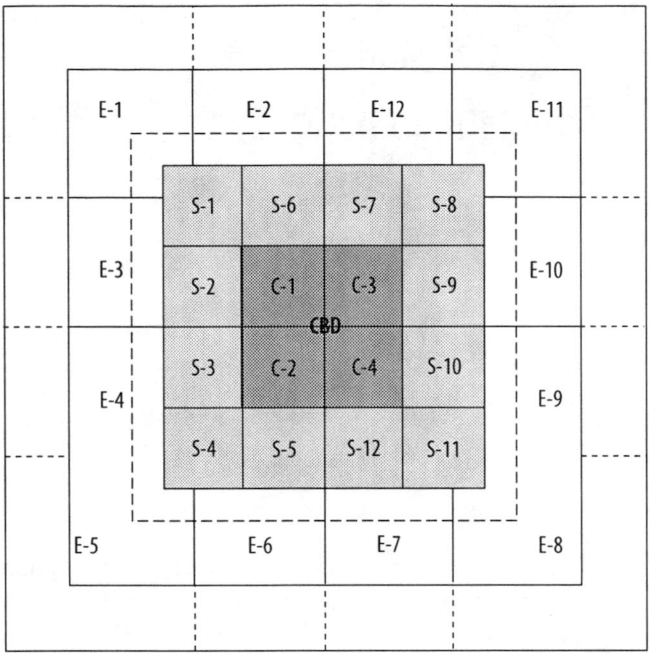

Source: Author's calculations.
Notes: C = central city; S = suburb; E = exurb; CBD = central business district.
The outermost solid line shows the 50-square-mile case; the base case region is shown by the solid lines inside this outermost solid line. The dashed lines within the base case region show the 30-square-mile case boundaries.
Job centers in the 50-square-mile case and the base case are located in the center of each sector. In the 30-square-mile case exurbs, job centers are located as follows: in the four corner exurbs, 1 mile horizontally and vertically from the outer corners of the suburban region; in the other exurbs, centered on the long dimension of each sector and 1.5 miles from the outer edge of the suburban region in the shorter dimension.

miles on each side. These dimensions produce a central city with a total area of 144 square miles, older suburbs with a total area of 432 square miles (24 times 24 minus 12 times 12), and outer suburbs or exurbs with a maximum area of 1,924 square miles (50 times 50 minus 24 times 24). The exurban subregion is divided into twelve sectors labeled E-1 through E-12, as shown on the map. The suburban subregion is divided into twelve sectors labeled S-1 through S-12, and the central city subregion is divided into four sectors labeled C-1 through C-4. The central business district is the center point in the diagram labeled CBD.

There are twenty-nine job centers in the basic version of this metropolitan area; all jobs are located in these centers.[1] They include the central business district in the area's center, four other in-city job clusters at the geometric centers of each city sector, twelve suburban job clusters each located 3 miles horizontally and vertically from the outer corners of the older suburban sectors, and twelve exurban job clusters located at approximately the geometric center points of the exurban sectors.

Various spatial distributions of population and jobs can be simulated by changing the outer boundaries of the model and changing the proportions within the central city, older suburbs, and exurbs of total jobs, total population, and the percentage of all workers employed in each job center. Workers' homes are spread across the entire area—although at different average densities in the city, suburbs, and exurbs. The average commuting distance from the center of each residential square mile to each job center can be calculated algebraically.[2]

Two different types of simulations are used. The first compares fully developed metropolitan areas that have different urban densities. A given total population is divided into three subgroups: central city residents, suburban residents, and exurban residents. The first two subgroups remain constant in area, total population, and therefore in density throughout the analysis. The exurban subgroup remains constant in total population but has varying areas and therefore varying densities. This type of simulation examines the impact of varying exurban densities on average commuting distances. Of course, spatially large metropolitan areas would have more jobs in their outer areas than smaller metropolitan areas. This outcome is simulated by varying the percentage of workers assigned to different job centers.

A second type of simulation starts with a total population and all jobs divided between the central city and suburban regions but no residents or job centers in the exurbs. It then assumes a certain annual rate of total population growth during an entire decade and places all that growth in the exurbs. By confining that exurban growth to areas of different sizes—and therefore different densities—this simulation can examine the impact of varying densities of future growth on average commuting distances in already established metropolitan areas. Future population growth rates can also be varied within this model.

Initial Calibration of the Basic Model

The base case version of the model consists of a square with 40 miles on a side, divided into zones, as described above. It makes use of all

TABLE D-1. Summary of Simulation Model Variations[a]

Variable	Low density exurbs	Base case	Denser exurbs	Even denser exurbs	No exurbs, dense suburbs	
					Low job dispersion	Great job dispersion
Spatial areas (square miles)						
Total region	2,500	1,600	900	784	576	576
Central city	144	144	144	144	144	144
Suburbs	432	432	432	432	432	432
Exurbs	1,924	1,024	324	208	...	...
Population (number)						
Total region	3,000,000	3,000,000	3,000,000	3,000,000	3,000,000	3,000,000
Central city	900,000	900,000	900,000	900,000	900,000	900,000
Suburbs	1,500,000	1,500,000	1,500,000	1,500,000	2,100,000	2,100,000
Exurbs	600,000	600,000	600,000	600,000	...	...
Population (percent)						
Total region	100	100	100	100	100	100
Central city	30	30	30	30	30	30
Suburbs	50	50	50	50	70	70
Exurbs	20	20	20	20	...	...
Density (persons/square mile)						
Total region	1,200	1,875	3,333	3,827	5,208	5,208
Central city	6,250	6,250	6,250	6,250	6,250	6,250
Suburbs	3,472	3,472	3,472	3,472	4,861	4,861
Exurbs	312	586	1,852	2,885	...	...
Job locations (percent)						
Total region	100	100	100	100	100	100
Central business district	7	7	7	7	7	7
Rest of central city	33	33	33	33	33	33
Suburban job centers	50	50	50	50	60	60
Exurban job centers	10	10	10	10	...	...

continued on next page

twenty-nine job sites. When this version was created for the first edition of *Stuck in Traffic*, it was initially populated and calibrated to resemble data available at that time for large U.S. metropolitan areas in population, number of jobs, population densities, and commuting travel times by various subgroups. Data from various travel surveys and censuses were used to determine targets that would resemble a typical large U.S. metropolitan area. Census data do not differentiate between exurbs and suburbs; both were combined in a category called "not in a central city."

At the time of writing this edition, more recent data from the 2000 Census and the 2001 Nationwide Household Travel Survey were avail-

TABLE D-1. Summary of Simulation Model Variations[a] (continued)

Variable	Low density exurbs	Base case	Denser exurbs	Even denser exurbs	No exurbs, dense suburbs	
					Low job dispersion	Great job dispersion
Average commuting distance by place of residence (miles)						
Total region	10.88	10.08	8.04	9.38	7.36	9.17
Central city	7.33	7.18	6.60	7.03	6.79	6.96
Suburbs	10.24	9.97	7.26	10.22	7.61	10.12
Exurbs	17.66	14.61	12.02	10.94	...	...
Average commuting distance by job location (miles)						
To CBD jobs from:						
Central city	5.12	5.12	5.12	5.12	5.12	5.12
Suburbs	12.28	12.28	12.28	12.38	12.28	12.28
Exurbs	24.54	21.40	21.40	16.52	...	...
To other central city jobs from:						
Central city	5.00	5.00	4.85	5.00	5.18	5.18
Suburbs	11.05	11.05	9.97	11.05	11.02	11.02
Exurbs	22.84	19.72	19.65	14.89	...	...
To suburban jobs from:						
Central city	9.26	9.26	5.78	9.26	8.85	8.85
Suburbs	9.04	9.04	5.37	9.83	5.84	5.84
Exurbs	14.26	11.10	8.52	7.70	...	...
To exurban jobs from:						
Central city	19.02	16.00	12.44	12.89	...	...
Suburbs	15.10	12.04	9.30	9.16	...	...
Exurbs	13.48	10.84	7.72	8.99	...	...

a. Low-density exurbs are represented by the 50-mile square; the base case, by the 40-mile square; the denser exurbs, by the 30-mile square; the even denser exurbs, by the 28-mile square; and the no-exurbs, dense-suburbs cases, by the 24-mile square.

able for only some of the key variables concerned. Therefore, a new model was developed that is not closely tied to empirical data about prevailing travel distances. Rather, it uses hypothetical density and travel assumptions to illustrate how the basic geometry of space inevitably leads to certain key relationships between residential and job densities on the one hand, and commuting travel distances on the other hand. It is my view that the basic conclusions drawn from this model are directly applicable to actual conditions in American metropolitan areas today.

The main simulations using this model are briefly described in table D-1. The base case version of the model has 30 percent of the total population living in the central city, 50 percent in the older suburbs, and 20 percent in the more distant exurbs. Because of the different areas of these zones, they have widely varying population densities. The central city has an average density of 6,250 persons per square mile, similar to the 2000 densities of Cleveland, Anaheim, Pittsburgh, and Milwaukee. However, that density is somewhat higher than the average central city density of 5,273 persons per square mile prevalent in the 50 largest urbanized areas in 2000. The suburbs have an average density of 3,472 persons per square mile—55 percent of the central city's density. This density is similar to that of Bellevue in the Seattle area, Columbus, Ohio, Dallas, Houston, Omaha, and Eugene, Oregon. That density is slightly higher than the average density of 3,173 in the "fringe areas" of the 50 largest urbanized areas in 2000. The exurbs in the 40-mile-square case have a very low average density of 586 persons per square mile—much lower than that of any large U.S. city or urbanized area.[3] However, when the overall size of the settled area—and therefore of the exurbs—is reduced in subsequent model cases, this exurban density rises significantly.

It is assumed that the population generates workers at the same rate of 478 per 1,000 total residents in each zone—a rate derived from national employment and population data.[4] Hence the percentage distribution of workers among these three zones by residence is the same as the distribution of population. But job locations are not spatially distributed in the same way as population. So a key step in developing the model is assigning percentages of total jobs to each zone. One fundamental assumption is that the central city contains a higher percentage of total jobs (40 percent including the central business district) than it does of total residents (30 percent), because some net inward commuting still occurs, especially to the central business district (which contains 7 percent of all jobs). Another fundamental assumption is that the suburbs contain the same percentages of total jobs and of residents (50 percent), since they attract workers inward from the exurbs but have many residents that work in the central city. So the exurbs contain a much smaller percentage of total jobs (10 percent) than total residents (20 percent).

These job assignments are then translated into specific numbers of jobs from each residential zone into each employment zone by means of a matrix shown in table D-2. This matrix is a vehicle for making the residential and job assignments mutually consistent. It serves as a basis for assigning percentages of all metropolitan area jobs to each job center in each of the model's three basic modules: one showing where all exurban-resident workers are employed, and two others showing where

TABLE D-2. Breakdown of Job and Residence Locations, Base Case

| | Location of residence | | | | | | | |
| | Central city | | Suburbs | | Exurbs | | Whole region | |
Job location	Number	Percent of all workers	Number	Percent of all workers	Number	Percent of all workers	Number	Percent of all workers
Exurbs								
Number	21,510	4.98	64,530	9.09	57,360	19.61	143,400	10.00
Percent of all workers	1.5		4.5		4		10	
Suburbs								
Number	164,910	38.21	437,370	61.62	114,720	39.22	717,000	50.00
Percent of all workers	11.5		30.50		8		50	
City outside CBD								
Number	193,590	44.85	164,910	23.23	114,720	39.22	473,220	33.00
Percent of all workers	13.5		11.5		8		33	
Central business district								
Number	51,624	11.96	43,020	6.06	5,736	1.96	100,380	7.00
Percent of all workers	3.6		3		0.4		7	
City total								
Number	245,214	56.81	207,930	29.29	120,456	41.18	573,600	40.00
Percent of all workers	17.1		14.5		8.4		40	
Total region								
Number	431,634	100.00	709,830	100.00	292,536	100.00	1,434,000	100.00
Percent of all workers	30		50		20		100	

all suburban-resident workers and city-resident workers are employed. These modules are then aggregated into a metropolitan-wide summary module and another summary module combining suburban and exurban job assignments.

Base Case Computation of Commuting Distances

The simulation starts by assigning a certain percentage of all the employed residents of each sector—city, suburban, and exurban—to each job center. This is done from the perspective of a single quadrant in the entire model (the upper left-hand, or northwest quadrant), assuming that residents of all four quadrants would have identical behavior patterns.

The distance that residents of a specific residential sector travel to jobs in a specific job center is calculated rectangularly and diagonally. This is done by measuring the east-west distance from the centerpoint of that residential sector to a north-south line passing through the job center, measuring the north-south distance from the centerpoint of the sector to an east-west line passing through the job center, adding those two distances (which form a right-angled line connecting these two locations) together, computing the direct straight-line distance between these two locations, which is the hypotenuse of the right angle formed by the horizontal and vertical distances described above, averaging (a) the sum of the two sides of that triangle and (b) the hypotenuse, and using that average as the estimated travel distance between these two locations. This method assumes that normal travel between two points is longer than a straight line connecting them directly but shorter than a rectangular distance connecting them by means of north-south and east-west lines.[5]

Using this method, a single average commuting distance can be computed for all exurban-resident workers, another for all suburban-resident workers, and another for all city-resident workers. These three averages can be altered by shifting the percentage distributions of workers among job centers within each category of centers. For example, shifting more of the total 39.22 percent of exurban-resident workers who are employed at suburban job sites from distant suburban job sites to closer ones reduces the average commuting distance for exurban workers. These assignments are based on my judgments about what fraction of the workers living in each sector are likely to work in each other sector. In many cases, no workers residing in a specific sector are assigned to commute to a relatively distant job center in another particular sector. The average commuting distance for all workers is then obtained by aggregating the separate calculations for city and suburban residents.

In the 40-mile-square base case, the average commuting distance for all metropolitan area workers is 10.08 miles, as shown under the column "Base Case" in table D-1. This is 9 percent lower than the actual 1983 average for metropolitan areas containing more than 3 million residents (11.03 miles), and 14 percent below the average of 11.7 miles for similar regions from the 1995 Nationwide Personal Transportation Survey.[6] The average commuting distance in 2001, according to the National Household Travel Survey, was 12.0 miles.[7] However, all the important conclusions drawn from this simulation depend on the relationships between residential densities and commuting distances, not on the absolute lengths of specific commuting trips. I believe this variance from recent empirical data has no significant impact on the validity of conclusions drawn from the simulation mode. The shortest average commuting distances from the model are for workers both living and working in the exurbs, workers both living and working in the suburbs, and workers both working and living in the central city. These simulation results are consistent with travel-time data that show the shortest commuting travel times in 1980 were for workers both living and working in the suburbs (which are equivalent to the exurbs and suburbs combined in the model). Analogous data from the 1995 and 2001 surveys were not available when this was written.

Exploring the Impacts of Differing Exurban Densities

What impacts on average commuting distances would result from settlement of the exurbs at higher average densities? A higher-density exurban population can be simulated by confining the same overall population to a total area 30 miles square, instead of 40 miles square. That reduces the total exurban area from 1,024 square miles to 324 square miles, or by 68 percent. In that case, the average density in the exurban area rises to 1,852 persons per square mile—3.16 times the analogous density in the 40-mile-square case. The overall density for the entire metropolitan area rises to 3,333 from 1,875 in the 40-mile-square case.

Under these conditions, the average commuting distance for all metropolitan-area workers declines to 8.04 miles. Hence, a 222 percent rise in exurban population density, causing a 78 percent rise in average metropolitan density, produces only a 20 percent decline in average overall commuting distance. The average commuting distance falls 18 percent for all exurban-resident workers (from 14.61 to 12.02 miles) and 27 percent for all suburban-resident workers (from 9.97 miles to 7.26 miles).

To shorten average commuting distances significantly, much higher exurban or suburban densities must be employed. One possibility would be concentrating the entire 70 percent noncity population in the older suburbs, thereby eliminating all exurban residences and job centers. The distribution of jobs would also have to be changed, say, to 60 percent in the suburbs and 40 percent in the central city. Population density in the suburbs would rise to 4,861 persons per square mile, 40 percent higher than in the 40-mile-square base case. That is about the same density as Springfield, Massachusetts, Erie, Pennsylvania, and Ft. Lauderdale and Coral Springs in Florida. The overall noncity population density would rise from 1,442 in the base case to 4,861 in the 24-mile-square case, an increase of 237 percent.

These data are shown in the last column of table D-1. Surprisingly, in this case, this greater concentration of population would reduce average commuting distances for the entire metropolitan area only from 10.08 to 9.17 miles, or by 9 percent. However, this small reduction results partly from assigning a greater dispersion of suburban-resident jobs across all sectors in the suburbs-only case than in the base case. That seems reasonable because there are 41 percent more workers residing in each suburban sector (83,615) in the suburbs-only case than in the base case (59,128). But if the same percentage assignments of residents to all job centers are used in the suburbs-only case as in the base case, the average commuting distance in the suburbs-only case for the entire region drops to 7.36 miles, as shown in the next-to-last column. Then the regional decline from the base case is 27 percent. That is still a much smaller proportional decline than the proportional rise in density necessary to attain that shorter average commuting distance.

This analysis implies that significant reductions in commuting travel can be achieved by raising overall suburban residential densities above typical American levels—but only if the density increases are substantial indeed. Yet most older suburban parts of U.S. metropolitan areas are already built up at not-very-high densities. It would be extremely difficult to alter their densities without encountering massive political and economic resistance from residents. This shifts the focus of the analysis to coping with future population growth.

What happens to commuting travel distances if exurban settlement densities become even lower than in the base case? This possibility can be simulated by expanding the boundaries of the exurbs out to those of a 50-mile-square territory, while leaving the total population of the exurbs unchanged from the base case. This is shown in the column "low-density exurbs" of table D-1. In this case, the exurbs cover a total area of 1,924 square miles, which drops the density of exurban residents to 312 persons per square mile. That is 47 percent lower than the exurban density in the base case. The average commuting travel distance among exurban residents rises from 14.61 miles in the base case to 17.66 miles in the 50-mile-square case, an increase of 20.9 percent. So a fall of 47 percent in density produces a fall of only 20.9 percent in average commuting distance. But exurban residents and jobs are a relatively small part of the region's total residents and jobs. Therefore, the impacts of this change on regionwide travel and density are much smaller than those on exurban travel and density. For the entire region, average density drops from 1,875 persons per square mile to 1,200—a decline of 36 percent. But the fall in regionwide commuting distance is only from 10.88 miles to 10.08 miles—a drop of 8 percent.

This analysis emphasizes an important but not obvious factor: the impact of greater dispersion of job sites in much larger exurban areas. Even though workers' homes are spread over much larger territories in low-density settlements, this need not generate proportionally longer commuting trips if jobs also become spread out more broadly. Given recent decentralizing trends in office construction, computers, and telecommunications, such a greater dispersal of jobs is likely.[8]

Possible Densities for Future Urban Development

Another way to analyze the relationship between residential densities and commuting travel is to examine alternative patterns of future exurban growth around basically unchanging central city and suburban zones. This approach essentially reverses the perspective of the first approach discussed. The first step is to assume a certain rate of population and job growth over the next decade and then convert that rate into absolute gains. The second step is examining the travel distance impacts of having that growth occur at different densities. The model described is used for these simulations. However, the initial situation is different from that in the previous discussion. In this analysis, an initial regional population of 2.4 million is assumed to reside wholly within the central city containing 144 square miles and the suburbs containing 432 square miles. Thus 32.5 percent of the region's total population is in the city and 62.5 percent in the suburbs. So the suburbs contain 1.5 million residents, and the city contains 900,000. Those are the same populations and areas for city and suburbs as in the base case.

This is similar to the previous situation in which the entire settlement pattern was confined to a square 24 miles on a side, with no exurban development outside the older suburbs. But in this case, the total initial population of the region is only 2.4 million instead of 3.0 million. Consequently, the initial densities are 6,250 persons per square mile in the city, 3,472 per square mile in the suburbs, and 4,166 per square mile in the entire metropolitan area. Moreover, all jobs are located in the city and suburbs—40 percent in the city and 60 percent in the suburbs. This situation produces an average commuting distance for the entire region of 9.17 miles (if a wide dispersion of suburban workers among job sites is assumed) or 7.36 miles (if a narrower dispersion of suburban workers is assumed).

It is then assumed that a decade of population growth occurs at an average annual growth rate of 2.257 percent per year, or 25 percent over ten years. Based on American experience, that is very rapid growth, but 37 U.S. metropolitan areas (out of 280 defined in 1999) attained or surpassed it in the 1990s.[9] All this growth takes place outside the original boundaries in the exurban zone. After ten years, the area's total population has grown by 600,000 to 3.0 million, and 286,800 additional workers reside in the new exurban area. The exurbs then contain 20 percent of the area's total population and its total resident workers, whereas the central city and suburbs contain 20 percent and 50 percent, respectively.

Clearly, the exurbs will also have developed some job centers and will contain a significant share of all jobs. It is assumed that this share is less than the exurban share of total population; so it has been set at 10 percent, with the suburbs containing 50 percent of all jobs and the central city 40 percent (including 7 percent in the central business district). These jobs are then distributed among the area's job centers, including the new exurban ones. Some outward commuting from the city and suburbs into these centers occurs, but the flows are predominantly inward or lateral. A key question is, what impact does varying the average density of this growth have on average commuting distances for the newly developing area and for the metropolitan area as a whole?

If this new growth has extended evenly outward through a square 50 miles on a side, the average exurban density is extremely low: 312 persons per square mile. (This situation is identical with the 50-mile-square case described earlier.) Furthermore, additional job centers have been created in the exurbs; so there are now twenty-nine job centers altogether. That generates an average commuting distance of 10.88 miles for the entire region and 17.66 miles for workers living in the exurbs. Substantial growth has added between 1.7 and 3.52 miles (18.5 percent or 47.8 percent) to the region's average commuting trip, depending on what assumptions are made about how widely dispersed suburban jobs were before the population growth occurred. In either case, the increased commuting distance is concentrated among the new exurban workers.

In contrast, if this new exurban development extends evenly out to fill a square only 30 miles on a side, the average exurban density is 1,852 persons per square mile, or 3.2 times that in the 40-mile-square case. This density produces average commuting distances of 8.04 miles for all workers and 12.02 miles for exurban-resident workers. Thus an exurban density 220 percent higher than in the 40-mile-square case produces an average exurban commuting distance of only 2.59 miles less, a drop of 17.7 percent. The fall in overall metropolitan area commuting distance is only 2.04 miles, or 20.2 percent.

How about even higher densities? If the same added population settles in a total area 28 miles square, the exurbs containing that population cover only 208 square miles. So exurban density rises to 2,885 persons per square mile. The average density for the entire metropolitan area reaches 4,437 persons per square mile, similar to the 2000 densities of the cities of Stockton, Grand Rapids, and Worcester, Massachusetts. Because the original exurban job centers are located outside this exurban territory, they have been moved closer to the central business district for this computation—2 miles closer for the corner E sectors, and 3 miles closer for the eight noncorner E sectors.

Thus raising exurban density from a low of 312 persons per square mile to a high of 2,885—an increase of 824 percent—lowers the average commuting distance of workers living in the exurbs from 17.66 miles to 10.94 miles, or 38 percent. That is a considerable reduction. The average commuting distance for all metropolitan area workers falls from 10.88 miles to 9.38 miles, a decline of 14 percent.

Conclusions

This entire simulation analysis leads to three main conclusions. First, if exurban growth occurs at medium to high average marginal densities, average commuting distances—especially for exurban residents—can be kept significantly below those that would be generated by the same population at very low densities. In short, residential density can make a notable difference in commuting patterns and in total commuting distances traveled per 1,000 workers. This conclusion has major implications for public policies concerning what densities should be sought in areas of new growth. It implies that very low-density settlement patterns will generate a lot more commuting travel than medium-density patterns, other things being equal.

Second, it takes huge percentage changes in average densities to produce relatively small percentage changes in average commuting distances. Policies aimed at reducing travel to and from work by changing residential densities cannot be effective if they have only small or moderate impacts on density levels.

Third, the biggest reductions in commuting distance occur when settlements are changed from very low to medium densities, rather than from medium to high densities. The biggest decline in average commuting distance for all metropolitan-area workers caused by shifting from low-density to higher-density exurban settlement results from moving from the 50-mile-square case to the suburbs-only, low-job-dispersion case. This move causes the average commuting distance for the entire region to fall from 10.88 miles to 7.36 miles, or by 32 percent. But 80 percent of that fall of 3.52 miles in average commuting distances occurs in the move from a regional density of 1,200 persons per square mile to one of 3,333 persons per square mile. That increase in regional density of 2,133 persons per square mile, or 78 percent, accounts for 2.84 miles of the total decline of 3.52 miles. In contrast, the shift in regional densities from 3,333 persons per square mile to 5,208 is a rise of 1,875 persons per square mile—also 78 percent. But it produces a drop in average regional commuting distance of only 0.68 miles, or only 8 percent (which equals 20 percent of the total drop from the 50-mile-square case to the 24-mile-square case with low job dispersion). This occurs because of the inexorable laws of geometry. As the total exurban territory gets smaller, relatively tiny further shrinkages in its diameter—holding total population constant—produce big changes in average density. In contrast, when the exurban territory is much larger, absolutely large movements in its boundary have only small impacts on its average density. This means that once a medium level of average density has been established, raising densities greatly beyond that level has relatively little impact on average commuting distances. To put it another way, if reducing commuting distances is a goal, it is more important to avoid very low densities than to achieve very high ones.

Admittedly, the above conclusions emerge from a specific model based on very particular assumptions. Hence it might be possible to construct another model from different assumptions that produced quite different results. The only basic way such a model could "prove" that residential densities have no significant impact on average commuting distances would be to scatter jobs far more widely and evenly across the landscape, in relation to where people live, than this model does. I believe this model has depicted actual job location patterns with reasonable fidelity to conditions in large U.S. metropolitan areas. Hence its generation of these conclusions should be considered reasonably reliable.

Impacts on Traffic Congestion

The analysis in this appendix focuses solely on relationships between commuting distances and settlement densities. That analysis does not tackle whether reducing commuting travel distances by encouraging higher-density settlements also reduces the traffic congestion generated by peak-hour commuting and other travel. In many metropolitan areas throughout the world, the greatest traffic congestion is found within the highest-density districts, regardless of the length of commuting journeys involved. However, since this issue is dealt with in chapter 12 and elsewhere in the book, it will not be explored further here.

Clustering High-Density Housing
Near Transit Stops

One way to increase use of public transit commuting would be to cluster relatively high-density housing near suburban transit stops, especially those served by fixed-rail systems. A 1977 study by Boris Pushkarev and Jeffrey M. Zupan showed that many people who live within 2,000 feet of a rapid transit stop are willing to use public transportation for daily commuting.[1] That distance is 37.9 percent of one mile. Pushkarev and Zupan depict the results of several studies of commuting behavior in the 1990s by persons living near transit stops in California, showing that the share of residents using transit fell from more than 25 percent living within 500 feet, to 20 percent within 1,000 feet, gradually declining to 10 percent within about 3,000 feet (57 percent of one mile). These shares were much higher among Canadian residents in Toronto and Edmonton.[2] To be generous, my analysis extends the range of high transit usage to half-a-mile (2,640 feet). A person walking 2.5 miles per hour could cover that distance in 12 minutes. Just how effective would this tactic be at reducing suburban or city traffic congestion?

The Basic Structure of the Model

A radius of one-half mile creates a circle containing 0.7854 square miles. If 50 percent of the land within the circle contains housing, as is common in most suburban areas, 0.393 square miles of housing lies within walking distance of each transit stop. If 25 percent of the land contains housing, as in many cities, 0.20 square miles would be within walking distance. The number of such circles within a metropolitan area would depend on how many stations there were.

In the model metropolitan area analyzed in appendix D, eight outlying employment centers were located on the diagonals of the square within the central city and suburbs (two on each diagonal), and twelve more in the exurbs. Figure E-1 shows the layout of this model metropolitan area. Assume four transit lines extend diagonally from the downtown through these outlying centers to the corners of the 24-mile-square encompassing the central city and older suburbs (but not into the newer suburbs, or exurbs). These lines would contain 68 linear route miles. Half would lie within the central city, half within the suburbs.

If transit stops are 0.75 miles apart in the central city and 1.5 miles apart in the suburbs—the approximate distances in the Washington metro system—each of the four transit lines would contain eleven stops in the city and six in the suburbs, for a total of 68. If residential land composed 50 percent of the land in the suburbs and 25 percent in the central city, the 24 suburban circles would have a combined net residential area of 9.42 square miles, and the 44 city circles a combined net residential area of 8.6 square miles (since only 25 percent of the land in them would be residential, versus 50 percent in the suburbs). These transit-oriented circles would contain 4.4 percent of all suburban residential land (216 square miles) and 24.0 percent of all central city residential land (36 square miles).

Calculating the Impact of Transit Circles

The impact of these circles on transit use would depend on the density of housing created within each circle and the percentage of workers living in that housing who chose to commute by transit. Higher densities can typically be achieved in central cities than in suburbs. Table E-1 shows the population that could live both within each circle and with all

FIGURE E-1. Region Used for Transit-Oriented Development Analysis

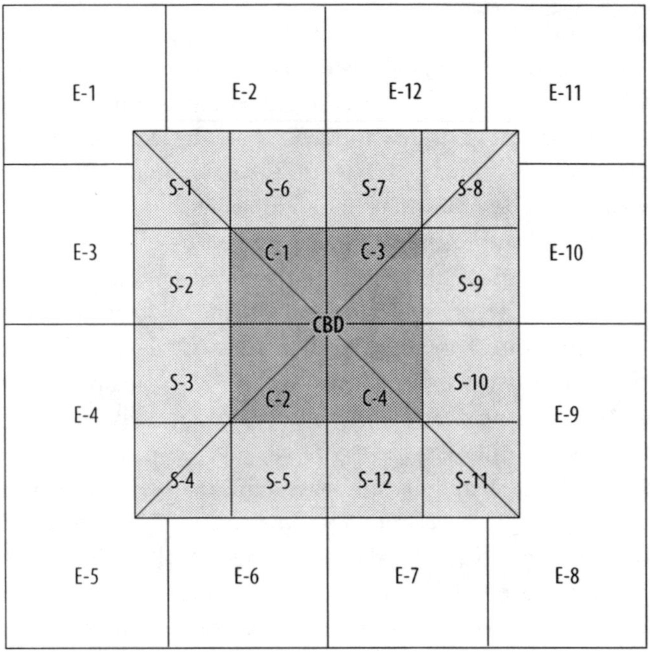

Source: Author's calculations.
Notes: C = central city; S = suburb; E = exurb; CBD = central business district.
For a description of the base case region shown here, see figure D-1. The solid lines extending from the CBD to the outer edges of the suburban sectors are fixed-rail transit lines.
Job centers are located in the centers of each sector except E-3, E-4, E-6, E-7, E-9, E-10, E-12, and E-2. In these sectors, they are centered in the long dimension of the sector and are 2 miles in from the suburban borders in the shorter dimension. Note that the transit lines do not enter the exurbs.

the circles in the model region combined under different net residential densities.

This model assumes that the central city and suburbs combined contain 2.7 million residents, 54 percent in the suburbs (1.620 million) and 46 percent in the city (1.080 million). Employed workers constitute 48 percent of this population: 777,600 in the suburbs and 518,400 in the city. For suburban transit circles, table E-1 calculates circle populations for net residential densities of 15 to 35 units per acre, assuming 50 percent of the gross land is for residential use, there are 2.5 persons per dwelling unit, and there are 24 circles in the suburban parts of the metropolitan area. The results for all the transit circles combined are shown in the seventh and ninth columns from the left. At a density of 25 units

TABLE E-1. Analysis of Transit Circles under Different Housing Densities

Part 1

Density (units/ net acre)	Square miles/ circle	Fraction of land in housing	Persons/ unit	Persons/ circle	Number of circles	Total population in circles	Total area population	Percent living in circles	Gross density/ square mile	Total working persons[a]
Suburbs										
15	0.7854	0.5	2.5	9,425	24	226,195	1,620,000	13.96	12,000	777,600
20	0.7854	0.5	2.5	12,566	24	301,594	1,620,000	18.62	16,000	777,600
25	0.7854	0.5	2.5	15,708	24	376,992	1,620,000	23.27	20,000	777,600
30	0.7854	0.5	2.5	18,850	24	452,390	1,620,000	27.93	24,000	777,600
35	0.7854	0.5	2.5	21,991	24	527,789	1,620,000	32.58	28,000	777,600
City										
20	0.7854	0.25	2.5	6,283	44	276,461	1,080,000	25.60	8,000	518,400
25	0.7854	0.25	2.5	7,854	44	345,576	1,080,000	32.00	10,000	518,400
30	0.7854	0.25	2.5	9,425	44	414,691	1,080,000	38.40	12,000	518,400
40	0.7854	0.25	2.5	12,566	44	552,922	1,080,000	51.20	16,000	518,400
50	0.7854	0.25	2.5	15,708	44	691,152	1,080,000	64.00	20,000	518,400

Part 2

Density (units/ net acre)	Working persons in circles[a]	Circle transit commuters if share of circle workers using transit is			Total transit commuters if share of circle workers using transit is			Percent of all workers using transit if share of circle workers using transit is		
		10 percent	20 percent	40 percent	10 percent	20 percent	40 percent	10 percent	20 percent	40 percent
Suburbs										
15	108,574	10,857	21,715	43,429	30,259	41,117	62,831	3.89	5.29	8.08
20	144,765	14,476	28,953	57,906	32,829	47,305	76,258	4.22	6.08	9.81
25	180,956	18,096	36,191	72,382	35,398	53,494	89,685	4.55	6.88	11.53
30	217,147	21,715	43,429	86,859	37,968	59,683	103,112	4.88	7.68	13.26
35	253,339	25,334	50,668	101,335	40,537	65,871	116,539	5.21	8.47	14.99
City										
20	132,701	13,270	26,540	53,080	53,768	67,039	93,579	10.37	12.93	18.05
25	165,876	16,588	33,175	66,351	53,603	70,190	103,366	10.34	13.54	19.94
30	199,052	19,905	39,810	79,621	53,437	73,342	113,152	10.31	14.15	21.83
40	265,402	26,540	53,080	106,161	53,105	79,645	132,726	10.24	15.36	25.60
50	331,753	33,175	66,351	132,701	52,773	85,949	152,299	10.18	16.58	29.38

a. 48 percent of population.

per net residential acre, which can be achieved with garden apartments, each circle would contain 15,708 persons, and all 24 together would contain 376,992 persons, or 23.3 percent of the entire suburban population. This net residential density is equivalent to a gross residential density (persons per square mile including all nonresidential uses) of 20,000. That is close to the overall gross density of New York City (26,402 persons per square mile in 2000). In the United States as a whole in 2000, 2.9 percent of all suburban workers commuted by transit. That percentage applied to the entire suburban population would be 22,550 transit commuters.

But if 24 suburban transit circles were created at the net density of 25 units per acre, as calculated above, and if 10 percent of the employed transit circle residents commuted by transit, then 18,096 transit circle residents would be transit commuters. In the rest of the suburbs there would be 1,243,008 residents (1,620,000 minus the 376,992 in transit circles); if 2.9 percent of the workers among them commuted by transit, that would be 17,302 such commuters. Thus there would be 35,398 transit commuters altogether, or 4.6 percent of all workers, compared with only 22,550 without any transit circles. This is a net gain of 12,848 transit commuters who presumably would otherwise use private vehicles. But among the total of 777,600 suburban workers, about 90 percent would have commuted by private vehicles if there were no transit circles, or 699,840. Thus the creation of 24 densely settled suburban transit circles would shift 12,847 out of 699,840 commuters from private vehicles to transit, or just 1.8 percent. So private vehicle commuting would only drop from 90 percent to 88.2 percent—hardly enough to affect suburban peak-hour traffic congestion significantly.

Impacts If Higher Fractions of Suburban Transit Circle Workers Commute by Transit

This result would be more impressive if more than 10 percent of the transit circle dwellers chose transit commuting. Robert Cervero analyzed the 1990 commuting behavior of residents of three East Bay Area counties served by Bay Area Rapid Transit (BART) and found that 9 percent lived within half a mile of a BART station and that about 18 percent of those residents commuted by rail transit.[3] If the fraction doing so in the model rose to 20 percent, then 36,191 transit circle residents would be transit commuters, and the total number of transit commuters would be

53,494. Hence 6.9 percent of all suburban workers would commute by transit, a gain of 4.0 percent over what would likely happen with no transit circles. That would drop commuting by private vehicles from 90 percent to 86 percent—a relatively small decline of only 4.5 percent in the number of such commuters. Whether that decline would notably affect peak-hour suburban traffic congestion is hard to tell.

This result would be still more impressive if 40 percent of the transit circle dwellers chose transit commuting. The four census tracts surrounding the Friendship Heights Metro stop in Chevy Chase, Maryland, a high-density neighborhood (tracts 7053, 7055, and 7056.02 in Montgomery County, Maryland, and 11 in the District of Columbia)—had 8,518 resident workers in 2000; 29.6 percent commuted by public transit (91 percent of those used the subway), and 53.6 percent used cars. The highest fraction using transit in any one tract was 45.8 percent. The census tract containing the Ballston subway stop in Arlington, Virginia (tract 1014), covers an area of about 1.28 square miles with 8,436 residents living in a high-density settlement developed around that subway stop over twenty years. In 2000, 42.6 percent of workers 16 and over living in that tract commuted by public transit.[4] If the fraction commuting by transit in the 24 model suburban transit circles rose to 40 percent, then 72,382 transit circle residents would be transit commuters, and the total number of transit commuters would be 89,685. Hence 11.5 percent of all suburban workers would commute by transit, assuming 2.9 percent of the remainder of all suburban workers did so. That would be a gain of 8.6 percentage points over what would likely happen with no transit circles. That would drop commuting by private vehicles from 90 percent to 81.4 percent—a decline of 9.6 percent in the number of such commuters. That is a significant reduction in private vehicle commuting.

However, the population density in the Ballston census tract is much lower than that assumed in the model suburban transit circles just analyzed, since the Ballston tract contains about 1.28 square miles and has 8,436 residents—or 6,590 residents per square mile. At that density, a circle containing 0.7854 square miles would hold about 5,180 residents. That is only about one-third as many as the 15,708 assumed to live there in a model transit circle at a net residential density of 25 units per acre. Hence the Ballston area appears to have a net residential density of only about 8.25 units per net residential acre, assuming 50 percent of its land is residential. Thus, the estimate that commuting patterns similar to that in the Ballston area would drop overall suburban commuting by private automotive vehicles from 90 percent to 81.4 percent is undoubtedly too high. To be conservative, that estimate should be cut in half to a decline from 90 percent to 85.7 percent. Whether that fall in private vehicle commuting would significantly reduce suburban peak-hour traffic congestion is not clear.

This analysis shows that even very high-density settlements in a great many suburban transit circles—capturing 23 percent of the suburbs' total population—accompanied by very high fractions of transit circle workers choosing transit for work trips, would still leave the vast majority of suburban commuters using private automotive vehicles. Up to now, wherever suburban transit stations have been created, a large fraction of them have had no high-density housing built around them, partly because they are surrounded by parking lots to encourage park-and-ride patronage. So the effort required to change this situation to virtually universally present high-housing-density settlements around all suburban transit stops would be immense for a relatively questionable pay off in terms of reduced congestion.

Calculating the Impact of Transit Circles on Central City Commuting Patterns

How about the situation in central cities? The bottom half of table E-1 shows similar calculations for cities. At a net residential density of 50 dwellings per acre, probably requiring midrise or high-rise buildings, a city transit circle would contain the same 15,708 residents as a suburban transit circle with half that net density, because only 25 percent of the land in cities would be used for residential versus 50 percent in suburbs. However, there are far more transit stops in the city than in the suburbs in this simulation model. Hence the total number of people living in such transit circles would be 691,152, or 64.0 percent of the entire city population. That is an extremely high fraction.

Moreover, the fraction of transit-circle-dwelling workers who would choose transit might be higher in cities, say, 20 percent. If there were no transit circles, about 10.5 percent of the city's 518,400 workers would commute by transit, or 54,432 (10.5 percent was the national average percentage for central cities in 2000). If transit circles were built at high density and contained 691,152 residents, then 331,752 would be employed workers. If 20 percent of them commuted by transit, that would be 66,351. Among the 186,647 workers living elsewhere in the city (518,400 minus the 331,752 living in transit circles), about 10.5 percent would use transit, or 19,598. Therefore, total transit commuters would equal 85,949, or 16.6 percent of all city workers. Thus the city's transit commuting share would rise from 10.5 percent to 16.6 percent, or by 6.1 percentage points. If 80 percent of city workers had previously been commuting by private vehicles, this fraction would drop to 73.4 percent, or by 8.3 percent. That might have some impact on traffic congestion in the city, although the vast majority of commuters would still be using private vehicles. But capturing two-thirds of the city's total population within high-density transit circles seems highly unlikely.

If the fraction of residents in model city transit circles commuting by transit rose to 40 percent, as in the Ballston area cited earlier, then the total number of transit commuters in the city would be 152,299, or 29.4 percent of all city workers. That is a rise of 18.9 percentage points and would reduce private vehicle commuting from 80 percent to 61.1 percent. That big a decline would undoubtedly reduce peak-hour traffic congestion in the city. However, this calculation is based on at least two very unrealistic assumptions: that 64 percent of the entire city population lived in transit circles, and that the net residential density in each circle was three times as high as the actual density in the Ballston census tract.

Extending Transit Lines and High-Density Circles into the Exurbs

One alternative to consider is extending transit lines far out into exurban areas and building high-density developments around the resulting exurban stations. If the four transit lines just noted were extended diagonally outward to the outer edges of the corner exurban zones (E-1, E-11, E-5, and E-8 in figure E-1), that would add 45.2 miles of transit lines. Assuming transit stations were built three miles apart in these low-density regions (twice as far apart as in the suburbs) this would result in a total of 15 additional transit stops. If a circular high-density settlement was built around each stop and developed at a net residential density of 25 units per acre, then all 15 circles would contain 235, 620 residents. These assumptions result in a gross population density within the transit circles of 20,000 persons per square mile—34 times as great as the low 585 persons per square mile in the entire exurban region in the base case as shown in figure E-1. The transit circle residents would constitute 39 percent of the entire exurban population (600,000 residents), assuming these developments attracted people from other parts of the exurbs rather than comprising a net addition to the total exurban population. (If these 235,620 residents were added to the pre-existing population, they would make up 28 percent of the total exurban population, which would then be 835,620.) Probably the share of transit circle residents using public transit for commuting would be somewhat lower in these far-out circles than in suburban or central city circles. If that fraction were 10 percent, then total transit usage among exurban residents would rise from 2.9 percent without such circles to 5.69 percent with them. If the share of transit circle residents using transit to commute equaled 20 percent, then total exurban transit commuting would reach 6.72 percent, or more than double what it would be without such developments. However, even then the share of exurban commuters using private vehicles would only decline from around 90 percent to 86 percent—not enough to reduce exurban traffic congestion significantly. This analysis implies that only if an extraordinarily high percentage of exurban transit circle residents decided to commute by transit would the extension of transit lines into exurban regions, and the creation of transit-oriented developments there, have a notable impact on exurban-generated traffic.

Comparing High-Density Residential Transit Circles with Park-and-Ride Transit Stops

An alternative method of stimulating more transit ridership would be to promote park-and-ride usage by surrounding outlying stations with parking lots aimed at attracting commuters from much farther than half a mile from each stop. This approach could tap into much larger residential areas than relying on people walking to transit stops from close-by housing units. This approach has been adopted at many outlying stations of the San Francisco Bay Area Rapid Transit system (BART) and the Washington metro system. BART's parking lots contain 42,230 spaces at 35 stations outside of downtown San Francisco, or an average of 1,206 parking spaces per station.[5] In the model just discussed, there were 24 suburban stations (excluding exurban stations). If each one had 1,500 parking spaces, and each car parked had 1.2 passengers, then 43,200 commuters could use those spaces daily. That is 19 percent more than the 36,191 suburban transit-circle dwellers who might use transit if the land around each station were developed at 25 units per net residential acre, and 20 percent of those living nearby commuted by transit. However, if 40 percent of those transit circle dwellers used transit for commuting, that would be 72,382, or 68 percent more than those would who use park-and-ride as just cited.

To put these figures another way, the fraction of transit commuters among residents of every suburban transit circle would have to exceed 23.9 percent in order for total commuting generated by those circles to surpass the amount that could be generated by park-and-ride parking lots there instead of high-density dwellings.

If it were possible to combine high-density housing near transit stops and large-capacity parking lots there too, then both sources of possible ridership could be tapped simultaneously. However, coordinating these two approaches is extremely complex and difficult because the two types of land uses involved are basically incompatible in the territory right around each transit stop. If each station is surrounded by large open parking lots convenient for park-and-ride commuters, then far fewer people can live close enough to walk to that station—and doing so across large parking lots would not seem a very desirable prospect. As Dena Belzer and Gerald Autler have pointed out, there is an inherent conflict between the strategy of using a transit stop as a *residential neighborhood center* in a transit-oriented development and using it as a *transit node* in a large-scale rail system.[6] These two strategies can only be carried out jointly by using very expensive types of parking—underground or structured—to get the parking out of the way of residential and commercial structures right around the station. That also requires complex multiuse planning by the developer and close coordination between the developer and the transit system. That is why so few successful examples of such dual-approach development have been achieved.

The Impact of High-Density Transit-Oriented Developments on Traffic Congestion

One aspect of transit-oriented development not always considered is the impact of the greater number of persons per square mile in such nodes on local traffic congestion. Even if a much higher proportion of all persons living close to a transit stop use public transit than is the case with housing elsewhere, that drop in private vehicle commuting may be offset by the greater number of households living in a small area. The normal density of most American suburbs is between 2,000 and 4,000 persons per square mile. The density in a transit circle necessary to generate significant transit ridership may be as high as 20,000 per square mile. Although a suburban transit circle contains only 0.393 square miles of housing, at a density of 20,000 persons per square mile (resulting from 25 units per acre), that would be 7,860 persons. If 48 percent were workers, that would be 3,772. If even 40 percent of them used transit, at least 50 percent—or 1,886—would most likely commute by private vehicles. In contrast, if the density of this area remained at 4,000 persons per square mile, then the 0.393 square miles would contain only 1,572 persons, including 755 workers. If 90 percent of them commuted by car, that would be 680 such commuters. That is only one-third the number of commuters living in this small area that would be using private vehicles at the higher density desired by advocates of transit-oriented development. Thus *the local traffic congestion within high-density transit circles themselves and their immediate vicinities is likely to be significantly more intense than if those circles were settled at more typical suburban densities, even if transit ridership among transit circle residents is high*. True, the number of vehicle commuters in the region as a whole would be lower if transit circles succeeded in raising public transit usage; hence overall regional traffic congestion might be less. But local congestion in the vicinity of the transit circles is likely to be greater.

Conclusion

There is little doubt that creating high-density housing around transit stops will increase transit ridership and therefore may be a tactic worth pursuing. However, for this tactic to have a notable impact on traffic congestion, especially in the suburbs, three conditions must be met. First, the number of transit stations developed with such high-density circles must be large—big enough to encompass a significant proportion of the total suburban population. This means there must be an effective regionwide program of developing high-density circles around nearly all fixed-rail transit stops, even though they may be in different local jurisdictions. Local resistance to such high-density settlements must somehow be overcome throughout the region. Second, the average density of housing units in each of those circles must be very high—much higher than densities in most U.S. suburban neighborhoods. Third, the proportion of transit circle dwellers who choose transit must also be high—at least 20 percent, and higher would be even better. Although the last two conditions have been met near individual transit stops in some suburban areas, no overall suburban areas in any U.S. metropolitan region have yet come close to achieving all of these conditions. Even if all these conditions were met, it is not clear that the results would reduce overall traffic congestion in the region concerned by any significant amount. However, it is reasonably clear that local traffic congestion in the vicinity of the transit circles would be greater than if "normal" suburban densities prevailed there. Thus careful analysis shows that this tactic is not nearly as promising a means of coping with traffic congestion as many of its proponents claim.

Notes

Chapter 1

1. Texas Transportation Institute, *The 2001 Urban Mobility Report* (College Station, Tex.: 2001), p. 15.

2. A Gallup poll of more than 1,032 adults taken in 2000 found that 62 percent thought that traffic congestion had gotten worse in the past five years, and 61 percent thought it would become even worse in the next five. Gallup Poll, *The Gallup Poll Monthly*, June 2000, pp. 44–47.

3. Texas Transportation Institute, *The 2002 Urban Mobility Report* (College Station, Tex.: 2002).

4. Ibid.

5. Ibid.

6. Anthony Downs, *Stuck in Traffic: Coping with Peak-Hour Traffic Congestion* (Brookings, 1992).

Chapter 2

1. See chapter 10 for citations by these advocates of road pricing.

2. Some methods of using tolls to reduce peak-hour congestion on a road do not force all drivers who do not want to pay off that road during peak hours. These methods charge tolls only on some of the lanes in the road, leaving other lanes available for drivers

unwilling to pay. These methods have a much better chance of being accepted as reasonably fair by American drivers and therefore by American elected officials.

3. Hong Kong experimented with such a system for six months but then dismantled it.

4. Data from Federal Highway Administration, Nationwide Personal Transportation Survey 1995, *1995 NPTS Data Book* (Department of Transportation, 1995), p. 6-30, table 6-17. See also table 11-1 in chapter 11 in this volume.

The 2000 Census reported that 3.6 percent of all employed persons sixteen years or older worked at home, so the share who traveled to work was 96.4 percent. However, 12.2 percent of all commuters used car pools. If the average car pool carried 2.2 persons, that would mean those carpoolers accounted for 5.5 percent of all commuting trips, not 12.2 percent. That removes 6.7 percent from the number of trips, leaving only 89.7 percent as many commting trips as commuters (96.4 minus 6.7). Assuming each person commuting by public transit counts as one trip, then 89.7 should be the base for computing what percentage of all trips occurred by each mode. That was assumed to be equal to 100 percent of all work trips. The share who traveled by transit was 4.73 percent of all workers, which equals 5.27 percent of all commuting trips (that is, 5.27 percent of 89.7). The share who commuted by SOVs was 75.7 percent, or 84.4 percent, of commuting trips. The share of trips consisting of car pools was 5.5 percent, or 6.1 percent of 89.7. Consequently, figure 2-1 assumes that POVs composed 90.5 percent of all peak-hour work trips (84.4 plus 6.1), and transit composed 5.3 percent. Data from factfinder.census.gov/servlet/DTTable?_ts=90436573302 (December 2003). For nonwork trips it was assumed that the transit share was 50 percent smaller, and the other 50 percent was added to the POV share. So transit accounted for 2.65 percent of all peak-hour nonwork trips, and POVs accounted for 93.2 percent. These were the coefficients used to compute the numbers in figure 2-1.

5. I am indebted to Martin Wachs for this point, which he presented in "Congestion in Cities: What? When? What Kind? How Much?" paper presented at the UCLA Symposium on Tackling Traffic Congestion, 2002.

6. Washington State Department of Transportation, "Traffic Tied to the Economy," *WSDOT News*, May 21, 2003. This article states, "New data from WSDOT show that the drop in employment is one factor that has contributed to a drop in traffic counts on several central Puget Sound highways. The trend lines for employment and average daily traffic counts are similar, reflecting rapid growth during the 1990s and dropping off in the past few years." (www.wsdot.wa.gov/news/may03/gray_notebook.htm). The author has hard copy on file for data cited from websites listed throughout this book.

7. Wachs, "Congestion in Cities."

Chapter 3

1. David Schrank and Tim Lomax, *The 2002 Urban Mobility Report* (College Station, Tex.: Texas Transportation Institute, June 2002), throughout. For details of how the congestion measures have been calculated see "Mobility Monitoring Program," "Keys to Estimating Mobility," chap. 5 (mobility.tamu. edu). Data for seventy-six regions were condensed to seventy-five statistics by merging data for Dallas and Fort Worth into combined numbers.

2. Texas Transportation Institute's (TTI's) set of regions contained most of the largest metropolitan areas. But there were actually 335 metropolitan statistical areas in the United States in 2000 (breaking up consolidated metropolitan statistical areas [CMSAs] into their smaller components). The size composition of TTI's sample differed from the actual size composition of those 335 metropolitan areas. TTI's sample population contained a much higher percentage of people living in very large areas and a much lower percentage of people living in small areas than exist in the nation as a whole. If TTI had calculated its overall estimates of key congestion measurements by using averages for the different size groups weighted with total group population from its own sample, then it would tend to overestimate the severity of congestion across the nation as a whole. That would occur because congestion measures are highest in very large areas, which TTI's sample overweights, and lowest in small areas, which TTI's sample underweights. But an analysis of TTI's estimates of these variables for all groups combined shows that those estimates are very close to estimates made by using weights based on the actual U.S. metropolitan-area population in each group. Hence TTI's estimates of these variables for all area size groups combined seem reasonable.

3. Surface Transportation Policy Project, *Easing the Burden: A Companion Analysis of the Texas Transportation Institute's Congestion Study*, May 2001, p. 5 (www.transact.org/PDFs/etb_report.pdf.)

4. These are data from regression analyses I performed.

5. The 2000 and 1990 statistics were taken from Census 2000, "Profile of Selected Economic Characteristics," table DP-3, Commuting to Work (http://censtats.census.gov/data/US/01000.pdf). The other statistics were from the Federal Highway Administration, *Nationwide Personal Transportation Study: Preliminary Results* (Department of Transportation, May 1997), p. 21. These two sources are not entirely consistent; the second source reported the 1990 average as 19.7 minutes.

6. Federal Highway Administration, *Our Nation's Travel: 1995 Nationwide Personal Transportation Survey Early Results Report* (September 1997), p. 13.

7. Federal Highway Administration, "System Congestion Trends," *Highway Statistics 2001* (www.fhwa.gov/ohim/hs01/chartv.htm).

8. TTI, *The 2001 Urban Mobility Report*, p. 54; and author's calculations.

9. *The 2002 Urban Mobility Report*, p. 42. This total is actually smaller than the total annual delay reported for 68 areas in *The 2001 Urban Mobility Report* (p. 42) because TTI shifted from measuring total delays caused by all congestion to measuring only peak-hour delays imposed on peak-hour travelers.

10. TTI, *The 2002 Urban Mobility Report*; and author's calculations.

11. Ibid.

12. P. B. Goodwin, "Solving Congestion: Inaugural Lecture for the Professorship of Transport Policy," University College, London, Centre for Transport Studies, October 23, 1997 (www.ucl.ac.uk/transport-studies/tsu/pbginau.htm), p. 9.

13. Ibid.

14. TTI, *The 2002 Urban Mobility Report*, p. 25.

15. TTI, *2002 Urban Mobility Study: The Short Report* (http://mobility. tamu.edu/ums/study/short_report.stm).

16. Patricia Mokhtarian and Ilan Salomon, "How Derived Is the Demand for Travel? Some Conceptual and Measurement Considerations," UCD-ITS-REP-01-15 (University of California at Davis, 2001), p. 706.

17. U.S. Bureau of the Census, *Statistical Abstract of the United States: 2001* (2001), p. 391.

18 . Martin Wachs pointed out this aspect of congestion in his presentation at the UCLA Symposium on Traffic Congestion, October 2002.

19. This point was suggested by Brian Taylor in his presentation at the UCLA Symposium on Traffic Congestion, October 2002.

20. See Glen Weisbrod, Don Vary, and George Treyz, "Measuring the Economic Costs of Urban Traffic Congestion to Business," paper presented at the Transportation Research Board annual meeting, January 2003. Clifford Winston of the Brookings Institution has stressed the same point in many of his writing on transportation policy.

21. I have personally encountered this view among regional leaders in various parts of the United States and Canada.

22. Gallup Poll, *The Gallup Poll Monthly*, February 2001, p. 7.

23. Federal Highway Administration, *Transportation Users—Views of Quality, Nationwide Personal Transportation Survey* (Department of Transportation, December 1997), p. 14.

24. National Association of Home Builders (www.nahb.com/news/survey. htm).

25. Pew Charitable Trusts (www.pewcenter.org/doingcj/research/ r_ST2000natl.html).

26. Bay Area Council (www.bayareacouncil.org/pubs/bap/2000BAP.pdf and bap/bap_mid.html.r_ST2000natl.html).

27. *Los Angeles Times*, June 1–4, 1996.

Chapter 4

1. U.S. Bureau of the Census, 2000 Summary File SF3 (factfinder.census.gov).

2. Data from Federal Highway Administration, *Our Nation's Travel: 1995 Nationwide Personal Transportation Survey Early Results* (Department of Transportation, September 1997), p. 14.

3. A metropolitan statistical area (MSA) is an urbanized area containing at least one city with 50,000 or more inhabitants, or an urbanized area with at least 50,000 inhabitants that is within a metropolitan region with at least 100,000 inhabitants (75,000 in New England). A consolidated metropolitan statistical area (CMSA) is a combination of several adjacent MSAs. The specific MSAs within a CMSA are designated as primary metropolitan statistical areas (PMSAs) to differentiate them from free-standing MSAs. U.S. Bureau of the Census, *Statistical Abstract of the United States: 2001* (2001), p. 892.

4. However, analysis in chapter 3 shows that high percentage increases in population alone are not closely linked with increasing traffic congestion.

5. Employment data from U.S. Bureau of the Census, *Statistical Abstract of the United States: 2001*, p. 367.

6. Data from the Center for Workforce Information of the Pennsylvania Department of Labor and Industry, telephone call on February 11, 2002. Employment in the Pittsburgh metropolitan area was 1,055,300 in 1980, 1,056,200 in 1990, and 1,106,500 in 2000.

7. Federal Highway Administration, *Our Nation's Travel: 1995 NPTS Early Results Report*, p. 17.

8. Federal Highway Administration, *Summary of Travel Trends: 1995 Nationwide Personal Transportation Survey* (Department of Transportation, December 1999), p. 40; and U.S. Bureau of the Census, *Demographic Profiles: 100 Percent and Sample Data* (www.census.gov/census2000/states/us.html), downloads of individual state data.

9. U.S. Bureau of the Census, "Aggregate Travel Time to Work (in Minutes) by Travel Time to Work by Means of Transportation to Work for Workers 16 Years and Over Who Did Not Work at Home," Census 2000 Summary File 3 (http://factfinder.census.gov/servlet/DTTable?_ts=71963412179 [December 2003]), table P33.

10. U.S. Bureau of the Census, *Statistical Abstract of the United States: 2001*, p. 690; and National Center for Statistics and Analysis, *Traffic Facts 2000* (Washington, 2000), p. 3.

11 . Federal Highway Administration website (www.fhwa.gov); and Bureau of the Census website (www.census.gov).

12. Department of Energy, *Energy Data Book: Edition 22* (September 2002), chap. 11, "Household Vehicle Ownership," table 11.4 (www-cta.ornl.gov/cta/data/Chapter11.html [December 2003]).

13. Bureau of Labor Statistics, "Consumer Spending in 2001" (www.bls.gov/cex/csxann01.pdf [April 2003]).

14. Gasoline and oil costs were 16.7 percent of transportation spending in 2001, compared with 17.4 percent in 2000 and 15.0 percent in 1999. Bureau of Labor Statistics, "Consumer Spending in 2001" (www.bls.gov/cex [April 2003]).

15. Data quoted from *Consumer Reports*, April 1991, pp. 248–49, in an article on the website of the Association for Manufacturing Technology, "Publications/prod__sect4.pdf, April 16, 2002" (www.mfgtech.org [December 2003]).

16. U.S. Bureau of the Census, *Statistical Abstract of the United States: 2000* (2000), p. 629.

17. Motor vehicle fuel rates from Department of Energy, Energy Information Administration, *Monthly Energy Review*, Average Motor Vehicle Miles per Gallon, updated September 12, 2001 (www.bts.gov/transtu/indicators/Environment/html/Average_Motor_Vehicle_Miles_Per_Gallon.htm [December 2003]). The source was also used for vans, sport utility vehicles, and light trucks.

18. Danny Hakim, "Fuel Economy Hit 22-Year Low in 2002," *New York Times*, Saturday May 3, 2003, pp. B-1–B-2.

19. Bureau of Transportation Statistics, *National Transportation Statistics 2000* (Department of Transportation, 2000), table 1-30.

20. Ibid.

21. David Shrank and Tim Lomax, *The 2002 Urban Mobility Report* (College Station, Texas: Texas Transportation Institute, June 2002), p. 149, table 5.

22. Boris S. Pushkarev and Jeffrey M. Zupan, *Public Transportation and Land Use Policy* (Indiana University Press, 1977), p. 177.

23. Catherine L. Ross and Anne E. Dunning, "Land Use Transportation Interaction: An Examination of the NPTS Data," in Federal Highway Administration, *Searching for Solutions: Nationwide Personal Transportation Symposium* (Department of Transportation, October 1997), p. 149.

24. Data from demographic website for 452 urbanized areas in 2000 (www.demographia.com/db-wa2000all.htm [December 2003]).

25. National Association of Home Builders, *Smart Growth: Building Better Places to Live, Work and Play* (Washington, 1999), p. 13.

26. Edward L. Glaeser and Jesse Shapiro, *City Growth and the 2000 Census: Which Places Grew, and Why* (Brookings Institution Center on Urban and Metropolitan Policy, May 2001), p. 12.

27. John Brennan and Edward Hill, *Where Are the Jobs? Cities, Suburbs, and the Competition for Employment* (Brookings Institution Center on Urban and Metropolitan Policy, November 1999), pp. 4–5.

28. Robert E. Lang, *Edgeless Cities: Exploring the Elusive Metropolis* (Brookings, 2003), p. 55. The remaining 6.0 percent was located in secondary downtowns.

29. Peter Gordon and Harry Richardson, "Are Compact Cities a Desirable Planning Goal?" "Smart Growth Network, Alternative Views of Sprawl," and "The Myth That Sprawl Causes Congestion," Thoreau Institute (www.ti.org/index.html).

30. Alan E. Pisarski, *Commuting in America II: The Second National Report on Commuting Patterns and Trends* (Washington: Eno Transportation Foundation, 1996), p. 87.

31. Estimates of the average commuting time for all commuters vary in different government sources. For example, the 1990 Census estimated average commuting time for all U.S. workers as 22.7 minutes, but the 1995 Nationwide Personal Transportation Survey stated that the 1990 average was 19.7 minutes. Federal Highway Administration, *Our Nation's Travel: 1995 Nationwide Personal Transportation Survey Early Results Report* (Department of Transportation, September 1997), p. 13. That is why differing estimates are cited in various parts of this book. The data were taken from the *Census 2000 Supplementary Survey Summary* tables. The overall average commuting time from that source was 24.3 minutes, but the final figure from the demographic data was 25.5 minutes.

32. Federal Highway Administration, *Our Nation's Travel: 1995 Nationwide Personal Transportation Survey Early Results Report*, p. 13.

33. William M. Rohe and others, *Travel to Work Patterns: A Preliminary Analysis of Selected Data from the Annual Housing Survey Travel-to-Work File* (University of North Carolina, Department of City and Regional Planning, 1980), p. 145.

34. U.S. Bureau of the Census, *Statistical Abstract of the United States: 2001*, p. 664.

35. Data from Federal Highway Administration, Office of Highway Policy Information, *Annual Highway Statistics* (Department of Transportation), volumes for the years 1995 through 2001, tables for state vehicle registrations and truck registrations (www.fhwa.dot.gov/ohim).

36. U.S. Bureau of the Census, *Statistical Abstract of the United States: 2002* (2002), p. 684.

37. Ted Scott, American Trucking Associations, "Trucking Industry Perspective," in Department of Transportation, *Federal Truck Size and Weight Policy: Looking beyond the Comprehensive Truck Size and Weight Study*, Symposium 2000, report issued June 30, 2000, p. 15.

38. Kiplinger, "Truck Weight Cap on Its Way Higher," *In the News*, July 26, 2002, Americans for Safe and Efficient Transportation (www.aset-safety.org/media/aset3.html [December 2003]).

39. I am indebted to Martin Wachs for pointing out the importance of nodes in creating congestion.

40. See Charles Lave, *Things Won't Get a Lot Worse: The Future of U.S. Traffic Congestion* (University of California at Irvine, Institute of Transportation Studies and the Department of Economics, 1990).

41. Data from Federal Highway Administration, Office of Highway Policy Information, *Annual Highway Statistics*, volumes for the years 1995 through 2001, tables for state vehicle registrations and truck registrations.

42. Federal Highway Administration, *1999 Conditions and Performance*

Report—Chapter 2, exhibit 2-7, "Highway Lane Miles by Functional System, Selected Years 1987-1997" (www.fhwa.dot.gov/policy/1999cpr/ch_02/cpg02_7. htm [December 2003]).

Chapter 5

1. Alice Reid and Patricia Davis, "A Jumper on Wilson Bridge Throws Area into Gridlock," *Washington Post*, November 5, 1998, p. A1.

2. A graph in J. Lindley, "Urban Freeway Congestion Problems and Solutions: An Update," *ITE Journal* (September 1989), p. 21, indicates that 61 percent of congestion was caused by incidents in 1984 and 64 percent in 1987 and predicts that 70 percent will be so caused in 2005.

3. P. B. Farradyne, *Traffic Incident Management Handbook*, prepared for the Office of Traffic Management, Federal Highway Administration (Department of Transportation, November 2000), pp. 1–2.

4. Cambridge Systematics, Inc., in association with JHK and Associates, Transmode Consultants, Inc., and Sydec, Inc., *Incident Management: Executive Summary, October 1990* (Alexandria, Va.: Trucking Research Institute, n.d.), p. 8.

5. Jeffrey A. Lindley, "Urban Freeway Congestion: Quantification of the Problem and Effectiveness of Potential Solutions," *ITE Journal* (January 1987), pp. 27–32, and "Urban Freeway Congestion: Problems and Solutions: An Update," *ITE Journal* (December 1989), pp. 21–23.

6. Data taken from National Highway Traffic Safety Administration (NHTSA), National Center for Statistics and Analysis, *Traffic Safety Facts 2001, Overview*, DOT HS 809 476 (http://www-nrd.nhtsa.dot.gov/).

7. NHTSA, 2001 National Statistics, *Traffic Safety Facts 2001* (December 2002), p. 1 (www-nrd.nhtsa.dot.gov/pdf/nrd-30/NCSA/TSFAnn/TSF2001.pdf).

8. Data from NHTSA, *Traffic Safety Facts 2000* (2001), tables 3 and 4. Posted on the NHTSA website as part of *2000 National Statistics* (www-nrd.nhtsa.dot.gov).

9. Ibid.

10. NHTSA, *Alcohol and Highway Safety: 2001, 4B Drinking Drivers, Pedestrians, and Bicycles* (Washington, 2001) (www.nhtsa.dot.gov).

11. Warren G. LaHeist, *Highway Safety Assessment: A Summary of Findings in Ten States*, DOT HS 808 796 (National Highway Traffic Safety Administration, June 1998) (www.nhtsa.dot.gov). The ten states were Connecticut, New Jersey, Pennsylvania, North Carolina, Ohio, New Mexico, Kansas, Colorado, Nevada, and Washington.

12. NHTSA, *Alcohol and Highway Safety: 2001, 4B Drinking Drivers, Pedestrians, and Bicycles* (www.nhtsa.dot.gov).

13. Ibid.

14. NHTSA, *Traffic Safety Facts 2000*, p. 10.

15. LaHeist, *Highway Safety Assessment*.

16. Department of Justice, *Bureau of Justice Statistics Bulletin,* Census of State and Local Law Enforcement Agencies (2000), p. 1 (www.ojp.usdoj.gov/bjs).

17. LaHeist, *Highway Safety Assessment.*

18. NHTSA, *Traffic Safety Facts 2001,* DOT HS-809-332 (Washington, 2001), p. 16.

19. U.S. Bureau of the Census, *Statistical Abstract of the United States: 1976* (1976), p. 600.

20. NHTSA, *Traffic Safety Facts 1999, Overview* (2000), p. 11.

21. In 1980, there were 30.022 million people 18 to 24 years old. That number declined to a low of 24.843 million in 1996 before rising to 26.011 million in 1999. In contrast, the number of people 75 and over was 9.969 million in 1980 and 16.322 million in 1999. U.S. Bureau of the Census, *Statistical Abstract of the United States: 2000* (2000).

22. U.S. Bureau of the Census, *Statistical Abstract of the United States: 2000,* p. 13.

23. Data from National Center for Statistics and Analysis, NHTSA, *Traffic Safety Facts 2001: A Compilation of Motor Vehicle Crash Data from the Fatality Analysis Reporting System and the General Estimate System* (Washington, December 2002), table 24 (www-nrd.nhtsa.dot.gov). Most of the information in this section is taken from this document.

24. Federal Highway Administration, *2000 National Statistics* (Department of Transportation, 2001), p. 45.

25. These calculations may seem inconsistent with the earlier data presented on the number of incidents reported to the Maryland Coordinated Highways Action Response Team (CHART) as arising on Washington's capital beltway. On an average day in 1999, CHART reported a total number of incidents that, when extrapolated to the entire beltway, including the Virginia portions, equals 46.7 per day. That is a much lower total than calculated as probable in this section. True, the beltway contains only 64 miles out of the hundreds of miles of roads in the Washington metropolitan area, but those are the 64 most heavily traveled miles in the area during peak hours. I have no persuasive means of reconciling these outcomes.

26. As of mid-2002, the Census Bureau's official projections of future population are based on pre-2000 Census data and are surely too low. Therefore, the projections used here are higher than the official projections.

Chapter 6

1. Elaine Murakami and Jennifer Young, "Daily Travel by Persons with Low Income," paper presented at Nationwide Personal Transportation Survey Symposium, Md., 1997, figure 2, table 4 (http://npts.ornl.gov/npts/1995/Doc/LowInc.pdf [December 2003]). "Low income" was defined in this study as less than $10,000 per year for 1-2 person households, less than $20,000 for 3-4 per-

son households, and less than $25,000 for households containing 5 or more persons (table 1).

2. See Federal Highway Administration, *Personal Travel in the U.S., vol. 1, 1983-1984* (Department of Transportation, 1986), p. 7-13, table 7-10 (www.fhwa.dot.gov/ohim/1983/vol1pt2.pdf [November 2003]).

3. Kenneth Small, University of California, Irvine, and Clifford Winston, Brookings, pointed out this possibility (personal communication).

4. For further discussion of the idea of convergence, see Anthony Downs, "The Law of Peak-Hour Expressway Congestion," *Traffic Quarterly*, vol. 16 (July 1962), pp. 393–409.

5. Kenneth Small of the University of California at Irvine and Frederick Ducca of the Bureau of Public Roads pointed out that modal convergence also takes place (personal communication).

6. Frederick Ducca pointed out this possibility (personal communication).

7. However, if such a public transit improvement occurs, there would not be a net increase in highway usage from modal convergence. Rather, improved public transit would cause a net shift away from the road system to the public transit system. The other two forms of convergence would still take place.

8. This point was made by Richard Tustian (planning director of Montgomery County in suburban Washington, D.C., during the 1970s and 1980s) in his extremely helpful comments on the original draft of this book.

9. It is true that much of the interstate highway system was built long after massive movements to the suburbs began. But any observer of how new housing and commercial real estate developments sprout along new roadways cannot help but conclude that roadways have influenced at least the location of such growth, if not its total amount.

10. See Arthur M. Winer, "Air Quality," University of California at Los Angeles Institute of the Environment (www.ioe.ucla.edu/publications/report98/air.html [November 2003]).

11. This observation may also apply to the central city in a region if it does not contain a high percentage of the region's total population. In case the central city does compose a large fraction of the entire region, that city's regulations limiting growth within its own boundaries might affect the growth rate of the entire region.

12. As Kenneth Small has pointed out, more commuters may travel during periods of maximum convenience both because travel capacity during those periods has risen and because the definition of such periods has changed as a result of altered traffic conditions (personal communication).

Chapter 7

1. Ken Retherford, "Two-Lane Roads Have More Fatalities," *Decatur [Alabama] Daily*, June 1, 2002.

2. James D. Carvell Jr., Texas Transportation Institute, "Dallas Urban Area Integrated Transportation Systems," Second National Symposium on Integrated Transportation Management Systems, 1995, *Plenary Session, Benefits of ITMS* (http://gulliver.trb.org/publications/circulars/circ474/toc.html [November 2003]).

3. Federal Highway Administration, press release, FHWA 60-99 (Department of Transportation, September 23, 1999), stated, "According to U.S. Department of Transportation statistics, drivers who run red lights are involved in 89,000 crashes a year, inflicting more than 80,000 injuries and nearly 1,000 deaths. In addition, from 1992 to 1998, the number of fatal crashes at intersections has increased by 16 percent, while all other types of fatal crashes have increased by only five percent."

4. Committee for Guidance on Setting and Enforcing Speed Limits, Transportation Research Board, National Research Council, *Managing Speed: Review of Current Practice for Setting and Enforcing Speed Limits,* Special Report 254 (Washington: National Academy Press, 1998), p. 161.

5. The program is directed by the CHART board, consisting of senior technical and operational personnel from the Maryland State Highway Administration, the Maryland Transportation Authority, the Maryland State Police, the Federal Highway Administration, the University of Maryland Center for Advanced Transportation Technology, and various local governments. The board is chaired by the chief engineer of the State Highway Administration.

6. Vincent Pearce, "What Have We Learned about Freeway, Incident, and Emergency Management and Electronic Toll Collection?" (Department of Transportation, December 2000), chap. 2, p. 23.

7. Federal Highway Administration and Federal Transit Administration, *Metropolitan Transportation Management Center—Concepts of Operation: A Cross-Cutting Study: Improving Transportation Network Efficiency,* FHWA-JPO-99-020/FTA-TRI-11-99-10 (Department of Transportation, October 1999), p. 28. This is an exceptionally comprehensive analysis of TMCs and their operations.

8. Alexander Skabardonis, Hisham Noeimi, Karl Petty, Dan Rydzewski, Pravin P. Varaiya, and Haitham Al-Deek, "Freeway Service Patrols Evaluation," Technical Report PATH Research Report UCB-ITS-PRR-95-5 (University of California, Berkeley, Institute of Transportation Studies, 1994).

9. Loral AeroSys, "The State-of-the-Practice, Task A Final Working Paper for Design of Support Systems for Advanced Traffic Management Systems," DTFH61-92C-00073 (Department of Transportation, Federal Highway Administration, Traffic Management Centers, June 1993), p. 22.

Chapter 8

1. If the 1980 population of this hypothetical region was 100,000, it would have contained 68,800 motor vehicles in that year. By 2000, the number of vehicles per 1,000 residents had risen from 688 to 787, and the population would be

10 percent larger by assumption, so there would have been 86,570 vehicles. Mileage traveled per vehicle rose by 28.4 percent in that period, so total mileage traveled would have increased from 688 million (at 10,000 miles per vehicle) to 1,111.6 million. That is an overall increase of 61.6 percent.

2. U.S. Bureau of the Census, *Statistical Abstract 2002* (2002); and Bureau of Transportation Statistics, *National Transportation Statistics 2002* (2002).

3. Expanding MPO powers was part of the Intermodal Surface Transportation Efficiency Act of 1991—known as ISTEA. For a summary of the ISTEA see http://ntl.bts.gov/DOCS/ste.html.

4. Don Pickerell, "Induced Demand: Definition, Measurement and Significance," Appendix A, in *Working Together to Address Induced Demand, Proceedings of a Forum, February 22-23, 2001* (Washington: Eno Transportation Foundation), p. 26.

5. In the language of economics, the increased capacity moves the "supply curve" of movement down and to the right. In the short run, this shifts the equilibrium point to the right along the initial demand curve. In the long run, the initial demand curve also moves to the right, causing a further increase in volume. This can be seen in the diagrams set forth in Don Pickerell's article, cited in note 4.

6. Pickerell, "Appendix A: Induced Demand," p. 28.

7. Robert Cervero, "Are Induced-Travel Studies Inducing Bad Investments?" *Access,* no. 22 (Spring 2003), p. 26; and Robert Cervero and Mark Hansen, "Road Supply-Demand Relationships: Sorting Out Causal Linkages" (University of California at Berkeley, October 2000). See also Douglas B. Lee Jr., "Induced Traffic and Induced Demand," World Bank publication, appendix B (www.worldbank.org/transport/roads/rpl_docs/apbinduc.pdf [January 2004]).

8. Pickerell, "Induced Demand," p. 35.

9. See appendix A in this book.

10. Cambridge Systematics, Inc., "Executive Summary, 9: Summary of Findings, Conclusions, and Recommendations" and "Appendix K – Technical Memorandum – Secondary Research" in *Final Report of the Twin Cities Ramp Meter Evaluation* (Cambridge, Mass., 2001).

11. The Cambridge Systematics, Inc., study cited in note 10 has many more detailed and useful analyses of various aspects of ramp metering.

12. According to Genevieve Giuliano (personal communication), the added delay of the car pooling necessary to be admitted onto an HOV lane averages about 15 minutes. So the travel time gain from using HOV lanes versus "normal" lanes must equal or exceed 15 minutes. This conclusion does not take into account the possible monetary savings of sharing driving costs. (Giuliano, professor, University of Southern California, and director of the Metrans joint USC and California State University Long Beach Transportation Center.)

13. Joseph L. Schofer and Edward J. Czepiel, *Executive Summary: High Occupancy Vehicle Facilities for the Chicago Metropolitan Area: A Review of*

National Experience, Success Factors and Decision Issues, prepared for the Metropolitan Planning Council and the Regional Transportation Authority (Northwestern University, May 1999).

14. Jennifer Nee, John Ishimaru, and Mark E. Hallenbeck, *HOV Lane Performance Monitoring: 2000 Report, Executive Summary*, WA-RD 506-2 (University of Washington, Washington State Transportation Center and Washington State Department of Transportation, February 2002), pp. 2–5.

15. Ibid., p. 2.

16. Metropolitan Washington Council of Governments, *Performance of 1997 Regional High-Occupancy Facilities on Interstate Highways in the Washington Region, An Analysis of Person and Vehicle Volumes and Vehicle Travel Times*, Publication 98605, and *1998 Performance of Regional High-Occupancy Vehicle Facilities on Interstate Highways in the Washington Region, An Analysis of Passenger and Vehicle Volumes*, Publication 99607 (Washington: May 1998, April 1999).

17. This calculation does not take into account the fixed costs of vehicle ownership. Rather, it assumes the commuter would own a car no matter how he or she was traveling to and from work. Operating costs are $0.10 cents per mile on a commuting trip of 9 miles each way. This method of calculation was suggested by Herbert Mohring, professor emeritus, Department of Economics, University of Minnesota.

18. If one-fourth is worth $4.80, a full hour is worth four times as much, or $19.20. Note, too, that free parking strongly encourages commuters to drive alone. If the commuter enjoys free parking, it is at lease $0.20 cents less expensive to travel alone than to use the bus, and it takes less time. The commuter would then be motivated to drive alone unless bus travel or ride sharing took less time than solo driving. That is unlikely unless peak-hour congestion in the area is horrendous, and HOV lanes are extremely effective at avoiding it.

19. See John R. Meyer and Jose A. Gomez-Ibanez, *Autos, Transit, and Cities* (Harvard University Press, 1981). Diverting existing lanes to HOV use can raise total capacity under some conditions. For example, if 200 vehicles save 10 minutes each on the HOV lane, and each carries an average of 2.5 persons, then 5,000 person-minutes are saved. If this causes 1,000 vehicles with solo drivers to lose 2 minutes apiece, they lose 2,000 person-minutes. Hence there is a net gain to society of 3,000 person-minutes. This example was furnished by Kenneth Small. But he did not point out that this exchange is a political loser. Five hundred people feel better because they saved 10 minutes each, but 1,000 people are angry because they not only lost 2 minutes each but also saw other people whizzing by on lanes they formerly used themselves. In a democracy, 1,000 votes outweigh 500—especially when the 1,000 have more intense emotions about the issue than the 500.

20. See Schofer and Czepiel, *Executive Summary*.

21. "Interstate 66 and the Metrorail Vienna Route" (www.roadstothefuture. com/Int66_MetroViennaRte.html [January 2004]); and Schofer and Czepiel, *Executive Summary*.

22. See Morgan State University, Center for Transportation Studies, *A Study to Assess the Importance of Personal, Social, Psychological and Other Factors in Ridesharing Programs* (Department of Transportation, 1984), pp. 66–67, 84. From surveys of ride-sharing commuters, this report concluded that "94 percent of the males and 84 percent of the females both suggested that economic factors influence their decisions on joining ridesharing programs" (p. 66). This survey showed that 73.7 percent of male respondents and 71.5 percent of female respondents cited economic factors as "very important" in this decision, followed by "personal" reasons (p. 67). Similar conclusions were reached by the National Capital Region Transportation Planning Board, *1987 Survey and Evaluation of Ride Finders Ridesharing Network* (Washington: Metropolitan Council of Governments, 1987).

23. 2000 Census, "Table P30. Means of Transportation to Work for Workers 16 Years and Over," and 1990 Census, "Journey to Work Trends in the United States and Its Major Metropolitan Areas, 1960–1990," Census of Population and Housing, Summary Tape File 3C.

24. I am indebted to Martin Wachs, director of the Institute of Transportation Studies, University of California, Berkeley, for pointing out these characteristics.

25. Personal description from William Waddill, my son-in-law, who used the system for several years to pick up passengers in Orinda on his way to South San Francisco.

26. Washington State Department of Transportation, *FLOW—A Two-Year Evaluation* (Seattle, 1983), p. 11.

27. Washington State Department of Transportation, *Six-Year FLOW Evaluation* (Seattle, 1989), pp. 3, 14.

Chapter 9

1. The independent variables were the population density of the metropolitan statistical area's (MSA's) central city, the percentage of all MSA workers living in the central city, the percentage of the total MSA population consisting of employed workers, and the total population of the MSA in 2000. If New York is included, only density and the percentage of all MSA workers employed within the city are statistically significant. If New York is excluded, the percentage of workers in the total MSA population also becomes significant. Central city population (including New York) has simple correlations of 0.782 with the percentage of MSA workers using transit and 0.528 with the percentage of central city workers using transit.

2. Data from the Federal Highway Administration, *1995 NPTS Data Book*, chapter 6, "Journey to Work," table 6-17, p. 6-30. See table 11-1, chapter 11 in

this volume, for more details. In this calculation, "work trips" include the following three types of trips in that table: journeys from home to work, journeys from work to home, and work-related business trips. See www.bart.gov/index/asp for Bay Area Rapid Transit system.

3. Chicago Transit Authority, Planning and Development Division.

4. Fiscal year 2002 data from American Public Transportation Association, *Public Transportation Fact Book*, table 5, "Unlinked Passenger Trips by Mode, Millions" (www.apta.com/research/stats/ridershp [February 2004]).

5. Department of Transportation, Federal Highway Administration, *Journey to Work Trends in the United States and Its Metropolitan Areas 1960-2000*, FHWA-EP-03-058 (June 2003), p. 4-1.

6. U.S. Bureau of the Census, 1990 and 2000 data, table DP-1, "Profile of General Demographic Characteristics for 1990, and 2000," and table DP-3, "Profile of Selected Economic Characteristics: 2000."

7. U.S. Bureau of the Census 2000, table DP-3, "Profile of Selected Economic Characteristics: 2000," and table GCT-P12, "Employment Status and Commuting to Work: 2000."

8. Federal Highway Administration, *Our Nation's Travel: 1995 Nationwide Personal Transportation Survey Early Results Report* (Washington, September 1997), p. 6; and U.S. Bureau of the Census, American Fact Finder, Census 2000 Summary File SF3—Table H44, "Tenure by Vehicles Available."

9. The Federal Highway Administration, *2001 National Household Travel Study* (Washington, 2002), showed that transit usage is concentrated among households that do not own automotive vehicles. Such households used transit for 19.1 percent of all their trips but automotive vehicles for 34.1 percent. Among households owning just one vehicle, transit usage dropped to 2.7 percent of all trips. It was less than 1 percent for those owning two or more vehicles and 1.7 percent among all households. Even households with low annual incomes—below $20,000—made 75 percent of all their trips by auto and only 4.6 percent by transit. In the next income group—$20,000 to $39,999—auto usage was 87.3 percent and transit usage, 1.4 percent. Higher-income groups had similar shares. Among all transit users, 37.8 percent had low incomes, and this fraction declined steadily with rising income to 14.1 percent who had incomes of $100,000 or more. John Pucher and John L. Renne, "Socioeconomics of Urban Travel: Evidence from the 2001 NHTS," *Transportation Quarterly*, vol. 57 (Summer 2003), pp. 49–77.

10. See note 4; and Bureau of Transportation Statistics, *National Transportation Statistics 2000* (Department of Transportation, 2001), p. 350.

11. However, buses accounted for 60.6 percent of all unlinked transit trips in 2000. See note 4.

12. Department of Transportation, Bureau of Transportation Statistics, *National Transportation Statistics 2002* (2002), table 1-34, "U.S. Passenger-Miles."

13. Surface Transportation Policy Project, "Decoding Transportation Policy and Practice no. 3," May 29, 2002 (www.transact.org [February 2004]).

14. Boris S. Pushkarev and Jeffery M. Zupan, *Public Transportation and Land Use Policy* (Indiana University Press, 1977), p. 177.

15. "USA Urbanized Areas: 2000 Alphabetical" (based on census data) (www.demographia.com/db-ua2000all.htm [February 2004]).

16. Surface Transportation Policy Project, Transportation Data from the 2000 Census, STPP Findings on the 2000 Census Journey-to-Work figures, June 4, 2002 (www.transact.org/report.asp?id=190 [February 2004]).

17. Nancy McGuckin and Elaine Murakami, "Examining Trip-Chaining Behavior," p. 6 (http://npts.ornl.gov/npts/1995/Doc/Chain2.pdf [February 2004]). In the 1995 Nationwide Personal Transportation Survey, the share of all commuting trips that were segmented was only 2.2 percent. However, segmented trips are defined as those that involve at least one portion of the trip on public transit; hence this is not the same as trip chaining. See *1995 NPTS Databook*, p. 6–30.

18. Patricia Mokhtarian and Ilan Salomon, "How Derived Is the Demand for Travel? Some Conceptual and Measurement Considerations," UCD-ITS-REP-01-15 (University of California at Davis, Institute of Transportation Studies, 2001), pp. 706, 710.

19. Surface Transportation Policy Project, *Transportation Costs and the American Dream,* table 1 (www.transact.org/report.asp?id=225 [February 2004]).

20. On the other hand, owning a car, or perhaps a second car, makes it possible for such households to commute farther out to where housing is typically less expensive. In regions with relatively high housing costs, such as San Francisco and Boston, the savings on housing achieved by longer commuting trips can more than offset the added time and fuel costs of making those longer trips. See Robert Burchell, Anthony Downs, and others, *Costs of Sprawl 2000,* Report 74 (Washington: Transit Cooperative Research Program, 2002), pp. 448–60.

21. Martin J. H. Mogridge, *Traffic in Towns: Jam Yesterday, Jam Today, Jam Tomorrow?* (London: Macmillan Reference Books, 1990); and Transport for London (www.tfl.gov.uk/tfl).

22. Light Rail Transit Association, "What Is Light Rail?" (www.lrta.org/explain/html [February 2004]).

23. The LRTA count of U.S. systems differs from the count made by the American Public Transit Administration, cited later. It is not clear why this is so. See "A World of Trams and Urban Transit" (www.lrta.org/world/worldind.html [February 2004]).

24. American Public Transit Association, table 107, "Light Rail National Totals, Fiscal Year 2001," and table 133, "Light Rail Transit Agencies Mileage and Station Data"(www.apta.com/research/stats/rail [February 2004]).

25. The Curitiba bus rapid transit system is described in detail in Federal Transit Administration, *Issues in Bus Rapid Transit* (Washington, 1998), chap.

3. Many of the ideas in this section of this book have been taken from that excellent paper.

26. General Accounting Office, *Mass Transit: Bus Rapid Transit Shows Promise*, GAO-01—984 (September 2001), p. 3.

27. David Schrank and Tim Lomax, *The 2002 Urban Mobility Report* (College Station, Tex.:Texas Transportation Institute, June 2002), p. 56, exhibit A-2.

28. Shrank and Lomax, *The 2002 Urban Mobility Report;* Dallas Area Rapid Transit, *DART Annual Report for 2001* (www.dart.org.); and American Public Transportation Association, "Light Rail Transit Ridership Report—First Quarter 2002, Estimated Unlinked Passenger Trips" (www. apta.com).

29. American Public Transportation Association, "Tri-County Metropolitan Transportation District of Oregon," annual reports for 1996, 1998, and 2000. Bus ridership in the Portland system rose by 11.1 percent from 1996 to 1998, whereas the population of the Portland region increased between 1990 and 2000 at a compound annual growth rate of 2.3 percent. Hence the region's population rose about 5.8 percent in those two years, or less than the region's transit ridership grew. Therefore, it is reasonable to assume that bus ridership would have risen at least as fast as the regional population from 1996 to 2000 if the light rail system had not been expanded.

30. Ridership and track mileage data for the Portland light rail system from American Public Transit Association, "Tri-County Metropolitan Transportation District of Oregon," reports for 1996 and 2000 (www.apta.com). If 43,705 added daily trips on the light rail system came from auto commuters, that is about 21,852 such commuters each day. So the hypothetical total of auto commuters in 2000 without the light rail expansion would have the actual total of 804,866 plus those 21,852, or 826,568. The shift of 21, 852 to light rail is a reduction of 2.6 percent.

31. The 208,700 total includes an adjustment downward to make Census 2000 data comparable to Census 1990 data, because the Census 2000 data used an estimate of 1990 figures that was higher than the count made in 1990. Without that adjustment, the gain in workers from 1990 to 2000 would have been 226,957. However, this adjustment does not make any significant difference in the analysis results.

32. Texas Transportation Institute, *The 2002 Urban Mobility Report*, various pages.

33. Bureau of Transportation Statistics, "Summary of Federal, State, and Local Transportation Finance by Mode" (www.bts.gov [February 2004]). The analysis is further complicated because total annual revenues collected by governments for transportation purposes are smaller than total annual expenditures made by the same governments for those purposes. Thus, in 1999, according to the federal Bureau of Transportation Statistics, the three levels of government took in $126.9 billion for transportation purposes, but spent $154.8 billion. Since spending has a greater impact on transportation services

than raising revenues, this analysis focuses on transportation spending. Another complication is that the Federal Highway Administration, the Bureau of Transportation Statistics, the Federal Transit Administration, and the American Public Transit Association publish many different data series about federal, state, and local government transportation spending in general and highway and transit spending in particular. These series are not fully consistent with one another.

34. Department of Transportation, *National Transportation Statistics, 2001,* "Transportation and the Economy, Section D–Government Finance," chap. 3, table 3-29a. Most of the data in this section are taken from this publication, which is posted on the Bureau of Transportation Statistics website (www.bts. gov [February 2004]).

35. This situation is cogently analyzed in Martin Wachs, *Improving Efficiency and Equity in Transportation Finance* (Brookings Institution Center on Urban and Metropolitan Policy, April 2003).

36. Federal Highway Administration and Federal Transit Administration, "Compilation of Spending Data from Adopted Long-Range Plans for Selected Metropolitan Areas, 1990-2000" (Department of Transportation, May 2002). As reported in Urban Mobility Corporation, *Innovation Briefs,* vol. 13 (July-August 2002), p. 2.

37. Two other groups also strongly advocate expanding transit: manufacturers of transit equipment, such as passenger buses and subway cars, and urban planners and environmentalists who are opposed to continued low-density settlement growth.

38. Wendell Cox, "MTA Riders Hurt by Union Contracts," *Los Angeles Daily News,* op-ed, August 22, 1999. Cox was a member of the Los Angeles County Transportation Commission from 1977 to 1985. In this article, he states, "In 1979, transit costs per mile in Los Angeles were approximately the same as in San Diego. Since that time more than 40 percent of San Diego's bus service has been competitively contracted, and costs have dropped 28 percent (inflation adjusted). At the same time, Los Angeles costs have risen 36 percent. If Los Angeles had contained its costs as well as San Diego, the same level of bus service could be provided for approximately $300 million less annually and more than $4.2 billion would have been available for other uses since 1979." See also John Walters, "Bus-jacking the Revolution," *Policy Review* (January-February 1996).Walters points out that the 104 Congress amended the Federal Transit Act to reaffirm "section 13c for the 1964 Federal Transit Act, which stipulates that any public-transit worker 'negatively impacted' by competition may receive six years of salary and benefits. By seconding this mandate, the GOP-controlled Congress institutionalized the government monopoly in American mass transit and hurt the poor urban residents that the federal subsidies were designed to help."

39. Dennis Polhill and Matthew Edgar, "RTD Is Afraid of Private Sector Competition," Independence Institute, Colorado, August 22, 2001.

40. Pushkarev and Zupan, *Public Transportation and Land Use Policy.*

Chapter 10

1. William S. Vickrey and Herbert Mohring are among the pioneers in devising analyses that indicate a need for peak-hour road pricing in order to achieve economic efficiency. See William S. Vickrey, "Some Implications of Marginal Cost Pricing for Public Utilities," *American Economic Review, Papers and Proceedings*, vol. 45 (1955) pp. 605–20; and Vickrey, "General and Specific Financing of Urban Services," in Howard G. Schaller, ed., *Public Expenditure Decisions in the Urban Community* (Washington: Resources for the Future, 1963), pp. 62–90; Herbert Mohring, "Urban Highway Investments," in Robert Dorfman, ed., *Measuring Benefits of Government Investment* (Brookings, 1965), pp. 231–75; and Herbert Mohring, "The Peak-Load Problem with Increasing Returns and Pricing Constraints," *American Economic Review*, vol. 60 (September 1970), pp. 693–705. For a brief bibliography of more recent articles on peak-hour road pricing see Kenneth A. Small, Clifford Winston, and Carol A. Evans, *Road Work: A New Highway Pricing and Investment Policy* (Brookings 1989), p. 87, notes 16–19.

2. In this discussion, collective costs are those experienced by an entire group, as opposed to individual costs. Where the time losses are caused by traffic congestion, both collective and individual losses are private costs, experienced by individuals, rather than social costs experienced by society as a whole, including groups and individuals. Hence collective costs can be private or social, whereas individual costs are always private. The capital costs of building more road capacity because of congestion are social costs if they are borne by society as a whole through general government expenditures.

3. Clifford Winston pointed out this distinction.

4. Tim Hau of the World Bank provided current information about which cities have adopted partial road pricing and which are considering broader systems (letter to the author).

5. Clifford Winston and Chad Shirley, *Alternate Route: Toward Efficient Urban Transportation* (Brookings, 1998), pp. 107–08.

6. See Elaine Murakami and Jennifer Young, "Daily Travel by Persons with Low Income," paper presented at Nationwide Personal Transportation Survey Symposium, Md., 1997, table 1 (http://npts.ornl.gov/npts/1995/Doc/LowInc.pdf [December 2003]). "Low-income" in this study was defined as under $10,000 per year for 1-2 person households, under $20,000 for 3-4 person households, and under $25,000 for households containing 5 or more persons.

7. Ibid., figure 2.

8. Data from a presentation made by Mark F. Muriello of the New York and New Jersey Port Authority at the Value Pricing Conference, sponsored by the Metropolitan Washington Council of Governments, Washington, 2003 (www. mwcog.org/pricingconference/presentations/Muriello.ppt [December 2003]).

9. C. Kenneth Orski, "Congestion Pricing: Promise and Limitations," remarks at the 1991 National Planning Conference, New Orleans, p. 8.

10. Small, Winston, and Evans, *Road Work*, p. 95.

11. Kenneth Small, University of California at Irvine, has suggested this policy.

12. Patrick DeCorla-Souza is an official with the Federal Highway Administration. He can be reached at patrick.decorla-souza@fhwa.dot.gov.

13. Kenneth A. Small, "The Incidence of Congestion Tolls on Urban Highways," *Journal of Urban Economics,* vol. 13 (January 1983), pp. 90–111.

14. Letter from Herbert Mohring, May 12, 1991. "Plowing congestion tolls back into road improvements is not necessarily efficient. Presume zero population and travel growth, infinitely durable roads, and an optimally designed road network. Marginal-cost tolls would then function as a normal return on the resources that society has invested in its road network. Efficiency would dictate using road-user tolls just as any other source of government revenues. Efficiency would not dictate spending these revenues on road improvements."

15. Another technique is called automatic vehicle identification (AVI). Electronic transponders are placed in or on each vehicle. Electronic sensors on which peak-hour prices are to be registered are buried in the roadways. Computers are used to track vehicle movements, calculate charges, and mail periodic bills to vehicle owners. One such system has been successfully demonstrated in Hong Kong. A small electronic number plate (ENP) the size of an audio- or videotape cassette is easily fitted onto the underside of any motor vehicle. The ENP needs no power from within the vehicle and can easily be removed, so the system will work only if drivers willingly leave their ENPs in place. When a vehicle passes over a buried loop, power from the loop energizes the ENP and causes it to transmit an identity signal back to the loop. This signal is transmitted to the central computer, which then calculates the appropriate charges for each vehicle, prepares a monthly or weekly bill, and sends it to the owner. Another device offered a means of identifying vehicles that crossed the loops but did not have ENPs. Identifying vehicles is vital in this system in order to catch drivers trying to use priced streets during peak hours without paying. The demonstration used closed circuit television cameras to photograph the rear license plates of any such vehicles. Once taken, these photos were transmitted to the system's control center, along with data concerning where and when they were taken. For a detailed description see Ian Catling and Brian J. Harbord, "Electronic Road-Pricing in Hong Kong: 2. The Technology," *Traffic Engineering + Control,* vol. 26 (December 1985), pp. 608–15.

16. Tim Hau provided this information about why the Hong Kong experiment was not extended into a permanent system.

17. Two analyses that have been done are Jose A. Gomez-Ibanez and Gary R. Fauth, "Downtown Auto Restraint Policies: The Costs and Benefits for Boston," *Journal of Transport Economics and Policy*, vol. 14 (May 1980), pp. 133–53; and Marvin Kraus, "The Welfare Gains from Pricing Road Congestion Using Automatic Vehicle Identification and On-Vehicle Meters," *Journal of Urban Economics*, vol. 25, no. 3 (1989), pp. 261–81.

18. Two studies from which much of this information has been drawn are Edward Sullivan, "Continuation Study to Evaluate the Impacts of the SR 91 Value-Priced Express Lanes: Final Report, Executive Summary" (Sacramento: State of California Department of Transportation, December 2000); and Edward Sullivan, "Evaluating the Impacts of the SR 91 Variable-Toll Express Lane Facility: Final Report" (Sacramento: State of California Department of Transportation, May 1998). For both reports http://ceenve.calpoly.edu/ (December 2003).

19. Patrick DeCorla-Souza of the Federal Highway Administration has suggested a form of HOT lanes he calls "FAIR Lanes," which stands for "fast and intertwined regular lanes." He advocates separating the lanes on existing expressways into two types: fast and regular. On the fast lanes, "fast, frequent, and high quality bus, jitney, and limousine-type para-transit services are provided. These services are subsidized using revenues obtained from tolls charged to low-occupancy vehicles for premium express service on the fast lanes. Carpools and vanpools with four or more persons are permitted to use the fast lanes free of charge" (e-mail from Patrick DeCorla-Souza, September 12, 2001). Regular lanes would remain congested, but drivers would be compensated with toll credits that could be used in the fast lanes. The toll costs of these credits would be funded from toll revenues collected on the fast lanes from low-occupancy vehicles. Since low-income users of the congested regular lanes would thus be receiving credits, which they could also use for bus fares and other transportation-related expenses, they would not regard being relegated to congested lanes as nearly as unfair as with "normal" peak-hour road pricing.

20. Robert W. Poole Jr. and C. Kenneth Orski, "HOT Networks: A New Plan for Congestion Relief and Better Transit," Reason Foundation Policy Study 305 (Los Angeles: Reason Foundation, February 2003).

21. This system is described in detail in David J. Forkenbrock and Jon G. Kuhl, *A New Approach to Assessing Road User Charges* (University of Iowa, Public Policy Center, 2002).

22. The Puget Sound Regional Council has initiated a demonstration project using this scheme that has been funded by the Federal Highway Administration. The project will put in-vehicle computers tied to GPS satellites in a selected group of private vehicles and charge the owners varying amounts per mile

driven, depending on what roads they use. Those charges will be subtracted from an initial balance placed in each participant's account, with the participants getting to keep whatever amount is left over in that account when the project is over. So the participants will have an incentive to respond to road prices without being charged overall for being part of the project. The driving behavior of a control group that does not have the equipment or such an account will be compared with that of the experimental group to determine to what extent drivers' behavior can be influenced by varying charges on specific roads. See Puget Sound Regional Council, "Transportation Pricing Demonstration Project," Issue Paper 4, February 2002 (www.psrc.org/projects/pricing/demo.pdf [July 2002]). I am indebted to Martin Wachs for pointing out this project.

23. Ng Guan Sim and Michael Li Zhifeng, "Singapore Road Pricing Scheme: Is Three Dollars Really Too High?" Nanyang Business School, Nanyang Technological University, Singapore (www.ntu.edu.sg/nbs/publications/regional_issues_in_economics/11-ngs96.pdf [December 2003]).

24. Todd Litman, "London Congestion Pricing: Implications for Other Cities," Victoria Transport Policy Institute, June 30, 2003 (www.vtpi.org/london.pdf [December 2003]).

25. Data for 2000 from Transport for London, "Congestion Charging 6 Months On," October 2003 (www.tfl.gov.uk/tfl/downloads/pdf/congestion-charging/cc-6monthson.pdf [December 2003]).

26. Ibid.

27. Information about the Lee County bridges came mainly from Leeway, a website sponsored by Lee County that describes how the variable pricing system works. See http://leewayinfo.com/index2.htm. and www.cutr.usf.edu/its/varprice.htm. Additional information was from notes I made at a conference at which John Albion of the Lee County Commission spoke about this subject.

28. See www.trafficcalming.org; and Federal Highway Administration, Office of Highway Policy Information, *Highway Statistics 2001* and *Highway Statistics Summary to 1995*, tables on highway finance (www.fhwa.dot.gov/policy/ohpi/hss/hsspubs.htm [December 2003]).

29. Martin Wachs, *Improving Efficiency and Equity in Transportation Finance*, Transportation Reform series (Brookings Institution Center on Urban and Metropolitan Policy, April 2003); and Robert Puentes and Ryan Prince, *Fueling Transportation Finance: A Primer on the Gas Tax*, Transportation Reform series (Brookings Institution Center on Urban and Metropolitan Policy, March 2003).

30. See Reid H. Ewing, *Traffic Calming: State of the Practice*, FHWA-RD-99-135 (U.S. Department of Transportation, Federal Highway Administration, 1999) (www.ite.org/traffic/tcstate.htm#tcsop [December 2003]).

31. Small, Winston, and Evans, *Road Work*, p. 97.

Chapter 11

1. Federal Highway Administration, *Our Nation's Travel: 1995 Nationwide Personal Transportation Survey, Early Results Report* (Department of Transportation, September 1997), p. 14. These data are somewhat misleading because trips with more than one purpose were counted as separate trips for each purpose, rather than a single trip. This probably understates the importance of work trips, which are often "chained" with other purposes.

2. Federal Transit Administration, Office of Technical Assistance and Safety, *TDM Status Report: Telecommuting*, prepared by K.T. Analytics (Department of Transportation, August 1992).

3. International Telework Association and Council, "Number of Teleworkers Increases by 17 Percent," ITAC press release, October 3, 2001 (www.telecommute.org). The survey was conducted by the Social Science Research Center of Old Dominion University and covered 1,170 randomly selected households after excluding all business phone numbers.

4. Bureau of the Census, *2000 Census Demographic Profiles: 100 Percent and Sample Data, Demographic Profile Search, U.S. Summary*, table DP-3. The 2000 Census reported that 3.26 percent of all workers 16 and over worked at home, but this figure presumably refers to those working at home all of the time and not employed elsewhere.

5. Judy Davis, "Portland Moves Ahead in Transit-Related Development," *Seattle Daily Journal of Commerce*, "Design '97" (www.djc.com [January 2004]).

6. Robert T. Dunphy and Ben C. Lin, *Transportation Management through Partnerships* (Washington: Urban Land Institute, 1990), pp. 159–60.

7. See COMSIS Corporation, *Evaluation of Travel Demand Management Measures to Relieve Congestion* (Department of Transportation, 1990).

8. Ibid.

9. Bureau of Labor Statistics, Consumer Expenditure Survey, "Income before Taxes," table 46 (www.bls.gov/cex/2002/share/income.pdf [January 2004]).

10. Data from Energy Information Agency, Department of Energy (www.eia.doe.gov [January 2004]).

11. A recent estimate of the price elasticity of gasoline was made by Hemanta Shrestha, Bobur Alimov, and Stanley McMillen of the University of Connecticut in *The Economic Impact of the Proposed Gasoline Tax Cut in Connecticut*, June 21, 2000 (http://ccea.uconn.edu ([January 2004]). Their estimate of price elasticity was −0.512975. Other recent estimates found on the Internet vary widely. They tend to be low for short-run estimates and rise as the time period increases. Therefore, the analysis in the text must be considered an approximation.

12. Department of Energy, *U.S. Retail Gasoline Prices* (www.eia.doe.gov).

13. This extrapolation assumes that the "point elasticity" of −0.51 estimate would remain valid over a large range of change.

14. "U.S. Automobile and Truck Motor Sales, 1970-2002" (www.senate. state.mi.us ([January 2004]).

15. John Pucher, "Urban Travel Behavior as the Outcome of Public Policy: The Example of Modal-Split in Western Europe and North America," *American Planning Association Journal*, vol. 54 (Autumn 1988), pp. 509–19.

16. www.expatsingapore.com/once/usedcar.shtml (January 2004).

17. Donald Shoup, "Evaluating the Effects of Cashing Out Employer-Paid Parking: Eight Case Studies," *Transport Policy*, vol. 4 (October 1997), pp. 201–16, quotation on p. 213.

18. Ibid.

19. Congressional Budget Office, "High-Tech Highways: Intelligent Transportation Systems and Policy," October 1995 (www.cbo.gov [January 2004]).

20. Intelligent Transportation Systems of America, *ITS America News* (August 2002), p. 8.

21. Lloyd Batzler, "All Over the Road," *Technews.com* (April 19, 2002).

22. The activities listed in the text were taken from Congressional Budget Office, "High-Tech Highways: Intelligent Transportation Systems and Policy," October 1995 (www.cbo.gov [January 2004]).

Chapter 12

1. See Robert Burchell, Anthony Downs, and others, *Costs of Sprawl 2000*, TCRP Report 74 (Washington: Transit Cooperative Research Program, 2002), for estimates of cost savings of many types from shifting less than half of all future growth from "sprawl" to "compact" development.

2. For example, see "The Loss of Community," in James Howard Kunstler, *The Geography of Nowhere* (Simon and Schuster, 1993), chap. 10.

3. A detailed discussion of these two measures of density and the relationships between them is presented in appendix C.

4. That growth rate over 10 years equals a compound annual growth rate of 4.26 percent.

5. Real Estate Research Corporation, *The Costs of Sprawl: Detailed Cost Analysis* (Washington, April 1974).

6. Cross commuting occurs when most people who live near job site A work at other sites—say, B through F—quite distant from their homes and from site A, whereas most people who reside close to job sites B through F work in other job sites—including site A—quite distant from their homes. Cross-commuting workers choose job and home locations that generate much longer-than-minimal commuting journeys. Consequently, many such commuters pass one another going to and from their homes and jobs each day.

7. Boris S. Pushkarev and Jeffrey M. Zupan, *Public Transportation and Land Use Policy* (Indiana University Press, 1977).

8. Concerning age, the higher the proportion of working adults as opposed to children or the elderly, the higher the area's incidence of automobile ownership and therefore the lower the propensity of residents to use transit.

9. The availability of commuter rail tends to increase the usage of public transit.

10. East-West Gateway Coordinating Council, "Demographic Patterns of the St. Louis Region as Reflected by the 2000 Census—Higher Public Transit Usage," January 21, 2003 (www.ewgateway.org/ourregion/trendicators/demopat-2000/DemoPat-PubTransit/demopat-pubtransit.htm [December 2003]).

11. University of South Florida, Center for Transportation Research, *Public Transit in America: Findings from the 1995 Nationwide Personal Transportation Survey*, NUT14-USF-4 (September 1998).

12. The independent variables were the population density of the MSA's central city, the percentage of all MSA workers living in the central city, the percentage of the total MSA population consisting of employed workers, and the total population of the MSA in 2000. If New York is included, only density and the percentage of all MSA workers employed within the city are statistically significant. If New York is excluded, the percentage of workers in the total MSA population also becomes significant. Central city population (including New York) has simple correlations of 0.782 with the percentage of MSA workers using transit, and 0.528 with the percentage of central city workers using transit.

13. Pushkarev and Zupan, *Public Transportation and Land Use Policy*, p. 177.

14. Computed as 7 units per net acre times 2.5 persons per unit times 320 acres. If only 30 percent of the land is used for housing, the gross density figure could be as low as 3,360 persons per square mile. But if 70 percent of the land is used for housing, that figure would be 7,840 persons per square mile.

15. See Gary Delsohn, "The First Pedestrian Pocket," *Planning Magazine*, vol. 55 (December 1989), pp. 20–22.

16. This point was taken from Dena Belzer and Gerald Autler, *Transit Oriented Development: Moving from Rhetoric to Reality* (Discussion Paper for the Brookings Institution Center on Urban and Metropolitan Policy and the Great American Station Foundation, June 2002), especially pp. 21–22.

17. Frederick Ducca pointed out this relationship.

18. The residential densities used in this analysis have been taken from the 2000 Census whenever possible. These are gross residential densities—that is, residents per square mile—including all the land within the borders of the community in the base of square miles counted. All the residents of each community are counted as living at the average gross density for that community. The land areas for individual communities used to compute densities have been taken from 1990 Census data. Most such land areas have not changed since 2000, but some have increased. In those instances, these data would overestimate the densities, since land areas would be larger but the population data are current.

19. The Census Bureau cuts off the edges of fringe areas at densities of around 1,000 persons per square mile. Hence few urbanized areas have fringes with average densities below that level. See U.S. Bureau of the Census, *Cartographic Boundary Files: Urbanized Areas* (www.census.gov).

20. The overall average density is computed by dividing the total population of the group by the total area of the group. The average individual density among members of the group is the average of all the individual densities in the group. In this case, the average individual density among fringe areas is 3,048, compared to the overall average density of 2,858.

21. Because of anomalies in the data, four urbanized areas have been omitted from much of this discussion (except total population figures). They are Jacksonville, Nashville, Oklahoma City, and San Antonio. All have very large central cities—two of which have been merged with surrounding counties—and this distorts their fringe area statistics.

22. See appendix C.

23. In this table, only Los Angeles is considered a central city in this urbanized area. Hence the population and area of the city of Los Angeles are not included in these data, but the population and area of the city of Long Beach are included.

24. Because these two counties are partly suburbs of Los Angeles and Orange counties, all of the cities in Riverside and San Bernardino county urbanized areas have been counted as suburbs—including Riverside and San Bernardino. Hence the populations and areas of those two cities are included in the table for these counties.

25. In table 12-4, data for the cities of San Francisco, Oakland, and San Jose have been excluded because these cities are considered central cities of their respective urbanized areas.

26. See Advisory Commission on Regulatory Barriers to Affordable Housing, *Not In My Back Yard: Removing Barriers to Affordable Housing* (Washington, 1991). This conclusion was more recently confirmed by the Millennial Housing Commission appointed by Congress in December 2000. Its report, *Meeting Our Nation's Housing Challenges* (Washington, May 20, 2002) is on the commission's website (www.mhc.org).

27. Gerald A. Carlino, "From Decentralization to Deconcentration: People and Jobs Spread Out," *Business Review* (Philadelphia: Federal Reserve Bank of Philadelphia, November-December 2000), pp. 15–27.

28. When the January temperature was used as an independent variable, the number of cases fell from 351 to 141 because data were not easily available on the January temperatures of many urbanized areas. Removing the January temperature from the regression increased the number of cases to 351 but dropped the adjusted r-squared to 0.6594 and rendered the total area of the urbanized area in 1990 statistically insignificant.

29. This subject is analyzed in more depth in chapter 17. The Advisory Commission on Regulatory Barriers to Affordable Housing concluded that existing exclusionary land-use policies adopted by local governments could best be changed through state governments' adopting statewide regulations requiring reexamination and alteration of such policies. See the commission's *Not In My Back Yard*, pp. 7-1 to 7-15, 13-16.

30. Under some circumstances, urban growth boundaries may also raise land and housing prices within the boundaries faster than they would otherwise rise and keep land prices outside the boundaries from rising as fast as they otherwise would. For discussions of their nature and effects, see Gerrit J. Knaap and Arthur C. Nelson, "The Effects of Regional Land-Use Control in Oregon: A Theoretical and Empirical Review," *Review of Regional Studies*, vol. 18 (Spring 1988), pp. 37–46, and Anthony Downs, "Have Housing Prices Risen Faster in Portland than Elsewhere?" *Housing Policy Debate*, vol. 13 (Spring 2002), pp. 7–31.

31. For a discussion, see Richard B. Peiser, "Density and Urban Sprawl," *Land Economics*, vol. 65 (August 1989), pp. 193–204.

32. See Advisory Commission on Reducing Regulatory Barriers to Affordable Housing, *Not In My Back Yard*, p. 8-2. The fifteen studies are listed on p. 8-11, note 1.

33. George Galster, "Review of the Literature on Impacts of Affordable and Multi-Family Housing on Market Values of Nearby Single-Family Homes," paper presented at a symposium on the Relationships between Affordable Housing and Growth Management, Brookings, May 2003.

Chapter 13

1. A description of jobs-housing imbalances, how they arise, and their negative effects is presented by Robert Cervero in "Jobs-Housing Balance and Regional Mobility," *American Planning Association Journal*, vol. 55 (Spring 1989), pp. 136–50, reprinted in Lincoln Institute for Land Policy, *Achieving a Jobs-Housing Balance: Land-Use Planning for Regional Growth, Resource Manual 1991* (Cambridge, Mass.: 1991), sec. 2.2.

2. Cervero, "Jobs-Housing Balance and Regional Mobility," p. 137.

3. Southern California Association of Governments, *The New Economy and Jobs/Housing Balance in Southern California* (Los Angeles: SCAG, April 2001).

4. Arnold Sherwood, "Job/Housing Balance," in Lincoln Institute for Land Policy, *Achieving a Jobs-Housing Balance*, sec. 2.5. The "targets" adopted by SCAG were to shift 9 percent of all new jobs into areas with a housing surplus and 5 percent of all new housing into areas with a job surplus. See Martin Wachs, "Thought Piece on the Jobs/Housing Balance," in Lincoln Institute for Land Policy, *Achieving a Jobs-Housing Balance*, sec. 2.4.

5. See Southern California Association of Governments, *The New Economy and Jobs/Housing Balance in Southern California*, p. 10.

6. See the Application Package for this program (www.hcd.ca.gov/ca/jhbig/ jhbig [December 2003]).

7. Richard T. LeGates, "Housing Incentives to Promote Inter-Regional Jobs-Housing Balance," January 2001 (www.abag.ca.gov/planning/interregional/pdf/ housing_incentives.pdf [December 2003]).

8. Data on California jobs from the Bureau of Labor Statistics website (www.bls.gov [December 2003]). State and local area employment and earnings from *California Statistical Abstract, 2001*, prepared by California Department of Finance Economic Research Unit (Sacramento, 2001), pp. 24–26. Population data for California from *California Statistical Abstract, 2001*, pp. 10–12. For the entire state, which is self-contained insofar as workers are concerned, there have typically been 20 to 25 percent more jobs than households from 1950 through 2000. Hence a local area "jobs-housing balance" based on state data would consist of the local area's having 20 to 25 percent more jobs than households, presumably because each household contains more than one worker. This indicates that the Riverside-San Bernardino counties area, which has more households than jobs, is still in a housing surplus condition. That is surely because it serves as a bedroom area for many workers employed in Orange and Los Angeles counties, as noted in the text.

9. Southern California Association of Governments, *The New Economy and Jobs/Housing Balance in Southern California*, p. 9.

10. U.S. Bureau of the Census, *Statistical Abstract of the United States: 2001* (2001), p. 430.

11. See Robert Burchell, Anthony Downs, Samuel Seskin, and others, *The Costs of Sprawl 2000* (Transit Cooperative Research Board, 2002), pp. 448–56.

12. Ibid.

13. National Association of Realtors, *Real Estate Outlook: Market Trends and Insights*, vol. 10 (April 2003), pp. 18–19.

14. City of Boulder Planning Department, "Jobs to Population Balance: A Literature Review and Summary of How Other Communities Have Addressed Jobs to Population Imbalances," Boulder, Colorado, July 10, 2002 (www.ci. boulder.co.us/buildingservices/jobs_to_pop/documents/Jobs-Pop%20in%20Other %20Cities4.pdf [December 2003]). This document reviews actions taken by many other localities to correct job-housing imbalances.

15. Robert B. Zehner, *Access, Travel, and Transportation in New Communities* (Ballinger, 1977).

16. Cervero, "Jobs-Housing Balancing," p. 138.

17. Hamilton, Rabinovitz, and Alschuler, "Thinking about Jobs-Housing Balance in Los Angeles," in Lincoln Institute for Land Policy, *Achieving a Jobs-Housing Balance*, sec. 3.3.

18. U.S. Bureau of the Census, *Statistical Abstract of the United States: 2001*, p. 28.

19. See Larry P. Arnn, "Jobs-Housing Balance: Too Good to Be True, Too Easy to Be Good—Some Lessons for the Inland Empire," *Golden State Briefings* (Montclair, Calif.: Claremont Institute, 1990).

20. Giuliano, "Is Jobs-Housing Balance a Transportation Issue?" pp. 14–15.

Chapter 14

1. See Anthony Downs, "What Does 'Smart Growth' Really Mean?" *Journal of the American Planning Association*, vol. 67 (April 2001), pp. 20–25.

2. Appendix E explores the feasibility of slowing down a region's peripheral growth by concentrating a significant portion of its future population growth in such areas.

3. IBI Group in association with various consultants, *Summary Report: Greater Toronto Area Urban Structure Concepts Study* (Greater Toronto Coordinating Committee, June 1990).

4. The Greater Toronto Area planning process is described in "How Many People Will There Be in the GTA?" (www.city.toronto.on.ca/torontoplan/pdf/flash_sec2.pdf [December 2003]).

5. Peter Gordon, Harry Richardson, and Genevieve Giuliano, *Travel Trends in Non-CBD Activity Centers* (University of Southern California, School of Urban and Regional Planning, 1989), p. 16.

6. Robert E. Lang, *Edgeless Cities* (Brookings, 2003), p. 77.

7. Edward L. Glaeser, Matthew Kahn, and Chenghuan Chu, *Job Sprawl: Employment Location in U.S. Metropolitan Areas* (Brookings Institution Center on Urban and Metropolitan Policy, May 2001).

8. The term *edge city* was coined by Joel Garreau, *Edge Cities: Life on the New Frontier* (Macmillan, 1991), p. 4.

9. The Twin Cities region in Minnesota has adopted regional sharing of commercial property assessed values as a means of reducing competition among communities for "ratables" and increasing the fairness of how local taxing resources are distributed. However, this is the only region in the nation that has adopted such an extensive sharing arrangement.

10. U.S. Bureau of the Census, *United States Census 2000: Demographic Profiles* (www.census.gov/prod/cen2000/dp1/2khus.pdf [December 2003]). See individual tables for each of the twenty-three regions.

11. U.S. Bureau of the Census, 2000 Census, STF3, detailed tables (www.factfinder.census.gov [December 2003]).

12. Some bus systems in less developed nations operate profitably. So do a few fixed-rail systems, such as those in Hong Kong and Singapore. But these are exceptional.

Chapter 15

1. The literature on growth management and growth management laws is too vast to cite extensively here. Hence only a few citations are made to highly relevant portions.

2. See Robert Cervero, *Suburban Gridlock* (Center for Urban Policy Research of Rutgers University, 1986); Madelyn Glickfield and Ned Levine, *The New Land-Use Regulation "Revolution": Why California's Local Jurisdictions Enact Growth Control and Management Measures* (University of California at Los Angeles Extension Public Policy Program, June 22, 1990); and Elizabeth Deakin, "Land Use and Transportation Planning in Response to Congestion: A Review and Critique," paper prepared for the annual meeting of the Transportation Research Board, 1989.

3. City of Boulder Planning Department, "Jobs to Population Balance: A Literature Review and Summary of How Other Communities Have Addressed Jobs to Population Imbalances," Boulder, July 10, 2002. This document reviews actions taken by many other localities to correct jobs-housing imbalances.

4. For a discussion of whether Florida's concurrency laws can work well, see Anthony Downs, "Why Florida's Concurrency Principles (for Controlling New Development by Regulating Road Construction) Do Not—and Cannot—Work Effectively," *Transportation Quarterly*, vol. 57 (Winter 2003), pp. 13–18.

5. See Glickfield and Levine, *New Land Use Regulation "Revolution."*

6. See William Fischel, *The Homevoter Hypothesis* (Harvard University Press, 2001), for an analysis of why local governments tend to adopt policies that local homeowners believe will increase the values of their homes.

7. See Seymour I. Schwartz, David E. Hanson, and Richard D. Green, "Suburban Growth Controls and the Price of Housing," *Journal of Environmental Economics and Management*, vol. 8 (December 1981), pp. 303–20; and Lawrence Katz and Kenneth T. Rosen, "The Interjurisdictional Effects of Growth Controls on Housing Prices, " *Journal of Law and Economics*, vol. 30 (April 1987), pp. 149–60.

8. This point was taken in part from the analysis of growth management policies carried out by William Fischel. See "What Do Economists Know about Growth Controls? A Research Review," in David J. Brower, David R. Godschalk, and Douglas R. Porter, eds., *Understanding Growth Management: Critical Issues and a Research Agenda* (Washington: Urban Land Institute, 1989), pp. 59–86.

9. Or perhaps *because of* higher prices, since the higher prices are a sign of greater exclusivity—and therefore a desirable attribute for people seeking exclusivity.

10. This discussion is based in part on Anthony Downs, "What Does 'Smart Growth' Really Mean?" American Planning Association, *Planning Magazine*, vol. 67 (April 2001), pp. 20–25.

11. Members of the other three groups may also support more compact growth, but this term has been selected because persons in this group are not trying to limit the amount of future growth, are not trying to promote more future growth than current trends would produce, and are not focused primarily on central city conditions but want the growth likely from current trends to occur in more compact patterns.

12. See chapter 9 for an analysis of the formidable overall challenges of greatly increasing public transit use.

13. See chapter 12 for a detailed analysis of the effects of higher-density development on traffic congestion.

Chapter 16

1. However, the competitiveness of their regions against many foreign regions is being undermined by other factors, especially lower labor costs.

2. True, there is immense variability among people, both within any given society and among societies, on their allocation of time each day to traveling. Yet people's desire to limit their total travel time to some "target" amount is widespread, even if "targets" vary among individuals.

3. Andreas Schafer, D. Victor, and Robert W. Johnson Jr., "The Future Mobility of the World Population," in *Transportation Research A*, Part A 34 (2000), pp. 171–205. Slides from this article were presented at the Transportation Vision 2050 Futurist Workshop, Washington, 2000. The figures cited are *group* average travel times for each location surveyed. Individual travel times varied considerably more than these group averages did.

4. Patricia Mokhtarian and Ilan Salomon, "How Derived Is the Demand for Travel? Some Conceptual and Measurement Considerations," UCD-ITS-REP-01-15 (University of California at Davis, Institute of Transportation Studies, 2001).

5. Data for gross national product per capita were taken from U.S. Bureau of the Census, *Statistical Abstract of the United Sates: 2002* (2002), p. 833. Data on the number of vehicles per 1,000 residents were taken from International Road Federation, *World Road Statistics 2002* (Geneva, 2002), global CD.

6. International Road Federation, *World Road Statistics 2002*, global CD.

7. These numbers are approximate because they were taken by eye from a graph. See Office of Transportation Technologies, "World Vehicle Sales, 1960–2020," Fact Sheet 147 (Department of Energy, November 6, 2000).

8. The nations included in the road survey but omitted from the vehicle population survey are Bahamas, Bosnia and Herzegovina, Dominica, Grenada, Guyana, Kiribati, Macedonia, Micronesia, Monaco, Nauru, Saint Kitt and Nevis, Saint Vincent and the Grenadines, Turkmenistan, Tuvalu, and Uzbekistan. Trinidad and Tobago is the only nation included in the vehicle population survey but not the road survey.

9. Data from auto industry, "World Vehicle Production since 1990," Economist Intelligence Unit (www.autoindustry.co.uk/statistics/production/world.html [January 2004]).

10. See note 7.

11. Data from United Kingdom Commission for Integrated Transport, "Published Reports: European Best Practice in Transport—Bench marking, Section III. Inputs and Outputs" (www.cfit.gov.uk/reports/ebptbench/03.htm [January 2004]).

12. Sutharsan Ganesan, "Rumble in Calcutta—City of Joy," October 31, 1997 (http://calcuttapolice.org/site/calcutta_traffic.htm [January 2004]).

13. Meera Smith, "Bakul: The Victim of Sacrifice" (www.prabasi.org/Literary/Shankha/Spring00/Item1_sp00.html ([January 2004]).

14. Kanchit Pianuan, Mingsarn Snatikarn Kaosa-ard, and Piyanuch Pienchob, "Bangkok Traffic Congestion: Is There a Solution?" *TDRI Quarterly Review*, vol. 9 (June 1994), pp. 20–23.

15. Thomas L. Friedman, "Bangkok Bogs Down," *New York Times,* March 20, 1996, sec. A, p. 19.

16. G. Giuliano, "Urban Travel Patterns," in B. Hoyle and R. Knowles, eds., *Modern Transport Geography*, 2d ed. (John Wiley and Sons, 1998).

17. Christian Gerondeau, "Moving People and Goods in Europe," Driving America Conference, highway users' national conference on mobility, Washington, 1999.

18. P. B. Goodwin, "Solving Congestion," Centre for Transport Studies, University College London, October 23, 1997 (www.ucl.ac.uk/tsu/pbginau.htm [January 2004]).

19. American Public Transit Association, "People on the Go: Mass Transit around the World, Case Study: Tokyo, Japan—A City in Motion," p. 3 (www.worldatlases.com).

20. Tang Yuankai, "Sound Transportation Network Makes Travel Easier in Beijing" (www.bjreview.com.cn). See also "Bikes Banned on Beijing Street," *China Energy Efficiency Information Bulletin*, vol. 4 (November 1998) (www.pnl.gov/china).

21. Ian Thompson and Alberto Bull, "Urban Traffic Congestion: The Scourge of Latin American Cities," *CEPAL Review*, no. 76 (April 2002), p.112.

22. Summarized by an article by Donella Meadows, "The City of First Priorities," *Whole Earth Review* (Spring 1995) (www.globalideasbank.org./BI/BI-262.html ([January 2004]).

23. Milton Keynes Chamber of Commerce, "About Milton Keynes and North Bucks" (www.mk-chamber.co.uk./aboutchamber/key facts.asp ([January 2004]).

24. Intelligent Speed Adaptation (www.ertico.com). Notes 24 through 28 are from ERTICO-Intelligent Transport Systems (ITS) (January 2004).

25. Autoroute-Info (www.ertico.com).

26. Intelligent Traffic Guidance System (www.ertico.com).

27. On-demand bus services on a variable route (www.ertico.com).

28. Motorway Control System (www.ertico.com/its_basi/succstor).

Chapter 17

1. Raising gasoline taxes would be most effective if done by the federal government, rather than by state governments, because many metropolitan areas contain parts of more than one state or are quite close to another state. If one state increased its gasoline tax to a level much higher than that in a nearby state, motorists would patronize service stations in the states with the lower prices. That would vitiate the impact of the tax increase and economically injure service stations in the state that raised taxes. Among the metropolitan areas or consolidated regions that cross state lines are New York City, Boston, Philadelphia, Chicago, Minneapolis-St. Paul, St. Louis, Kansas City, Cincinnati, Providence, Washington, D.C., and Portland, Oregon. States in which major population centers are relatively distant from neighboring states could successfully avoid this problem. Probably the most important such states are California, Florida, and Texas, in which a sizable share of U.S. population growth has occurred since 1970.

2. Kathryn A. Foster, *Regionalism on Purpose* (Cambridge: Lincoln Institute of Land Policy, 2001), p. 18.

3. Martin Wachs and Jennifer Dill, "Regionalism in Transportation and Air Quality: History, Interpretation, and Insights for Regional Governance," in A. Altshuler, W. Morrill, H. Wolman, and F. Mitchell, eds., *Governance and Opportunity in Metropolitan America* (Washington: National Academy Press, 1999), p. 261.

4. Ibid., p. 262.

5. Ibid., pp. 253–80. The authors were referring to Brian D. Taylor, "Unjust Equity: An Examination of California's Transportation Development Act," *Transportation Research Record No. 1297* (1991), pp. 85–92.

6. Sternlieb was a colleague and friend. He made this statement on many occasions.

7. These evaluations include U.S. Advisory Commission on Intergovernmental Relations, *MPO Capacity: Improving the Capacity of Metropolitan Planning Organizations to Help Implement National Transportation Policies*, A-130 (Washington, May 1995); W. M. Lyons, *The FTA-FHWA MPO Reviews—Planning Practice under the ISTEA and the CAAA* (Washington: Federal Transit Administration, n.d.) (www.fta.dot.gov/library/planning/ftafhwa/fta.html [January 2004]); and Paul S. Dempsey, Andrew Goetz, and Carl Larson, *Metropolitan Planning Organizations: An Assessment of the Transportation Planning Process* (University of Denver and Mississippi State University, 1998).

8. Dempsey, Goetz, and Larson, *Metropolitan Planning Organizations*, executive summary, p. 3.

9. Ibid., pp. 3–4.

10. Ibid., pp. 5–6.

11. www.planning.dot.gov (January 2004).

12. Foster, *Regionalism on Purpose*, p.1.

13. Ibid., p. 9.

14. Ibid; and Anthony Downs, *Stuck in Traffic: Coping with Peak-Hour Traffic Congestion* (Brookings and Lincoln Institute of Land Policy, 1992), chap. 10.

15. Some parts of interstate highways do charge tolls. They are mainly portions incorporated into the system from pre-existing toll roads. Examples are the Pennsylvania Toll Road, the Ohio Toll Road, the toll road system around Chicago, and the parts of Interstate 95 through Delaware. However, the federal government is now very reluctant to permit placing tolls on any additional parts of the interstate system.

16. For a study of bureaucratic resistance to change, see Anthony Downs, *Inside Bureaucracy* (Little, Brown, 1967).

17. California Environmental Protection Agency, Air Resources Board, "LEV II—Amendments to California's Low-Emission Vehicle Regulations" (www.arb. ca.gov [January 2004]).

18. This list is taken from David R. Godschalk, "Smart Growth Efforts around the Nation," in *Growing Smart in North Carolina*, a special issue of *Popular Government*, vol. 66 (Fall 2000), p. 17. Godschalk included Georgia and Vermont in his list, but they have been omitted because local government participation in their plans is voluntary.

19. Alexis de Toqueville, *Democracy in America*, vol. 1 (Knopf, 1972), p. 198. This tendency was more recently celebrated in Robert N. Bellah and others, *Habits of the Heart: Individualism and Commitment in American Life* (Harper and Row, 1985).

20. The processes most useful for creating and managing such organizations are comprehensively analyzed in Lawrence Susskind, Sarah McKeranan, and Jennifer Thomas-Larmer, *The Consensus Building Handbook: A Comprehensive Guide to Reaching Agreement* (Thousand Oaks, Calif.: Sage Publications, 1999).

21. This description of the consensus-building process was taken in part from Susskind, McKeranan, and Thomas-Larmer, *The Consensus Building Handbook*.

22. This point is best made by William Fischel in *The Home-Voter Hypothesis* (Harvard University Press, 2001).

23. However, those metropolitan areas that encompass parts of more than one state include some of the largest in the nation, such as New York, Chicago, Philadelphia, Boston, Washington, and Minneapolis-St. Paul.

24. For a detailed analysis of how this arrangement works in a democracy,

and why it is an advantage of democracy over other systems, see Anthony Downs, *An Economic Theory of Democracy* (Harper and Row, 1957).

25. See Anthony Downs, "Up and Down with Ecology: The Issue-Attention Cycle," in *Political Theory and Public Choice: The Selected Essays of Anthony Downs, Volume One* (Northampton, Mass.: Edward Elgar, 1998), pp. 100–12.

Chapter 18

1. In theory, extensive adoption of peak-hour road pricing or peak-hour long-term parking surcharges within a metropolitan area could substantially reduce peak-hour traffic congestion without the use of other tactics, as discussed further later. But neither is likely to be adopted on a sufficient scale to accomplish that goal at one stroke.

2. The United States has 22.9 kilometers of roads per 1,000 inhabitants. The following nations have more: Australia (43.7), Canada (29.8), Austria (24.7), Ireland (24.2), New Zealand (24.0), and Sweden (23.9). Data from the International Road Federation, *World Road Statistics* (Geneva, 2002).

3. One tactic—creating separate and exclusive roadways for trucks—has been included in the summary ratings of tactics but is not specifically discussed in the text.

4. In Europe, large shares of the public revenues collected from very high sales taxes on gasoline are shifted away from transportation uses into general government revenues. Such "diversion" reduces public support for any increased taxes or tolls on roads. But if the increased revenues were certain to be spent improving roads and other means of transportation, public resistance to them might be greatly reduced.

5. Concerning the fickleness of public opinion, see Anthony Downs, "Up and Down with Ecology—The Issue-Attention Cycle," in *Political Theory and Public Choice, the Selected Essays of Anthony Downs*, Volume One (Edward Elgar, 1998), pp. 100–12.

Appendix A

1. Karl Petty, "Data for Datta," Caltrans Performance Measuring System (PeMS) Lane 2 chart for Speed versus Flows (http://paleale.eecs.berkeley.edu/FSP/Datta/index.html [June 2002]).

2. The actual points shown on figure A-1 may be from average counts of 1-second observations aggregated into 30-second or 1-minute groups, since the number of 1-second observations would be larger and more scattered. This point was suggested to me by Kara Maria Kockelman, Clare Boothe Luce Assistant Professor of Civil Engineering at the University of Texas in Austin, who made many excellent suggestions on an earlier draft of this chapter.

3. The relationships between key speed-flow variables can be stated in equation form as follows:

S = speed in miles per hour

F = flow rate in vehicles passing a given point per hour

D = density, or number of vehicles in each lane mile of road

I = interval between vehicles (from the back of one to the front of the next) in feet

L = average vehicle length in feet

5,280 = number of feet in one mile

Therefore:

F = S times D [Flow rate = Speed times Density]

I = [5,280 – (L times D)] / D [Interval between vehicles = {5,280 minus (average length times density)} divided by density].

4. Kara Maria Kockelman, "Modeling Traffic's Flow-Density Relation: Accommodation of Multiple Flow Regimes and Traveler Types," *Transportation*, vol. 28, (2001), pp. 363–74, and "Changes in the Flow-Density Relation due to Environmental, Vehicle, and Driver Characteristics," *Transportation Research Record No. 1644* (1998), pp. 363–74.

5. Zhangfeng Jia, Pravin Varaiya, Chao Chen, Karl Petty, and Alex Skabardonis, *Congestion, Excess Demand, and Effective Capacity in California Freeways* (PeMS Development Group, University of California Berkeley, December 9, 2000) (http://paleale.eecs.berkeley.edu/~varaiya/papers_ps.dir/delay7-eff.pdf).

6. In this analysis, the term "interval between vehicles" refers to the distance from the back of the first vehicle to the front of the second or trailing vehicle. Among traffic experts, the same term is often defined as the distance from the front of the first vehicle to the front of the second or trailing vehicle, known as "headway." I prefer the former definition because it is what drivers themselves can perceive while driving. The second definition results in a longer distance because it includes the length of the first vehicle; whereas the former definition excludes that length. There is some confusion about which of these definitions is referred to by the two-second rule that drivers should stay two seconds apart. Since drivers cannot in practice see the front of the vehicle ahead of them but can see its back, it seems to me more practical to conceive of the two-second rule as applying to the first definition—the back of the first vehicle to the front of the second vehicle.

7. As discussed in note 6, Kara Maria Kockelman measures the distance between vehicles as the distance from the front of any vehicle to the front of the following vehicle. Since the average vehicle length assumed in this analysis is 18.65 feet, her measure would add that amount to the measures used in this analysis, which are from the rear of any vehicle to the front of the following vehicle. She also stated that observations on California freeways sometimes

record short periods of 3,000 vehicles per hour moving past a given point at a speed of 60 miles per hour. That combination produces an interval between vehicles measured front-to-front of only 1.2 seconds, or 105 feet. When translated into the measure of interval between vehicles used in this analysis (rear-to-front), that produces an interval of 0.99 seconds, or 86.9 feet. However, it is rare that drivers moving 60 miles per hour are willing to stay so close together for any long period of time. She stated that intervals of 1.5 seconds, front-to-front, are more common. At 60 miles per hour, that would produce a flow rate of 2,400 vehicles per hour and a front-to-front interval of 132 feet. In the measures used in this analysis, that equals an interval of 113 feet, or 1.29 seconds. Correspondence with Kara Kockelman, November 2002.

8. See also Zhanfeng Jia, Pravin Varaiya, Chao Chen, Karl Pctty, and Alex Skabardonis, *Maximum Throughput in LA Freeways Occurs at 60 mph* (University of California Berkeley, PeMS Development Group, January 16, 2001) (http://paleale.eecs.berkeley.edu/~varaiya/papers_ps.dir/throughoutput4.pdf).

9. The distance of 300 feet was suggested by Kara Kockelman, based on her reading of American Association of State Highway and Transportation Officials, *A Policy on Geometric Design of Highways and Streets, 2001* (www.fhwa. dot.gov/programadmin/y2kgb.htm [January 2004]). The California Highway Patrol publishes a table entitled "Stopping Distances for Passenger Vehicles" showing car stopping distances at various speeds. It indicates that at 60 miles per hour, perception and reaction distance is 132 feet and braking distance is 171 feet, for a total stopping distance of 303 feet. (www.chp.ca.gov/html/ stopping.html [January 2004].) Under the two-second rule, vehicles moving at 60 miles per hour (88 feet per second) should stay 176 feet apart from the rear of the first vehicle to the front of the second (by the author's interpretation). That is about ten car lengths if the average passenger car is 17 feet long. Since the stopping distance required at 60 miles per hour under dry pavement conditions is 304 feet, it may appear that the two-second rule does not provide safe intervals at that speed. But this appearance is deceiving; in fact that rule does work under these conditions. If the leading car encounters an obstacle and begins to brake, the trailing car will see the brake light of the leading car, then take about 132 feet to react, and then take another 171 feet to bring the trailing car to a stop. But in the meantime, the leading car will have moved another 171 feet forward in the process of braking itself. So the trailing car has a total space in which to stop of 347 feet—the initial 176 feet between the two vehicles before either begins braking, and the additional 171 feet that the leading car takes to stop after it begins braking. This 347 feet should be enough for the trailing car to stop before hitting the leading car. However, under other pavement conditions—such as wet or icy pavement—the two-second rule may not provide a big enough interval between cars moving at 60 miles per hour to prevent crashes if the lead car has to stop suddenly.

Appendix B

1. This diagram is a version of a well-known set of relationships that has appeared in many previous analyses of this subject. For a more elaborate version, see Timothy D. Hau, "Economic Fundamentals of Road Pricing: A Diagrammatic Analysis" (World Bank, 1992). Timothy Hau provided information on road pricing systems throughout the world.

Appendix C

1. Boris S. Pushkarev and Jeffrey M. Zupan, *Public Transportation and Land Use Policy* (Indiana University Press, 1977), exhibit 7.2.

2. Note that 69,333 divided by 2.0 persons per dwelling equals 34,666 dwellings per square mile. If there are 210.6 dwellings per net residential acre, those 34,666 dwellings occupy 164.6 acres. That is 25.7 percent of the 640 acres in the one square mile containing the 69,333 persons.

3. See Pushkarev and Zupan, *Public Transportation*, p. 202, for a conversion chart for relating gross population per square mile to dwelling units per net residential acre.

4. U.S. Bureau of the Census, *Statistical Abstract 2002* (2002), p. 49.

Appendix D

1. Concentrating all jobs in these twenty-nine nodes greatly simplifies the calculation of average travel distances from each of the 1,600 square miles in this model. Because there are twenty-nine such centers, five in the city, twelve in the older suburbs, and twelve in the exurbs, jobs can still be spread widely across the map while remaining within these centers. Hence this simplification does not distort reality significantly, even though real-world jobs are much more widely distributed across the landscape.

2. This distance can be calculated rectangularly (assuming all movements are purely vertical or purely horizontal or some combination of those) or diagonally (assuming all movements are in straight lines directly connecting the center of each residential square mile with each job center). Because actual street patterns combine rectangular and diagonal elements, the average of these two distances has been used to represent the average commuting distance between each square mile and each job center.

3. The urbanized area with the lowest overall density in 2000 is Barnstable Town in Massachusetts, with a density of 851 persons per square mile. The average density of all 476 urbanized areas is 2,148 persons per square mile. Data from the 2000 Census, Bureau of the Census website (www.census.gov).

4. The total residential population of the United States in 1999 was 279.295 million. U.S. Bureau of the Census, *Statistical Abstract of the United States:*

2002 (2002), p. 8, and total civilian employment in that year was 133.488 million (p. 367). The ratio between them is 0.478.

5. However, if the two locations are on the same north-south line or the same east-west line, the calculated travel distance between them is the same as a direct line drawn from one to the other.

6. The commuting distances for large U.S. metropolitan areas shown in table D-1 are from Federal Highway Administration, *Personal Travel in the U.S., Volume I: 1983-1984 Nationwide Personal Transportation Study* (Department of Transportation, 1986), pp. 7-3, 7-5. The metropolitan average commuting distance shown is from 1983 for areas containing 3 million or more residents (p. 7-5). However, this source contained no breakouts for the suburbs or the central city. Hence the average commuting distances for exurbs and suburbs combined (similar to the Department of Transportation's category "not in a central city") and for the central city have been extrapolated to large metropolitan areas from the data for all metropolitan areas (p. 7-3). Travel distance data for 1995 are from Federal Highway Administration, *1995 NPTS Databook,* ORNL/TM-2002/248 (Oak Ridge, Tenn.: Oak Ridge National Laboratory, October 2001), pp. 6-11 to 6-20 (www-cta.ornl.gov [January 2004]).

7. Federal Highway Administration, Bureau of Transportation Statistics, "Changes in Demographics and Travel," *Inklings: Preliminary Results from the 2001NHTS* (http://nhts.ornl.gov/2001/presentations/inklings/inklings1.pdf [January 2004]).

8. Fundamentally, the relationship between travel distances and densities in this model—as in the real world—reflects the difference between measures of distance (which are straight lines) and measures of area (which are products of multiplying the lengths of straight lines). This difference is most obvious in a circular-shaped metropolitan area. The distance from the outer edge to the center is the radius of the circle (R). But the area of the circle (A) is determined by the formula $A = Pi * R^2$. Any change in the region's radius produces a proportionally much greater change in its area because computing the area involves squaring the radius. Thus a region with an initial radius of 10.0 miles has an area of 314.2 square miles. Raising the radius by 50 percent to 15.0 miles raises the area to 706.8 miles, an increase of 125 percent. Conversely, reducing the radius of a region from 15.0 miles to 10.0 miles drops the travel distance to the center from the outer edge by 33 percent. But it drops the area of the region from 706.8 miles to 314.2 miles, or by 56 percent. If the region's population remains the same—say 1 million persons—the average density rises from 1,414 persons per square mile to 3,183 persons—an increase of 125 percent. Thus it is inevitable that changes in the size of a region without altering its population are bound to affect its density more than the length of movements within it.

9. Census 2000 redistricting data, Bureau of the Census website (www.census.gov).

Appendix E

1. See Boris S. Pushkarev and Jeffrey M. Zupan, *Public Transportation and Land Use Policy* (University of Indiana Press, 1977), p. 39.

2. Transit Cooperative Research Program, *Research Results Digest Number 52, October 2002–Transit-Oriented Development and Joint Development in the United States: A Literature Review* (Washington: Tansportation Research Board, 2002), p. 42. (http://gulliver.trb.org/publications/tcrp/tcrp_rrd_52.pdf [January 2004]).

3. Robert Cervero and Kara Kockelman, "Travel Demand and the 3Ds: Density, Diversity, and Design," Transportation Research D 2D, 3: 199-219, cited in John Niles and Dick Nelson, "Measuring the Success of Transit-Oriented Development: Retail Market Dynamics and Other Key Determinants, " paper prepared for the American Planning Association National Planning Conference, Seattle 1999. (www.globaltelematics.com/apa99.htm [January 2004]).

4. American Fact Finder for 2000 on the Bureau of the Census website (www.census.gov). The census tract for Ballston is number 1014 in Arlington County, Virginia.

5. Bay Area Rapid Transit System, "BART System Facts" (www.bart.gov [January 2004]).

6. Dena Belzer and Gerald Autler, *Transit-Oriented Development: Moving from Rhetoric to Reality* (Brookings Institution Center on Urban and Metropolitan Policy and the Great American Station Foundation, June 2002).

Index